Post-mortem Divine Retribution

A Study in the Hebrew Bible and Select Second Temple Jewish Literature Compared with Aspects of Divine Retribution in Deuteronomy

Angukali Rotokha

MONOGRAPHS

© 2023 Angukali Rotokha

Published 2023 by Langham Monographs
An imprint of Langham Publishing
www.langhampublishing.org

Langham Publishing and its imprints are a ministry of Langham Partnership

Langham Partnership
PO Box 296, Carlisle, Cumbria, CA3 9WZ, UK
www.langham.org

ISBNs:
978-1-83973-605-6 Print
978-1-83973-865-4 ePub
978-1-83973-867-8 PDF

Angukali Rotokha has asserted her right under the Copyright, Designs and Patents Act, 1988 to be identified as the Author of this work.

All rights reserved. No part of this publication may be reproduced, stored in a retrieval system or transmitted, in any form or by any means, electronic, mechanical, photocopying, recording or otherwise, without the prior written permission of the publisher or the Copyright Licensing Agency.

Requests to reuse content from Langham Publishing are processed through PLSclear. Please visit www.plsclear.com to complete your request.

All Scripture quotations marked (NRSV), are from the New Revised Standard Version Bible, copyright © 1989 National Council of the Churches of Christ in the United States of America. Used by permission. All rights reserved.

All Scripture quotations marked (NET), are from the New English Translation (NET). NET Bible® copyright ©1996-2006 by Biblical Studies Press, L.L.C. www.bible.org. Used by permission. All rights reserved worldwide.

British Library Cataloguing-in-Publication Data
A catalogue record for this book is available from the British Library

ISBN: 978-1-83973-605-6

Cover & Book Design: projectluz.com

Langham Partnership actively supports theological dialogue and an author's right to publish but does not necessarily endorse the views and opinions set forth here or in works referenced within this publication, nor can we guarantee technical and grammatical correctness. Langham Partnership does not accept any responsibility or liability to persons or property as a consequence of the reading, use or interpretation of its published content.

Dr. Rotokha's fascinating study of post-mortem retribution in the Old Testament and Second Temple Jewish writings is cogent, coherent, and compelling. She presents a balanced and thorough case on an under-researched topic that provides important background for the New Testament. This is a fine example of careful research, deserving of careful reading.

Paul Barker, PhD
Assistant Bishop, Anglican Diocese of Melbourne
Visiting Lecturer in Old Testament,
Myanmar Evangelical Graduate School of Theology

Angukali Rotokha's excellent study, carefully examining and comparing the multidimensional aspects of the concept of divine retribution in Deuteronomy with four post-mortem texts, addresses a significant lacuna in biblical scholarship, and thereby makes an important contribution to the field. While adopting primarily an intertextual and synchronic approach, Rotokha does not ignore the historical questions related to authorship and the dating of the various texts she examines. Her careful and nuanced approach to the topic demonstrates an impressive knowledge of the relevant scholarly literature, while she presents a fair assessment of the various arguments and views. Written in a lucid and engaging style, Rotokha's wonderful study demonstrates that there is both continuity and discontinuity as well as significant development in the portrayal of the nature of divine retribution in the texts about the afterlife. This book is a welcome and significant addition to the research and conversation on this important topic.

Rebecca G. S. Idestrom, PhD
Professor of Old Testament,
Tyndale University, Toronto, Canada

Contents

Acknowledgments xi

Abstract xiii

Abbreviations xv

Chapter 1 1
  Introduction
    1.1. Focal Statement 1
    1.2. Definition of Retribution 2
    1.3. Rationale 2
    1.4. Selection of Texts 4
      1.4.1. Texts with Linguistic but No Conceptual
           Post-mortem Import 5
      1.4.2. Section Conclusion 7
      1.4.3. Texts with Debatable Post-mortem Import 7
      1.4.4. Section Conclusion 28
    1.5. Review of Literature 29
      1.5.1. Section Conclusion 32
    1.6. Method: Intertextuality 32
      1.6.1. Origin 33
      1.6.2. Intertextuality and Biblical Studies 36
      1.6.3. Production and Reception-Centred Intertextuality ... 40
      1.6.4. Questioning Intertextuality 43
      1.6.5. Intertextuality As a Method in This Dissertation 44

Chapter 2 47
  The Aspects of Divine Retribution in the Book of Deuteronomy
    2.1. Introduction 47
    2.2. Divine Retribution in the Hebrew Bible:
         The Traditional View 48
    2.3. Klaus Koch's Challenge 49
    2.4. Towards a More Nuanced Understanding of Divine
         Retribution 51
    2.5. The Aspects of Divine Retribution in the Book of
         Deuteronomy 54
      2.5.1. Impersonal Aspect of Divine Retribution 54
      2.5.2. Anthropocentric Aspect of Divine Retribution 62

  2.5.3. Theocentric Aspect of Retribution 67
  2.5.4. Dissolution of Retribution 72
 2.6. Conclusion 80

Chapter 3 83
 Post-mortem Divine Retribution in Isaiah 26:19
 3.1. Introduction 83
 3.2. Isaiah 24–27: A Distinct Textual Complex 85
 3.3. Date of Isaiah 24–27 85
  3.3.1. Lack of Dateable Historical Data 87
  3.3.2. Circular Argument of Theological Concept as a
   Basis for Date 88
  3.3.3. Literary Genre 89
  3.3.4. Redactional History 90
 3.4. Structure of Isaiah 26 92
 3.5. Text: Isaiah 26:19 94
  3.5.1. Grammatical Problem 94
  3.5.2. Identity of the Speaker in Isaiah 26:19 96
 3.6. Resurrection: Metaphorical or Literal 98
 3.7. Basis and Aspect of Post-mortem Divine Retribution in
  Isaiah 26:19 103
  3.7.1. The Dead Who Rise 104
  3.7.2. The Dead Who Do Not Rise 107
  3.7.3. Differentiated Fates in Isaiah 26:19 112
 3.8. Conclusion 116

Chapter 4 119
 Post-mortem Divine Retribution in Daniel 12:1–3
 4.1. Introduction 119
 4.2. Date of the Book of Daniel 120
 4.3. Resurrection: Literal or Metaphorical 127
  4.3.1. Literal Interpretation 127
  4.3.2. Problems of Metaphorical Interpretation 128
  4.3.3. Section Conclusion 131
 4.4. Resurrection and Post-mortem Divine Retribution in
  Daniel 12:1–3 131
  4.4.1. Double Resurrection 133
  4.4.2. Section Conclusion 137
 4.5. Basis and Aspect of Post-mortem Divine Retribution 138
  4.5.1. "Many" As "All" 138
  4.5.2. "Many" As "Some, Not All" 141

  4.5.3. Section Conclusion 142
  4.5.4. Post-mortem Reward for the "Wise One"....................143
  4.5.5. Section Conclusion 150
 4.6. Nature of Divine Retribution: An Emphasis on Individuals 151
 4.7. Conclusion 152

Chapter 5 155
Post-mortem Divine Retribution in the Book of Watchers 22

 5.1. Introduction 155
 5.2. 1 Enoch 157
 5.3. Enochic Judaism..160
  5.3.1. Insignificance of Moses and Torah in 1 Enoch.............162
  5.3.2. Torah and 1 Enoch 164
  5.3.3. Distinct Explanation of the Origin of Evil 166
 5.4. Post-mortem Divine Retribution in BW 22..........................174
  5.4.1. The Spirits of the Souls of the Dead 175
  5.4.2. The Differentiated Dead 176
  5.4.3. Foretaste of Final Retribution.....................................177
  5.4.4. Coming Final Judgment 178
 5.5. Basis and Aspect of Post-mortem Divine Retribution 179
  5.5.1. The Theocentric Aspect 180
  5.5.2. The Anthropocentric Aspect.......................................180
 5.6. Nature of Post-mortem Divine Retribution: Individual or
  Corporate..192
 5.7. Conclusion 196

Chapter 6 199
Post-mortem Divine Retribution in 2 Maccabees 7

 6.1. Introduction 199
 6.2. The Book of 2 Maccabees: Contents and Provenance 200
 6.3. Historiographic Value of 2 Maccabees 202
 6.4. 2 Maccabees 7: Story and Background 205
 6.5. Post-mortem Divine Retribution in 2 Maccabees 7 209
  6.5.1. Resurrection in the Speeches of the Mother and
   Her Seven Sons 209
  6.5.2. Post-mortem Divine Retribution Via Physical
   Resurrection..212
  6.5.3. Section Conclusion 215
  6.5.4. Divine Retribution for Antiochus IV..............................215
  6.5.5. Section Conclusion 218
 6.6. Basis and Aspects of Post-mortem Divine Retribution............219

  6.6.1. Dying for the Law: Anthropocentric Aspect of
    Divine Retribution 219
  6.6.2. Section Conclusion 224
  6.6.3. Dying for Their Sins: The Theocentric Aspect of
    Divine Retribution 225
  6.6.4. Section Conclusion 229
 6.7. Nature of Post-mortem Divine Retribution: Corporate
   and Individual...230
  6.7.1. Corporate Nature of Divine Retribution...........................230
  6.7.2. Individual Nature of Post-mortem Divine Retribution 232
  6.7.3. Section Conclusion 234
 6.8. Excursus: Divine Retribution for the Agent of Divine
   Punishment 235
 6.9. Conclusion 236

Chapter 7 239
Conclusion
 7.1. Introduction..239
 7.2. Summary of the Chapters..240
 7.3. Overall Observations 251
  7.3.1. Post-mortem Divine Retribution Is Predominantly
    Anthropocentric..252
  7.3.2. Theocentric Aspect of Divine Retribution Underlies
    the Anthropocentric Aspect..253
  7.3.3. The Impersonal and the Dissolution Aspects
    Become Defunct 253
  7.3.4. Post-mortem Divine Retribution Is Both Corporate
    and Individual in Nature 254
 7.4. Potential for Further Research: The Nature of Post-
   mortem Divine Retribution in the New Testament....................255
  7.4.1. Discerning Post-mortem Divine Retribution
    in the NT 256
  7.4.2. The Basis of Post-mortem Divine Retribution in the
    NT...259
  7.4.3. Nature of Divine Retribution: Corporate or
    Individual 262
  7.4.4. Section Conclusion 263
 7.5. Conclusion 264

Appendix 265
    Annotated Bibliography for the Themes of Divine Retribution
    and Afterlife in the Hebrew Bible and Second Temple Period
    Jewish Literature
        Introduction 265
            Divine Retribution 265
            Afterlife and Related Themes 269

Bibliography 275

Subject Index 301

Scripture Index 303

Acknowledgments

The thesis bears my name, but I owe a debt of gratitude to many people and institutions who invested as much as I did to see it completed.

My first offering of thanks is to God whose faithfulness I experienced in so many tangible and unexpected ways during my four-year doctoral program. Knowing that he is quietly bringing all things together gave me the conviction I needed to persevere.

I am deeply indebted to my supervisor, Dr. Havilah Dharamraj, for her academic acuity, efficiency, and encouragement at all stages of my doctoral program which helped give shape and direction to my thesis. Her knack for knowing when to point me in the right direction and when to walk along with me was crucial to my academic progress and I truly appreciate it.

I also owe special thanks to Dr. Eric Montgomery, Dr. Mark Awabdy, and Dr. Ernest Clark, who read various chapters of my thesis. Their incisive and detailed feedback helped further sharpen my work.

I have been able to pursue my studies because of the generous scholarship I received from Langham Partnership International, for which I am truly grateful. Their support, however, was more than financial. They have worked closely with me to provide all the help I needed to progress academically by sending me on fully paid research residency trips, and organizing annual consultations for Langham scholars, among other things. Langham also provided me with pastoral support, especially through Dr. Federico Villanueva and his wife Rosemarie, and I thank them for the constant love and care I received from them over the years.

My Langham supported research trips helped me access resources that were not readily available in India, and I want to thank the following institutions and people:

i) Ridley College, Melbourne, Australia, whose library resources I used for two months. My heartfelt gratitude to Ruth Weatherlake, the librarian at Ridley College, who hosted me for the entire duration of my stay and showed me how wonderful Australia and Australians are. During my stay in Melbourne I was also able to use the resources of the Dalton McCaughey Library for which I am very grateful.

ii) Nagel Institute, Grand Rapids, MI, USA, whose hospitality I enjoyed for three months. They took care of all my needs and gave me access to the library resources at Calvin College. My special thanks to Donna Romanowski who did everything to ensure that my stay there was productive and comfortable.

iii) Tyndale House, Cambridge, UK, where I stayed for two months using their vast library resources and met some amazing women. Tyndale House also provided me access to the Cambridge University Library and database which were invaluable for my work.

My sincere gratitude also goes to my external examiners, Dr. K. Jesurathnam and Dr. Rajkumar Boaz Johnson, for insightful comments and encouragement. I am also immensely grateful to my parents, parents-in-law, and siblings for consistently and earnestly praying for me through these years. Lastly, I thank my husband, Luke Haokip. I do not have words good enough to express my gratitude for the unswerving dedication and support he has shown to me and my work every single day in the past four years. From reading my every chapter to rearranging his life and schedule around mine, he did everything possible so that I can pursue my studies unhindered. I could not have asked for a better partner, and I am excited for what God has in store for us together and it is to Luke that I dedicate this study.

Abstract

The concept of post-mortem divine retribution is a minor theme in the Hebrew Bible ("HB") when compared to the concept of divine retribution that is focused on this life. However, if the locus of divine retribution is the same God, then it is probable that divine retribution in this life and in the afterlife will share some features. As such, this study attempts to investigate the concept of post-mortem divine retribution in four post-mortem texts – two from the HB: Isaiah 26:19 and Daniel 12:1–3, and two from the Jewish literature of the Second Temple period ("STP"): Book of Watchers 22 and 2 Maccabees 7 – by studying them alongside the concept of divine retribution in Deuteronomy, whose orientation is solely on this side of death. Examining the post-mortem texts alongside the concept of divine retribution in Deuteronomy highlights the continuities and discontinuities between earthly and post-mortem divine retribution.

Divine retribution as presented in the Book of Deuteronomy exhibits at least four aspects or facets: impersonal, anthropocentric, theocentric, and dissolution. These aspects are the varying emphases, rather than distinct types, that emerge in the way divine retribution is expressed in Deuteronomy. Further, these aspects are operational both corporately and individually, although the corporate expression seems to be predominant in Deuteronomy.

The aspects of divine retribution in Deuteronomy are read alongside the four post-mortem texts. Each text is examined to see if in their presentation of post-mortem divine retribution there is any continuity with the aspect of divine retribution in Deuteronomy. This examination is done through the lens of intertextuality that reads the connection between texts synchronically.

It emerges that the post-mortem divine retribution in these four texts does reflect some continuities with the earthly life-oriented divine retribution.

As in life, human deeds become one of the determinative factors for one's post-mortem fate and hence are reflective of the anthropocentric aspect. However, again as in life, the theocentric aspect underpins this anthropocentric aspect in that the judgment of those deeds is rooted in God's law and covenant with the community. Thus, earthly life becomes determinative for one's post-mortem fate, and the impersonal and dissolution aspects become defunct when divine retribution is transposed to the afterlife.

Abbreviations

AB	Anchor Bible
AOTC	Abingdon Old Testament Commentary
AJS	Association for Jewish Studies
ARG	Archiv für Religionsgeschichte
BASOR	*Bulletin of the American Schools of Oriental Research*
BCOTWP	Baker Commentary on the Old Testament Wisdom and Psalms
Bib Int	*Biblical Interpretation*
BTCB	Brazos Theological Commentary on the Bible
BWANT	Beiträge zur Wissenschaft vom Alten und Neuen Testament
BZAW	*Beihefte zur Zeitschrift für die alttestamentliche Wissenschaft*
CB	Coniectanea Biblica
CBC	Cambridge Bible Commentary
CEJL	Commentaries on Early Jewish Literature
DCLS	Deuterocanonical and Cognate Literature Studies
DSBS	Daily Study Bible Series
EGL & MWBS	Eastern Great Lakes and Midwest Biblical Societies
FAT	Forschungen zum Alten Testament
FOTL	Forms of the Old Testament Literature
HALOT	*The Hebrew and Aramaic Lexicon of the Old Testament*
HCOT	Historical Commentary of the Old Testament
HSM	Harvard Semitic Monographs
HSS	Harvard Semitic Studies

HTS	Harvard Theological Studies
IBT	Interpreting Biblical Text
ICC	International Critical Commentary
IJPR	International Journal for Philosophy of Religion
IOSCS	International Organization for Septuagint and Cognate Studies
ITC	International Theological Commentary
JAAR	*Journal of the American Academy of Religion*
JANER	*Journal of Ancient Near Eastern Religions*
JATS	*Journal of the Adventist Theological Society*
JAOS	*Journal of the American Oriental Society*
JBL	*Journal of Biblical Literature*
JBR	*Journal of Bible and Religion*
JCTCRS	Jewish and Christian Text in Context and Related Studies
JEBS	*Journal of European Baptist Studies*
JHS	*Journal of Hebrew Scriptures*
JLA	*Judaism in the Late Antiquity*
JSJ	*Journal for the Study of Judaism*
JSJSup	Journal for the Study of Judaism Supplements
JSNTSup	Journal for the Study of the New Testament Supplement
JSOT	*Journal for the Study of the Old Testament*
JSOTSup	Journal for the Study of the Old Testament Supplement
JSPSup	Supplements to Journal for the Study of Pseudepigrapha
JTS	*The Journal of Theological Studies*
LCIB	Literary Currents in Biblical Interpretation
LBI	Library of Biblical Interpretation
LHBOTS	Library of Hebrew Studies/ Old Testament Studies
LSTS	Library of Second Temple Studies
NAC	New American Commentary
NCBC	New Century Bible Commentary
NIBC	New International Biblical Commentary

NICOT	New International Commentary of the Old Testament
NTS	*New Testament Studies*
OTL	Old Testament Library
OTM	Old Testament Message
OTS	Old Testament Studies
CBQ	*Catholic Bible Quarterly*
SBJT	The Southern Baptist Journal of Theology
SBLMS	Society of Biblical Literature Monograph Series
SBLSP	Society of Biblical Literature Seminar Papers
SBLSS	Society of Biblical Literature Symposium Series
SHBC	Smyth and Helwys Bible Commentary
SJT	*Scottish Journal of Theology*
SNTS	Society for New Testament Studies
SR	*Studies in Religion/Sciences Religieuses*
STDJ	Studies on the Texts of the Desert of Judah
TOTC	Tyndale Old Testament Commentary
VT	*Vetus Testamentum*
VTSup	Supplements to Vetus Testamentum
WBC	Word Biblical Commentary
WUNT	Wissenschaftliche Untersuchungen zum Neuen Testament
ZNW	*Zeitschrift für die Neutestamentliche Wissenschaft*

CHAPTER 1

Introduction

1.1. Focal Statement

The concept of divine retribution in the Hebrew Bible ("HB") is primarily conceived of and presented in relation to earthly life, that is, the rewards and punishments are intended to be realized in this life, and post-mortem divine retribution is a minor theme in the HB. However, it is possible there are shared features in the way divine retribution operates in life and in the afterlife. To determine if it is the case this dissertation attempts to investigate post-mortem divine retribution by studying it alongside earthly divine retribution, especially as presented in Deuteronomy. This is done by first examining the earthly life oriented divine retribution in Deuteronomy. Divine retribution in Deuteronomy comprises at least four aspects or emphases, each of which is examined and illustrated with a text, and operates both corporately and individually. Then, four texts that speak of post-mortem divine retribution are selected, two each from the HB and the Second Temple period ("STP") Jewish literature. The HB does not focus on post-mortem divine retribution, and this necessitates seeking texts outside the HB to test the idea; hence Jewish texts from the STP are used. Each of the four texts is read alongside the aspects of divine retribution found in Deuteronomy. This allows continuities and discontinuities to emerge between earthly divine retribution and post-mortem divine retribution.

1.2. Definition of Retribution

Since this dissertation studies divine retribution and the term "retribution" is not always understood uniformly, a definition of its use in this study is in order. Divine retribution is sometimes understood as referring only to punishments resulting from God's wrath. However, in biblical studies, it can refer to both rewards and punishments[1] and will be used accordingly in this dissertation. Retribution is one of the ways in which the interaction between the divine and the human is experienced.[2] Thus divine retribution is a tangible manifestation of divine-human interactions and of God's justice experienced as rewards or punishments by humans.

1.3. Rationale

As stated, the interest of this study is the concept of post-mortem divine retribution, in particular seeking to examine the continuities or discontinuities between post-mortem divine retribution and divine retribution in Deuteronomy. The rationale for this extrapolation of divine retribution in Deuteronomy, which is earthly life oriented, to post-mortem divine retribution is that divine retribution is an expression of God's just character. Justice is a central theme in the HB, whether it is presented positively as in Abraham's bargain with the angels and the punishment of the cities of Sodom and Gomorrah (Gen 18:17–32), or negatively as in Job, or in the cries of the psalmist for God to vindicate him; except the purview of this justice in the HB was largely bound to life on earth. However, once the exilic situation brought the Israelites face to face with foreign oppression and persecution on a large scale, the problem of theodicy became more apparent.[3] It challenged the conception of the boundary of justice. As John Walton puts it, "Since God is just, the Israelites held that it was incumbent on him to uphold the retribution principle."[4] So if it is God who sanctions retribution, whether applied to this life or the afterlife, divine retribution can be seen as operating in a continuum

---

1. Walton, "Retribution," 647–655; Koch, "Doctrine of Retribution" 59; Wong, *Idea of Retribution*, 2; Kiel, *"Whole Truth"*, 1–2, 4; Kaminsky, "Would You Impugn My Justice?" 300; Rottenberg, "Reward and Punishment," 827.
2. Chapman, "Reading the Bible," 175–176.
3. Sigvartsen, *Afterlife and Resurrection*, 9–10.
4. Walton, "Retribution," 647.

of life and afterlife and God's justice is dispensed, either in life or after death. If that is the case, the consequences of retributions may differ; retribution in this life may mean prosperity or plague, while it could be crowns or fire in the afterlife, but the principle of justice should be the same between the mechanics of earthly and post-mortem retribution.

Also, application of divine retribution to this life is well known. For instance, the whole Deuteronomistic History is an exercise in interpreting the Israelite history and its crisis as an outworking of divine retribution;[5] the prophetic literature draws heavily upon the justice of God and its call for repentance is couched in terms of divine retribution;[6] as for wisdom in the HB, it has been studied as crisis literature[7] that questions and re-examines the Deuteronomic principles of retribution. If wisdom indeed re-examines the divine retribution principle, then it is worth looking at where it goes from there. Hence, instead of focusing on this-life retribution, this dissertation is an attempt to investigate the concept and outworking of divine retribution beyond earthly life.

Further, there is the question of why one should use Deuteronomy as a theological and theoretical interpretive framework for divine retribution. First, divine retribution in the HB is rooted in the covenant that Yahweh made with Israel, and Deuteronomy is a restatement of that covenant. Second, as stated above, that the HB is rooted in Deuteronomic thought has been recognized in the narrative, prophetic and wisdom sections of the HB as well as in the literature of the STP.[8] Such an identification of Deuteronomic redactional activities in books outside Deuteronomy and the Deuteronomistic History is often called pandeuteronomism.[9] Thirdly, Deuteronomic retributive theology in particular is pervasive in the HB, so much so that Brueggemann proposes retributive justice (or "contractual theology" as he calls it) as the

---

5. Nelson calls theology of retribution the "guiding principle" of the DtrH. Nelson, *Double Redaction*, 100; also for Chronicles see Kelly, *Retribution and Eschatology*.

6. For instance, Wong, *Idea of Retribution*.

7. For instance, Gese, "Crisis of Wisdom"; Crüsemann, "Unchangeable World."

8. For instance, Kiel, *"Whole Truth,"* 82; Barrett, "Disloyalty and Destruction," 9; Adams, *Wisdom in Transition*.

9. The uncritical use of the designation has been criticized, for instance, see Schearing, *Those Elusive Deuteronomists*. However, on the whole it is acknowledged that Deuteronomy lies at the heart of the OT.

theological centre for the HB.[10] No other book in the HB has this range of influence or provides as good a theological category for investigating the concept of divine retribution. Thus, this dissertation, while not arguing for pandeuteronomism in the post-mortem texts, takes its cue from the centrality of Deuteronomy in the HB to make reasoned connections between the various aspects of Deuteronomic divine retribution and the HB and STP texts' engagement with retribution in the hereafter. The aim is to see which aspects of Deuteronomic divine retribution are discernible and if they diverge when retribution is transposed to the afterlife.

Lastly, a study on the theme of divine retribution evokes the possibility of a comparative study with the concept of *karma* in Hinduism or at least of drawing some contextual implications from the perspective of *karma*. However, two important considerations lead to the conclusion that such an endeavour is better reserved for separate research. First, the difference in the worldviews between the Judeo-Christian tradition and Hinduism as a belief system is vast. Consequently, a conceptual parallel between divine retribution in the HB and *karma* in Hinduism is not easily drawn. Secondly, the variety of slants within Hinduism does not permit the use of one view within Hinduism as the typical or authoritative view. As such, though at the outset the seeming parallel is inviting, the work required to draw this parallel for a comparative study is beyond the scope of the present investigation.

1.4. Selection of Texts

In the STP Jewish literature, explicit post-mortem references are plentiful and hence, the selection of texts to be examined is based on two criteria: i) date of composition of the text – the selected text are composed during or before the first century BCE, keeping the purview of the research to the time before the beginning of the New Testament era; and ii) the length of the text – the selected texts are at least a chapter or more in length. There are numerous texts of varying lengths among the STP Jewish literature that refer to post-mortem existence, hence it makes sense to examine the ones that are most substantial.

---

10. Brueggemann, "A Shape for Old Testament," 28–46. McConville also states, "Deuteronomy offers some of the most vivid reflections on the theme of divine justice in the Hebrew Bible." McConville, "Retribution in Deuteronomy," 289.

Selection of texts to be studied from the HB is a little more complicated. As mentioned earlier divine retribution in the afterlife is not a major focus of the HB. However, there is a vast array of texts in the HB that seem to speak of or allude to some kind of post-mortem existence or retribution. These passages are examined below to see if they have any afterlife or post-mortem divine retribution content. This survey categorizes the texts into three sections in increasing degree of the presence of the post-mortem retribution theme: i) texts with linguistic but no conceptual post-mortem import, ii) texts with debated post-mortem import, and iii) texts with actual post-mortem import. This last category of texts that have post-mortem content is studied in the succeeding chapters and hence not included in this survey.

1.4.1. Texts with Linguistic but No Conceptual Post-mortem Import

There are two passages in this category of texts, both of which are songs. The language in these passages evoke the concept of resurrection. However, upon closer examination these texts seem to use the language of resurrection to express the idea of Yahweh's power and potential.

1.4.1.1. Deuteronomy 32:39 – Song of Moses

"I kill and I make alive; I wound and I heal." (NRSV)

Deuteronomy 32, read as either a divine indictment of Israel for covenantal breach[11] or a wisdom instruction text,[12] contains this line attributing to Yahweh the acts of killing and giving life.[13] Yahweh as the speaker in this verse has engendered some curiosity regarding what Yahweh making alive means. Leila Leah Bronner's view is perhaps the most optimistic when she notes that the sequence of life mentioned after death denotes at least the possibility of resurrection on a poetic level.[14] Scholars like Eugene Merrill, Christopher Wright, Richard Nelson, and Duane Christensen view in this

---

11. Wright, "Law-Suit of God," 26–67.
12. Boston, "Wisdom Influence," 198–202.
13. See Steven Weitzman who argues that both the wisdom and legal strains are integral to the song in its present setting within the narrative. Weitzman, "Lessons from the Dying," 377–393.
14. Bronner, *Journey to Heaven*, 22–23.

statement an assertion of Yahweh's traditional attributes of sovereignty, power, and mercy.[15] Others like Gerhard von Rad and Walter Brueggemann do not particularly dwell on it.[16]

The verse is part of the claim the poem makes that Yahweh alone is God. It serves to contrast Yahweh from the gods of the other nations who are shown to be weak and incompetent; Yahweh is the source of life and human welfare, whereas the other gods are "poisonous in their source and effect."[17] Edward Woods states the verse is a statement of Yahweh's uniqueness and draws a contrast with the other gods whose impotence prove that they are not gods at all.[18] Aaron Jonathan Chalmers's analysis of thirteen occurrences of Yahweh striking and healing concludes that such expressions are formulaic and the employment of such language is "a means of denoting the supreme power of the deity."[19] It was a belief that Yahweh's power was indeed limitless,[20] and is expressed in the affirmation that both death and life reside in his hands. Thus, while the language is evocative of the concept of resurrection, at this point it seems to be only expressing a belief in Yahweh's sovereign power.

1.4.1.2. 1 Samuel 2:6 – Song of Hannah

> "The LORD kills and brings to life;
> he brings down to Sheol and raises up." (NRSV)

The vocabulary of this verse, similar to the previous one, is likewise very suggestive of an afterlife. Joyce Baldwin states that this verse envisages a resurrection from the dead.[21] However, such an interpretation is in the minority with most scholars not seeing a clear reference to resurrection from the dead. The closest readings are perhaps those of Hans Wilhelm Hertzberg and Robert Gordon who see it as a starting point to the belief in resurrection.[22] Ralph Klein states that resurrection was probably not originally in view although it

---

15. Merill, *Deuteronomy*, 424; Wright, *Deuteronomy*, 303; Nelson, *Deuteronomy*, 377; Christensen, *Deuteronomy 21:10–34:12*, 819.
16. See von Rad, *Deuteronomy*, 199–200; Brueggemann, *Deuteronomy*, 281–281.
17. Merill, *Deuteronomy*, 424.
18. Woods, *Deuteronomy*, 315.
19. Chalmers, "Critical Analysis," 16.
20. Crenshaw, "Love Is Stronger," 56.
21. Baldwin, *1 and 2 Samuel*, 57.
22. Hertzberg, *I and II Samuel*, 30; Gordon, *I and II Samuel*, 80.

has contributed towards the later development of the concept of resurrection in an apocalyptic breakthrough.[23]

Others take a more metaphorical interpretation. Francesca Aran Murray reads it as a reference to spiritual resurrection from the long spiritual death during the period of the judges,[24] while reformation scholars like Viktorin Strigel and Johann Gerhard see it as denoting conversion, or sin and repentance.[25] Some scholars do not focus on rising up from Sheol but rather speak of Yahweh as the source of life with his ability to end barrenness,[26] or his power and sovereignty over life and death as the extreme opposites which God both holds and bestows.[27] The writer seems to be playing off contrasting actions against each other in such a manner that together they bring home the message of the comprehensiveness of God's rule and his power to turn life's seeming tragedy into joy.

1.4.2. Section Conclusion

The general assessment of these two texts seems to be that they are a traditional formulation expressing God's power over life and death in contrast to the powerlessness of human beings, or the gods of the other nations, to bring people back to life. Johnston argues convincingly, giving four reasons why in both the songs of Moses and Hannah a resurrection in afterlife is most probably not in view, nor is it witnessed in the contexts, but rather is cited as a potentiality – "this is who [Yahweh] is, not what he has done."[28] As such, regardless of if or how these two passages contributed to the later development of the afterlife concept, in context they use language reminiscent of resurrection to articulate the concept of Yahweh's ultimate power and sovereignty over human life and situations.

1.4.3. Texts with Debatable Post-mortem Import

Moving on from texts in which the concept of any afterlife existence is absent, this section explores passages that are seemingly polyvalent in terms of the

---

23. Klein, *1 Samuel*, 17–18.
24. Murray, *1 Samuel*, 20.
25. Cooper and Lohrmann, *1-2 Samuel, 1-2 Kings, 1-2 Chronicles*, 12.
26. So Firth, *1 and 2 Samuel*, 61.
27. Brueggemann, *First and Second Samuel*, 18; Cartledge, *1 and 2 Samuel*, 47.
28. See Johnston, *Shades of Sheol*, 219.

extent to which they allude to the possibility of an afterlife or post-mortem retribution. There is much support for both sides of the debate. Most such texts are found in the poetic and prophetic sections of the HB, both genres that lend themselves well to more than one meaning.

1.4.3.1. Psalms
Psalm 1:5

> "Therefore the wicked will not stand in the judgment,
> nor sinners in the congregation of the righteous;" (NRSV)

The question immediately arises: does the judgment here refer to the experience in the present life or the afterlife? According to Peter Craigie, the judgment here implies a place of judgment, such as the court of law or where the righteous meet for justice and governance. Consequently, he interprets the verse to mean that the wicked will have no place, respect or recognition in these places. He states that this line of interpretation is strongly supported by the synonymous parallelism of the second line, "congregation of the righteous," and thus infers that there is no implication of a final judgment.[29] Hans-Joachim Kraus likewise sees this verse as speaking of judgment in a sacral juridical context.[30] Edward Kissane is more categorical in stating that there is no reference to final judgment or resurrection in this verse.[31] Nahum Sarna likewise states that later exegetes saw a reference to the final judgment but that in the text itself the judgment referred to is in "the here and now."[32] J. W. Rogerson and J. W. McKay are somewhere in the middle; they state that there are definitely "overtones of final judgment" although they agree the author may not have intended it.[33] Many others simply do not discuss the presence or absence of afterlife in this verse.

Mitchell Dahood has a different view.[34] He sees an adaptation of Canaanite mythological motif into this imagery, and reads judgment as the final

---

29. Craigie, *Psalms 1–50*, 58.
30. Kraus, *Psalms 1–59*, 119–120.
31. Kissane, *Book of Psalms*, 3–4.
32. Sarna, *On the Book*, 45.
33. Rogerson and McKay, *Psalm 1–50*, 17.
34. Dahood's eschatological reading of the Psalms is well known, although other scholars have not received it with equal enthusiasm. See for instance John Goldingay, who states that

judgment that "will take place in the heavenly council" in which the wicked will not be admitted but "will be condemned in *absentia*." He admits that this reading assumes a rather advanced understanding of the concepts of resurrection and immortality, but posits that there is sufficient basis in the psalter for this supposition. He cites several texts to support his interpretation of the heavenly council and the advanced concept of resurrection.[35] H. C. Leupold similarly sees in the word "judgment" a reference "primarily" to the final judgment which is the "most drastic demonstration" of the overthrow of the wicked.[36]

The Hebrew word קוּם ("to arise, stand") is translated in the LXX by the Greek word ἀνίστημι ("to rise"). In Joachim Schaper's view the LXX Psalms has a heightened interest in the afterlife, and in this verse the Greek word ἀνίστημι lends this psalm its eschatological perspective although there is no reference to eschatology in the Hebrew.[37] He sees it as a reference to resurrection of the righteous and hence the judgment spoken of in this psalm as the final judgment. He translates this verse as: "Therefore unbelievers will not rise [from death] in judgment, nor will sinners [rise] in the counsel of righteous men."[38] His approach has however been criticized.[39] Karen Jobes and Moises Silva say that such Greek translations for the same Hebrew word, קוּם, exists in the LXX even when there is no possible reference to resurrection and hence Schaper's view, although it proposes a fresh perspective, remains "ambiguous."[40] As can be seen, although those who do not see any reference to an afterlife are in the majority, others find some support for an eschatological reading.

Dahood's "thesis has not carried conviction," and takes issue with Dahood's methodology. Goldingay, "Death and Afterlife," 61, 74–75.

35. See Dahood, *Psalm I, 1–50*, 4–5.

36. Leupold, *Exposition of the Psalm*, 38.

37. Schaper's overall orientation and approach to the LXX Psalter in this work is eschatological, and according to Schaper this reinterpretation is substantiated by other Jewish writings like 2 Maccabees. He dates the LXX Psalter to the second century BCE during the Hasmonean period and persecution of the Jews, and says that during this crisis the theology of earthly retribution was insufficient and hence the interest of the LXX translator in the afterlife. See Schaper, *Eschatology*, 47–48.

38. Schaper, 46–48.

39. See Leonard Greenspoon who cites other scholars who have taken issue with Schaper's eschatological reading of the LXX. Greenspoon, "Afterlife in the Septuagint," 52–54.

40. See Jobes and Silva, *Invitation to the Septuagint*, 342–343.

Psalm 16:10–11

> "For you do not give me up to Sheol,
> or let your faithful one see the Pit.
> You show me the path of life. In your presence there is
> fullness of joy;
> in your right hand are pleasures forevermore." (NRSV)

Here too a conclusion is elusive with opinions divided between an eschatological reading and deliverance from immediate threat. Dahood and Artur Weiser favour the eschatological interpretation, and both go even further to say that the psalmist had Enoch and Elijah's assumption in mind.[41] Weiser is convinced that the psalmist had the resurrection from the dead in mind and the "path of life" is the life lived in communion with God both in this life and after.[42]

In the middle are those who consider the possibility of a reference to an afterlife though they feel there is not enough for a conclusive reading. According to Johnston Psalm 16 builds on the delight of the present experience and projects it into the future, without spelling out what exactly he means by "future."[43] Kissane weighs the possibility of the verses referring to resurrection, a complete escape from death, or being saved from untimely death, and he concludes that it is a reference to premature death.[44] Schaper continues his eschatological reading of the LXX Psalter. He states clearly that in the Hebrew these verses speak of premature death, but that in Greek it introduces the concept of physical resurrection.[45]

On the other end of the spectrum are those who contend against all eschatological interpretation. Craigie, for instance, states that the psalmist's concern was the immediate crisis that threatened him with an "untimely termination in *Sheol*," and thus his praise is for deliverance in the face of the imminent threat. According to him, the path of life is not a reference to afterlife but to this life that is enriched by rejoicing out of an awareness of God's presence.[46]

---

41. Dahood, *Psalm I, 1–50*, 19; Weiser, *Psalms: A Commentary*, 178.
42. Weiser, 178.
43. Johnston, *Shades of Sheol*, 217.
44. Kissane, *Book of Psalms*, 65.
45. Schaper, *Eschatology*, 49.
46. Craigie, *Psalms 1–50*, 158.

John Goldingay argues against the likelihood of the redactors of the book of Psalms endorsing the expectation entertained by an individual to be taken up in the manner of Enoch or Elijah. He explains that rather the psalmist is speaking of the delight and fullness in God's presence that "belongs to this life." Goldingay argues against Dahood's references to Enoch and Elijah stating that such expectations by individuals of the community are unlikely to have been endorsed by the editors or redactors of the Book of Psalms.[47]

This verse has a neat lineup of scholars at every possible point on the eschatological spectrum. It is likely that the psalmist was referring to a deliverance from an untimely death which later, as the LXX seems to indicate, came to be read as a reference to resurrection.

Psalm 17:15

> "As for me, I shall behold your face in righteousness;
> when I awake I shall be satisfied, beholding your likeness."
> (NRSV)

Psalm 17 is a plea from the psalmist to God to hear his prayer and vindicate him. The verb קִיץ (hiph "to awake") in this verse is an infinitive and does not have pronominal suffice to indicate the subject. Hence some translate it as "you awake."[48] Kissane argues that the grammar favours the translation as "you awake" and states that God's awakening implies God has stopped his seeming inactivity and intervenes in human affairs, and hence sees no reference to resurrection.[49]

Others translate the infinitive as "I awake." According to Leupold the hope of resurrection is clearly stated here and such a hope had always been part of Israelite faith.[50] However, some who also read the subject as the psalmist have argued that it is unlikely that this was the original focus of the psalm. Several scholars see this as being in the context of the cultic practice of staying the night in the temple and awaiting the morning. Nancy Declaisse-Walford, Rolf Jacobson and Beth Laneel Tanner read it as "I awake." Poetically they understand morning as a time of "deliverance and hope," and awaking as the

---

47. Goldingay, "Death and Afterlife," 77.
48. So Vulgate and LXX; also Kissane, *Book of Psalms*, 71.
49. Kissane, 71.
50. Leupold, *Exposition*, 160.

banishing of fear. The psalmist, having been exhausted by praying in distress, trusts the morning will bring hope.[51]

Similarly, James Luther Mays says that it could be a reference to the psalmist spending the night in the temple. However on the basis of Christian faith he also thinks that the Christian interpretation of resurrection is possible.[52] Craigie allows for the possibility of a theological dimension of afterlife in the Christian and later Jewish theology as providing hope for both immediate crisis, as for the psalmist, and also a greater hope for the ultimate deliverance from a more dangerous enemy, a hope that reaches beyond death itself.[53] However, he regards this psalm as non-eschatological in its original meaning. He focuses instead on the psalmist's awareness of God's presence as opposed to being dominated by the enemies, and that on "awakening from the restless sleep of night" God's "actual presence would be a reality for the psalmist."[54] Weiser at this point is more in agreement with Craigie, negating any eschatological import in this verse but suggesting instead a possible expectation of a theophany in the worship place the next morning.[55]

Although eschatological reading for this verse still exists, the cultic, non-eschatological explanation is a reasonable one which over time may have gained eschatological overtones.

Psalm 49:15

> "But God will ransom my soul from the power of Sheol,
>   for he will receive me." (NRSV)

This is a psalm of the Korahite tradition in which the motif of redemption figures prominently.[56] Psalm 49 speaks of being persecuted by the wealthy who put their confidence in their riches and have no fear. The psalmist, however, teaches that one should not be amazed at their prosperity because despite their wealth they do not endure and end in the grave.

---

51. Declaisse-Walford, Jacobson and Tanner, *Books of Psalms*, 189.

52. Mays, *Psalms*, 91.

53. So also, Tremper Longman according to whom the NT afterlife perspective allows it to be read in its fuller sense as a reference to the afterlife. Longman, *Psalms*, 109–110.

54. Craigie, *Psalms 1–50*, 164–165.

55. Weiser, *Psalms*, 182.

56. See Mitchell, "'God Will Redeem,'" 371.

Classified as a Wisdom Psalm, the designations "rich," "poor," "wise," "foolish," etc. are not without moral implications. Dahood says that in this psalm the rich and the poor are to be identified as referring to the *unjust* and the *just* (so Targum, and warranted by the interpretation of other biblical texts).⁵⁷ On the surface verse 15 sounds like a clear assertion of an afterlife; however, a conclusive answer is not forthcoming.

Weiser, Dahood, Mitchell, Johnston, Clinton McCann, and Janet Smith all see in this verse a reference to life after death, albeit to varying degrees. According to Weiser the psalmist is confident that the power of God is able to reach beyond death and redeem him from the power of the underworld. How this redemption from death is achieved – whether by "assumption" like Enoch and Elijah (alluded to using the term לָקַח in Gen 5:24 and 2 Kgs 2:3–10) or by resurrection after death – is something that Weiser says the text does not explain and hence it is futile for us to ask. He also sees post-mortem retribution for the wicked rich who have no hope beyond death and are destined for destruction and darkness.⁵⁸ While in line with Weiser's eschatological reading, for Dahood, as also Mitchell and Bronner,⁵⁹ this is a clear expression of the psalmist's belief in "assumption" like that of Enoch and Elijah.⁶⁰

Johnston and Clinton McCann are more cautious. Johnston says the psalmist wrestles with the issue of unjust reward in this life and asserts that it will be reversed at death,⁶¹ without getting into the specifics. McCann also asserts that there is a distinction between the final fate of the fool, who is destined for *Sheol*, and the psalmist who is certain that not even death can separate him from God. McCann observes that the psalmist revisits the concept of ransom from the preceding verses. While the rich cannot secure their ultimate destiny with their riches, God will redeem the psalmist from the grave. McCann sees this assertion of God's power over *Sheol* as a departure from the view of life and death generally seen in the HB. While admitting that it is not a developed doctrine of resurrection, he states that it does "push beyond the normal limits."⁶²

---

57. Dahood, *Psalm 1, 1–50*, 296.
58. Weiser, *Psalms*, 390–391.
59. Mitchell, "'God Will Redeem," 375; Brommer, *Journey*, 28–29.
60. Dahood, *Psalms I, 1–50*, 301. So also Smith, *Dust or Dew*, 128–129.
61. Johnston, *Shades of Sheol*, 217.
62. McCann, "Book of the Psalms," 483–484.

Craigie and Goldingay see very little in that direction. For Craigie this passage does not have an eschatological point of view. He reads this verse as the rich man's "(imaginary) words of self-confidence," a misplaced self-confidence that leads to destruction. Craigie's interpretation is placed in the context of wisdom teaching where a teacher warns his audience that they should not make the same mistake of relying on or seeking riches as the basis for a position of privilege when it comes to death.[63] Goldingay finds the psalmist here similar to Qohelet, as speaking of happenstances that overtake everyone. The rich despite their wealth cannot ransom their life, nor can even the wise for that matter. He argues that the sense in which the word לָקַח ("take") has been used finds better comparison in Psalm 18:17 where it is used in the sense of "rescue," that Enoch and Elijah were translated from the earth while alive, and that it was not an assumption from Sheol. He further points out that לָקַח ("take") is not a technical term, and 2 Kings 2 uses both לָקַח ("take") and עָלָה ("to go up" in 2 Kings 2:1) to describe Elijah's translation into the heavenly realm.[64] Hence he states that this psalm is a juxtaposing of one's security in life – God versus riches – and not of the dead rich and the resurrected wise, and as such finds the afterlife reference in this psalm unconvincing.

The emphasis of redemption in the Korahite tradition together with the reference to death in the preceding verse (v. 14) makes it plausible to read an afterlife concept in its embryonic form; however, it is far from a clear expression of the afterlife as some others have claimed, and it especially does not indicate an Enoch-like translation into the heavenly realm.

Psalm 73:24

> "You guide me with your counsel,
> and afterward you will receive me with honour." (NRSV)

This psalm centres on the theme of the righteous sufferer and the prosperous wicked; distraught by such disparities the psalmist visits the sanctuary and gains understanding. Discussions on this verse centre around the terms "counsel," "afterwards," "honour," and "take/receive."

Dahood finds in these a clear expression of a life in the world beyond and interprets them as such; for instance he sees in it a reference to the heavenly

---

63. Craigie, *Psalm 1–50*, 360–361.
64. Goldingay, "Death and Afterlife," 78.

council, being led into paradise or the eternal assembly, and a reference to "assumption" like that of Enoch.[65] Tremper Longman also views this text as a rare example of a clear expression of the hope of an afterlife for the righteous.[66]

Bauckham views this text, along with Psalm 49, as an example of texts that are precursors to the hope of resurrection prominent in the STP Jewish writings. According to Bauckham, the psalmist seems to take a step further to express a hope of deliverance from death itself by using a language that is reminiscent of God receiving (or taking) Enoch and Elijah. He argues that the situation that gives rise to a hope of deliverance are not of physical sickness or threat of enemies, but rather the issue that these two psalms grapple with is those of justice, that is, the prosperity of the wicked, and gives rise to a radical hope that God's reach "extends even beyond death."[67]

Other scholars are not so certain. Marvin Tate's examination leads him to tentatively conclude that this verse does not have an afterlife reference but is likely a reference to the worth and fulfilment of a life lived under God's counsel. However, he states that the context does allow space for "a perception of ultimacy" and hence the statement remains open to interpretations with greater eschatological orientation.[68] Goldingay, on the other hand, rejects the possibility of a reference to the afterlife. He explains that the use of כָּבוֹד ("honour") here is an expression of the psalmist's confidence that God will restore his honour; it is not a reference to an individual's sharing in God's glory as a beatific afterlife reading of the text may imply, as such a usage does not exist in the HB.[69]

Among the psalms examined this is perhaps one of the clearest in terms of a detectable afterlife conception. There are several instances in which the psalmist expresses a steady faith that God would deliver him from situations that threaten the him with premature death. However, here the context is that of injustice and it does seem possible that the texts offer a glimpse of the afterlife although it remains inconclusive.

---

65. Dahood, *Psalm II, 51–100*, 194–195; similarly, Bronner, *Journey*, 29.
66. Longman, *Psalms*, 215.
67. Bauckham, "Life, Death, and Afterlife," 85.
68. Tate, *Psalms 51–100*, 236.
69. Goldingay, "Death and Afterlife," 81.

1.4.3.2. Section Conclusion

In an examination of all psalms mentioned above it emerges that in a debate regarding the presence of the concepts of an afterlife and post-mortem retribution, the arguments can go both ways. There are staunch believers in their interpretation on both sides of the debate. While it is impossible to determine what the psalmist's intent was, it is safe to say that these psalms have influenced the growth of the idea of an afterlife, and later exegetes could look back and see glimpses of the life to come in these lines.

1.4.3.3. Ecclesiastes 3:21

> "Who knows whether the human spirit goes upward and the spirit of animals goes downward to the earth?" (NRSV)

The question here is whether this verse affirms or denies a possible differentiated post-mortem fate. Longman says that while this does not deny the possibilities of an afterlife, it does deny the possibility of certitude.[70] Murphy, on the other hand, takes the verse to mean that Qoheleth rejects any claim of differentiated post-mortem fates; however, he adds that it is not possible to deduce from this verse his view on *Sheol* and afterlife.[71] Seow clearly states that for Qoheleth there is no scope for separate destinies of man and animals and that "people and animals have the same fate."[72]

Thus, Qoheleth seems to be speaking of the equalizing force of physical death, where not only the distinction between human beings dissolves but even that between humanity and animals fade. If it deems the equality of the grave as unfair, it does not postulate a differentiated afterlife; at best it rejects the idea that one can know of the afterlife with certitude.

1.4.3.4. Job 19:25–27

> "For I know that my Redeemer lives, and that at the last he
>   will stand upon the earth;
> and after my skin has been thus destroyed, then in my flesh I
>   will see God,

---

70. Longman, *Book of Ecclesiastes*, 130.
71. Murphy, *Ecclesiastes*, 37.
72. Seow, *Ecclesiastes*, 176.

whom I shall see on my own side, and my eyes shall behold,
  and not another.
My heart faints within me!" (NRSV)

This verse is often perceived in Christian circles as an expression of Job's faith that he would meet God in the afterlife, and such a reading is probably right in its *sensus plenior*. However, it is difficult to conclusively say that the author envisaged an afterlife. Further, this is a grammatically difficult verse and has been translated variously,[73] adding to the ambiguity.

In Norman Snaith's view, the exact meaning of this passage may remain cryptic but the need for individual justice seems to lead Job to foray into the possibility of an afterlife vindication.[74] Johnston finds that while it is possible Job envisaged some form of vindication after death, and may indicate a growing belief in the resurrection, it was hardly Job's understanding. In Job 42:5, Job says that he has seen God with his eyes, hence it seems that Job's vindication happens in this life and not post-mortem.[75] It could signify an understanding that judgment and redemption require the participation of a realm that is beyond the merely human, but there is no reference to post-mortem life or retribution here. Fischer likewise argues that this passage "is a juridical statement" that expresses Job's hope of vindication. According to him, the author of Job "discusses the idea of a second life on earth but he denies it."[76] Sigvarten makes an important observation when he states that to argue that Job envisaged a resurrection would resolve, and hence effectively ruin, the tension of theodicy that lies at the centre of the book.[77]

Elsewhere in the book the finality of death is clearly envisioned – Job contrasts the tree that is cut down but "at the scent of water" it sprouts again (Job 14:7–9) with that of mankind who once dead "do not rise again" (Job 14:10–12). The author of Job speaks of going to Sheol and coming back (Job 14:13). However, it is not in the sense of dying and resurrecting, but rather, in his despair, he wishes he could relocate to Sheol for the duration of God's

---

73. For instance, see Mombert, "On Job Xix. 25–27," 27–39; Carson, "Word 'Aphar," 387–397.
74. Snaith, "Justice and Immortality," 316–317.
75. Johnston, *Shades of Sheol*, 123.
76. Fischer, "How God Pays Back," 31.
77. Sigvartsen, *Afterlife and Resurrection Beliefs*, 6.

wrath and be brought back when the wrath is past. Hence, the author of Job seems to momentarily begin exploring the afterlife idea but stops short (Job 14:14), as though it was too absurd an idea to even entertain. Further, in the end Job states that he has seen God with his own eyes (Job 42:5), and God declares him more righteous than his friends. This eventuates in Job being vindicated not post-mortem but in this life. As such, the resurrection language here seems to be functioning as a hypothetical possibility describing a circumstance that a tired and desperate Job longed for.

1.4.3.5. Ezekiel
Ezekiel 32:18; 21–23

> [18] "Mortal, wail over the hordes of Egypt, and send them down,
>   . . . to the world below . . .
>
> [21] The mighty chiefs shall speak of them, with their helpers,
>   out of the midst of Sheol: 'They have come down, they lie
>   still, the uncircumcised, killed by the sword.'
> [22] Assyria is there, and all its company, their graves all around
>   it, all of them killed, fallen by the sword.
> [23] Their graves are set in the uttermost parts of the Pit . . ."
>   (NRSV)

This passage is a divine oracle of judgment pronounced on Egypt.[78] Ezekiel is assigned the task of bewailing the coming defeat of Egypt, and hence the death of the hordes or the many (vv. 17–18). Egypt's dead are sent to the earth below with those who go down to the pit, and "they bear their shame with those who go down to the pit" (vv. 24, 25, 30). The oracle gives a list of nations who greet Egypt on her arrival to Sheol. It is a lament[79] or lament parody[80] for a foreign ruler, with Egypt being perhaps singled out to symbolize the last of a long line of kingdoms (Ezekiel 25–32) that have spread terror.[81]

Daniel Block studies the theme of death in the book of Ezekiel and brings his study to bear on the individual passages. According to him Ezekiel has

---

78. Block, "Beyond the Grave," 132.
79. Doak, "Ezekiel's Topography," 607–624.
80. Shipp, *Of Dead Kings*, 46. John Barclay Burns calls it a "lament intended as an ironic celebration." See Burns, "Consolation of Pharaoh," 123.
81. Burns, 124.

a view of the afterlife and this passage, although it primarily deals with a foreign nation, does not preclude doctrinal implications of Yahweh's power extending beyond life, and the continuity of life after death.[82] On the seeming indication in this passage that there is a separate place in Sheol for those who spread terror, Block explains it as Ezekiel's use of the local practice of the tomb of the king being surrounded by that of other lesser individuals to describe an afterlife scene.[83]

Eichrodt states that those who had tried to spread terror on earth are now subjected to contempt. Here, Sheol not only levels all the dead by reducing them to a shade-like existence, but seems to assign a separate place of dishonour, executing some "sort of punitive justice, in which unforgiven guilt meets with its retribution." Eichrodt however says that this is not a moral judgment but rather a reflection of the condition of the corpse serves to impact the condition of "the human ghost," which here is seen in the fact that those slain in the battle are more likely to not receive a proper burial.[84] Doak argues that Ezekiel's bewailing of Egypt as a fallen (anti-)hero is subversive and polemical against ancient Mediterranean forms of hero cults. In doing so Ezekiel is stripping such practices of any power in the eyes of his audience. Themes of heroic dead and afterlife from the Mediterranean appear in this passage but Ezekiel adapts them to convey his own message.[85]

The topography of Sheol portrayed in this passage is not in itself an affirmation of its fact, but rather it is likely the prophet's adaptation and employment of known beliefs and customs to counter forbidden or pagan ideas among the Israelites who might have believed that a special place awaits the heroic dead.[86] The expectation seemed to be that heroes will be treated in a special manner in the afterlife. But in this case Egypt is now not in a place of honour. She along with others are depicted as in a state of shame. Further, Egypt is unburied and there is a repeated reference to being laid among the uncircumcised (vv. 19, 21, 28, 32). The implication is that since the Egyptians

---

82. Block, "Beyond the Grave," 121–136. Allen also says that there seems to be a distinction between Sheol proper and the lower regions to which Egypt's dead are sent. Allen, *Ezekiel 20–48*, 137.

83. Block, "Beyond the Grave," 121–136.

84. Eichrodt, *Ezekiel*, 436–437.

85. Doak, "Ezekiel's Topography," 613–623.

86. Doak, 619.

practiced circumcision, to be left among the uncircumcised was dishonourable, something well understood by the Israelites, and is compounded by the fact that they are said to be left unburied.[87] That it is not to be taken literally is further signalled by parallels in Ezekiel 31 that speaks of a cedar tree in very similar terms. The tree, compared again to the king of Egypt, is portrayed as the envy of all, but is later brought down and lies in the netherworld among the uncircumcised who were killed by the sword. Hence, it is likely that Ezekiel 32:17–32 too is a derision of a mighty nation using what was known or thought of the underworld.

Ezekiel 37: 1–14 – the Valley of Dry Bones

The vision describing the valley of dead bones is arguably the most well-known prophecy of Ezekiel. It consists of a vision (vv. 1–10) followed by an interpretation (vv. 11–14). Ezekiel receives this vision during Judah's Babylonian captivity. The objective of the vision was to give hope and encouragement to the disheartened exiled people. The terminology of this passage is picked up in the NT and many see a clear foreshadowing of the concept of resurrection in this passage.

Block understands the primary message of the vision in Ezekiel 37 to be the restoration of Israel. However, he states that the text also speaks of individual resurrection by implication. He states that Ezekiel's concept of resurrection had several gaps that would only develop later, but the message of national revivification stems from "the conviction that the grave need not be the end."[88] Albert Hogeterp draws attention to the Qumran *Pseudo-Ezekiel* that evinces eschatological readings of Ezekiel 37 in Jewish circles that incorporated the ideas of resurrection of the righteous to the eschatological restoration of Israel in the land.[89] Among those who do not view the text as speaking of the resurrection of the dead are Michael Fox and John Strong.[90] Fox states that although the excellent rhetoric of the vision persuades its readers of the possibility of reversing death, the text itself is speaking not of a corporeal resurrection but a figurative one. He however agrees that this

---

87. Strong, "Egypt's Shameful Death," 493.
88. Block, "Beyond the Grave," 136–140.
89. See Hogeterp, "Resurrection and Biblical Tradition," 59–69.
90. Strong, "Egypt's Shameful Death," 475–503, although he only notes this position in a cursory manner.

vision creates an avenue contributing to the development of the concept of physical resurrection because the vision takes the ultimate polarity, that of life and death, and shows that Yahweh can bridge it.[91]

Of all the texts examined in this survey, this is perhaps the most powerfully graphic, yet it is also in a way the most unambiguous because of the clear interpretation that followed of the vision's application to reality. There is no denying that the image of the reversal of death and the dramatic process involved in achieving it is appealing, not least of which is contributed by the fluidity of the word רוּחַ ("wind" but also "Spirit") which is at once a natural element and the divine agency by which transformation is affected. The vivid portrayal has captured the imaginations of its readers down the centuries. That the text may have arisen from a known supposition of the resurrection of the dead is a possibility, although it remains indeterminate. Nonetheless, the immediate context makes it abundantly clear that the vision uses resurrection imagery to speak of the revival of a people who considered themselves finished.

1.4.3.6. Section Conclusion

In their literary contexts, the two Ezekiel passages do not seem to be speaking about the afterlife or resurrection. Rather the prophet probably had at his command contemporarily held beliefs regarding Sheol and resurrection and used them to address false beliefs in his community – the false belief regarding the fate of the fallen heroes, and the disbelief about the ability and willingness of Yahweh to remedy their situation. The passages, especially Ezekiel 37, are vivid and detailed in their description and have most likely contributed to the development of concepts surrounding the afterlife.

1.4.3.7. Hosea 6:1–2

> [1] "Come, let us return to the Lord;
>   for it is he who has torn, and he will heal us;
>   he has struck down, and he will bind us up.
> [2] After two days he will revive us;
>   on the third day he will raise us up,
>   that we may live before him." (NRSV)

---

91. Fox, "Rhetoric of Ezekiel's Vision," 12.

The context of this prophetic text is the Assyrian crisis in the northern kingdom of Israel in the eighth century BCE. Exile was looming over Israel with Assyria wiping out several of the smaller states in the Ancient West Asia (AWA).

For those who see in this passage a reference to resurrection, the argument is that the usage of terms like חָיָה ("to live") and קוּם ("to rise"),[92] and the shared reference to the third day both here and in the NT indicate that resurrection is in view. Hubbard understands the wounds as fatal and consequently understands חָיָה and קוּם as references to resurrection.[93] For Stuart the "basic promise" is that of God's renewal of his people, but the concept of resurrection is detectable in the phrase בַּיּוֹם הַשְּׁלִישִׁי ("on the third day"), although he does admit the difficulty of knowing with certainty if Hosea 6:2 points to Jesus' resurrection. He comes to this conclusion by arguing that the reference to the third day makes the connection to Jesus' resurrection viable, despite having stated earlier that two and three days "should not be taken literalistically."[94] J. Wijngaards likewise finds references to death and resurrection, albeit reading terms like חָיָה and קוּם as reflective of covenantal terminology.[95]

That the passage is speaking of a national restoration is the alternate view espoused by other scholars. Barré takes a comparative approach in his two articles and studies cognate verb pairs[96] in Hosea 6:1-2 and some Aramaic and Akkadian texts, demonstrating that the word pairs found in Hosea 6:1-2 extend to other Semitic languages as well. He also compares the temporal expressions (two days, on the third day) in Hosea with similar expression in the Akkadian text that appear in conjunction with the verb pairs. He finds that the verb pairs and the temporal expressions are common in medical texts with the temporal expression providing an estimated time for healing. He concludes that although the texts do not share a direct literary connection, the

---

92. Bronner, *Journey*, 31–32.
93. Hubbard, *Hosea: An Introduction*, 125.
94. Stuart, *Hosea and Jonah*, 164–165.
95. Wijngaards, "Death and Resurrection," 236–239.
96. The word pairs being רָפָא - חָבַשׁ ("to heal" - "to bind") and קוּם - חָיָה ("to live" - "to rise") in Hosea 6:1-2 and *balatu* - *riksu/sindu* ("heal" - "bind") and *balatu* - *tebu* ("live" - "get up") in the Gula Hymn. See Barré's two articles, Barré, "New Light," 129–41, and Barré, "Bullutsa-rabi's Hymn," 241–245.

identical word pairs in the texts suggests that Hosea 6:1–2, like the Aramaic and Akkadian texts, is not a reference to the future resurrection of the dead but refers primarily to healing, which the prophet then uses to express the hope of restoration for Israel.[97] This conclusion finds some degree of corroboration in 2 Kings 20:5 where the word רָפָא ("to heal") occurs again in conjunction with the temporal expression בַּיּוֹם הַשְּׁלִישִׁי ("on the third day") in Yahweh's message of healing to King Hezekiah.[98] Others have found the book as using the motif of dying and rising fertility gods of the Canaanite cult while opposing the cult.[99]

Johnston argues that throughout the book the prophet wrestles with the fate of the nation and holds in tension both Yahweh's messages of coming destruction on Israel and the hope of restoration eventuating in a merging of the images of healing and revivification of a dying nation.[100] According to Bo Lim Hosea 6:1–3 are the words of the people,[101] who superficially confess their return and trust in Yahweh, rather than words of the prophet.[102] It is a plausible reading. If the prophet is understood as the speaker of 6:1–3 it does not explain why Yahweh continues to be frustrated and disappointed with the people in vv. 4–10; one must assume that the people perhaps did not heed the prophet's words. Whereas reading vv. 1–3 as the words of the people would explain the sudden change in the tone between vv. 1–3 and vv.4–10. Lim sees no place for interpreting vv. 1–2 as references to resurrection, national or individual.

Even if it is read as the words of the prophet to the people, immediately preceding the passage are Yahweh's words – Ephraim and Judah are diseased and look to Assyria for healing in vain, and Yahweh like a lion will tear them to pieces and would not turn to them until they admit their guilt and earnestly seek him (Hos 5:13–15). The shared words רָפָא ("to heal") in 5:13 and 6:1 and טָרַף ("to tear") in 5:14 and 6:1 link 6:1–2 to the preceding verses in 5:13–14,

---

97. Barré, "New Light," 129–41, and Barré, "Bullutsa-rabi's Hymn," 241–245.

98. Bo H. Lim makes the same observation, however he mentions perhaps mistakenly that the word קוּם ("to rise") is present in 2 Kings 20:5 as well, whereas the text there uses עָלָה ("to go up") instead. See Lim and Castelo, *Hosea*, 133.

99. See May, "Fertility Cult in Hosea," 84–84; Roubin, "On Canaanite Motifs," 109–110.

100. Johnston, *Shades of Sheol*, 221–222.

101. Wijngaards also identifies the speaker of vv. 1–3 as the people, a prayer, rather than as the prophet. See Wijngaards, "Death and Resurrection," 236.

102. Lim and Castelo, *Hosea*, 133.

which is a description of Israel's current political crisis. It is in this context that the prophet calls Israel to return to Yahweh consequent to which Yahweh will heal and revive their nation.

Further, the verbs are plural and hence most likely refer to the people rather than to an individual, and it is unlikely that a prediction of an individual resurrection of the messiah would have instilled a sense of urgent repentance in the prophet's immediate wayward audience. Reading back with the NT in view it would perhaps be short-sighted to not consider, as Duane Garrett says, the possibility of this passage being a typological foreshadowing of the resurrection of Christ.[103] That said, in context the text was most likely speaking of the repentance of the people, whether by the people themselves or a call to them from the prophet, and the consequent national reconstitution (as promised in 5:15), and uses the metaphor of healing and revivification to portray this restoration.

1.4.3.8. Isaiah

Isaiah 53:10–12

> [10] Yet it was the will of the Lord to crush him with pain.
> When you make his life an offering for sin,
>   he shall see his offspring, and shall prolong his days;
> through him the will of the Lord shall prosper.
> [11] Out of his anguish he shall see light;
> he shall find satisfaction through his knowledge.
>   The righteous one, my servant, shall make many righteous,
>   and he shall bear their iniquities.
> [12] Therefore I will allot him a portion with the great,
>   and he shall divide the spoil with the strong;
> because he poured out himself to death,
>   and was numbered with the transgressors;
> yet he bore the sin of many,
>   and made intercession for the transgressors. (NRSV)

---

103. Garrett, *Hosea, Joel*, 159–159. She agrees that the author was referring to national restoration in the original context.

The Christian understanding of Jesus' death is often seen as explained in Isaiah 53. One of the major problems with this passage is that the text of Isaiah 53:10–12 is corrupted, with the LXX differing quite significantly from the MT, and scholars have often despaired of restoring it or recovering its meaning.[104] This has meant that often the analysis of the text comes with the scholar's reconstruction of it (which often vary at significant points) on which depends their interpretation.

Dahood's reconstruction of Isaiah 53:8–12 leads him to conclude that the Servant was put to death publicly.[105] John Day focuses on the translation of the noun דַּעַת (בְּדַעְתּוֹ in Isa 53:11) which he translates as "humiliation," as opposed to the older translation as "knowledge," and in contrast to H. G. M. Williamson's "rest." Day argues that Daniel 12:4 is dependent on Isaiah 53:11 and both are in the context of death and resurrection.[106] Alternatively, others see no reference to either death or resurrection. Johnston states that there is no mention of resurrection, but the descriptions of the new life are strongly reminiscent of earthly existence – the text portrays the Servant returning to life in some unspecified form.[107] Others assert that the text does not mention the death of the Servant and hence there is no reference to resurrection. Isaiah Sonne reconstructs and reads v. 10a–b as Yahweh's healing of the Servant from the pain and affliction mentioned in 53:3, and restoring him in community so that the Servant is not shunned anymore.[108] Based on a verbal connection with 2 Chronicles 26:21, Barré argues that Isaiah 53:8 speaks of cutting off the Servant from the land of the living and is often understood as indicating the Servant's death, refers not to killing but to exclusion of the Servant, perhaps from the temple. And just as he was counted among the transgressors, the reference to his grave in v. 9 refers to the decision to assign him a grave with the wicked. He then reconstructs and reads vv. 10c–11b as a prayer for

---

104. See Sonne, "Isaiah 53:10–12," 335; Breytenbach, "Septuagint Version," 345–347.

105. See his translation and interpretation of v. 9, which according to him was a problematic verse primarily because of the erroneous division of the words. Dahood, "Isaiah 53," 568.

106. John Day, "Daʿat 'Humiliation,'" 97–103.

107. Johnston, *Shades of Sheol*, 228.

108. For the reconstruction see Sonne, "Isaiah 53:10–12," 336.

the Servant's restoration after his affliction; he sees no reference to either his death or resurrection.[109]

The textual corruption means that this passage continues to be a point of contention making it quite impossible, as of now, to determine with certainty which reconstruction and reading is the correct one. Further, as part of the Servant Song, the passage in the *sensus plenior* is applied to Christ. However, in context the identity of the Servant is a much-discussed subject with no resolution in sight and hence this passage is placed in this category.

Isaiah 66:24

> And they shall go out and look at the dead bodies of the people who have rebelled against me; for their worm shall not die, their fire shall not be quenched, and they shall be an abhorrence to all flesh. (NRSV)

Often considered a late interpolation, this verse seems to suggest that the dead bodies of those who rebel against Yahweh suffer some kind of unending punishment.[110] This verse is thought to underlie the later references to *Gehenna* or hell in passages like Mark 9:43–48, and is often quoted in discussions concerning the emergence of the idea of hell.[111] This verse was later considered too negative for ending the synagogue reading and was read before v. 23 so that the reading ended on a positive note.[112]

Discussions abound on whether it is a figurative reference to a temporal punishment or an eschatological one. The text depicts a scene of Yahweh's worshippers leaving from the temple and looking down to see the burning-decaying yet unconsumed dead bodies of Yahweh's enemies. The location is thought to be in the Valley of Hinnom (*ge'hinnom*), which emerges when this text is studied in conjunction with Jeremiah 7:31–33 and 19:5. This valley was also called Topheth and had gained notoriety during the Judean monarchy,

---

109. For details of the argument see Barré, "Textual and Rhetorical-critical Observations," 18–23.

110. The majority of scholars have followed Duhm's suggestion that chapter 65–66 is a later addition, dating to around the mid-fifth century BCE. Duhm, *Das Buch Jesaia*, 489; Marti, *Das Buch Jesaja*, 414, both cited in Smith, *Rhetoric and Redaction*, 1; Westermann, *Isaiah 40–66*, 428; Olyan, "Fire and Worms," in Olyan and Wright, *Supplementation and the Study*, 155.

111. For instance, see Bernstein, *Formation of Hell*, 171.

112. Peterson, *Hell on Trial*, 31.

particularly the reigns of Ahaz and Manasseh, as the place for human sacrifice to Molech, the Ammonite god. This place was desecrated during Josiah's reform (2 Kgs 23:10). It however retained its evil reputation and eventually came to be the designation for *Gehenna* or hell.[113]

Claus Westermann states that this is a description of an eschatological scene where the world order centres around juxtaposing scenes – one of a universal and perpetual worship at the temple and the other of the everlasting suffering of Yahweh's enemies by fire and worm.[114] Brevard Childs likewise states there is a consensus in critical scholarship that this is a later addition of an apocalyptic portrayal of *Gehenna*. However, he opines that even if it is a later addition it is fundamental in the final shaping of the book that retains the righteous-wicked divide "into the eschaton."[115]

For those who argue for the temporal interpretation, the language here is figurative, a "prophetic symbolism."[116] In the wider context of the chapter, the author describes God executing his judgment with fire and sword on his enemies with the climactic result that many are slaughtered (Isa 66:15–16); Yahweh's enemies perish and the righteous survive who come to worship Yahweh. For Edward Fudge this setting indicates that it is symbolic.[117] Robert Peterson states that Isaiah uses a battlefield imagery to portray those slain by Yahweh and the terrible consequence.[118] Kim Papaioannou likewise sees this passage as "simple battle language" and there being no one to bury the dead they are eventually eaten by worms and burnt.[119] Others have found in the unquenchable fire a reference to the altar fire that was to be continually burning.

The term דֵּרָאוֹן ("abhorrence") is found elsewhere only in Daniel 12:2 that speaks of the final judgment, and hence seems to suggest that this text also should be read eschatologically. However, the imageries of fire as punishment and of worms devouring decaying bodies in the grave are commonly used in the HB for temporal judgment – fire in Isaiah 1:31; 26:11; 30:33; Jeremiah

---

113. Peterson, 31.
114. Westermann, *Isaiah 40–66*, 428.
115. Childs, *Isaiah*, 542.
116. Fudge, "Final End," 329.
117. Fudge, 329.
118. Peterson, *Hell on Trial*, 31; Finney similarly opines that hell as a place of eternal punishment does not exist in the OT, Finney, *Resurrection, Hell*, 158.
119. Papaioannou, *Geography of Hell*, 31.

4:4; 7:20; 17:27; Ezekiel 20:47–48; Amos 5:5–6; worms in Job 17:14; 21:26; 24:20; Isaiah 14:11. These texts are prophetic oracles speaking of divine judgment, similar to Isaiah 66:24.[120] Described as unquenchable and deathless, Isaiah 66:24 and several other passages cited above seemed to have had some bearing on the emergence of the idea of a state of eternal perdition. As such, regardless of whether the author intended it or not, this imagery has made a lasting impression and at the very least contributed to the later development of the concept of a place of unending punishment for the wicked.

1.4.3.9. Section Conclusion

In context, it is arguable that the Isaianic texts examined above, like the rest of the passages in this category, are not primarily speaking of resurrection or eschatological judgment. However, the language is suggestive enough for some to postulate it, and the texts lend themselves to be easily adopted into the resurrection/afterlife concept. It is not hard to see how they contributed to the rich reservoir of texts that later readers and writers could rehash to more clearly express the concepts of, and relating to, the afterlife.[121]

1.4.4. Section Conclusion

The first category of texts examined speak of Yahweh bringing people back to life as an expression of Yahweh's potentiality and his status as the sovereign over life and death. These are part of the more formulaic expressions that draw contrasts between Yahweh's power and the powerlessness of other gods or human beings. In the second category of texts, some have stronger detectable beats of the afterlife than others. These texts, occurring in the poetic and prophetic sections of the HB, can and have been read eschatologically. It is probably not wrong to see more than one level of meaning in these texts, especially in their fuller sense. And Claudia Setzer is right in saying that metaphors are meaningful only if they have a reference to the way people

---

120. Papaioannou, 31.

121. Isaiah 25:8a speaks of Yahweh swallowing up death forever, which may be read as indirectly implying some kind of immortality or post-mortem existence. Some see this as the ultimate overcoming of death (Blenkinsopp), others have objected to such a reading citing that death in Hebrew and English do not have the same range of meanings and could refer to terrible affliction or anything that limits one from living to the fullest (Wildberger), or have understood it as an expression of Yahweh's infinite power (Crenshaw). See Blenkinsopp, *Isaiah 1–39*, 359; Wildberger, *Isaiah 13–27*, 532–533; Crenshaw, "Love is Stronger," 56.

actually think and live.¹²² Hence while the textual evidence is not concrete, it is reasonable to surmise that the idea of afterlife retribution did not suddenly emerge but that texts such as these must have been formative. These texts were like seeds laying in fertile ground, and at the least, their language provided an easy transition from language to substance when the time was ripe.

1.5. Review of Literature

Post-mortem divine retribution sits at the point of intersection of two broad themes in the HB and STP Jewish literature: divine retribution and the afterlife. There is robust literature available on both themes. However, the study of this point of intersection is largely unexplored. The literature review will present an overview of the significant works that sit at the confluence between the two. These are not presented chronologically but in order of their relevance to my work. An annotated bibliography of some of the significant works on the themes of retribution and afterlife are in the Appendix.

One significant work on post-mortem retribution is that of Samuel Adams.¹²³ He traces the transition of the idea of retribution, or act and consequence as used in Adams's book, in the wisdom tradition of Israel – Proverbs, Qohelet, Ben Sira, and 4QInstruction (Job being excluded in his analysis). This transition in Wisdom literature is seen in terms of the concerns for the afterlife, which sets the purview of retribution in a much larger context by extending retribution from limited to this world to the afterlife. Adams connects the themes of divine retribution and afterlife and posits a linear development of the theme of afterlife – from lack of belief in the afterlife in Proverbs to increasing engagement with ideas of afterlife to affirmations of it in the 4QInstruction.

Adams demonstrates that a study of the themes of post-mortem retribution as an intersection of the themes of divine retribution and afterlife is warranted, but since his work concentrates on four wisdom texts it leaves ample room for other works such as this present study. Moreover, this dissertation goes a step further by asking about the basis of retribution in order to determine which aspect of divine retribution is emphasized in a particular

---

122. Setzer, *Resurrection of the Body*, 8.
123. See Adams, *Wisdom in Transition*.

instance of post-mortem divine retribution. Further, on one hand, Adams takes a historical approach to develop his thesis of a linear development of the concept of afterlife in Jewish thought, although his dating for Proverbs and Qohelet seem rather circular. On the other hand, the approach adopted in this dissertation is primarily synchronic and intertextual and does not depend on historical issues in the selected texts.

Apart from Adams, other works do not primarily focus on post-mortem divine retribution but rather on questions surrounding the afterlife, while touching upon post-mortem divine retribution in varying degrees. For instance, George W. E. Nickelsburg[124] focuses on the three themes of resurrection, immortality and eternal life, demonstrating that early Judaism and Jewish texts exhibit a diverse and complex view of the afterlife. He argues that the three themes are closely related to three literary forms –the story of a righteous person falsely accused but vindicated, the judgment scene, and the two-way covenantal theology at Qumran – and proposes a setting in Jewish history that led to their emergence. He analyses how prior traditions have contributed to the formal and theological development of the themes and their transformation of the traditions through the impact of their historical environment. In his analysis, it emerges that the theme of resurrection features prominently though not exclusively. This leads to the second part of the book that examines the adaptation of the concept of resurrection in the NT, an examination of the Markan passion narrative, and the Son of Man tradition as appropriated from its Jewish origins.

Particularly relevant to my dissertation is his analysis of the function of resurrection vis-à-vis judgment, which leads to a discussion of the presentation and conception of post-mortem existence and post-mortem divine retribution in the texts. One of his conclusions is that resurrection functions either as a reward itself or as a means through which the post-mortem judgment is realized. Moreover, while in some texts resurrection has the whole of humanity in its purview, in others it is more exclusive. These conclusions find resonance in my findings as well. However, the treatment of the post-mortem divine retribution in Nickelsburg's book is brief and it does not examine the basis of post-mortem divine retribution. This is understandable since his primary interest is on the three themes *per se*, and it covers a much wider

---

124. Nickelsburg: *Resurrection, Immortality*.

range of Jewish texts than does this dissertation. Further he primarily uses form critical approach to analyse the texts, but uses literary and historical approaches as well, which affects his conclusions, some of which he later finds amiss and mentions in his expanded edition.

One of the most recent works in this area is Jan Age Sigvartsen's[125] recently published two volume work which is a valuable addition in the field of afterlife beliefs in the STP Jewish literature. It provides a comprehensive and systematic overview of the diversity of afterlife and resurrection beliefs presented in the Apocrypha and Pseudepigrapha. One of the expressed interests of the book is to analyse the references and allusions to the language and imagery of the HB in the presentation of these concepts in the later Jewish and Christian works. The analysis shows that resurrection language and symbolism were abundant in the HB and the readings of these texts by the Jews of the STP contributed to the development of beliefs in afterlife and resurrection in Judaism and Christianity. While the afterlife and resurrection beliefs that coexisted during the STP were varied and complex, it finds that a common predominant thread at the core of these beliefs was theodicy.

In analysing these texts Sigvartsen touches upon the theme of post-mortem divine retribution which is of relevance to this present study. The analysis of the numerous texts includes an examination of the concept of resurrection in the two STP texts this study examines, 2 Maccabees 7 and Book of Watchers (BW) 22. However, these references to post-mortem retribution, though significant and well-examined, occur more as a by-product of the discussions of afterlife and resurrection, which are the central focus of the book, rather than as an interest in itself.[126]

Hans Clements Caesarius Cavallin's[127] work is an older but comprehensive study on the theme of afterlife in Judaism. His investigation centres around the questions rising from Paul's arguments on the resurrection of the dead in 1 Corinthians 15. He poses four questions to a wide range of Jewish texts to gain insight into the Jewish background of 1 Corinthians 15: (i) Does the text really speak of life after death? If so (ii) does it speak of resurrection, or

---

125. Sigvartsen, *Afterlife and Resurrection*; and Sigvartsen, *Afterlife and Resurrection Beliefs*.

126. I have tried to incorporate this work in my study but because it was published 19 September 2019, after I had finished writing, I have not been able to engage with it as extensively as I would have liked.

127. Cavallin, *Life After Death*, 1.

immortality, or something else? (iii) Do the resurrected ones return to earthly life or live a glorified existence in heaven? (iv) When exactly does the new life begin, and how does it relate to the final judgment? He concludes that the conception of afterlife in Judaism during the STP was indeed variegated.

Relevant to this dissertation is the second part of question (iv) which looks for a relationship between life after death and final judgment. He finds that in almost all the texts under examination the discussion of the afterlife was explicitly set in the context of judgment, although it is not always clear if the judgment is an eschatological one. The judgment nonetheless expresses interest in the establishment of divine justice and restoration of just balance in either Israel or the order of cosmos. The large number of texts considered in Cavallin's study means that the treatment of the post-mortem retribution aspect of the texts is not as comprehensive, however, it does bring the diversity of Jewish post-mortem conception to the fore and highlights the connection between divine justice and post-mortem divine retribution.

1.5.1. Section Conclusion

The theme of post-mortem divine retribution is one that has been recognized but appears mostly in tandem with or in the process of the explorations of the afterlife and related subjects. There is very little work, if any, that directly investigates or addresses this subject. The preceding discussion highlights the validity as well as the scope for an investigation into the basis or aspect of post-mortem divine retribution.

Having discussed the works relevant to examination of the concept of post-mortem divine retribution, we now note how these texts are to be examined. This dissertation will be using the method called *intertextuality*. Since the dissertation compares the concept of divine retribution in Deuteronomy and in post-mortem texts in HB and STP literature, intertextuality is most suited for the purpose as it maximizes the interconnections between texts. An intertextual reading of the biblical texts is a relatively new approach, hence the value of a brief explanation of what it is.

1.6. Method: Intertextuality

Intertextuality as a method can be described as the reading of one text in conjunction with another or others. It is based on the presumption of the interrelatedness of texts, and derives from the understanding that texts do not exist in isolation, rather encoded in any text are the voices of other related texts "bounded only by human culture and language itself" as Danna Nolan Fewell puts it.[128] The dissertation examines the post-mortem divine retribution texts in the HB and two works of STP Jewish literature in terms of the aspects of divine retribution found in the book of Deuteronomy. It studies the concept in the selected texts by placing each one alongside the Deuteronomic concept of divine retribution and hence intertextuality is well suited for the purpose.

1.6.1. Origin

As a literary theory intertextuality came into currency in the second half of the twentieth century. The theory can be said to be anticipated in the Russian literary theorist Mikhail Bakhtin's notion of *dialogism* – the idea that words or utterances have multiple meanings and are characteristically polyphonic, that, is they express a plurality of voices, regardless of the author's or speaker's intentions.[129] It posits that no word or utterance is read or heard in isolation; it is always in a living context where a word or an utterance presupposes past words and anticipates future responses from its receiver.[130] Thus every expression is an ongoing network of statements and responses that presuppose past statements and anticipates future responses.[131] In Bakhtin's view a word or text is historically contingent because it is "always already embedded in a history of expressions by others in a chain of ongoing cultural and political moments."[132] A discourse, which is a chain of utterances, is hence "fundamentally dialogic and historically contingent, that is, positioned within, and inseparable from, a community, a history, a place."[133] Thus according to

---

128. Fewell, "Introduction: Reading, Writing," 17.
129. Grohamann and Kim, "Introduction," 3. Bakhtin's dialogism was not just a literary formulation but had socio-political implications. See Allen, *Intertextuality*, 21–30.
130. Bakhtin's views on language can be found in Bakhtin and Medvedev, *Formal Method*; Beal, "Ideology and Intertextuality," 29; Claassens, "Biblical Theology," 129.
131. Irvine, "Mikhail Bakhtin."
132. Irvine.
133. Irvine.

Bakhtin a text is the product of an author's dialogue with existing texts as well as with current reality.[134]

However, Bakhtin never used the word intertextuality to describe his specific view of language. It was Julia Kristeva, the Bulgarian-French literary critic and semiotician, who coined the term "intertextuality" in the late 1960s and used it to articulate her theory.[135] Kristeva's work emerged in the backdrop of a transition from structuralism (which was bound by formal objectivity) to post structuralism (where emphasis fell on subjectivity, instability, and indeterminacy).[136] She used the word intertextuality to describe both spoken and written discourses.[137] Her work was influenced by both Ferdinand de Saussure[138] and Bakhtin.[139] She modified Bakhtin's dialogue model by limiting its application to relationship between texts or discourses, rather than between texts and reality.[140] Within her intertextual theory, intertextuality challenges the textual boundaries, that is, the fixed elements that allow the reader to speak of "*the* meaning, subject, or origin of a writing."[141] Thus texts are not self-contained but dynamic, not fixed but unstable. Kristeva describes "literary word" as "an intersection of textual surfaces rather than a point (a fixed meaning), as a dialogue among several writings."[142] As such "each

---

134. van Wolde, "Texts in Dialogue," 2.

135. Kristeva, "Word, Dialogue and Novel," 66, also 15.

136. Allen, *Intertextuality*, 3; Grohamann and Kim, "Introduction," 3.

137. Beal, "Ideology," 22.

138. The Swiss linguist Ferdinand de Saussure, also known as the founder of modern linguistics, who developed the notion of a linguistic sign as composed of two elements: the signified, or the concept, and the signifier, or the sound-image. He also posited that linguistic signs are arbitrary and non-referential (that is, a linguistic sign does not directly refer to the concept or the thing in the real world, but derives its meaning by referring to the linguistic system), and differential (that is, any particular sign has meaning because of its similarity to and difference from other related signs within the linguistic system). Although not as directly influential on the concept of intertextuality as Bakhtin's idea of dialogism, this reconceptualization of language and words had implications for how words and texts are understood in intertextuality. Saussure's work in linguistics is considered the origin of literary and cultural theory including structuralism. See Allen, *Intertextuality*, 8–10.

139. Allen, 11.

140. van Wolde notes that Kristeva expands the idea of text to the extent that "reality becomes a text too," van Wolde, "Texts in Dialogue," 2; See also Stahlberg, *Sustaining Fiction* 57, who also notes that Kristeva's approach is ahistoric unlike that of Bakhtin for whom the historicity of the word was important.

141. Beal, "Ideology," 22–23.

142. Kristeva, "Word, Dialogue," 65.

word (text) is an intersection of other words (texts) where at least one other word (text) can be read."[143] This opens up the texts, making them dynamic where a text is always in conversation with other texts. Thus, intertextuality argues that for a full appreciation and understanding of a text it is necessary to recognize texts as essentially interconnected to other texts.[144]

The works of other scholars like the French theorist Roland Barthes and Michael Riffaterre supplemented this movement towards the polyvalence of a word and the shift of centre of meaning from the author to the readers by underscoring the role of the readers in the creation of meaning. Barthes challenged the authorial role in meaning-making to the point that he would declare the author dead.[145] Riffaterre would go in another direction and posit that the reader approaching the text is also a plurality hence making the act of reading active in the process of making meaning.[146] Thus the multiplicity that is embedded in and makes up the text is focused on one place, that is, the liberated reader.[147] These propositions destabilized the text by divorcing the author from the text and positing a plurality not only of the words that make up the text but also a plurality of the reader in whom now rested all the powers of meaning-making.

The brief overview shows that intertextuality as a literary theory explains the phenomenon of the interrelatedness of texts. It challenges and reshapes the fundamental conception of the way meaning is created and understood. In doing so it also deconstructs the concept of source, the idea of author in relation to text and meaning, and the vector of influence, more of which will be seen shortly. It posits the interaction between the reader and the text as determinative for meaning-making, and transgresses the textual boundaries between texts.

---

143. Kristeva, 66.
144. Oropeza, "Intertextuality: Brief History," 3.
145. Barthes, *Image, Music, Text*, 148.
146. Riffaterre, cited in Grohamann and Kim, "Introduction," 4.
147. Grohamann and Kim, 4.

1.6.2. Intertextuality and Biblical Studies

Intertextuality was soon appropriated in biblical scholarship as a method by those interested in exploring relationships between texts.[148] It has been argued, however, that biblical texts have been read intertextually long before the word was coined. The use of the HB in the NT and the STP Jewish literature, Scripture citing Scripture, inner-biblical interpretation, and the idea of influence and reception have all been cited as intertextual approaches. Hence the claim that intertextuality is not new in the field of biblical studies, since exegetes have had to study intertextually before it came to be called intertextuality.[149] Further, because of such an understanding of intertextuality in biblical studies Peter D. Miscall could say: "'Intertextuality' is a covering term for all the possible relations that can be established between texts."[150] Thus intertextuality in biblical studies came to be used as a broad term for methods that read biblical texts from the perspective of their relation to other texts.

One of the most important works in intertextual reading in biblical studies is by Michael Fishbane who used inner biblical exegesis (IBE) to denote the interpretation of Scripture in ancient Israel.[151] IBE's interest lies in the subsequent interpretations of an authoritative text within scripture. Fishbane makes two important points regarding IBE: (i) it is in the nature of scripture to be reinterpreted, and (ii) reinterpretation arises out of some need or crisis.[152] IBE focuses on biblical texts that demonstrably cited older texts in the process of (re)interpreting them. Thus, IBE reads the text to discern "traces of exegesis within Scripture," and the process of discerning the authoritative

---

148. The use of intertextuality as a method is not limited to biblical studies. Barton notes such a use of intertextuality among French literary critics too, including Kristeva herself. See Barton, "Déjà Lu," 8.

149. See de Moor, *Intertextuality in Ugarit*, ix; Clayton and Rothstein, cited in Barton, "Déjà Lu," 1–2.

150. Miscall, "Isaiah: New Heavens," 44.

151. Fishbane, *Biblical Interpretation*, 6, 7, 14. He identified four types of IBE; see Fishbane, "Inner Biblical Exegesis," 19–37. The term "inner biblical exegesis" was coined by Nahum Mattathias Sarna. See Sarna, "Psalm 89," 29–46. Further, the first explicit use of the term intertextuality in biblical studies in credited to Tryggve Mettinger in his study of the Book of Job, 1993. Dell and Kynes, "Introduction," xvii.

152. Fishbane, "Inner Biblical Exegesis," 17, 43.

scripture, or *traditum*, from the subsequent interpretation of it, called *traditio*, is central in IBE.[153]

Essential to Fishbane's IBE is the discernibility that the *traditio*'s use of the *traditum* is a deliberate act, and that the direction of influence is demonstrable as well. Lyle Eslinger takes issue with these aspects. He questions whether every instance of interconnectedness between texts can be laid down to authorial intent since shared features between texts could arise without authorial intent or awareness. A reader may perceive a connection which the author may not have intended. Further, to establish the direction of influence necessitates that historical questions for both the authoritative text and the subsequent interpretation be answered, and historical issues are not always definitive in biblical studies.[154]

As such Eslinger proposes a more synchronic approach as an alternative to IBE which he calls inner biblical allusion (IBA). IBA, according to Eslinger, does require "some literary reasons to assume a vector of influence," but does not pretend to be using a "'scientific' historical framework" to determine accurately the priority of the given texts.[155] While Eslinger's proposition has its merits by sitting lightly on authorial intent, Benjamin Sommer rightly points out that IBE and IBA belong to two separate categories:

i. IBE is historical while IBA is more ahistorical, and hence Eslinger's proposition that IBA replace IBE is not viable.[156] IBE comes with its own sets of problems owing to its historical diachronic approach, IBA does not proceed by overcoming those problems but rather by somewhat bypassing them. Hence, Sommer is right in seeing them as two categories rather than one as a replacement of the other. However, he also points out that allusion

---

153. See Fishbane, *Biblical Interpretation*, 10–11. Further, Fishbane differentiates IBE from tradition-historical criticism which looks backwards from the text to the oral tradition that forms the received authoritative text, while IBE goes forward from the authoritative text to its subsequent interpretations. He states, "In tradition-history, written formulations themselves become authoritative; by contrast inner-biblical exegesis begins with the authoritative *traditum*." Hence in IBE the authoritative text is the fixed base and the adaptations of or responses to it within the Scripture are the interpretations. See Fishbane, *Biblical Interpretation*, 7.

154. Lyle Eslinger, "Inner-Biblical Exegesis," 49, 53. See also Sommer, "Exegesis, Allusion and Intertextuality," 481. James L. Kugel had already questioned whether every instance of textual allusion could be termed as exegesis since some may simply evoke another text without necessarily exegeting it. Kugel, "Bible's Earliest Interpreters," 280, cited in Leonard, "Identifying Inner-Biblical Allusions," 242.

155. Eslinger, "Inner-Biblical Exegesis," 56.

156. Sommer, "Exegesis, Allusion, and Intertextuality," 479.

is not entirely free of historical and temporal considerations since it does posit the question of sequence of the text – which text came first – in order to determine the vector of influence.[157]

ii. Further, IBA differs from IBE in that IBE requires some reworking or reinterpretation of the source text in the receptor text, but IBA simply evokes the source text without making any changes.[158] The allusion simply evokes "for the reader a larger textual field"[159] through the use of shared terms, similar contextual or thematic elements and peculiar grammatical usages and motifs.[160] Allusions are indirect references and hence its success depends on the ability of the reader to recall or access the evoked text which then influences the reader's understanding of the alluding text.[161]

It may be noted here that some scholars differentiate between IBE and IBA on one hand, and intertextuality on the other. They contend that the term intertextuality should not be applied to IBE and IBA. The difference between the two types, that is, IBE/IBA vs. intertextuality, according to Russell Meek for instance, lies in whether or not authorial intent is part of the hermeneutical presuppositions, arguing that intertextuality "precludes author-centred and diachronic studies."[162] This is discussed further below.

Thus, intertextual approaches in biblical studies showed greater interest in diachronic aspects of the text, albeit some lean more heavily on the diachronic elements than others. This historical approach, the need for distinguishing the source or authoritative text from its interpretations in the case of IBE and the need to determine the sequence of the text in IBA, contrasts with intertextuality as formulated by Kristeva, and other literary theorists after her, that does not concern itself with source or influence. Barthes objects to the domestication of the theory by biblical scholars.[163]

The difference in the understanding and use of the term intertextuality between literary critics and biblical scholars, can be seen in Kristeva's disapproval of the use of the term intertextuality as a "study of sources," which

---

157. Sommer, 486–488.
158. Meek, "Intertextuality, Inner-Biblical Exegesis," 290.
159. Beal, "Glossary," 21.
160. Meek, "Intertextuality," 289–290; Sommer, "Exegesis, Allusion," 485.
161. Tooman, *Gog of Magog*, 7.
162. See Meek, "Intertextuality," 283; Sommer, "Exegesis, Allusion," 486–489.
163. Barton, *"Déjà Lu,"* 16.

is a feature of several intertextual approaches in the field of biblical studies. Kristeva's articulation of intertextuality itself is more ahistorical. She is not concerned about the flow of influence or a supposed source and hence she later seemed to prefer the word "transposition" over "intertextuality."[164] Ellen van Wolde similarly notes that the difference between comparative approaches used in biblical studies and intertextuality is that comparative approaches rely on detectable chronological order and thus are necessarily diachronic, while intertextuality is synchronic.[165]

Further, it can be said that for literary theorists like Kristeva intersubjectivity, the influencing of an author by another, is not intertextuality since a text is "not simply equivalent to their subjects (i.e. their writer's intentions)."[166] Intertextuality does not seek the authors intention; to Kristeva intertextuality, more than being a method to unpack texts, was a "condition of all texts."[167] Hence the point of intertextuality was to look at a word or text as a complex intersection of various other texts that are invoked in the process of reading and interpreting.

Nonetheless, biblical scholars have largely adapted and used intertextuality as a method without necessarily embracing all its theoretical assumptions like Kristeva's textual polyvalence and ahistorical approach or Barthes' disregard for authorial intention. While acknowledging the underpinnings of intertextuality as a literary theory, such as the nature of text as essentially intertextual and the transgression of the textual boundaries unintended by the author, the use of intertextuality as a method in biblical studies retains an interest in the vector of influence and authorial intent whenever possible.

Regardless of the differences in some respects in the conception of intertextuality between literary critics and biblical scholars, as a method intertextuality has seen a sustained use in the field of biblical studies. In biblical studies, intertextuality as a wider term for intertextual relations can be broadly classified into two types: (i) production-centred intertextuality and (ii) reception-centred intertextuality. Others prefer to designate them

---

164. Kristeva, *Revolution in Poetic Language*, 60; Meek, "Intertextuality," 283.
165. van Wolde, "Trendy Intertextuality?," 45–46.
166. Barton, "*Déjà Lu*," 3; Beal, "Ideology," 30.
167. Huizenga, *Isaac*, 49, cited in Kiel, "Interpreting Tobit Two Ways," 294. Similarly, Carol Newsome states that Bakhtin's approach is not a method but rather a way of conceptualizing the nature of discourse. Newsome, "Bakhtin, the Bible," 306.

as diachronic and synchronic,[168] or alternatively as temporal and spatial.[169] Both types have as their fundamental presupposition the interrelatedness of text but are differentiated by their emphases. One approaches the relations between the given texts and the creation of meaning from the perspective of the author, and the other from that of the reader.

1.6.3. Production and Reception-Centred Intertextuality

Production-centred intertextuality looks at intertextual relations between texts from an author-centred perspective and is necessarily diachronic and historical. This means that the connection between any given texts is presumed as originating during the process of writing; that is, it arises from the author's intentional use of an earlier text. Hence the meaning of the text is perceived as determined by the author.[170] Production-centred intertextuality is guided by the principle of causality that looks for connections between the texts indicated "by means of quotations, allusions and so forth,"[171] which are determined by indexing the words of the later texts against the earlier text. As such it posits a compulsory relationship between texts established by the author, and discovering the purpose of that inter-textual relationship becomes the focus. IBE and IBA as discussed above fall under this category.[172] Thus intertextuality applied to intertextual readings that are production-oriented is a broad use of the term, and used in this sense it does not describe a new method but rather designates methods that were already in practice, as some biblical scholars observed. It can be said of this type of intertextuality that

---

168. Barton, "Déjà Lu," 2.
169. Stephen Granowski, cited in Barton, "Déjà Lu," 5–6.
170. Meek, "Intertextuality," 282.
171. van Wolde, "Texts in Dialogue," 5.
172. IBA is not strictly intersubjective in that allusion are not necessarily author intended, however IBA still posits a later text referencing an earlier one, and concerns itself with the vector of influence, something that Sommer pointed out and was noted earlier. As such IBA has a production-centred emphasis and falls under diachronic approach. Clayton and Rothstein, cited in Barton, "Déjà Lu," 5, fn. 15. Further, Stephen Hinds notes that allusions are thought to be interpretively meaningful only when intended and controlled by the author. Although he himself argues for some fluidity between intentional allusion and "mere accidental confluence" without which according to him we lose some interpretive possibilities. This shows that allusions can be intention-bearing and hence not absolutely free of assumptions of authorial control in every instance. See Hinds, *Allusion and Intertext*, 25, 47.

what is new is the application of the term to denote the methods rather than the methods themselves.

Where the term intertextuality as a method makes a difference in biblical studies is the second category, called reception-centred intertextuality. It is based on the premise that texts grow within a larger system of literary culture with shared "linguistic, aesthetic or ideological contexts."[173] The various aspects of reception-centred intertextuality can be enumerated as:

i. Reader Oriented: Reception-centred intertextuality is reader oriented, that is, the reader rather than the author postulates connections between texts.[174] It posits that the links perceivable between texts are inherent in the texts themselves and it is the reader who discerns these interrelations between any given texts; authorial intent at this point becomes irrelevant.[175] Consequently it does not concern itself with authorial intent in meaning making, but rather orients itself towards the reader.

ii. Synchronic and Literary: It is synchronic and literary in its approach and as such questions of intersubjectivity (author influencing author), direction of influence, and temporal sequence of the given texts do not arise. It simply reads texts side by side as they exist at that point of time without asking the question of which text came first. Thus, for example, establishing the dates of the selected texts is not a prerequisite for this approach. This has led some to prefer its description in terms of spatiality as opposed to temporality as noted earlier.

iii. Principle of Analogy: By conceiving of texts as being placed side by side, rather than sequentially as earlier and later texts, the principle of causality between texts is replaced by the principle of analogy.[176] Rather than indexing or listing words of one text against the other as in production-centred intertextuality, relations between texts are pursued by comparing shared images, themes, concepts, narratological features, etc., that are analogous or comparable and are called signs or icons.[177] Thus, the transgression of textual

---

173. Sommer, "Exegesis, Allusion," 486.
174. van Wolde, "Texts in Dialogue," 6.
175. Sommer, "Exegesis, Allusion," 486–488; Meek, "Intertextuality," 288.
176. van Wolde, "Texts in Dialogue," 6.
177. van Wolde lists various of features which when repeated can be considered as signs or icons for comparing texts, such as repetitions in words and semantic fields, larger textual

boundaries is achieved thorough related iconicity.[178] For instance, this dissertation approaches the selected texts though the analogous theme of divine retribution and wherever possible shared images that refer to resurrection (like the verb "to rise up") are compared without positing these linking features as necessarily intended by the author of the texts.

iv. Potential Relations: The shared features (signs or icons) evoked in the texts that the reader perceives are not a result of cause and effect, that is, a text is not seen as emerging out of an earlier one. Rather its interest is in the potential links that the reader perceives by comparing repetitions and similarities, and by observing the transformations that occur when these texts are compared side by side.[179] This, according to van Wolde, is "the new text created by the interaction of both texts."[180]

v. Effects: The interest of this approach is to discover the effect of such an intertextual relationship. In other words, reception-centred intertextuality does not ask, "Why did the later author cite or allude to the earlier one?" Rather it asks, "What happens when two or more texts are read together?" "How do they affect our understanding of the subject in view?"

Therefore, reception-centred intertextuality deemphasizes the historical process of text production and the accompanying issues, and focuses on the interaction between the texts and the reader for "discerning literary, thematic, and theological linkages."[181] Van Wolde's table, slightly modified here, gives an overview of the differences between the two types:[182]

Text Production	Text Reception
Author centred	Reader centred
Diachronic and historical	Synchronic and literary
Causality and indexicality	Analogy and iconicity
Compulsory relations	Potential relations
Purpose	Effects

---

units or structures, similar themes or genres, character description or types, actions or series of actions, narratological representations. See van Wolde, "Texts in Dialogue," 7–8.

178. van Wolde describes iconicity as a term "used to denote the principle that phenomena are analogous or isomorphic." van Wolde, "Trendy Intertextuality?" 46.

179. van Wolde, "Texts in Dialogue," 6.

180. van Wolde, 8.

181. Hayes, "Forward to the English," xiii.

182. van Wolde, "Texts in Dialogue," 5.

1.6.4. Questioning Intertextuality

It may be noted, however, that intertextuality does not enthuse everyone. William Irwin makes this abundantly clear. He proposes that intertextuality be "stricken from the lexicon of sincere and intelligent humanists."[183] Because of the broad and varied application of the term Graham Allen feels that it "is in danger of meaning nothing more than whatever each particular critic wishes it to mean."[184] In light of such scepticism the question of controls arises: What are the controls in the production of meaning if there are "indeterminate surplus of meaningful possibilities"?[185] Theoretically, there is no limit to the number of meaningful possibilities but in practice and as a method it necessarily narrows "the intertextual domain" to specific and identifiable texts.[186] Thus, as Marianne Grohamann and Hyun Chul Paul Kim state, intertextuality is not "a limitless web of deferred meanings." There are controls, for the code narrows the theoretically limitless possibilities; for instance, the specificity of the texts to be studied intertextually, a logical relationship between the given texts, adherence to the logic or principles of language, and interpretation of the text with the principles by which it was constructed.[187] Further, as noted earlier, some have advocated for a dichotomy between production- and reception-centred intertextuality, but others like Barton and Will Kynes consider the polarization to be "probably exaggerated."[188] Regarding production-centred intertextuality, it may be argued from an epistemological point of view that often the authorial intention is difficult to ascertain, and as such the author is "ultimately and necessarily a figure whom we ourselves read out from the text."[189] Thus the dichotomy between production- and

---

183. See, Irwin, "Against Intertextuality," 227–242.
184. Allen, *Intertextuality*, 2.
185. Beal, "Ideology," 31.
186. Culler, "Presupposition and Intertextuality," 1384.
187. See Grohamann and Kim, "Introduction," 4; van Wolde, "Trendy Intertextuality?" 47.
188. So Barton, "Déjà Lu," 7. See also Barton, "Historical Criticism, 3–15. Will Kynes likewise uses both approaches to date Job in relation to Deutro-Isaiah; Kynes, "Job and Isaiah 40–55," 94–105. Similarly, other contributing writers in *Reading Job Intertextually* also gainfully combine the synchronic and diachronic approaches in their intertextual readings.
189. See Hinds, *Allusion and Intertext*, 47–48

reception-centred intertextuality is one of emphasis rather than an absolute, a point of view which this dissertation will also adopt.[190]

1.6.5. Intertextuality As a Method in This Dissertation

The dissertation posits an intertextual reading of the theme of divine retribution, more specifically between the analogous concepts of divine retribution in the book of Deuteronomy and post-mortem divine retribution in four distinct texts, two from the HB (Isaiah 26:14, 19 and Daniel 12:1–3) and two from the STP Jewish literature (the Book of Watchers 22 and 2 Maccabees 7). It will primarily use intertextuality with reception-centred emphasis; hence it will read relationships between the texts synchronically.

While the intertextual reading of the concepts of divine retribution in Deuteronomy and post-mortem divine retribution in the four texts itself is synchronic, the examination of the post-mortem texts may identity some historical questions to help illuminate the interpretation of that text. For instance, investigating the date of composition of a text is a historical quest. However, the dating of the text often influences the interpretation, as will be seen for instance in the Danielic text, and hence is examined to illuminate the interpretation the text. But once the line of interpretation is decided, the intertextual reading of the concepts of post-mortem divine retribution in Daniel with the aspects of Deuteronomic divine retribution is done synchronically. Further, when features of the text-production process are explicit it will also take those into consideration. For instance, where there is an explicit reference or a strong allusion in the post-mortem texts to Deuteronomy, that bolsters the intertextual connection by explicitly linking the given text to an earlier authoritative text, as will be seen in 2 Maccabees 7, this will be noted. The dissertation otherwise will not concern itself with matters related to intersubjectivity or vector of influence.

Further, it is possible to say in broad terms that Deuteronomy is earlier than the other four texts, and some degree of temporality regarding Deuteronomy relative to each of the four other texts could surface throughout the discussion. However, the dissertation otherwise will not make any

---

190. Ferdinand de Saussure, the Swiss linguist who coined the terms "diachronic" and "synchronic" to apply to semiotics, said the diachronic and synchronic approaches "are both autonomous *and* interdependent," cited in Dell and Kynes, "Introduction," xxii.

arguments or assumptions regarding the temporal sequence or dependence of the texts. Rather each of the four post-mortem texts are read alongside the concept of divine retribution in Deuteronomy. The four texts are not read alongside each other as it is beyond the scope of the present exercise, although a few references between texts are made when explicit. I approach the text looking for fruitful ways in which selected texts may be connected to each other (even if unintended by the original author).

Chapter 2 examines the concept of divine retribution in the book of Deuteronomy by investigating the different facets or aspects of divine retribution presented in the book. It examines four aspects of divine retribution – impersonal, anthropocentric, theocentric, and dissolution of retribution. Each of these four aspects are illustrated with a text from Deuteronomy. The next four chapters explore the concept of post-mortem divine retribution in the four texts, reading each one intertextually with the concept of divine retribution in Deuteronomy to see if there are continuities and discontinuities when divine retribution is transposed to the afterlife.

Chapters 3 and 4 read Isaiah 26:19 and Daniel 12:1–3 with Deuteronomic divine retribution, and since the conceptions of afterlife in the HB constitute a minor strand, it is not surprising the texts consists of only two to three verses on post-mortem divine retribution. Nonetheless these are significant, being the early and only expressions of post-mortem divine retribution in the HB.

The STP post-mortem texts, BW 22 and 2 Maccabees 7, are more substantial both in terms of content and length, and make up Chapters 5 and 6. These texts exhibit similarity to the Deuteronomic divine retribution but its projection to the afterlife show some major and distinct transformations as well. Thus, in postulating an intertextual relation between these texts the dissertation seeks to explore the potential relations between the concepts of divine retribution in Deuteronomy, whose outworking is bound to the earthly life, and the divine retribution that is deferred but effective in the afterlife.

The intertextual relations posited between the selected texts in this dissertation may not have been author-intended; instead it is possible that they arose out of the larger system of shared linguistic, cultural and theological contexts from which the authors drew. The overall effect of reading these texts side by side is that while still exhibiting continuity in some respects, the concept of divine retribution which is bound to earthly life in Deuteronomy is pushed to expand to make room for divine retribution as a post-mortem possibility. The conception of death as the end in every practical sense is now challenged and transformed by positing a potential post-mortem existence. Each of the four intertexts transcends the boundary of Deuteronomic earth-bound divine retribution so that the concept of divine retribution is compelled to expand and accommodate the viability of a post-mortem divine retribution.

CHAPTER 2

The Aspects of Divine Retribution in the Book of Deuteronomy

2.1. Introduction

Divine retribution in the HB has often been conceived of as a one-dimensional concept characterized by corresponding divine blessings and punishment attendant upon human obedience and disobedience. This is perceived as characteristic of the traditional view of divine retribution in the HB, which was challenged by Klaus Koch who presented his own single-dimensioned view of divine retribution. This chapter is driven by the question, "What is the nature of divine retribution in the HB?" It contends that the concept of divine retribution in the HB is more nuanced than it has been credited with, and that a one-dimensional understanding of retribution, whether it is the traditional view or Koch's view, does not do justice to the complexity of the idea as found in the HB. To demonstrate this, the chapter traces the salient features of the traditional view of divine retribution as well as Koch's understanding of divine retribution to provide a background against which to understand a multi-dimensional view of divine retribution in the HB. To illustrate that the nature of divine retribution in the HB is indeed multi-faceted, this chapter takes the concept of divine retribution in Deuteronomy and highlights its various aspects, elucidating each aspect with a textual example from Deuteronomy.

2.2. Divine Retribution in the Hebrew Bible: The Traditional View

Among scholars the place and meaning of the concept of divine retribution in the HB has been variously judged. Earlier, as Stephen Chapman says, "Old Testament theologies agreed that a single, consistent depiction of retribution lay at the heart of Old Testament faith."[1] He is referring to the traditional view of divine retribution that was dominant at the beginning of the twentieth century. The traditional view of divine retribution is represented by the metaphor of God as a judge, and hence is known as the juridical view. This was the category within which divine retribution was traditionally conceived, and it had proponents like Hermann Gunkel[2] and Walther Eichrodt.[3] Some of the basic features of the traditional view of divine retribution are:

i) God is the Judge: In the traditional conception of retribution, the emphasis was on the role of God as a judge.[4] God as the higher authority judges human deeds and metes out appropriate rewards or punishments.

ii) God intervenes personally to punish: The traditional understanding takes an interventionist view of God's involvement in retribution. Eichrodt states that God "intervenes with fearful jealousy against any contempt shown to him" and punishments are seen "as the personal actions of an offended God."[5] Norman Gottwald, with particular reference to Lamentations, likewise argues that the concept of retributive justice in the HB is "interventionist" and "more vivid and direct" than "the slow working out of requital through the process of moral 'sowing and reaping.'"[6]

iii) Retribution works according to the principle of *lex talionis*: Traditionally, retribution was perceived as corresponding and proportionate to the offense, giving it an almost mathematical exactitude – following the principle of *lex talionis*;[7] Chapman says this principle of "an exacting,

---

1. Chapman, "Reading the Bible," 176.
2. Gunkel, *RGG2* V: col. 1529, cited in Koch, "Doctrine of Retribution," 57.
3. Eichrodt, *Theology of Old Testament*.
4. Terms such as "divine Lord and Judge," "universal Judge," "supreme Judge and Lord," "incorruptible Judge," etc. are common in Eichrodt's *Theology of Old Testament*; Chapman, "Reading the Bible," 178.
5. Eichrodt, *Theology of Old Testament*, vol. 2, 425.
6. Gottwald, *Studies*, 72, quoted in Boase, *Fulfilment of Doom?*, 144.
7. According to Eichrodt the principle of *lex talionis* was a human attempt in their legal retributive punishment to reflect God's judicial activity and righteousness, e.g., judgment at the

imitative correspondence" lies at the heart of the judicial model of retribution (Exod 21:23–25; Lev 24:17–21).[8]

iv) Divine retribution is not arbitrary: Everything God does in retribution, intervening directly and punishing, is not perceived as "unbridled revenge of a wrathful one" because it is all within the already established norm of the covenant between Yahweh and Israel.[9] Hence, divine retribution was not thought of as "arbitrary" but as a legitimate divine response to disobedience within the framework of a predictable covenant law known to man (e.g., Deut 5:9–10; 7:12–15).[10]

Thus, the traditional view of retribution may be characterized as God's intervening action with appropriate judgments on human deeds based on established, known norms of the covenant. This was the category within which divine retribution was traditionally conceived.

2.3. Klaus Koch's Challenge

However, Koch challenged this traditional conception of retribution in his seminal paper in 1955.[11] He bemoaned that despite significant developments in the study of the history and religion of the HB, the concept of retribution remained unchanged. He particularly objected to and denied the idea of God as a judge, who through a *"judicial process,"* metes out recompense "according to a previously established norm" – a recompense which is neither *"part of the person's nature nor part of the essence of the action"* (italics Koch's).[12] He argued that actions had "built-in consequences" so that an evil deed "inevitably

---

Fall (Gen 3), judgment at the Tower of Babel (Gen 11). Eichrodt, *Theology of Old Testament*, vol. 2, 425–426. The basic idea underlying the principle of *lex talionis* in the OT was to prevent retribution from going overboard. It set the upper limit and ensured that the punishment is commensurate as well as limited to the harm caused by the perpetrator. However, as McConville says, in Deuteronomy "proportionality . . . is not absolute," as in Deuteronomy 25:1–3 where the maximum number of stripes for any offender is limited to forty. Thus, proportionate punishment is also tempered by concerns for human dignity. McConville, "Retribution in Deuteronomy," 296.

8. Chapman, "Reading the Bible," 176.

9. Eichrodt, *Theology of Old Testament*, vol. 2, 425.

10. Eichrodt, *Theology of Old Testament*, vol. 2, 260; and Chapman, "Reading the Bible," 176–178.

11. Koch, "Doctrine of Retribution," 57.

12. Koch, 59.

result(ed) in disastrous consequences." Koch called it the act-consequence connection.[13] He questioned therefore not how God dispenses retribution but whether it is actually God who does so.

K. Fahlgren preceded Koch in espousing such an understanding. Fahlgren noted that Hebrew uses the same word to denote both the sin and its consequences; for instance the word עון is used both for trespass or iniquity and punishment as in Cain's use of the word in Genesis 4:13. Fahlgren concluded that at some point in history Israel considered the act and its consequence as a "whole." He called it the "synthetic view of life" (*synthetische Lebensauffassung*).[14] Koch developed the idea further. According to Koch, each human action is a "fate-producing deed," generating a sphere of influence that naturally leads the action to its fruition. That is, an evil deed will naturally result in grievous consequences. God's intervention, if any, was considered minimal, like that of a midwife, facilitating the successful completion of the fate-producing process set into motion by the deed.[15] Thus in Koch's view, retribution ceases to be a forensic act executed by God external to the act-consequence nexus. In other words, retribution is not a juridical act of the divine but a natural and inevitable consequence of a human action.

Koch's thesis provoked much criticism. It was perceived as being "too extreme," and as postulating "a worldview that cannot be fully supported."[16] His non-theistic conception of the working of retribution was considered not tenable in the ancient world.[17] A major flaw of Koch's proposal is his claim that the act-consequence model is valid for the whole of the HB. Placing the weight of the entire HB on a case he built on selectively chosen texts of Proverbs, Hosea, and Psalms, while overlooking witnesses to the contrary, was an added disservice to his claim. However, there is validity in Koch's observation. It shed

---

13. Koch, 58. Koch emphasized this aspect of retribution when he concluded in his important and controversial article that there is no retribution in the HB if by retribution it is meant that God took on a juridical role.

14. Fahlgren, *S'daka, nahestehende*, 17, 24–25, 50–52, cited in Wong, *Idea of Retribution*, 3–4; von Rad, *Old Testament Theology*, vol. 1, 265; Eichrodt, *Theology of Old Testament*, vol. 1, 413. However, Wong further notes that the assumption that "linguistic structure reflects or corresponds to the thought structure" has been refuted in Barr, *Semantics of Biblical Language*, 22.

15. Koch, "Doctrine of Retribution," 61.

16. Boase here cites Barton, "Natural Law," 10–11, Boase, *Fulfilment of Doom?*," 148.

17. Feder, "Mechanics of Retribution," 119–120, 123, 144, 150.

light on the aspects of retribution generally neglected – the dynamistic or impersonal aspect of retribution in the HB. Being as polyphonic as the HB is, there is a place for the dynamistic or impersonal aspect of retribution,[18] only not as the sole model of the operation of the principle of divine retribution.

2.4. Towards a More Nuanced Understanding of Divine Retribution

Other scholars have increasingly recognized the nuanced and multi-faceted nature of divine retribution in the HB. For instance, Jože Krašovec, examining the presence of collective retribution in the HB, states that divine retribution can be direct or indirect, that is, suffering directly for one's own sin, or indirectly for someone's sin as in a community, and can either be interventionist or allowing natural consequences for actions.[19] Joel Kaminsky asserts that divine recompense in the HB is more nuanced than a simplistic, straightforward correlation between deeds and results.[20] Chapman concludes that in the HB the judicial-traditional and Koch's act-consequence connection models of divine retribution "exist side-by-side."[21] Both John Barton[22] and Patrick Miller[23] come to a similar conclusion in discussing the prophetic section of the HB. Stefan Fischer outlines five concepts of retribution in the HB,[24] and John Gammie, earlier than all the scholars cited above, proposed that divine retribution in Deuteronomy has at least four aspects. One of his aspects is similar to the act-consequence while the other three are the anthropocentric, the theocentric, and the dissolution aspects.[25] In examining the aspects of divine retribution in Deuteronomy, this dissertation employs Gammie's

---

18. If not Koch's act-consequence connection itself.
19. Krašovec, "Is There A Doctrine of 'Collective Retribution'?," 38.
20. Kaminsky, "Would You Impugn My Justice?," 299–310.
21. Chapman tests these two models on 2 Samuel 12. Chapman, "Reading the Bible," 185.
22. Barton, *Ethics in Ancient Israel*, 211–221.
23. Miller, *Sin and Judgment*, 121ff.
24. Fischer examines the Book of Job against the following five concepts of retribution: i) the classical concept (judicial), ii) world-order concept (Koch's act-consequence), iii) retribution extending to the community (corporate or inherited), iv) retribution to community in the afterlife, and v) retribution for the individual in the afterlife. Fischer, "How God Pays Back," 26–29.
25. Gammie, "Theology of Retribution," 1–12.

designations for the aspects of retribution since his is the only article that concentrates on retribution in Deuteronomy.

However, these different facets of divine retribution the scholars highlight in their works are not altogether new. Though Eichrodt is recognized as a proponent of the traditional view within the studies on retribution in the HB, he is aware of the nuances and limitations of the concept of judicial divine retribution, except he does not categorize them as distinct aspects but rather discusses them all as one. These other aspects of retribution are not organized systematically nor are they fully elaborated; however, they are traceable and are highlighted here.[26]

Eichrodt acknowledges the presence of the concept of objective guilt in ANE societies, including Israel, as deriving from a dynamistic worldview. This is similar to the impersonal aspect of divine retribution discussed later in the chapter. In such a conception of guilt "the incidence of punishment and offence was simultaneous, because the latter immediately placed men under the dominion of the demonic powers" or brought the offender under the taboo. He argues that while in the other ANE societies "the dominating fear of demons was able to keep the curse-like quality of guilt much more strongly alive," Israel's covenant with Yahweh gave them a "clear knowledge of the will of God" that enabled Israel to see in the conception of dynamistic guilt the operation of God's justice and to overcome the fear of having unwittingly offended or disrupted some power or force.[27] So although Eichrodt identifies the impersonal aspect of retribution, for him it is subsumed under the direct rule of God and not considered distinct.

Eichrodt also perceives the pedagogical functions of reward and punishment when he says that in the prophetic literature the view of Israel's history in relation to "[a]ll punishments experienced hitherto" was that God had been waiting for them and everything they had suffered until now "were but efforts to purify and educate," even though Israel will eventually meet "an inescapable eschatological doom."[28] Such instances are discussed later in the chapter as cases of the dissolution of retribution.

---

26. It is expected that a seminal work like Eichrodt's *Theology of the Old Testament* would resist attempts at schematization. However, at the risk of being reductionist, the other aspects are listed here briefly.

27. Eichrodt, *Theology of Old Testament*, vol. 2, 413–415.

28. Eichrodt, *Theology of Old Testament*, vol. 1, 267.

Further, Eichrodt acknowledges the limitations of the traditional concept of divine retribution. He states that Israel recognized "that fullness of the divine nature was not to be comprehended in the scope of such purely rationalist categories as reward and punishment." Eichrodt cites Job and Ecclesiastes as instances demonstrating that the only right attitude is one of "wondering adoration" and worshipping of God "by humble resignation to the relativity of human existence." He says that though Israel did not reduce "divine wrath entirely to the exercise of retributive justice," it was undoubtedly "its proper and principal sphere of operation."[29] Thus, although God's judicial role was preponderant in Eichrodt's discussion of divine retribution, it was not oblivious to testimonies that suggested otherwise.

It may be said that among scholars, retribution has come to be understood and accepted as a complex concept, although reaching a consensus regarding all its nuances is another matter. Further, divine retribution in the OT operates at the individual as well as corporate level. Individual retribution is more easily understood since the judicial systems of modern governments are based on the principle of individual retribution.[30] In individual retribution, the sinner or the perpetrator is held responsible, and not anyone else.[31] Corporate retribution, on the contrary, comes into play when people other than the offender(s) are either held liable for the offense or the retributive consequences affect or include them. The corporate body could be family, clan, or in case the offender "occupies an exalted position" it could involve his tribe and or even the entire nation.[32] Corporate retribution can come into force either on a group of people living at one particular time or trans-generationally, in that ancestral guilt is perceived as inheritable.[33] Kaminsky explains that such a corporate focus in retribution can be attributed to the

---

29. Eichrodt, 263.

30. Although there are instances of corporate retribution still being used, like in some rural areas in India governed by khap panchayats.

31. Paul Joyce challenges the developmental hypothesis that sees the early period of Israel as characterized by a strong sense of collectivism and attributes the development of the concept of individualism to the exilic, post-exilic period. Joyce, *Divine Initiative*.

32. Eichrodt, *Theology of Old Testament*, vol. 2, 428.

33. At times, there may not be a very sharp distinction to be made between corporate retribution on a group of people living at the same time and a trans-generational corporate retribution as three or four generations can be living at the same time and in such a case the horizontal and the vertical application of corporate retribution can be applied to the same group of people.

covenant between God and Israel that "maintains a corporate understanding of reward and punishment."[34] Krašovec argues that only God can execute corporate retribution and that too "only in special circumstances" while "human institutions are not allowed to practice it" (Deut 24:16).[35] Jeffery Tigay also states that such cross-generational retribution was "recognized as an aspect of divine governance."[36] This chapter will make brief notes on this individual-corporate application of retribution for each aspect of divine retribution in examining its sample texts.

2.5. The Aspects of Divine Retribution in the Book of Deuteronomy

The above summary demonstrates the idea of different aspects to divine retribution in the HB is not a particularly new one, and that it has been gaining greater currency. This chapter builds on it, albeit limiting itself to the book of Deuteronomy. The different aspects of divine retribution in Deuteronomy are not proposed as hermetically sealed categories. Rather they are each a facet of divine retribution but with the emphasis falling on one or the other aspect in any particular instance. In this chapter, four aspects of retribution observable in Deuteronomy will be discussed with an exegesis of a text for an example.

2.5.1. Impersonal Aspect of Divine Retribution

In its impersonal aspect, retribution is presented as a natural consequence of sin rather than the direct, personal judgment of God. This aspect of retribution comes to the fore in passages where retribution is expressed in terms that do not refer to the divine as the agent of retribution but portrays it as a natural consequence of the deed. Eichrodt uses the term "dynamistic" to describe a similar understanding of the way retribution sometimes operates.[37] Brueggemann affirms the presence of this aspect of retribution in Deuteronomy. He states that divine retribution in the form of personal judgments of God within the covenant is intrinsic to the teachings of the

---

34. Kaminsky, *Corporate Responsibility*, 12.
35. Krašovec, "Is There A Doctrine of 'Collective Retribution'?," 35–36, 73–74.
36. Tigay, *Deuteronomy*, 436.
37. Eichrodt, *Theology of Old Testament*, vol. 2, 413–414.

Torah, especially Deuteronomy. However, he adds, Deuteronomy also exhibits "awareness that certain acts produce certain consequences in a quasi-'automatic' way, that is 'automatic' given YHWH's governance and purposes."[38]

Other scholars have also recognized that retribution is sometimes operative as an "impersonal principle"[39] or "a natural process."[40] Gammie states that in its impersonal aspect retribution can be described as the principle *"according to which an evil deed will inevitably bring guilt upon the wrongdoer"*[41] (italics Gammie's). He proposes that instances of impersonal retribution in Deuteronomy are detectable in passages that command the people to "purge the evil from your midst" and are related to offenses that pollute the land. Examples of such passages are Deuteronomy 13:2–6; 17:2–7; 19:11–13; 16–19; 21:1–9; 21:18–21; 22:13–29; 24:7. Alan Bernstein expresses a similar impersonal conception of retribution when he states that in the Deuteronomic view the "world is so composed that the perpetrator of evil becomes his or her own victim." He calls it "reflexive justice."[42] Thus evil circles back on its perpetrators and there is no need to explain why their suffering was just; the fairness of their suffering is evident. This is similar to Koch's act-consequence connection, but unlike Koch who argued that the HB evinced no other forms of retribution than the act-consequence connection, Gammie maintains that this impersonal aspect is only one among several aspects of divine retribution discernible in Deuteronomy.

Further, this impersonal formulation of retribution does not assume an impersonal world order operating mechanistically. Retribution may sometimes operate in a seemingly impersonal manner, but only because God chooses it to be so. In Karsovec's view God, as "the highest authority," can choose whether to intervene or leave people to "the consequences of their own behaviour." He is free to intervene, but "it may not be necessary for him to do so."[43] Yitzhaq Feder examines Mesopotamian and Hittite texts that describe oath-curses and bloodguilt "as self-contained dynamic" and compares them to similar texts in the HB. While acknowledging that in cases dealing

---

38. Brueggemann, *Deuteronomy*, 104.
39. Gammie, "Theology of Retribution," 6.
40. Krašovec, *Reward, Punishment, and Forgiveness*, 151.
41. Gammie, "Theology of Retribution," 6.
42. Bernstein, *Formation of Hell*, 151.
43. Krašovec, *Reward, Punishment, and Forgiveness*, 151.

with homicides there was "a tendency to view retribution as a self-contained mechanical process," he argues that a non-theistic conception of retribution would be foreign to the ANE thought even when "the blood is depersonalized and the role of God deemphasized."[44] Therefore if human actions have built-in consequences it is because God created the world and organized it to function in that manner, and the impersonal aspect of retribution is subsumed within the overarching covenantal framework that governs the interactions between God and Israel.

2.5.1.1. Deuteronomy 21:1–9 As an Example of Impersonal Aspect

The case of an unsolved homicide in Deuteronomy 21:1–9 typifies the impersonal aspect of retribution. The discovery of a body within Israelite boundaries in verse 1 sets the stage. That the body is described as חָלָל ("one pierced"; Deut 21:1) indicates that it was not a natural death. It was a case of either murder or manslaughter. What is unusual about this case, however, is that the perpetrator is not found and yet liability is assumed. Generally, if a homicide is unsolved there is nothing more to be done – it "would be simply ignored in many societies."[45] However, in Israel "an unpunished homicide"[46] incurs bloodguilt. Similar beliefs seem to have been known in ANE societies – Timothy Willis notes the existence of laws and rituals to deal with unsolved homicides in the Ugaritic, Hittite, and Babylonian documents. Such cases, as well as the law in Deuteronomy 21:1–9, give us a glimpse into "other aspects of the conceptual world concerning homicide."[47]

Bloodguilt in the HB refers to the liability for punishment and contamination of the land for shedding of הַדָּם הַנָּקִי ("the innocent blood"; ref. Deut 21:9), for wrongful killing outside of the legal prescription such as killing in a battle, a judicial death sentence, etc.[48] It was not a personal feeling of guilt; rather as Brueggemann explains, bloodguilt "is understood as an almost substantive, palpable danger as a residue of wrong killing that will contaminate the land and make it unlivable."[49] The blood of the innocent victim remains,

---

44. Feder, "Mechanics of Retribution," 119–120, 123, 144, 150.
45. Miller, *Deuteronomy*, 161.
46. Tigay, *Deuteronomy*, 191.
47. Willis, *Elders of the City*, 145–147.
48. Warmuth, "נָקִי", 558; Sperling, *AB* I, 764, quoted in Butler, *Hosea, Joel*, 155.
49. Brueggemann, *Deuteronomy*, 199.

in Feder's words, "in a state of seething hostility with a single-minded demand for vengeance."[50]

Further, the primary interest of the rite prescribed to deal with the bloodguilt is neither in the perpetrator nor in the victim, but in the "protection of the land."[51] The land is adversely affected by the shedding of innocent blood. The earliest case of bloodguilt in the HB is in Genesis 4:10–12. Abel's blood is received by the ground and is described as crying out (צעק "to cry out" Gen 4:10) to God for vengeance. The same verb is used to describe the Israelites' cry about making bricks without straw (Exod 5:8). It is also used when Yahweh says that if oppressed widows and orphans cry to him, he will hear (Exod 22:22 or 23 EV; so also, I Kgs 20:39 and Lam 2:18). As a consequence, Cain is cursed, but his curse is tied to the land – the land will now resist Cain's agricultural efforts and no longer bear its fruits for him. Thus, the consequence of bloodguilt is portrayed as infertility of the land. Similarly, 2 Samuel 21 links the enduring famine in the land during the reign of David to the bloodguilt incurred by Saul's killing of the Gibeonites. Hence it is reasonable to say that the consequence of the bloodguilt in Deuteronomy 21:1–9 is the potential infertility of the land. Bloodguilt is usually compensated for in kind; for instance, the execution of the perpetrator in the case of a premeditated murder absolves the bloodguilt (Deut 19:11–13; cf. Lev 17:11). But for cases where the perpetrator is not found, this text prescribes a distinct ritual for the removal of the bloodguilt.

The first step for removing the bloodguilt is to identify the city nearest to the body (Deut 21:2). The actors in this task are the elders and the judges of Israel who measure the distance between the body and the surrounding cities. The assumption is that "the perpetrator lived nearby."[52] Once identified, the city nearest to the body bears the responsibility of performing the ritual and provides an unworked heifer for the rite (Deut 21:3).[53] In this verse, the name of Yahweh is mentioned once but only to qualify the land as a gift from

---

50. Feder, "Mechanics of Retribution," 139.
51. Brueggemann, *Deuteronomy*, 199; Christensen, *Deuteronomy 1:1–21:9*, 455.
52. Merrill, *Deuteronomy*, vol. 4, 288.
53. It has been argued that the term עֶגְלָה is better translated as "cow" rather than "heifer." However, since this has no particular bearing on the present work the standard translation "heifer" has been retained here. For arguments in favour of translating עֶגְלָה as "cow" see Zevit, "The 'Eglâ Ritual," 254, note b.

Yahweh. There is no mention of the bloodguilt being the direct, personal judgment of God. It is simply assumed that bloodguilt has been incurred as the consequence of the homicide and hence needs to be dealt with.

The ritual includes two symbolic acts and a verbal declaration. The first symbolic act is the killing of the heifer. This takes place in a wadi with perennial water (Deut 21:4). The significance of performing the rite in an uncultivated plot of land, Wright states, is that it relocates the negative consequence of bloodguilt to the unused plot of land, thus removing the threat of infertility from the land.[54] This ritual is most probably not a sacrifice to Yahweh.[55] Wright lists the following reasons against the rite being a sacrifice. First, the verb used here to describe the killing of the heifer is עָרַף ("to break the neck"; Deut 21:4). Breaking the animal's neck is prescribed only in the case of a ritually unclean firstborn donkey that is not redeemed with a lamb (Exod 13:13; 34:20), and in Isaiah 66:3 it describes the killing of a dog. If this rite was intended to be a sacrifice, one would expect the verb זבח ("to slaughter"). Secondly, it is זִקְנֵי הָעִיר הַהִוא ("the elders of that city" Deut 21:4) and not the priests who kill the heifer. Thirdly, this rite performed outside the sanctuary, with no altar, and out in the field, does not fit well with Deuteronomy's emphasis on centralization of worship (Deut 12).[56] All these factors point to the rite not being a sacrifice to Yahweh.

If not a sacrifice, what was the purpose of the rite? The text only describes the rite; it does not explain its purpose or significance and scholars have put forward various possibilities. For instance, Anthony Philips views the killing of the heifer as the symbolic execution of the murderer as well as transferring the guilt of the community to an unused land.[57] Hooke proposes a substitutionary sacrifice for the community "devoted to the underworld."[58] Ziony Zevit posits that the rite, in the form in which it now stands in Deuteronomy, is a polymorphic collection of pre-Deuteronomic sacrifices. He argues that in the pre-Israelite stage the rite served as a "propitiatory sacrifice" to "ward

---

54. Wright, "Deuteronomy 21:1–6," 395.

55. Even among scholars who have considered this rite a sacrifice qualifies it as pre-Deuteronomic – for instance Elhorst considered it a sacrifice to the gods of the underworld, Elhorst, "Eine verkannte Zauberhandlung," 66–67, cited by Zevit, "'Eglâ Ritual," 378.

56. Wright, "Deuteronomy 21:1–6," 391.

57. Phillips, *Deuteronomy*, 138–139.

58. Hooke, "Theory and Practice of Substitution," 10–11.

off a curse"; later when it was adopted by Israel it was considered as a "combination of free-will and expiatory offering." Subsequently it was adapted into its present Deuteronomic form and the sacrifice was "replaced by sacral neck-breaking." Changes such as the presence of priests (in Deut 21:5) were included to reflect a more Deuteronomic view.[59] Other suggested purposes of the rite include the killing of the heifer as representative of the penalty the elders will face if their declaration of innocence is false,[60] that the ritual prevented the animal carrying the guilt from returning to the community,[61] or that the ritual was a re-enactment of the murder to eliminate the negative consequences of the bloodguilt by transferring it to an unused piece of land.[62] Such varied explanations only serve to substantiate the point that the bloodguilt was assumed as a natural consequence of shedding innocent blood and not as a direct judgment from Yahweh, in which case the rite should have been a sacrifice to Yahweh.

The killing of the heifer is followed by the second symbolic act, that of the city elders washing their hands over the heifer (v.6). This washing of the hands is a "symbolic expression of innocence," in the HB (Ps 73:13).[63] Later in the NT, Pontius Pilate would also wash his hands at the sentencing of Jesus (Matt 27:24). However, while Pilate knew exactly what he was doing it for, here the city elders are ignorant about the particulars of the homicide and declare it to be so (Deut 21:7–8). Both of these acts – killing the heifer and washing of the hands – central to the rite for removal of bloodguilt, are devoid of any references to Yahweh.

---

59. Zevit, "'Eglâ Ritual," 377–390.

60. Benjamin, *Deuteronomy and City Life*, 198–210, 297–298; Garnet, "Salvation and Atonement," 71, note 3, cited by Wright, "Deuteronomy 21:1–6," 389, note 7.

61. Grad, *Studies in Biblical Uses*, 80–83, and Mayes, *Deuteronomy*, 297–300; both cited by Wright, "Deuteronomy 21–1–9," 389, note 8.

62. Patai, "'Egla 'Arufa," 59–69; Roifer, "Breaking of Heifer's Neck," 129–43, cited by Zevit, " 'Eglâ Ritual," 378; and Wright, "Deuteronomy 21:1–6," 393–398. Wright argues that the explanation of the ceremony as an elimination rite is the most convincing among those proposed. He also provides brief, helpful critiques of all the other explanations in this article. Willis draws a parallel from Isaiah 66:3 that compares the breaking of a dog's neck to the killing of a man and speculates that perhaps here in Deuteronomy 21 too, by breaking the heifer's neck the murder is reenacted and by doing it in an uncultivated land the bloodguilt of the actual murder is transferred to unused land and the guilt is removed through hand-washing. Willis, *Elders of the City*, 155.

63. Zevit, "'Eglâ Ritual," 386; Merrill, *Deuteronomy*, 289.

Sandwiched between these two acts is the appearance of the priests of Yahweh (Deut 21:5). However, they enter the scene only after the heifer is slaughtered and remain silent spectators outside the ongoing action. Structurally, as Christensen states, the priests are at the centre of the literary unit; however their precise role in the ritual remains unclear. They are "merely observers and not the officiants in this symbolic act."[64] What is more, in this verse, the description of the role of the priests highlights their conflict-resolving capacity – וְעַל־פִּיהֶם יִהְיֶה כָּל־רִיב וְכָל־נָגַע "and by their word every dispute and every assault will be settled" – rather than officiating a "religious ceremony as such."[65] The Targums attempt to ease the awkward presence of the priests by attributing to them the prayer in Deuteronomy 21:8.[66] Scholars, however, generally agree that Deuteronomy 21:5 is a secondary addition.[67] For instance, Welch argues that by including the priests in a supervisory role the Deuteronomist ensures that the pre-Deuteronomistic rite "would be minimally Yahwistic."[68]

The hand washing is followed by a declaration of innocence – וְעָנוּ וְאָמְרוּ יָדֵינוּ לֹא שָׁפְכוּ אֶת־הַדָּם הַזֶּה וְעֵינֵינוּ לֹא רָאוּ ("And they shall answer saying, 'Our hands did not shed this blood, and our eyes did not see'" Deut 21:7). This declaration of innocence is also rather irregular; it is not a prayer *per se*. It consists of a "secular denial of complicity" in Deuteronomy 21:7, as though responding to an accusation, and only in verse 8 is an appeal addressed to the LORD.[69] Zevit notes "the recitation is strange in that it does not begin with an invocation nor does it contain any indication that the words are directed to Yahweh until the middle of v. 8."[70] Moreover, a corporate orientation of impersonal retribution is seen in this instance. Scholars observe that since the prayer requests absolution for "your people Israel whom you have redeemed" the bloodguilt was assumed to be on the whole nation rather than on the

---

64. Christensen, *Deuteronomy 1:1–21:9*, 458.
65. Christensen, *Deuteronomy 1:1–21:9*, 454.
66. *Targum Neofiti 1: Deuteronomy*, 103–104; *Targum Pseudo-Jonathan: Deuteronomy*, 58; *Targum Onqelos: Deuteronomy*.
67. Wright, "Deuteronomy 21:1–6," 391–392; Mayes, *Deuteronomy*, 297–300; Zevit, "'Eglâ Ritual," 381–382; and L'Hour, "Législation Criminelle," 1–28, cited by Gammie, "Theology of Retribution," 6.
68. Zevit citing Welch, "Remarks on the Article," 164, in Zevit, "'Eglâ Ritual," 382.
69. Zevit, 386–387.
70. Zevit, 386.

nearest city and its people.⁷¹ This prayer is in line with the conception that the community as a whole is responsible for innocent bloodshed (Deut 19:10).⁷² Zevit states that the prayer (in Deut 21:8) itself is in "disharmony with the denial" (in Deut 21:7) but functions to "Yahwehize" the pre-Deuteronomic ritual.⁷³ Thus if the rite of killing the heifer on uncultivated land on a wadi with perennial water removed the bloodguilt from the land, this prayer appeals for the LORD's forgiveness on the people. Here again, it is the city elders who utter these words; the priests continue to remain on the sidelines.

What emerges from the analysis of Deuteronomy 21:1–9 is that when the culprit is not found, the negative consequence of the bloodguilt engulfs both the land and its people and hence the rite is prescribed to remove it from the human sphere of concern. This pericope creates a distance, verbally and syntactically, between the assumption of bloodguilt and the rite on one hand, and the name of Yahweh and his priests on the other. The distance thus created lends this instance of retribution its impersonal undertones, with only direct reference to Yahweh being the prayer, which is arguably a secondary addition. However, such a rite even if originally pre-Deuteronomic is incorporated into the Yahwistic belief in Deuteronomy's canonical form and hence subsumed within the framework of the covenant that entails the purity of the chosen nation and governs the divine-human interactions. Thus, while still being an instance of divine retribution, there are elements in this expression of retribution that are distinct enough to merit consideration as a separate aspect of divine retribution.

2.5.2. Anthropocentric Aspect of Divine Retribution

In the anthropocentric aspect of retribution, human actions and their consequences are described so that God appears mainly as a "reactor" to man's actions. Gammie credits Johannes Hempel with having identified the anthropocentricity in the "many expressions of the OT idea of history."⁷⁴ In

---

71. Nelson, *Deuteronomy*, 258; Christensen, *Deuteronomy 1:1–21:9*, 458; Craigie, *Book of Deuteronomy*, 280.

72. Later Jeremiah cites this verse to make a case for his own life (Jer 26:15).

73. Zevit, "'Eglâ Ritual," 387. Some scholars consider the prayer in Deuteronomy 21:8a a secondary addition, for instance, Phillips, *Deuteronomy*, 139; Dillmann, *Numeri*, 337; and Bertholet, *Deuteronomium*, 65, all cited by Zevit, "'Eglâ Ritual," 378, note 6.

74. Gammie, "Theology of Retribution," 8.

Hempel's words "the action of God is conditioned by the action of men."[75] In discussing theodicy in the context of Deuteronomistic History, Antti Laato also recognizes the human agency in the idea of retribution. He says that if human beings, who "have the capacity to fulfil the will of god" fail to do so, they receive punishments. But "if they are loyal to god they will be blessed." He uses Ronald Green's term, "free-will theodicy," to describe this anthropocentricity.[76] Gammie explains anthropocentric aspect of retribution as one in which "the faithful are assured" that obedience to God will surely be rewarded.[77] It may be added here that in Deuteronomy this assurance of God's "reaction" is not restricted to obedience but also applicable to disobedience. He says that such anthropocentricity can be seen in Deuteronomy 28:1–45 which lists a series of blessings and curses, or in Deuteronomy 5–26 where this aspect is seen in passages that contain the conjunction לְמַעַן ("in order that" or "so that"). In such passages "the plea to keep the commandments is based on an appeal to the operation of a principle of retribution."[78] For instance, in Deuteronomy 11:18–21 the commandment to fix God's words in their hearts and to teach them to their children is followed by "*so that* your days and the days of your children may be many . . ." (emphasis added).

2.5.2.1. Deuteronomy 11:13–21 As an Example of Anthropocentric Aspect of Divine Retribution

The anthropocentric aspect of divine retribution in Deuteronomy can be illustrated through Deuteronomy 11:13–21. This passage is part of a larger section, Deuteronomy 10:12–11:32, that is primarily an exhortation[79] to love and fear[80] Yahweh and to keep his commands. It focuses on God's giving of

---

75. Hemplen, *Altes Testament und Geschichte*, 15, quoted by Gammie, "Theology of Retribution," 8.

76. This is a category of theodicy in Ronald M. Green's five types of theodicy in a monotheistic context, in Green, 'Theodicy', 430–41, cited by Laato, "Theodicy," 183.

77. Gammie, "Theology of Retribution," 7.

78. Gammie, 7.

79. von Rad states that this section constitutes "a whole series of fragments of the formal covenant pattern" and that "they have appeared in a definite hortatory style." von Rad, *Deuteronomy: A Commentary*, 83.

80. In Deuteronomy, the people are often commanded to love the LORD as well as to fear him. This may seem like a contradiction. Arnold argues that in Deuteronomy love and fear are not contrary to each other but rather complementary. He says that love and fear are used together to "demarcate the connotation of each," so that fear restricts love that is "devoid

the land as a conditional promise. As Christensen states, the land that Yahweh is giving them is a "special land, which YHWH himself takes care of" (Deut 11:12). However, possession of this land is "contingent on their obedience to YHWH's commandments."[81] Thus the people's obedience and disobedience to Yahweh will determine their occupation (Deut 11:8) and continued possession (Deut 11:9-21) of the promised land.

Deuteronomy 11:13-21 draws attention to a time when the people will already be settled in the promised land. The basic commandments to obey, love, and serve Yahweh are expressed as a condition.[82] This passage lays before the people the consequences of their obedience as well as disobedience. אִם ("if"; Deut 11:13) indicates the conditional clause that needs to be fulfilled before God can bless them. The condition is that the people שָׁמֹעַ תִּשְׁמְעוּ [lit. "you (pl) shall indeed heed"] God's commands and it is expressed emphatically by using the double form of the verb שמע ("to listen or heed") – infinite absolute and imperfect forms. The command is further explained couched in words that echo the Shema (Deut 6:5), the essence of the Deuteronomic covenant, which is a single-minded, wholehearted devotion to the one God, Yahweh. So, the condition for the blessing is laid out – if the people indeed keep his commands, then Yahweh will respond with blessings.

The promised blessing in this case is that Yahweh will provide them with timely rainfall (Deut 11:14).[83] The importance of rain, particularly timely rain, for an agricultural society cannot be overstated. This was especially true for the land where the Israelites were about to settle. Unlike in Egypt (Deut 11:10)[84] where the agricultural land was watered by the flooding of the Nile

---

of reverence" and love restricts the kind of fear that is "devoid of delight." Arnold, "Love-Fear Antinomy," 552.

81. Christensen, *Deuteronomy 1:1–21:9*, 212.

82. Christensen, 215.

83. Not only is having rainfall important but also the timing of it is crucial. As Tigay says delayed or early rainfall, or rainfall at the wrong time, can have adverse effects on the growth and harvesting of the crops. Hence unseasonal rainfall was often considered a curse. See Tigay, *Deuteronomy*, 113–114.

84. The discussion of Deuteronomy 11:10–11 is generally seen as presenting a desirable picture of the promised land, even if it were a utopian vision, in contrast to Egypt. The idea proposed is that in comparing Egypt and the promised land (Deut 11:10–11), the author is portraying Egypt as being watered by urine while the promised land drinks "the very waters of heaven" [Eslinger, "Watering Egypt (Deuteronomy XI 10–11)," 89], or that the land of Egypt is small, comparable to a vegetable garden while the promised land is spacious, "a broad land of hills and valleys [Nicol, "Watering Egypt," 348]. However, the view that the advantage of the

into the canals and reservoirs,⁸⁵ Israel was a land of הָרִים וּבְקָעֹת ("hills and valleys"; Deut 11:11) and relied on rainfall for agriculture – לִמְטַר הַשָּׁמַיִם תִּשְׁתֶּה־מָּיִם ("it drinks the water from the rain of heaven"; Deut 11:11). There were two rounds of rain that were important for the crops. יוֹרֶה (the "early or autumn rain"; Deut 11:14) started in October-November after a hot dry summer and softened the soil and commenced the sowing season.⁸⁶ מַלְקוֹשׁ (the "late or spring rain"; Deut 11:14; cf. Zech 10:1) referred to the final showers that come before the summer around March-April that "refresh and advance the ripening of the crops."⁸⁷ Yahweh as the subject of the verb נתן ("to give"; Deut 11:14) is portrayed as directly responsible for the timely rainfall because of which the crops flourish and the people and their cattle have plenty and are satisfied (Deut 11:15). Thus, when the people obey, Yahweh will respond by blessing their land with timely showers.

Ironically though, apostasy is especially likely when the people are sated;⁸⁸ hence the people are warned that there would be negative consequences for their disobedience (similar warnings of being satisfied and abandoning Yahweh are given in Deuteronomy 6:10–15 and 8:10–11; see also 32:13–18). Just as single-hearted devotion to Yahweh captures the essence of obedience, disobedience is presented as apostasy – turning away from Yahweh and worshipping other gods (Deut 11:16). In verses 16 and 17 there is probably, as Woods observes, a "polemic against Baal."⁸⁹ The Canaanites worshipped Baal as the god of rain and fertility, whose conflict with and victory over other gods was, as the Canaanites believed, mirrored in the seasons of dryness and fertility of the land. Once in Canaan Israel would be completely dependent on the cycles of rainfall for farming, and as Merrill says, "it would be easy for Israel to share the naturalistic point of view that forces of nature must be acknowledged and appeased if productivity of animal and vegetable life was

---

divinely watered land could also turn against the people is recorded by Herodotus. Herodotus writes of an Egyptian priest who wondered that since Greece was watered by water from heaven what the fate of the Greeks would be if Zeus for some reason decides to withhold the rain. Herodotus 2:13 cited by Tigay, *Deuteronomy*, 112.

85. Tigay, 112.
86. Tigay, 113.
87. Driver, *Deuteronomy*, 130. von Rad, *Deuteronomy*, 85.
88. Driver, 130; Woods, *Deuteronomy*, 179.
89. Woods, 179.

to be achieved."[90] This was borne out in Israel's history. Hosea records that when Yahweh gave Israel grain, wine, and oil – the very same things listed in Deuteronomy 11:14b – they did not acknowledge him; instead they credited these to Baal and turned away from Yahweh to worship Baal (Hos 2:10–15 [Eng. 8–13]; also, Deut 32:13–18).[91]

The Israelites are warned that worshipping other gods for fertility of the land would have the opposite effect – וְעָצַר אֶת־הַשָּׁמַיִם וְלֹא־יִהְיֶה מָטָר Yahweh will shut up the heavens and there will be no rain (Deut 11:17). The Israelites experience this first-hand, as Tigay points out, during the reign of King Ahab and his queen Jezebel when worship of Baal in Israel was flourishing (1 Kgs 17–18). Yahweh withheld the rain for 3 years and sent rain after the contest between the prophets of Baal and the prophets of Yahweh led by Elijah on Mount Carmel, thus demonstrating that "only He, and not Baal, controls the rain."[92] If the people abandon Yahweh, instead of rain and plenty they will face drought, famine, and destruction.[93] The land drinking water directly from the heavens highlights the desirability of the promised land (Deut 11:11). However, if they do not keep the commandments this advantage can work against them as עָצַר אֶת־הַשָּׁמַיִם "he (Yahweh) will shut the heavens" and there will be no rain thus initiating famine and destruction, and possibly jeopardizing their possession of the land. In this instance of anthropocentric retribution, the whole of Israel is in view. The perspective here is that the entire community is a single entity and timely rain and productivity of the land, or drought and famine are promised to the people collectively as a nation.

In order to remain faithful to Yahweh and to avoid the disastrous consequence, Moses instructs the Israelites to take necessary measures – internalizing Yahweh's commandments, teaching them to their children, and using visual symbols (Deut 11:18–20). These verses recall the words that immediately follow the Shema (Deut 6:6–9).[94] The people are both to internalize[95]

---

90. Merrill, *Deuteronomy*, 211.

91. Lundbom, *Deuteronomy: A Commentary*, 406.

92. Tigay, *Deuteronomy*, 114.

93. Drought, famine, and destruction were "standard curses all over the Ancient Near East," and found in several ancient treaties. Woods, *Deuteronomy*, 179.

94. Christensen, *Deuteronomy 1:1–21:9*, 215; Merrill, *Deuteronomy*, 211.

95. Internalization was necessary in an oral education system as is seen in Proverbs (Prov 3:1; 4:4; etc.). Tigay also compares this to Enuma Elish where the instruction is for the father

Yahweh's commandments conveyed to them by Moses, and use visual symbols as memory and teaching aids. Not only are they to tie the words on their bodies but also have it on their doors and city gates[96] (Deut 11:20), thus covering the personal, private, and public spheres of life. Verse 19, using merisms, instructs the parents to teach their children "wherever you are, at all times."[97] This was crucial as the future of Israel depended on the successful transmission of their faith to every new generation.[98] The breakdown of this chain of transmission could lead to a situation as in the book of Judges when the new generation that came after Joshua's generation did not know Yahweh or what he had done (Judg 2:10–11) and so forsook the God they did not know. But if the people do as Moses commands – love and serve Yahweh and teach his commandments to their children – they will ensure that they remain on the good land that Yahweh is giving them and enjoy it forever as was originally intended (Deut 11:21). The expression כִּימֵי הַשָּׁמַיִם עַל־הָאָרֶץ "as long as the heavens are above the earth" means "forever" as "the sky and other heavenly bodies symbolize longevity and permanence"[99] (cf. Ps 72:5, 7, 17; 89:29 [Eng. 30]; Job 14:12). The word לְמַעַן "so that" indicates that the plea to keep the LORD's commandments is made based on the assurance that Yahweh would reward their faithfulness with longevity on the land.

In this example of anthropocentric retribution, the whole of Israel is in view. The perspective is that the community is a single entity and timely rain and productivity of the land, or drought and famine are promised to the people as a whole.

Thus, in the anthropocentric aspect of divine retribution mankind's action remains primary. Yahweh's actions are contingent on humankind's actions. Human beings are portrayed as the determiner of their fate through the choices they make. However, this must not be mistaken for humans being

---

is to repeat the teachings as well as to teach it to his son although the content is not religious. Tigay, *Deuteronomy*, 78.

96. Tigay states that the שַׁעַר refer to city gates as "houses rarely had gates." City gates were the center of public life and the most effective place to publicize important matters. Such a placement of God's commandments would ensure "widest visibility." Tigay, *Deuteronomy*, 79.

97. Tigay, 78.

98. The imperative to remember the commands and to teach it to their children is repeated several times in Deuteronomy and is reflective of the primary function of "religious education" that Deuteronomy served for the Israelites. Christensen, *Deuteronomy 1:1–21:9*, 81, 135.

99. Tigay, *Deuteronomy*, 115.

the movers of history, for it is all subsumed under the understanding of "Yahweh as the God of the covenant" and "the belief in the absolute rule of God over history."[100] In other words, even the anthropocentric aspect is rooted in a theistic worldview, and in the covenant in particular. Further, this anthropocentric aspect of retribution is balanced by the theocentric aspect in which God takes the lead.

2.5.3. Theocentric Aspect of Retribution

The emphasis in the theocentric aspect of retribution is on God's initiative in his dealing with people. Here God is no longer the reactor but the initiator; his actions are directed to achieving his own purposes and no longer dependent on the deeds of human beings. According to Gammie, this is the concept "*by which Yahweh's past and present actions may be described*" (italics Gammie's). The focus in this aspect of retribution is on God's relationship with Israel.[101]

Gammie states that instances of this aspect of retribution are seen in God initiating a covenant with Israel. Deuteronomy clearly states the covenant is independent of Israel's prior actions or merit (Deut 7:7–8). Another example is the giving of the law, which is for man's own good (Deut 10:12–13). This too was God's initiative and not based on Israel's behaviour. Furthermore, even though man seems to possess control over their fate in that very frequently retribution comes as a reaction to man's action, Gammie states that God's action is not "unalterably contingent" on human action because often punishment does not come in full force. God may choose to show mercy, such as when God's punished the Israelites for their rebellion at Horeb but chose not to exercise the "full measure of judgment" warranted by their actions because of his relationship with them (Deut 7:9b–10:11).[102]

2.5.3.1. Deuteronomy 7:6–11 As an Illustration of Theocentric Aspect of Divine Retribution

Deuteronomy 7 begins with a repetition of the instructions found in Exodus and Numbers to exterminate the nations and their religious symbols when

---

100. Hempel, *Studien des apologetischen Seminars*, 15, cited by Gammie, "Theology of Retribution," 8.
101. Gammie, 9.
102. Gammie, 9.

they enter the Canaan (Deut 7:1–2, 5).[103] The motivation behind the command to completely destroy the nations is the preservation of Israel's holiness; it is a preemptive measure against apostasy (vv. 2b–4).

Deuteronomy 7:6 explains that Israel's holiness was an absolute necessity because of her status as God's chosen people (Deut 7:6–8). Wildberger calls Deuteronomy 7:6–8 "the classical OT text for Israel's election."[104] The word בחר itself ("to choose" Deut 7:6), as Emile Nicole says, has no intrinsic theological meaning,[105] however, in HB studies it has come to function almost as a technical term for the concept of election.[106] Along with other terms,[107] it conveys the theologically rich idea of Israel's divine election.[108] It also underlies concepts such as "the people of the LORD" (Judg 5:11), "treasured possession" (Deut 7:6 and Exod 19:5), "holy nation" (Exod 19:6), and "covenant" (Deut 5:2).[109] The meaning of being chosen by God is further explained by two phrases – i) עַם קָדוֹשׁ ("holy people") indicates that Israel's chosen status also entails holiness, and ii) [110]עַם סְגֻלָּה ("special people" or "treasured people") which expresses the idea of God's sovereignty over and attachment to Israel (Deut 7:6).[111] Thus, God's election of Israel lies at the heart of God's relation-

---

103. Also in Exodus 32:20–33; 34:11–16; Numbers 33:50–56. The instructions in Exodus, Numbers and Deuteronomy vary in detail. In Exodus 23 the people are told that an angel will lead Israel. However, Deuteronomy and Numbers do not mention an angel. Further, the command to drive out the nations in Exodus and Numbers is replaced in Deuteronomy by חָרַם, the command to totally annihilate them. This command, given by the LORD himself, presents a problem that is not completely resolved however one explains it and stands in tension with Deuteronomy's concern for the alien, the widow, the orphan, etc. Thompson, *Deuteronomy: A Theological Commentary*, 82–83.

104. Wildberger, "בחר bhr to choose," in Jenni and Westermann, eds., *Theological Lexicon*, vol. 1, 216.

105. Nicole, "בחר" in VanGemeren, ed., *NIDOTTE*, vol. 1, 638.

106. Wildberger, "בחר bhr to choose," 213.

107. Other terms used to express the concept of election are יָדַע "to know" (Gen 18:18; Amos 3:2), בָּדַל "to separate" (1 Kgs 8:53), לָקַח "to take" (2 Sam 7:8), כּוּן "to establish" (2 Sam 7:24), קָרָא "to call" (Hos 11:1). Nicole, "בחר," 638.

108. This concept of election of the whole people is in contrast to that of the Egyptian and other ANE nations where only the king is chosen by their gods or is a son or representative of the gods.

109. Nicole, "בחר," 638.

110. This term is used to describe special private treasure like those accumulated by a housewife, or a slave, or a royal privy purse. Thus, in this context it would indicate that though everything belongs to the LORD, he cherishes Israel in a special way. Weinfeld, *Deuteronomy 1–11*, vol. 5, 368, and Tigay, *Deuteronomy*, 87.

111. Tigay, xv.

ship with Israel, which is expressed in several ways in the HB and formalized using the בְּרִית "covenant" metaphor.

Choosing Israel out of all the other nations is completely God's doing without any contribution from Israel. As Gammie says, "the divine election of Israel was not dependent at all upon Israel's *actus primus*."[112] In fact, in this divine election, God's decision to choose Israel was the *actus primus*, or the "first act."[113] God's initiative was the "first actuality"[114] that culminated in the covenant at Mt. Sinai. From Israel's perspective, the relationship might be considered to have begun at Mt. Sinai when Israel pledged their allegiance to Yahweh and agreed to serve him. However, the initiation of the relationship began long before Israel was even formed – God's promise to their ancestor Abraham to bless him and make him into a great nation (Gen 12:1–3). Thus, the relationship that God and Israel enter in making the Sinai covenant is a result of and reliant on God's past action, and not on Israel's. The initiative lies with Yahweh; the interaction between God and man in the covenant framework was the God act of grace, and not a reward for Israel's deeds.

The explanation for why Yahweh chose Israel to be his people is given in Deuteronomy 7:7–8. Deuteronomy unambiguously locates the basis of God's choice of Israel in God's unmerited love for Israel and his faithfulness to his promise to Israel's ancestors. If the people of Israel had any delusions about being chosen because of some inherent quality as a people, Deuteronomy is quick to dispel it. In these two verses, Yahweh is consistently the subject, and Israel the object, in these two verses – it is Yahweh who חשק ("to set") his heart on Israel, Yahweh בחר ("to choose") Israel, Yahweh אהב ("to love") Israel, Yahweh שמר ("to keep") his promise made to their ancestors, and Yahweh פדה ("to ransom or redeem") them from Egypt. The word חשק means "to set one's heart" and can be used to describe the affection or desire of a man for a woman (as in Gen 34:8; Deut 21:11) and is "always used in a positive sense."[115] It can also be used to describe the bond between God and Israel as used here (also in Deut 10:15; Ps 91:14). In the case of Yahweh being the subject of חָשַׁק

---

112. Gammie, "Theology of Retribution," 9.

113. Doran and Corken, eds., *Collected Works*, 655

114. "The first actuality (actus primus) begins a series; it supposes no other actuality preceding it in the same series, but calls for a further complement, namely, the second actuality (actus secundus)." "Actus Primus," http://www.catholic.org/encyclopedia/view.php?id=166.

115. Talley, חשק in *NIDOTTE*, vol. 2, 318; Wallis, "חָשַׁק hasaq" *TDOT*, vol. 5, 262.

("he set"), James Baxter's definition of the term is apt – "a strong emotional attachment that runs beyond any reasonable act."[116] There was no reason to choose Israel; it was "his own past decision, incomprehensible to mankind,"[117] yet Yahweh did this, in Thompson's words, "simply because God has wed Godself to Israel."[118]

Deuteronomy explains that the reason God set his heart on Israel and loved them goes back to their forefathers (Deut 7:8) – God's commitment to the promise made to Abraham, Isaac, and Jacob,[119] which itself was a pure act of grace.[120] In redeeming Israel from Egypt, a defining event in the Yahweh-Israel relationship, God was keeping his promise to their forefathers.[121] Thus, the reason for Israel's special status as God's chosen people has its origin in the LORD himself. It is nothing that Israel has done to merit, just as they did nothing to merit the possession of the land (Deut 9:4–6).

While the choosing of Israel was a matter of God's grace, their "future well-being" was contingent on their adherence to his commandments.[122] The people are told to ידע ("to know, or keep in mind") that God is faithful and they must obey the law because "the integrity of God's character threatens individual retribution upon apostate (v.10)."[123] Moreover, the use of the terms אהב ("to love") and שנא ("to hate") "leave no middle ground or room for half measures" (vv. 9b–10).[124]

In this passage, Deuteronomy 7:6–11, while God's choosing of Israel has a corporate focus, the warning of punishment to those who hate Yahweh seems to have a more individualistic orientation –

הָאֵל הַנֶּאֱמָן שֹׁמֵר הַבְּרִית וְהַחֶסֶד לְאֹהֲבָיו וּלְשֹׁמְרֵי מִצְוֹתָו לְאֶלֶף דּוֹר׃

וּמְשַׁלֵּם לְשֹׂנְאָיו אֶל־פָּנָיו לְהַאֲבִידוֹ לֹא יְאַחֵר לְשֹׂנְאוֹ אֶל־פָּנָיו יְשַׁלֶּם־לוֹ׃ (Deut 7:9b–10). Deuteronomy 7:9b–10 is a restatement of Deuteronomy 5:9–10, but with

---

116. Baxter, *Book of Deuteronomy*, np.
117. Wallis, "חָשַׁק hasaq," 262.
118. Thompson, *Deuteronomy*, 86.
119. Calvin, *Commentaries on Last Four*, 353, cited in Thompson, *Deuteronomy*, 87, and Tigay, *Deuteronomy*, 87.
120. Wildberger, "בחר bhr to choose," 21 and Christensen, *Deuteronomy 1:1–21:9*, 156.
121. Weinfled, *Deuteronomy*, 101.
122. Tigay, *Deuteronomy*, 87.
123. Nelson, *Deuteronomy*, 101–102.
124. Nelson, 101–102.

a significant difference. In both passages, reward for covenant faithfulness applies to אֶלֶף דּוֹר ("a thousand generations"). However, the expression of the second part of the covenant in Deuteronomy 7:10 deviates from its earlier expressions in Exodus 20:5 and 34:6–7, Numbers 14:18, and Deuteronomy 5:9. Exodus 20:2 and its counterparts reflect a collective view of retribution even when punishment is in view, but the unique expression of negative retribution in Deuteronomy 7:10 has a more individualistic view – אֶל־פָּנָיו יְשַׁלֶּם־לוֹ ("he will repay to his face"). Merrill takes this expression as an indication that the punishment perhaps affects only the offending person and is not passed on to the "unborn generations."[125] Weinfeld states that the author of Deuteronomy "changes altogether the clause about the view that God visits the father's sin upon its descendants but, on the contrary, requites the sinner personally."[126] Nelson[127] and Tigay[128] also agree that Deuteronomy 7:10 supports the view that punishments affect only those who had sinned and is not carried over cross-generationally. The Targum of Pseudo-Jonathan reflects this individualistic understanding in its translation as well.[129]

While this view of individual retribution is radical in its deviation from the traditional expression of cross-generational retribution, it nevertheless remains in tandem with Deuteronomy 5:9–10 (and its parallel passages in Exodus and Numbers) where the collective aspect is explicitly stated. Hence, in Deuteronomy as a whole, the two views are held in tension and that tension is not completely resolved.

The election and redemption of Israel was a demonstration of God's faithfulness; they are to know that he is "reliable and steadfast."[130] The practical implication of the passage is that God has been faithful to Israel and hence they are also to respond with their own faithfulness[131] by observing and fol-

---

125. Merrill, *Deuteronomy*, 182.
126. Weinfeld, *Deuteronomy*, 371.
127. Nelson, *Deuteronomy*, 101–102.
128. Tigay, *Deuteronomy*, 437.
129. Translation of Deuteronomy 7:10 in Targum Pseudo-Jonathan "... who pays, *in this world*, to those who hate him, *the rewards of their good works* in order to destroy them in *the world to come* and who does not delay (the retribution) of those who hate him *but while they are living pays them, in this world, their recompense*." Clark, trans., *Targum Pseudo-Jonathan, Deuteronomy*, vol. 5B, 27–28.
130. Tigay, *Deuteronomy*, 87.
131. Tigay, 88.

lowing all the commandments and laws they have received (Deut 7:11). This would ensure that they continue to remain in God's favour.

Thus, the emphasis in the theocentric aspect of retribution is on God's relationship and initiative in his dealing with people. In this aspect, God's actions are independent of the deeds of mankind and directed towards the realization of his goals. Israel is bound by the covenant to respond to God in love and obedience, and is subject to the covenant stipulations, and hence there is an element of the anthropocentric aspect of retribution. However, the election of Israel itself was an act of God that is completely independent of any inherent quality or merits of Israel. It was God who chose Israel and bound himself to her in a covenant, and that covenant remains the basis of all the interactions between God and Israel. So, while at times God's dealings with Israel brings the anthropocentric aspect to the fore, it is always operative within the framework of the covenant that is quintessentially theocentric, and it is within this framework that God's dealings with his people are best understood.

2.5.4. Dissolution of Retribution

Dissolution of retribution describes instances where the principle of retribution ceases to work as a "conceptual vehicle"[132] to describe God's dealings with people. This is where "the limitations of the idea of retribution are pointed out."[133] According to this aspect, not all misfortune can be attributed to human sin, nor all prosperity correlated to righteousness. There may be other reasons. The idea that privations may not be retributory is also expressed by Rankin when he states, "That adversity may be sent by God to test man's faith – the probationary view of suffering – or to discipline and train character – the pedagogical explanation – appears to have been an early Hebrew conception."[134] God may choose to test or teach his people, or achieve other goals through adversities or affluence. As Irene Nowell states, "God blesses the righteous and punishes the wicked; yet he is free."[135] Laato states that educative theodicy can be found in Deuteronomistic History. Educative theodicy refers to the

---

132. Gammie, "Theology of Retribution," 10.
133. Gammie, 10.
134. Rankin, *Israel's Wisdom Literature*, 19.
135. Irene Nowell, "Book of Tobit," 233, cited by Kiel, *"Whole Truth,"* 5.

understanding that "modest suffering can enrich the sufferer's life by giving him a deeper understanding of life."[136]

Gammie proposes that Deuteronomy 8:1–9:6 brings out four cases to make the point that there need not be a situation-morality correlation every single time. He asserts that these four points have been intentionally put together in the pericope to counter the dogmatizing of anthropocentric understanding of retribution by the Israelites[137] as evident in the books of Job and Ecclesiastes and in other cultures including Egypt.[138] In these four cases in Deuteronomy 8:1–9:6 God's actions are understood as God's suspending the retributive principle to achieve other objectives. The objectives could be

1. to test the Israelites (8:2)
2. to discipline and teach the Israelites lessons through adversity (8:3)[139]
3. to remind them that the power to generate wealth or prosperity comes from God (8:18) and
4. to undercut any idea that Israel's inheritance of the land was because of their goodness by attributing Israel's inheritance of the land to the wickedness of the other nations (9:4–6).[140]

A closer examination of the three examples contained in Deuteronomy 8, out of the four cited above, should suffice to illustrate the point.

2.5.4.1. *Deuteronomy 8:1–20 As an Illustration of Dissolution of Retribution*

Deuteronomy 8:1–20 presents three instances where either adversity or blessing cannot be correlated to human actions, that is, some instances of adversity are not divine punishments for wrong deeds and some instances of blessing are not divine rewards for faithfulness. The outer frames of the pericope, Deuteronomy 8:1 and 19–20, affirm the operation of the retribution principle:

---

136. This is a category of theodicy in Green's five types of theodicy in a monotheistic context, in Green, "Theodicy," cited by Laato, "Theodicy in Deuteronomistic History," 184.

137. Gammie, "Theology of Retribution," 11.

138. Gammie here cites Hans H. Schmid who examines the dogmatization of the concept of retribution in Israel and other ANE cultures, in Schmid, "Wesen und Geschichte," 173–196. Gammie, "Theology of Retribution," 11.

139. So also Kaminsky, "Would You Impugn my Justice?" 304.

140. Gammie, "Theology of Retribution," 10.

Verse 1 exhorts Israel to obey the commands לְמַעַן תִּחְיוּן וּרְבִיתֶם וּבָאתֶם וִירִשְׁתֶּם אֶת־הָאָרֶץ ("*so that* you may live, and multiply, and go, and possess the land"), very much in the style of anthropocentric aspect of retribution where divine blessings follow human obedience.

Verses 19–20 exhibit the same pattern except in its negative aspect that divine sanctions will follow covenant violation –

וְהָיָה אִם־שָׁכֹחַ תִּשְׁכַּח אֶת־יְהוָה אֱלֹהֶיךָ . . .
הַעִדֹתִי בָכֶם הַיּוֹם כִּי אָבֹד תֹּאבֵדוּן׃
. . . תֹּאבֵדוּן עֵקֶב לֹא תִשְׁמְעוּן בְּקוֹל יְהוָה אֱלֹהֵיכֶם׃

("If you do forget the Lord your God . . . I solemnly warn you today that you shall surely perish . . . so shall you perish, because you would not obey the voice of the Lord your God" Deut 8:19–20, NRSV). It is unambiguous in its warning that spiritual amnesia and apostasy will be met with destruction, thus drawing a clear cause and affect connection.

However, within this frame is the exposition of instances where the expected correlation between human deed and divine sanction ceases to work. This pericope is an exhortation to Israel to maintain her fidelity to Yahweh amid the prosperity that living in the land will bring. As typical of Deuteronomy, the pericope looks back at Israel's past as well as forward to their future in the promised land. The text anticipates that arrogance and self-reliance could stem from living in a bountiful land (Deut 8:7–9), making disobedience and infidelity highly plausible (Deut 8:12–14),[141] a concern also expressed in Deuteronomy 6:10–12. Thus, it attempts to counter this possibility by drawing lessons from Israel's wilderness experiences and employing them in the service of driving home a theological point – not to forget the LORD.[142] The emphasis is evinced in the text by its repeated use of terms like שמר ("to keep, observe" Deut 8:1, 6, 11), זכר ("to remember" Deut 8:2, 18), ידע ("to know" Deut 8:5), and שכח ("to forget" Deut 8:11, 19).

Offering perspective from the past, two adversities experienced by the Israelites in their exodus from Egypt to Canaan are recalled – the long duration of their journey in the perilous wilderness (Deut 8:2, 15a), and the hunger

---

141. Nelson, *Deuteronomy*, 108.

142. Deuteronomy 7 warns of the dangers of forgetting the LORD as a result of following the people of the land, and now Deuteronomy 8 highlights the perils of forgetting the LORD being blinded by their economic prosperity in the land.

they experienced that led to the provision of manna (Deut 8:3). These two instances are examples of Deuteronomy's understanding that adversities are not always divine punishments but are part of God's design to achieve other purposes. The future view portrays two positive, albeit potentially dangerous, prospects – the possession of the promised land (Deut 8:7; 9:1) and material prosperity in the land (Deut 8:8–9; 12–13). In these instances, we can see Deuteronomy's cases against equating prosperity with righteousness or merited blessings. The lessons behind the three examples do overlap to some degree rather than stand as distinct unrelated purposes. The point is that all these experiences, whether in the past or those awaiting them in the future when understood in the right perspective, can help Israel remain loyal to the LORD. The first example of the dissolution of retribution in Deuteronomy 8 is that of adversity as divine tests or the probationary view of suffering.

i. Adversities as a Divine Test

According to Deuteronomy, the hardships Israel faced in the wilderness were by design – to test the Israelites. Both the forty years of wandering and the experience of hunger were intended by God as a process of humbling and testing Israel (Deut 8:2–3). ענה in the Piel form is generally translated "to humble," and can also mean to degrade, afflict, violate, or slight.[143] According to Giessen Gerstenberger the term can indicate the use of force to change someone's status "for the worse."[144] He states that applied to the people as a whole it could also indicate a loss of status in that "hunger (Deut 8:3) is not part of the covenant design" and yet God imposed hunger on them as "a test of faith."[145] Paul Wegner explains, "God sometimes uses affliction for correction or to bring about a desired goal,"[146] and in this instance God used these privations to test and teach the Israelites.

The word נסה ("to test" Deut 8:2b) is used in the sense of testing someone or something to "determine something about them."[147] The objective of the test here is to expose what is in the לֵבָב of the people. Though generally

---

143. Wegner, "ענה," in VanGemeren, ed., *NIDOTTE*, vol. 3, 450; Gerstenberger, "עָנָה II 'ānâ" in Botterweck, Ringgren, and Fabry, eds. *TODT*, vol. XI, 237.

144. Gerstenberger, 237.

145. Gerstenberger, 237.

146. Wegner, "ענה," 450.

147. Brensinger, "נסה" in VanGemeren, ed., *NIDOTTE*, vol. 3, 111.

translated "heart," לֵבָב can also refer to the mind, will, or inner person. Here it refers to the "inner attitude of the people,"[148] implying testing with hardships would reveal whether the people would obey Yahweh or not. Nelson refers to their time in the wilderness as "a tempering of national character and a test of faith and obedience."[149] As such, it can be said that their forty years' journey in the wilderness was a testing period designed to reveal Israel's true intentions; a training period paradigmatic of their covenant life in the land. Further, the book of Numbers explains Israel's extended forty years' wilderness journey as a judgment for their disbelief and rebellion (Num 14:26–35). However, here in Deuteronomy 8 the event is interpreted[150] through a pedagogical lens – God used those years to teach their absolute dependence on him and to test whether Israel would obey his decrees.[151] Thus the present text makes a theological point by highlighting the testing and teaching aspect of God's dealing with Israel in recalling their wilderness journey. What we have here is that Numbers's portrayal of forty years in wilderness as a punishment, which can be classified as the anthropocentric aspect of divine retribution, which is downplayed in Deuteronomy and the dissolution aspect of retribution is amplified by presenting the wilderness journey as a testing and teaching period. Thus, two aspects of divine retribution are present in this one event, but interpreted in Deuteronomy with the emphasis falling on the dissolution aspect to make a theological point.

While Deuteronomy explains the long period of Israel's wilderness journey as a divine test, it also portrays hunger and the provision of manna as God's ways of disciplining and teaching Israel. This pedagogical aspect receives more emphasis in the second example of the dissolution of retribution in Deuteronomy 8.

ii. Adversities As Disciplining and Teaching Periods

The hunger that the Israelites experienced and the daily provision of manna are also explained as a process of reminding them of truths about God and

---

148. Christensen, *Deuteronomy 1:1–21:9*, 173.

149. Nelson, *Deuteronomy*, 107.

150. Helfmeyer states that such interpretations result from the need to provide meaningful answers in the face of national disaster. Helfmeyer, "נָסָה *nissaâ*; מַסּוֹת *massôt*; מַסָּה *massâ*," in *TDOT*, vol. IX, 449.

151. Tigay, *Deuteronomy*, 92.

what being his people entails. In the wilderness, stripped of their usual ways of providing necessities like food and water for themselves, Israel was learning by experience what total reliance on God meant.[152] The Hiphil form of the verb רעב, וַיַּרְעִבֶךָ "and he caused you to hunger," shows that it was God who made them hunger (Deut 8:3). At the same time, God also fed them (יַאֲכִלְךָ "he caused you to eat") with manna, something neither they nor their fathers knew.[153] The desired goal was a movement from self-reliance to absolute reliance on God. Tigay says it was to "teach the people that nature alone could not be relied upon for food." The provision of manna demonstrated that nourishment is "whatever God decrees to be nourishing."[154] Further, provision of manna was a lesson in obedience. Manna could not be hoarded, except on the sixth day. This meant that they had to go out every morning to gather manna, and to gather only as much as they needed (Exod 16:16–26) – an experiential lesson in obedience and in trusting God daily for their sustenance (Deut 8:4).

These experiences in the wilderness were meant to יסר ("to correct, chasten"; Deut 8:5) them. Although God taught them through adversities it was a fatherly discipline designed for Israel's own good "in order to shape specific conduct."[155] Merrill states that although יסר could have the connotation of punishment, the fact that it is used in conjunction with ענה "to humble," and נסה "to test," "it may be best to see the desert itinerary as a learning experience rather than a punishing one."[156] God's parental concern is demonstrated further in the preservation of their clothing from the normal wear and tear, and protection of their feet during their years in the wilderness (Deut 8:4).[157] Thus, deprivation and provision are spoken of not in terms of punishment and rewards but as a process of disciplining Israel leading them to recognize (לְמַעַן הוֹדִעֲךָ "so that you recognize/know") that life itself was dependent on God.

---

152. Craigie, *Book of Deuteronomy*, 185.

153. Christensen cites Sarna who notes that there is no known substance that corresponds exactly to the manna of biblical description. The closest thing to manna is the substance secreted by sucking insects on tamarisk bushes. However, the best available quantity in the whole Sinai Peninsula, about 600 pounds, is found only for about six weeks in a year. Sarna, *Exploring Exodus*, 117, cited by Christensen, *Deuteronomy 1:1–21:9*, 173; also Tigay, *Deuteronomy*, 93.

154. Tigay, 92.

155. Branson, "יסר *yāsar*" in Botterweck and Ringgren, *TDOT*, vol. 6, 129.

156. Merrill, *Deuteronomy*, 187.

157. Tigay, *Deuteronomy*, 72.

The idea of the discipline being for Israel's own long-term good is expressed again in Deuteronomy 8:16b, in the context of their imminent entry to the promised land. Recalling God's past provision for their sustenance is also meant for Israel to "recognize human dependence on God, thereby preventing arrogance"[158] amid prosperity and abundance in the land, a theme prominent in the passage, and to which we now turn.

iii. Ability to Generate Wealth Comes from God

The perspective of the pericope transitions from the past to now envision the future when the people are already settled in the land (Deut 8:7–18). A hymn[159] praising the qualities of the land highlights its inherent goodness (Deut 8:7–9) and becomes the basis for further instructions to the people. Tigay notes that in Halakhic literature the agricultural products listed here are known as "the seven species for which the land of Israel is praised."[160] The triple use of the verb רבה "to be many" in verse 13, variously translated as multiplied, grow, increased, prospered, etc., underlines the increase of wealth that is to be expected in the land. But there is a catch – their newfound material prosperity could become a snare for them. The text warns of the dangers of taking credit for their prosperity.

Tigay observes that although wealth generation would obviously require the people's labour, the construction of the sentence as "when your herds and flocks have multiplied" rather than "when you have multiplied your herds and flocks," subtly undercuts any attempts to construe their prosperity as a reward for their deeds.[161] Such dismissal of the people's labour may seem unreasonable, but first, there was a greater risk at stake if the people took credit for their wealth – they would become self-reliant and arrogant and it would

---

158. Helfmeyer, "נָסָה nissaâ; מַסּוֹת massôt; מַסָּה massâ," 450–451.

159. Several scholars have noted that vv. 7–9 constituted an independent poem, similar to Sinuhe's poem on the land of Yaa, in *ANET*, cited by Nelson, *Deuteronomy*, 112; Craigie, *Book of Deuteronomy*, 186; von Rad, *Deuteronomy*, 72.

160. Tigay, *Deuteronomy*, 94. Some have questioned the validity of the reference to iron and copper as a resource of the land, especially in the west Jordan (for instance, von Rad, *Deuteronomy*, 73). Tigay explains that there were significant deposits in Transjordan Gilead and "in the Jordan Rift south of the Dead Sea, and in the southern Negev," and it would make sense if the text is referencing areas later controlled by Israel. The reference here of iron may also include basalt which is around 20% iron. Tigay, *Deuteronomy*, 9; see also Craigie, *Book of Deuteronomy*, 187.

161. Tigay, *Deuteronomy*, 95.

eventually result in their forgetting (שׁכח) Yahweh (Deut 8:11–17). Secondly, it was fundamentally true that the ability to generate wealth was not their own, it was a blessing concomitant with the covenant that Yahweh made with them. As Merrill states, "[T]here is a reciprocal dynamic in which covenant produces blessing and blessing proves the reality of covenant."[162] Hence rightly, the antidote to pride and forgetting Yahweh was זכר, "to remember" that it is Yahweh who is the source of all ability to generate wealth. Any success they enjoyed was primarily a confirmation of the covenant favour (Deut 8:18).[163]

In the HB, שׁכח ("to forget")[164] and זכר ("to remember")[165] are not merely mental activities. Preuss states that forgetting God is not unconscious or because of the inevitable passage of time. It is "a wilful, culpable act from conscious disinclination and renunciation" invoking Yahweh's punishment (Deut 8:19–20). In concrete terms the people forget Yahweh because they apostatize and do not keep his commandments.[166] Allen says, "Especially Israel was liable to forget the significance of God and his past saving acts," and this is manifested in disobedience and apostasy.[167] As such, Israel forgot the LORD to her own peril, and remembering is prescribed as a remedy.

Like forgetting, remembering "often implies an appropriate action that one is moved to take."[168] It is not just a recollection of the past "but also consequences their memory entails,"[169] and here in Deuteronomy 8:18 remembering God and his gifts should move them to keep his commandments and obey him. To remember was to continue to be connected to the source of their life and to forget was to forsake that source of life and so doom themselves to the very fate of the Canaanites before them (Deut 8:19–20). In essence, to remember was life and to forget was death. Thus, in Deuteronomy's view, economic prosperity was the LORD's gift to them, and any self-congratulatory attitude was misplaced and a sure path to destruction. Israel's prosperity in

---

162. Merrill, *Deuteronomy*, 188.
163. Merrill, 188.
164. Allen, "שׁכח," in *NIDOTTE*, vol. 4, 104.
165. Allen, "זכר,"1102.
166. Preuss, "שָׁכַח šākah" in *TDOT*, vol. 14, 674.
167. Allen, "שׁכח,"104.
168. Allen, "שׁכח,"104.
169. Eising, "זָכַר zākhar" in *TDOT*, vol. 4, 67.

the land came part and parcel with God's covenant promise to their ancestors and was not a reward for their deeds.

These three instances demonstrate that there are instances when the deed-consequence correlation breaks down. It is instead put aside to achieve other objectives. Also, the perspective presented in these instances of dissolution of retribution is corporate. The past experiences of the people and their significance are treated as belonging to the collective whole; it does not pause to consider, for example, whether some individuals' deeds were definitive in delaying the whole nation's entry to the promised land. This corporate perspective is maintained in speaking of their future in the land. God does reward and punish human deeds; however, he is not compelled to work exclusively within the framework of retribution. In Deuteronomy 8 the outer frame affirms the operation of the retributive principle in its more familiar garb, expressing a correlation between human deeds and consequences. Contained within the frame is an exposé on the dissolution of retribution where human experience of blessings or hardship is related not to human deeds but rather to God's purposes, such as to test, discipline, teach, or to remind them of some fundamental truths.

2.6. Conclusion

Divine retribution in the book of Deuteronomy is a complex idea that cannot be represented by any single model of retribution, nor reduced to an axiom, convenient and appealing as that might be. This was seen in both the traditional formulation of divine retribution as juridical, which viewed God as directly intervening in every instance of retribution, and in Koch's proposition of the act-consequence connection model which deemed consequences as built into the deeds themselves so that retribution was inevitable in an almost mechanical way with divine involvement reduced to the minimal at best.

Instead it was argued that divine retribution is a more nuanced and multi-faceted concept and it was seen that several scholars have recognized and acknowledged this multi-faceted nature of divine retribution in the HB. In the book of Deuteronomy, it was seen that divine retribution is expressed with four distinct emphases or aspects, namely impersonal, anthropocentric, theocentric, and dissolution. Each of these aspects were further illustrated with a passage from Deuteronomy. In all these aspects, it was noted that God is involved. God's involvement in the anthropocentric and theocentric aspects was evident since God is either presented as intervening and responding directly to the deeds of human beings, or as blessing or showing mercy to human beings for his own purposes. However, even in the impersonal aspect when retribution is expressed in terms that deemphasizes the role of God, this is so because he allows the natural process to bring to fruition the consequences of a human deed. The nuanced understanding of divine retribution also preempts the dogmatizing tendency that a monochromatic understanding of divine retribution often fosters by allowing for privation and prosperity to be God's purview and yet be detached from a retributional understanding, as espoused in the dissolution aspect. Further, it was observed that divine retribution in Deuteronomy is presented as operational both corporately and individually, although the corporate expression is predominant. These two voices are allowed to sit side-by-side with no attempt to harmonize them.

CHAPTER 3

Post-mortem Divine Retribution in Isaiah 26:19

3.1. Introduction

As examined in the last chapter, divine retribution in the book of Deuteronomy is a multi-faceted concept. It is expressed with at least four different emphases, namely, the impersonal aspect, anthropocentric aspect, theocentric aspect, and dissolution of retribution. These aspects are not mutually exclusive but rather are distinguished by where the emphasis is placed in each case of retribution. Further, these aspects of divine retribution could work out corporately or individually, although the corporate nature seemed predominant in Deuteronomy.

From this chapter on, the focus is on placing the concept of divine retribution in Deuteronomy side-by-side with post-mortem texts to examine the continuities and discontinuities between earthly and post-mortem divine retribution. In the HB, the presence of the concept of life after death is a debated subject. Richard Freidman and Shawna Overton capture the essence of the problem when they state that the problem of paucity of material in the HB regarding a subject as common as death is "mysterious," and while it might have been better if the HB was altogether silent on the issue, there is "just enough suggestive text to confuse the issue."[1] The difficulty this subject poses is not novel considering how even during Jesus' time the

---

1. Freidman and Overton, "Death and Afterlife," 35.

Pharisees and the Sadducees, the theological scholars of the day, did not see eye-to-eye on the matter of afterlife (Mark 12:18). This highlights the fact that disagreement regarding the interpretation of texts on the afterlife in the HB is a long-standing one. Scholarly discussions have followed suit until this day and a sustained consensus is hard to come by.

The following two chapters will examine texts from the HB that have possible post-mortem import and observe if and how divine retribution is carried out. Potentially there are two such passages in the HB – Isaiah 26:19 and Daniel 12:1–3. What follows is a study of these passages from the perspective of post-mortem divine retribution driven by three questions:

1. Is there a detectable reference to an afterlife in the text under consideration? If so,
2. Are there traceable elements of continuities and discontinuities between the text and the aspects of divine retribution delineated from the book of Deuteronomy, or does it introduce a different emphasis?
3. Does divine retribution in these texts operate as a corporate or an individual phenomenon, or both?

The quest here is to see how these texts function as part of the larger tradition of the HB and later flow into the Jewish literature of the Second Temple period.

Isaiah 26:19 is not as well-known as the resurrection passage in Daniel 12, however several scholars have considered it as expressing a belief in a literal resurrection of the dead in the HB. That opinions on this matter are diverse is obvious; nevertheless, the perspective presented in Isaiah 26:19 regarding the nature of post-mortem divine retribution is worthy of consideration. This chapter begins by considering the immediate textual context of Isaiah 26:19, that is, Isaiah 24–27, which forms a textual unity. It then discusses two aspects regarding Isaiah 24–27: i) the issues revolving around the dating of Isaiah 24–27 since it has a bearing on its interpretation, and ii) the structure of the unit, which helps locate the verse of interest (Isa 26:19) within its larger literary context. From there on the chapter focuses on Isaiah 26:19, considering the grammatical issues in the verse, and the question of the identity of the speaker, both of which help illuminate the interpretation of the text. The chapter next considers whether the resurrection image in the verse is used metaphorically or literally to see if there is a defensible reference to an afterlife divine retribution. It then examines the post-mortem retribution as presented in this verse against the aspects and nature of divine retribution that was seen in Deuteronomy.

3.2. Isaiah 24–27: A Distinct Textual Complex

Isaiah 24–27 is commonly accepted as a distinct unit within proto-Isaiah (Isaiah 1–39) and has been treated as such by scholars.[2] Chapter 24 begins with an introductory *hinneh* (24:1), which often marks the beginning of a new section or thought. Chapter 28 is likewise introduced by *hoy* ("woe!" 28:1), denoting the unfolding of a distinct emphasis – the experience of the nation of Ephraim and its implications for Judah. Isaiah 24–27 follows chapters 13–23, which are chiefly concerned with the oracles against nations, whereas chapters 24–27 mark a shift in interest by turning its focus to the entire earth (*'eres*). It speaks of a worldwide divine judgment and restoration for Israel. There are repeated references to בַּיּוֹם הַהוּא ("on that day," 24:21; 25:9; 26:2; 27:1, 2, 12, 13), and it looks forward to a banquet לְכָל־הָעַמִּים ("for all peoples"), which Yahweh will host on his mountain (25:6). All these lend the unit a comparatively universal outlook to these chapters.[3] However, its distinctiveness as a unit should not be overstated. While it is unique, and there are disagreements regarding the degree of distinctiveness of Isaiah 24–27 from the rest of the book, there exists a broad consensus that in its present form it is both internally cohesive and well-integrated with the rest of the book of Isaiah.[4]

3.3. Date of Isaiah 24–27

Isaiah 24–27 is a part of the proto-Isaiah corpus, however, most scholars do not assign its composition to the prophet Isaiah of Jerusalem. There are a few

---

2. Duhm, *Das Buch Jesaja*, 10–12; Redditt, *Isaiah 24–27*, 151–152, both cited in Doyle, *Apocalypse of Isaiah*, 12.

3. Sweeny, *Isaiah 1–39*, 312; Wildberger, *Isaiah 13–27*, 446.

4. Scholars have also noted the redactional unity of the book, for instance, Childs, *Introduction to Old Testament*, 325–334; Brueggemann, "Unity and Dynamic," 89–107, Johnson, *From Chaos to Restoration*, 15–17. Sweeny argues that there is a strong intertextual relationship between Isaiah 24–27 and other parts of the book of Isaiah, and as such although compositionally distinct, functionally Isaiah 24–27 is integral to the book. Sweeny, *Reading the Prophetic Books*, 64–78.

who defend the Isaianic date and authorship, like Oswalt who considers the alternatives to Isaianic authorship not strong enough to preclude an Isaianic authorship.[5] But this view does not have a wide following today. Duhm was the first to date the unit to the Maccabean era.[6] But the discovery at Qumran of a complete scroll of Isaiah dating to the second century BCE established the *terminus ad quem*, and Duhm's Maccabean dating has been largely abandoned now.[7] Consequently it is more commonly accepted among scholars that it was composed after the time of prophet Isaiah of Jerusalem and before the second century BCE.

Precisely when between these two dates, however, is another question. Scholars are acutely aware that Isaiah 24–27 defies certitude in dating, and hence when they propose a date, or a set of dates, most do so tentatively. The proposed dates range over half a millennium – from the seventh to the third century BCE[8] with each century being proposed as the possible date of composition (seventh century BCE;[9] sixth century BCE;[10] fifth century BCE;[11] fourth century BCE;[12] third century BCE[13]). Further, some scholars date the unit over a couple of centuries or more, for instance, Polaski dates the textual unit to late sixth to fifth century,[14] Hibbard to late sixth to early fourth century,[15] Rudolph Smend to 500–300 BCE,[16] Kaiser fourth to second century

---

5. John Oswalt, *Book of Isaiah 1–39*, 23–28, 441–442. As also Hayes and Irvine, *Isaiah*, 295–320, cited by Doyle, *Apocalypse of Isaiah*, 31.

6. Duhm, *Das Buch Jesaja*, 172. He dated some sections of Isaiah 24–27 to 135 BCE, and 25:9–11 to 103–76 BCE, with others in between, cited in Hibbard, *Intertextuality in Isaiah 24–27*, 36.

7. Sweeny, *Isaiah 1–39*, 316; Hibbard, *Intertextuality in Isaiah 24–27*, 36; Wildberger, *Isaiah 13–27*, 462.

8. Brian Doyle briefly outlines the various date hypotheses; Doyle, *Apocalypse of Isaiah*, 30–36.

9. Bleek, *Introduction to Old Testament*, 57, cited by Doyle, *Apocalypse of Isaiah*, 31.

10. Driver, *Isaiah, His Life and Times*, 119–125; March, "Study of Two Prophetic," 271ff, cited in Doyle, *Apocalypse of Isaiah*, 32; Cross, *Canaanite Myth*, 345; Hanson, *Dawn of Apocalyptic*, 313–314; Millar, *Isaiah 24–27*, 120.

11. Redditt, *Isaiah 24–27*, 247, cited in Doyle, *Apocalypse of Isaiah*, 33.

12. Sawyer, *Isaiah*, vol. 1, 204.

13. Procksch, *Jesaja I*, 343–346; Mulder, *Die Teologie*, 78–93; Frost, *Old Testament Apocalyptic*, 147–148; Plöger, *Theocracy and Eschatology*, 96–97, all cited in Doyle, *Apocalypse of Isaiah*, 34–35.

14. Polaski, *Authorizing an End*, 58, 215.

15. Hibbard, *Intertextuality in Isaiah 24–27*, 36, 145–148.

16. Smend, "Anmerkungen zu Jes 24–27," 161–224, cited in Young, *Book of Isaiah*, 253.

BCE.[17] This inability to be more precise in dating the unit is illustrative of the elusiveness of the issue based on the data currently available. Among the dates proposed, the sixth century date is gaining relative currency,[18] however, it is also still not indisputable. There is no indispensable reason to privilege or neglect this date; it is simply a probability among other possible dates. For instance, Hays dates the textual complex to the reign of Josiah based on comparable themes, and "historical and literary features" with "older" ANE texts.[19]

However, similarity between texts is not evidence that they are from the same period. Konrad Schmid rightly critiques Hays' approach by pointing out that the biblical book of Job, the *Ludlul bēl nēmeqi*, and the Babylonian Theodicy share several similarities, but they do not help date the book of Job.[20] So although a majority of scholars prefer a post-exilic date, until now no single proposition has gained the general approval of scholars. The frustration arising from the inability to date Isaiah 24–27 with any certainty has been the inevitable fate of scholars dealing with this section of Isaiah. Some reasons behind the difficulty reflected by this array of dates can be briefly summarized as follows:

3.3.1. Lack of Dateable Historical Data

Isaiah 24–27 evinces no indisputable allusions to a dateable historical person or situation. This referential ambiguity opens it up to multiple interpretations, making it challenging to locate the text in any historical period with precision. In the text, Egypt and Assyria (27:12–13) are mentioned, but only as places Israel has lived in. The only city clearly mentioned is Moab (25:10). However, attempts to locate Moab in time have not been fruitful.[21] Similarly, the unnamed city that figures so prominently in this unit (24:10; 25:2; 26:1, 5; 27:10) lacks specific historical allusion so that its proposed identity has also

---

17. Kaiser, *Isaiah 13–39*, 178–179, 215–217.

18. More scholars have begun dating Isaiah 24–27 to the early exilic period, i.e., around the sixth to fifth centuries, rather than later as was true in the past. See Johnson, *From Chaos*, 11–17, and Doyle, *Apocalypse of Isaiah*, 36.

19. Polaski, *Authorizing an End*, 353.

20. Konrad Schmid, "Review of Christopher B. Hays," *Journal of Hebrew Scriptures*, vol. 12.

21. Polaski explains why this route of inquiry is suspect. See Polaski, *Authorizing an End*, 53–54.

remained conjectural at best.[22] Moreover, as Wildberger rightly observes, trying to determine the date on the basis of correctly identifying the city presupposes the same situation at the backdrop of all the city songs.[23] Further, scholars like Wildberger and Polaski point out that the future orientation of the text precludes the identification of the city from being a useful factor in dating. Greenspoon rightly warns that these references are veiled allusions given the fact that the efforts to date this unit of Isaiah based on references to historical events has resulted in such varying dates. He seems to have assessed the situation fairly in doubting that scholarly analysis can achieve anything more than "scholarly illusions" as far as dating Isaiah 24–27 based on historical reference is concerned.[24]

3.3.2. Circular Argument of Theological Concept as a Basis for Date

Some scholars have perceived the presence of the concept of resurrection as tipping the balance in favour of a late date. The argument assumes that resurrection as a concept emerged in the Hebrew theology only in the later period, presumably developing out of the metaphorical usage of resurrection for national revivification. Consequently Isaiah 24–27 is dated to a later period.[25] However it is easy to see why such an argument often ends up as a circular exercise. Additionally, some scholars have countered this late development argument by positing that the idea of resurrection was prevalent among the people of the ANE during the Bronze Age because of their familiarity with the Baal cult and the accompanying concept of the dying and rising gods.[26] As such, dating based on the presence of certain theological concepts is slippery ground. Moreover, the argument that resurrection was a late development assumes, as Polaski highlights, that ideas become democratized and accepted at

---

22. Johnson provides an overview of the various suggestions for the identification of the unnamed city in Johnson, *From Chaos*, 11–14. Even an agreement on the identity of the unnamed city, does not guarantee a consensus date; for example, one of the proposals is that the city is Babylon, however, does the text refer to Babylon's destruction by Cyrus (538 BCE), or Xerxes (485 BCE), or Alexander the Great (332 BCE)?

23. Wildberger, *Isaiah 13–39*, 462; Polaski, *Authorizing an End*, 56.

24. Greenspoon, "Origin of the Idea," in Halpern and Levenson (eds.), *Traditions in Transformation*, 285.

25. For instance, Kaiser, *Isaiah 13–39*, 178–179; Sawyer, *Isaiah*, 204.

26. Hays, "Date of Isaiah 24–27," 8–9. Also, Smith, *Isaiah 1–39*, 452–453.

all places around the same time;[27] this is difficult to sustain. Hence, assigning a particular concept to a specific historical time and context and then arguing for the date of a text on that basis is not an approach that withstands scrutiny.

3.3.3. Literary Genre

In the past, it was common to refer to Isaiah 24–27 as the Isaiah or Isaianic Apocalypse[28] following Smend,[29] and Duhm whose readings of Isaiah as an apocalypse led him to date it to the Maccabean era.[30] But over the years scholars have become wary of classifying Isaiah 24–27 as an apocalypse,[31] at least in the full sense.[32] It has been noted that Isaiah 24–27 lacks several features that characterize the later apocalyptic literature, and does not qualify according to John Collin's somewhat broad but generally accepted definition[33] of apocalypse as a genre. Hence some scholars prefer to call it proto-apocalyptic.[34] Other suggested designations include lamentation of the people,[35] prayer[36] in

---

27. Polaski, *Authorizing an End*, 55, 332. Polaski later points out that a diverse outlook on the concept of resurrection probably co-existed in Israel as seen in the physical revivification of the boy the text clearly referred to as "dead" (2 Kgs 4:18-37), and David's rhetorical question in the context of the death of his son born of Bathsheba, ". . . why should I fast? Can I bring him back?" (2 Sam 12:23).

28. For instance, Box, *Book of Isaiah*, 112, cited in Polaski, *Authorizing an End*, 50.

29. Smend, "Anmerkungen," 210–211; he dated the material to 500–300 BCE, cited by Doyle, *Apocalypse of Isaiah*, 28.

30. Duhm, *Das Buch Jesaja*, 172–194, Kaiser, *Isaiah 13–39*, 174. Hibbard states that Duhm was evidently so convinced of the theological similarity between this text and Daniel he opined that the same person could have written both. Hibbard, *Intertextuality in Isaiah 24–27*, 35.

31. Hibbard says that classifying Isaiah 24–27 as apocalyptic "has been abandoned." Hibbard, *Intertextuality in Isaiah 24–27*, 35; G. Fohrer, at the opposite end of the spectrum from Duhm, asserts that Isaiah 24–27 exhibits no characteristics of apocalyptic; Fohrer, "Der Aufbau der Apokalypse," cited by Wildberger, *Isaiah 13–27*, 464.

32. For instance, Redditt designates Isaiah 24–27 as an eschatological prophecy of the post-exilic period. He however notes that there is some relationship between Isaiah 24–27 and apocalyptic literature. Redditt, *Form Critical Analysis*, 309ff; Doyle similarly says that Isaiah 24–27 is not an apocalypse, however, he sees the later apocalyptic literature as being influenced by Isaiah 24–27. Doyle, *Apocalypse of Isaiah*, 26–27.

33. "'Apocalypse' is a genre of revelatory literature with a narrative framework, in which a revelation is mediated by an otherworldly being to a human recipient, disclosing a transcendent reality which is both temporal, insofar as it envisages eschatological salvation, and spatial insofar as it involves another, supernatural world." Collins, "Introduction: Towards the Morphology," 9.

34. Cross, *New Direction*, 157–165; Miller, *Isaiah 24–27*, 1–9; Doyle, *Apocalypse of Isaiah*, 27.

35. So Lindblom, *Die Jesaja-Apokalypse*, 63, cited in Polaski, *Authorizing an End*, 50; and Kaiser, *Isaiah 13–39*, 210.

36. So Robert Martin-Achard, *From Death to Life*, 131.

the form of a national lament,[37] and early apocalyptic prophecy.[38] Some others, like Willem Beuken, Cook, and Polaski, retain the term "Isaiah Apocalypse" without identifying its genre as an apocalypse.[39] Hence, along with rejecting apocalypse as the literary genre for the textual complex, dating it based on the genre has also been abandoned.

3.3.4. Redactional History

Duhm in 1892 was the first to contest the unity of the composition.[40] While the details of redactional history proposed by Duhm may no longer hold sway, it is generally accepted that Isaiah 24–27 is composite in nature, coming into its present form gradually.[41] This complicates dating even further[42] with scholars assigning various dates to different subunits of Isaiah 24–27.[43] Even when scholars view Isaiah 24–27 as an early composition, consideration has to be given to possible later redactional activity. This is particularly true for Isaiah 26:19, which several scholars consider a later interpolation.[44] Therefore, the redactional history of this unit adds to the myriad of issues scholars grapple with in dating it.

As such, it has been quite impossible to locate Isaiah 24–27 to a precise date or to even delineate the possible context from which it grew. This

---

37. Eissfeldt, *Old Testament: An Introduction*, 324.

38. Cook, "Deliverance as Fertility," 165, n. 1.

39. Beuken, "Mount Zion," 91; Polaski, *Authorizing an End*, 49–51.

40. Duhm, *Das Buch Jesaja*, 148–149, cited by Polaski, *Authorizing an End*, 57; Kaiser, *Isaiah 13–39*, 174. Scholars like Kaiser also posit that there was significant expansion through redaction and rereading of Isaiah 24–27. Kaiser, *Isaiah 13–39*, 177–178.

41. Polaski, *Authorizing an End*, 57. Wildberger points out, however, that there are a few scholars, like Lindblom, *Die Jesaja-Apokalypse*, and following him Ringgren, "Some Observations on Style," 107–115, cited in Doyle, *Apocalypse of Isaiah*, 20, who argue for the original coherence of Isaiah 24–27. Wildberger himself is more cautious. He admits that the developmental process of the text, although hard to demonstrate, is plausible considering that the editorial hand is often observed in other parts of Isaiah, especially in terms of unevenness or tensions in the text, and there is no reason why Isaiah's Apocalypse would be different. Wildberger, *Isaiah 13–27*, 450–451.

42. Hibbard, *Intertextuality in Isaiah 24–27*, 32.

43. Wildberger concludes that Isaiah 24–27 developed in various stages between 500–300 BCE. Wildberger, *Isaiah 13–27*, 467. Sweeny locates Isaiah 27 in the seventh century BCE, and the rest in the sixth century BCE. Sweeny, *Isaiah 13–39*, 55–57. Vermeylen proposes three layers of growth assigning them dates between the fifth and third centuries BCE. "La Composition Littéraire," 5–38; cf. idem, *Du Prophete Isaie*, 2–3, 249–381 cited by Hibbard, *Intertextuality in Isaiah 24–27*, 32.

44. For instance, Kaiser, *Isaiah 13–39*, 216–217.

has often meant that the dates assigned by scholars are not entirely based on objective reasoning or evidence but rather, broadly speaking, driven by underlying biases or interests. This is more reflective of the elusiveness of the task of dating the material than of the inability or lack of objectivity of scholars. Nonetheless there is currently no agreement on either its date of composition(s) or the context of its final form.

The question relating to the dating of Isaiah 24–27 pertinent to this study is whether it affects interpretation. There is a broad pattern evident between the date one assigns to the text and the interpretation of the concept of resurrection in Isaiah 26:19. Those who prefer the earlier date, around the sixth or fifth century BCE, tend to interpret resurrection in Isaiah 24:19 metaphorically as a reference to the national restoration of Israel, whereas the literal interpretation of resurrection as the resurrection of the dead is more common among those who date the textual unit to the fifth century BCE or later. This split however is not absolute. For instance Oswalt, who maintains Isaianic authorship of the unit, interprets resurrection literally.[45] Roberts dates the unit to the late seventh to early sixth century BCE and argues that the concept of resurrection in Isaiah 26:19 is metaphorical. However, he accepts the possibility that the author used the concept of resurrection in verse 19 in a way that "transcend(s) this limited sense of resurrection" to indicate the overcoming of death for all people.[46] Blenkinsopp dates it to the sixth century BCE, shortly after 539 BCE, but states that although resurrection may have been intended metaphorically, it refers to literal resurrection in its final form.[47] Alternatively, Clements dates it to the fifth century Persian period and Wildberger dates it between 500–400 BCE yet both read resurrection as a metaphor.[48] As such, interpretation of the idea of resurrection in Isaiah 26:19 is not strictly divided on dating lines.

Hence, since the dating of Isaiah 24–27 remains an ongoing quest, and because the date of the unit does not conclusively determine the interpretation

---

45. Oswalt, *Book of Isaiah*, 23–28, 441–442, 485–486.

46. Roberts, *First Isaiah*, 333.

47. According to Joseph Blenkinsopp, the concept of resurrection in Isaiah 26:19 is used metaphorically, however, the fact that נְבֵלָתִי ("my corpse" v. 19) is used instead of *rephaim* ("shades") to him indicates that in the text's final form the author wanted to express with greater clarity the idea of a belief in individual, physical resurrection. Blenkinsopp, *Isaiah 1–39*, 348, 370–371.

48. Clements, *Isaiah 1–39*, 19, 199; Wildberger, *Isaiah 13–27*, 445–447, 567–568.

of the concept of resurrection one way or the other, instead of trying to interpret the text against any specific date or historical context this study will look at the text from the perspective of its general temporal orientation. Although there is at least one scholar in whose view the perspective of Isaiah 24–27 is that of the past,[49] it is more commonly held that the orientation of the text is futuristic.[50] Whether this future perspective includes a historical event that inaugurates the eschatological era,[51] or is it one that leaves history completely out of its purview[52] is debated. For instance, according to Johnson the future in the purview of the text is the imminent destruction of Jerusalem, followed by the later destruction of Babylon, and the national restoration for Israel leading to the eschatological era.[53] On the contrary, Wildberger argues that the future time indicated is one of "universal, eschatological-apocalyptic turn of events." He argues that even if specific historical referents were intended during its composition, in its present literary context, it is to be understood eschatologically since the coming judgment of Yahweh specifies no nations or people. Hence the orientation of Isaiah 24–27 is beyond history.[54] Considering that a clear historical referent is impossible to detect in Isaiah 24–27, taking the temporal perspective as eschatological without locating it to any particular historical city or event would be a reasonable reading, and is adopted in this study.

3.4. Structure of Isaiah 26

The structural unity of Isaiah 26 has also been the subject of scrutiny.[55] Nevertheless from the canonical point of view, Isaiah 26 exhibits a reasonable

---

49. Previously, Duhm, who divided the unit into songs and eschatological oracles, considered the perspective of the songs as referring to events of the past, whereas Rudolph maintained the oracles were predictive and hence future oriented; cited in Johnson, *From Chaos*, 15.

50. Kaiser, *Isaiah 13–39*, 177; Wildberger, *Isaiah 13–27*, 446–447; Johnson, *From Chaos*, 15; Doyle, *Apocalypse of Isaiah*, 27–28.

51. Cf. Johnson, *From Chaos*; Doyle, *Apocalypse of Isaiah*, 28.

52. Kaiser and Wildberger espouse this view. Cf. Kaiser, *Isaiah 13–39*, 177; Wildberger, *Isaiah 13–27*, 446–447.

53. Cf. Johnson, *From Chaos*.

54. Wildberger, *Isaiah 13–27*, 446.

55. For a brief overview of the issue see Hibbard, *Intertextuality in Isaiah 24–27*, 120.

unity in its present form and can be broadly divided into two segments – vv. 1–6 and vv. 7–21.⁵⁶ The first section (vv. 1–6) is a song,⁵⁷ a song to be sung בַּיּוֹם הַהוּא ("in that day,"⁵⁸ 26:1). It celebrates the singers' strong city,⁵⁹ with exhortations to trust in Yahweh, their צוּר עוֹלָמִים ("eternal rock," v. 4), who ensures *shalom* for those who trust in him (v. 3). Alongside the celebration of the strong city is praise of Yahweh for bringing low the once lofty city (vv. 5–6).⁶⁰ However, this victory lies somewhere in the future.

The celebratory mood soon dissolves into a lament (vv. 7–21)⁶¹ as their current dismal state comes to the fore. The community prays to Yahweh pleading for the destruction of the evildoers and deliverance for the righteous. They acknowledge their dependence on Yahweh (v. 12) despite having been dominated by "other lords" (v. 13). Having been chastised by Yahweh (v. 16) they declare, employing the image of fertility, or the lack thereof in this instance, the ineffectiveness of their own efforts to overturn their situation

---

56. Some degree of agreement exists regarding this broad division of Isaiah 26. Scholars like Johnson, Blenkinsopp and Doyle have offered reasons for dividing Isaiah 26 into two sections. Cf. Johnson, *From Chaos*, 67–68; Blenkinsopp, *Isaiah 1-39*, 362–365; Doyle, *Apocalypse of Isaiah*, 282–283. However, there is disagreement regarding the compositional and redactional unity between the two sections; for instance, Hibbard views the two sections of Isaiah 26 as disparate compositions, even in their redacted form, while Polaski, even though he also divides Isaiah 26 in to two between vv. 6 and 7, argues for the thematic unity of Isaiah 26. Hibbard, *Intertextuality in Isaiah*, 123–124 and Polaski, *Authorizing an End*, 207, 216.

57. Variously designated as a hymn, Wildberger, *Isaiah 13-27*, 455; a thanksgiving song, Blenkinsopp, *Isaiah 1-39*, 360; a song of trust, Johnson, *From Chaos*, 68; an eschatological and processional song of thanksgiving, Cook, "Deliverance as Fertility," 166.

58. Hibbard states that within the Isaiah 24-27 complex the formula "in that day" indicates a day, sometime in the future, when Yahweh will execute his judgment and deliverance. Hibbard, *Intertextuality in Isaiah*, 125.

59. Although the city is unnamed, some scholars, like Blenkinsopp and Hibbard, think that it is a reference to Jerusalem. Marvin Sweeny, "Textual Citations," 48; Blenkinsopp, *Isaiah 1-39*, 365; Hibbard, *Intertextuality in Isaiah*, 125–165.

60. Based on linguistic parallels, it has been surmised that the exalted city (Isa 26:5) could be a reference to Moab as described in Isa. 25:11b–12 or the city described in Isa. 2:6–21. It must be mentioned however that the direction of influence remains difficult to determine. See Kaiser, *Isaiah 13-39*, 204; Sweeny, "Textual Citations," 47–48; Hibbard, *Intertextuality in Isaiah*, 131–134.

61. The second section is often further subdivided. Scholars generally agree that the second section is a lament or a complaint of some kind. However, there is a variety of ways in which the second section is subdivided. Cook divides vv. 7–21 into vv. 7–10 and 11–19 and 20–21. Cook, "Deliverance as Fertility," 166. While other subdivisions often include 27:1 – Qswalt's division is made up of 26:7–15, 26:16–19, 26:20–27:1, Oswalt, *Isaiah 1-39*, 469–470; Sweeny as well as Hibbard divide the section as follows: 26:7–10; 26:11–19; 26:20–27:1. See, Sweeny, *Isaiah 1-39*, 337–338 and Hibbard, *Intertextuality in Isaiah*, 123–124. Gary Smith's divides the second section into two parts: 26:7–18 and 26:19–27:1, Smith, *Isaiah 1-39*, 441.

(vv. 17–18). It is in response to the community's supplication that deliverance is promised in terms of resurrection (v. 19), the meaning of which will be explored shortly. This verse is followed by instructions for Yahweh's people in view of his coming judgment on earth (vv. 20–21).

3.5. Text: Isaiah 26:19

יִחְיוּ מֵתֶיךָ נְבֵלָתִי יְקוּמוּן הָקִיצוּ וְרַנְּנוּ שֹׁכְנֵי עָפָר כִּי טַל אוֹרֹת טַלֶּךָ ¹⁹
וָאָרֶץ רְפָאִים תַּפִּיל׃

The interpretive question regarding Isaiah 26:19 germane to this study is whether rising of the dead ones here refers to the resurrection of the dead,[62] or does it metaphorically refer to a national restoration.[63] Both interpretations have been supported by a good number of scholars. However, two issues need to be addressed before that – the identity of the speaker and the grammatical problems that impede precise translation.

3.5.1. Grammatical Problem

The translation of Isaiah 26:19 suffers from grammatical problems. For this analysis verse 19 is further divided into smaller units. The change of possessive pronouns and their number in Isaiah 26:19a–b is problematic and adds to the difficulty of interpretation. Otto Kaiser calls it an "irritation."[64]

19a	יִחְיוּ מֵתֶיךָ		Your dead ones will live
19b	נְבֵלָתִי יְקוּמוּן		My corpse will rise
19c	הָקִיצוּ וְרַנְּנוּ		Awake and shout for joy
19d	שֹׁכְנֵי עָפָר		dwellers of the dust
19e	כִּי טַל אוֹרֹת טַלֶּךָ		for your dew is a dew of lights
19f	וָאָרֶץ רְפָאִים תַּפִּיל׃		but the earth will cast down the *rephaim*

---

62. Martin-Achard, *From Death to Life*, 130–131; Kaiser, *Isaiah 13–39*, 215–217; Gray, *Critical and Exegetical Commentary*, 444–446; Sawyer, *Isaiah*, 204; Brueggemann, *Isaiah 1–39*, 208; Nickelsberg, *Resurrection, Immortality*, 31–32; Cook, "Deliverance as Fertility," 175.

63. Clements, *Isaiah 1–39*, 16; Collins, *Daniel*, 395; Wildberger, *Isaiah 13–27*, 567–60; Schmitz, "Grammar of Resurrection," 148; Day, *Yahweh and the Gods*, 124; Finney, *Resurrection*, 29–32.

64. Kaiser, *Isaiah 13–39*, 215.

The word נְבֵלָתִי ("my corpse" 19b) in the Masoretic Text (MT) has a difficult reading. Translators commonly accept the MT reading as the *lectio difficilior*, however, translations into English usually translate the noun as plural and the suffix as third person plural – "their corpses" – following the reading in the Syriac and the Targums. For instance, the RSV, the ESV, and the NIV follow this reading. The Vulgate translates it as *interfecti mei resurgent* (lit. "my dead shall rise again") and thus maintains the consonantal form of the word in the MT, but interprets the noun as a collective.[65] Further, in the LXX (καὶ ἐγερθήσονται οἱ ἐν τοῖς μνημείοις "and those who are in the tombs shall be raised") and the 1QIsa[a] (Qumran Isaiah[a] Scroll) the injunction in v. 19b is changed so that it reads in the future tense expressing a belief in the future resurrection of the dead.[66] However the various readings are reflective, as Hays states, not so much of actual textual variant as they are of the scribes' and translators' attempts to grapple with the difficult reading presented by the text.[67]

This study retains the MT reading נְבֵלָתִי ("my corpse") with the first person singular suffix, "my," denoting Yahweh and the noun "corpse" understood collectively to refer to the righteous dead.[68] Reading נְבֵלָה as a collective noun does not require an emendation of the text. Further, the lack of noun-verb number concord in נְבֵלָתִי יְקוּמוּן, where the governing verb is a third person plural is not uncharacteristic for Hebrew collective nouns.[69] Further, in Psalm 79, which is also a lament, נְבֵלָה (in v.2) is in the singular form but functions as a collective, referring to the dead faithful servants of Yahweh – נִבְלַת עֲבָדֶיךָ (lit. "body of your servants"). Polaski recognizes the possibility of this close association between the righteous dead and Yahweh within the text of Isaiah 26, although he admits that it is still odd. He argues that the righteous community is identified with Yahweh; for instance, in Isaiah 26 the word צַדִּיק describes Yahweh (in Isaiah 24:16) as well as the community and what they

---

65. Schmitz, "Grammar of Resurrection," 146.
66. Blenkinsopp, *Isaiah 1-39*, 370; Schmitz, 146.
67. Hays, *Covenant with Death*, 323.
68. Kaiser also takes the corpses as a collective noun. Cf. Kaiser, *Isaiah 13-39*, 215. However, see Wieringen who says that נְבֵלָה "has no collective meaning in Tanakh." Wieringen, "'I' and 'We,'" 246.
69. See Young, "Collectives: Biblical Hebrew," 477-478. Young notes that scholars agree there is no "convincing grammatical explanation" for an author's choice of singular or plural in every case.

learn from Yahweh (26:7). As such, Yahweh claiming the dead ones as "my corpse" is plausible.[70]

3.5.2. Identity of the Speaker in Isaiah 26:19

One of the ambiguities that readers of this text must wrestle with is the difficulty in identifying the speaker of Isaiah 26:19.[71] There are three possible speakers in this section – the community and the prophet, both or either of whom could be speaking the lament, and Yahweh who responds to the lament. Hence, the possible speakers are: i) the community ii) Yahweh, or iii) the prophet, albeit the prophet's identity is "fluid" in that he could represent the community to Yahweh[72] as well as be God's mouthpiece to the community.[73]

The first possibility is that the preceding dialogue continues and there is no change in the communication situation in v. 19 – the community, or the prophet speaking for them, continues to address Yahweh. Read from this perspective, v. 19 becomes part of the group's plea to Yahweh to intervene. Beuken takes this interpretation, reading the first person singular in v.19b, "my corpse," as indicating the prophet.[74] Grammatically, יִחְיוּ ("they will live" v. 19a) and יְקוּמוּן ("they will rise" v. 19b) are third person imperfect verb forms, and can function as jussives.[75] Hence it is possible to read v. 19a–b as a petition within the lament: "Let your dead ones live; let my body rise!"[76] Further, regarding the form of the two verbs in v. 19c – הָקִיצוּ ("Awake") and וְרַנְּנוּ ("shout for joy") – the MT (as also the Vulgate) reads them as imperatives. This is a more difficult reading than the one preserved in the 1QIsaᵃ, which translates it as an imperfect, יָקִיצוּ ("they will rise up") and וִירַנְּנוּ ("they will shout for joy") respectively, thus making v. 19a–c a chain of four imperfects.

---

70. Polaski, *Authorizing an End*, 264–266.

71. For instance, van der Woude, "Resurrection or Transformation," 154; Hibbard, *Intertextuality in Isaiah*, 146.

72. So Willem Beuken, *Jesaja 13–27*, 380–385, cited in van der Woude, "Resurrection or Transformation," 155.

73. See Wieringen for the "I"-figure as the speaker, addressing the people on behalf of the community. Wieringen, "'I' and 'We,'" 247.

74. Beuken, *Jesaja 13–27*, 380–385, cited by van der Woude, *Resurrection or Transformation*, 155.

75. This possibility is briefly mentioned by André LaCocque in LaCocque and Ricoeur, *Thinking Biblically*, 158.

76. Although in this case the plural form of the verb יְקוּמוּן ("they will rise) in v. 19b gets translated as a singular "... my body rise."

LXX and a few other mss. seem to follow the reading similar to the one in 1QIsaᵃ translating the address to the dead in the future tense.[77] Accordingly, the lament is read as concerning the present affliction of the community, and their petition is for deliverance from their current state, rather than a literal resurrection in the indeterminate future time.[78]

Alternatively, if the speaker is Yahweh, as most scholars now think[79] it becomes *Heilsorakel*,[80] a salvation oracle. In the lament the change in the mood in v. 19 is quite drastic, so much so that some have considered v. 19 a later interpolation.[81] However, this shift in mood can be explained instead by positing a change in speaker – Yahweh answers their petition in v. 19a–d. Formally speaking, this is not unprecedented in laments. Johnson cites Westermann who explains that although it is more common for a lament to close with a vow of praise, there are instances, especially in the prophets, where instead of ending with a vow, the lament closes with Yahweh's positive response, for example, Jeremiah 11:20–23 and 15:19–21. Yahweh responding to the community's lament fits the pattern found in prophetic literature.[82] The one difficulty with this reading is that v. 19e כִּי טַל אוֹרֹת טַלֶּךָ ("for your dew is a dew of lights") reverts to referring to Yahweh in the second person. This requires a shift in speaker once more so that the community or the prophet addresses Yahweh between 19a–d and vv. 20–21.

This difficulty is removed if the speaker is identified as the prophet speaking on behalf of Yahweh.[83] It is still a *Heilsorakel* and retains all the arguments above regarding Yahweh being the speaker, except now Yahweh speaks

---

77. Other mss. like Peshitta, Aquila, Symmachus, and Theodotion. Cf. Martin-Achard, *From Death to Life*, 130; Day, "טַל אוֹרֹת in Isaiah 26:19," 265; Hasel, "Resurrection," 271, n. 37; Schmitz, "Grammar of Resurrection," 148; van der Kooij, "Isaiah 24–27," 15; Bailey, "Intertextual Relationship," 307.

78. For instance, Sweeny, *Isaiah 1–39*, 340–341. Martin-Achard also reads v. 19 as a prayer but one that is uttered by the prophet. He, however, views v. 19 expresses the prophet's hope and prayer for physical resurrection. cf. Martin-Achard, *From Death to Life*, 130–131.

79. See Kaiser, *Isaiah 13–39*, 215–216; Johnson, *From Chaos*, 80; Smith, *Isaiah 1–39*, 452; Wieringen, "'I' and 'We,'" 246–247; Roberts, *First Isaiah*, 332–333; van der Woude, "Resurrection or Transformation," 158–159.

80. Johnson, *From Chaos*, 79–80.

81. For instance, Kaiser, *Isaiah 13–39*, 216–217.

82. Johnson, *From Chaos*, 80. So also, Begrich, "Das Preissterliche Heilsorakel," 81–92, cited in LaCocque and Ricoeur, *Thinking Biblically*, 158; Smith, *Isaiah 1–39*, 452.

83. Wieringen proposes that in v. 19 the prophet, the I-figure, is addressing the people, the "we" group, on God's behalf. See Wieringen, "'I' and 'We,'" 246–247.

the salvation oracle through his prophet, and in v. 19e כִּי טַל אוֹרֹת טַלֶּךָ ("for your dew is a dew of lights"), the prophet addresses Yahweh. This study will continue to read, as stated earlier, נְבֵלָתִי (my corpse") with the first-person singular suffix, "my," as denoting Yahweh on whose behalf the prophet delivers the salvation oracle, and the noun "corpse" as collectively referring to the righteous dead.

3.6. Resurrection: Metaphorical or Literal

Among those who hold that verse 19 is a *Heilsorakel* are some who understand resurrection as referring metaphorically to national restoration, and others who interpret it literally as indicating the resurrection of the dead. Read metaphorically, resurrection in the oracle is a symbol for Israel's national resuscitation, and not an actual resurrection of the dead.[84] The loss of land and political autonomy spells death for the Judeans. Hence, God's promise to reverse Israel's situation is expressed in terms of bringing the dead back to life.

In the metaphorical reading the lament and the response are seen as constituting an organic whole – the community prays for relief from their present anguish caused by the exile, and God responds with a promise that he will remedy that precise situation by restoring their nation. For instance, Wildberger states that if the community is lamenting the threat to the very existence of Israel in vv. 7–18, then the response "must be speaking" about eliminating this threat.[85] Hibbard likewise says that literal interpretation places Yahweh's solution somewhere in the future with no intervention in their present political crisis; as such it would not be something the community wanted.[86] There are two objections to this point. First, what the community wanted cannot be the criterion for the interpretation of Yahweh's response. God is not bound to answer in a certain way because of the supplicant's expectation; that the answer should logically and exactly fit the request is not a given. Hence, while the naturalness of lament-response is appealing, it cannot be a determining factor in interpretation. Second, Cook rightly

---

84. Collins, *Daniel*, Hermeneia, 395; Johnson, *From Chaos*, 80–81 Hibbard, *Intertextuality in Isaiah*, 147–149.

85. Wildberger, *Isaiah 13–27*, 567.

86. So Hibbard, *Intertextuality in Isaiah*, 147–148.

observes that in the book of Isaiah, even in Second Isaiah which is considered pre-apocalyptic, the purview of salvation is not just political or historical. It presents a vision of new life that is in the far future, supernatural and abundant. This picture of the prolific future of Zion (40:1–5; 41:18; 43:20; 44:1–5; 51:3) is a reversal of the fate of Zion mourning her children.[87] That the scope is beyond nationalism is also sensed in Isaiah 26:21 which, as Polaksi says, "stands as a universal crescendo."[88] It speaks of Yahweh leaving his dwelling and coming out to punish not just the other lords or rulers, but the יֹשֵׁב־הָאָרֶץ ("the inhabitants of the earth"). Hence, a nationalistic interpretation is likely to be a narrowing of the perspective of the text.

Most scholars[89] who interpret resurrection metaphorically date the Isaiah Apocalypse around the time of the Babylonian exile, around the sixth to fifth century BCE. This date makes the metaphorical function of resurrection attractive by anchoring the textual unit to a known historical crisis. The HB uses death as a metaphor for exile (Gen 3[90]; Isaiah 5:13, 14; Ezek 37), consequently resurrection is considered a metaphor for national restoration, and dating the composition of the unit close to the exile makes this interpretation seem natural. One of the weaknesses of the view that resurrection refers to national restoration is that it requires a firm situation of the text in the historical context of the Babylonian exile. The metaphorical interpretation uses a provisional dating of the text close to the time of exile as *a priori* to argue that resurrection is meant metaphorically in response to the exilic setting. As stated earlier, the text is referentially ambiguous as far as historical events are concerned.

The date of this text remains a contentious subject and there is no indisputable reason yet to privilege the sixth or fifth centuries BCE date over other dates. As the current state of research on this issue stands, the sixth

---

87. Cook, "Deliverance as Fertility," 176, 178.
88. Polaski, *Authorizing an End*, 231.
89. Wildberger, *Isaiah 13–27*, 445–447, 567–568; Sweeny, *Isaiah 1–39*, 55, 57, 320, 340–341; Johnson, *From Chaos*, 16–17, 80–81; Polaski, *Authorizing an End*, 58, 215; Hibbard, *Intertextuality in Isaiah 24–27*, 36, 145–148; Hays, "Date and Message," 22–23.
90. Mitchell Chase observes that death as denoting exile goes back to Genesis 3. In Genesis God pronounces the penalty for eating the fruit from the forbidden tree as death, but upon eating from it Adam and Eve are not met with immediate physical death, rather they are exiled from Eden. He states that the author of Genesis viewed death dynamically and that the exile "was a kind of death." Chase, "'From Dust,'" 21–22.

or fifth centuries BCE date is one possibility among others. Moreover, the metaphorical interpretation also works well for a date earlier than the sixth or fifth centuries BCE. For instance, Gary Smith dates Isaiah 24–27 to the end of the eighth century BCE Sennacherib's attack on Judah, in King Hezekiah's time c. 703–701 BCE. He interprets resurrection metaphorically but, drawing from Psalms (16:10–11; 18:5–6; 49:14–15), reads it as a reference to God's potentiality to restore to life one destined for death, as in the case of King Hezekiah.[91] Further, on the other end of the spectrum of those who favour the Babylonian exile setting for the text are those like Christopher Seitz who flatly deny any semblance of the exilic setting to the overthrow of the city in Isaiah 24–27.[92] This demonstrates that the dating of this text cannot be used as *a priori* to determine the interpretation.

Even without the exilic setting, a metaphorical interpretation is impeded by a cluster of death-life phrases in v. 19. First, the root word נְבֵלָה ("corpse" or "carcass;" נְבֵלָתִי in v. 19b) occurs around 41 times in the HB. Except for Jeremiah 16:18 where it refers to the "carcass" of idols,[93] and excluding the present case of Isaiah 26:19 which is under discussion here, in every other instance נְבֵלָה is used literally. Out of the 41 times, 20 times it refers to animal carcasses[94] and 19 times (excluding Isaiah 26:19) to human bodies. When the referent is a human corpse, it refers to criminals who are buried (Deut 21:23) but often in places that indicate that their death was a punishment (Josh 8:29; 1 Kgs 13:22–30; Jer 26:23). Other occurrences refer to unburied dead bodies (Deut 28:26; 2 Kgs 9:37; Ps 79:2; Isa 5:25; Jer 7:33; 9:21; 16:4; 19:7; 34:20; 36:30). Hence, if the resurrection in v. 19 is indeed metaphorical, this would be the only instance in the HB where נְבֵלָה is used metaphorically to refer to a nation in exile. Often Ezekiel 37 is cited as similar to Isaiah 26:19 to say that both texts use metaphorical language.[95] However, Isaiah 26:19

---

91. Smith, *Isaiah 1–39*, 454–455.

92. Christopher Seitz, *Isaiah 1–39*.

93. The reference to idols as corpses was probably to convey the point that worshipping idols made the people ritually unclean just as touching corpses did. Alexander, "נְבֵלָה," in *NIDOTTE*, vol. 3, 15.

94. The other twenty occurrences refer to the dead body of an animal, mainly in the context of ritual cleanness, sixteen occurrences of which are in Leviticus. "H5038 נבלה," Strong's Hebrew Lexicon Number. So also Polaski, *Authorizing an End*, 240, n. 98.

95. For instance, Johnson says, "The message of 26.19 is the same as that of Ezekiel 37," Johnson, *From Chaos*, 80; also Collins, *Daniel*, Hermeneia, 395.

lacks the clarity of Ezekiel 37 whose metaphorical interpretation is clearly provided in the text itself. Polaski argues that the dead bodies are exposed corpses and hence similar to Ezekiel 37.[96] However, apart from the fact that the word נְבֵלָה (dead body) is not used in Ezekiel 37, what lie exposed is not נְבֵלָה (dead body), but הָעֲצָמוֹת הַיְבֵשׁוֹת (dry bones); moreover, once covered with sinews, flesh and skin they are soon animated and not left exposed. Hence a parallel with Ezekiel 37 is not so easily drawn.

Secondly, the phrase שֹׁכְנֵי עָפָר ("dwellers of the dust" v. 19d) favours a literal reading for resurrection. Genesis 3:19 refers to dying as returning to עָפָר ("dust") – "By the sweat of your face you shall eat bread, till you return to the ground, for out of it you were taken; for you are dust, and to dust you shall return." This passage is significant as it is the first reference to physical death in the HB. Genesis 3:19 in turn alludes to God's creation of humans using עָפָר מִן־הָאֲדָמָה "dust from the ground" (Gen 2:7). As such, it sets the paradigm for the HB's use of the language of dust to indicate physical death. Further, just as the HB identifies the dead with dust, it also describes the dying ones as those who "go down to the dust" (Ps 22:29) or "lie down in the dust" (Job 7:21; 21:26).

Thirdly, the dead are to הָקִיצוּ וְרַנְּנוּ ("awake and shout for joy," 19c). This command implies that the dwellers of the dust were previously unable to do so; they were asleep and unable to shout for joy. The HB describes the physically dead as sleeping (2 Kgs 4:31; Jer 51:39, 57; Job 3:13, 14:12), and Sheol is often described as a place of silence[97] whose inhabitants cannot sing (Ps 6:6 [Eng 6:5]; 30:10 [Eng 30:9] 94:17). Hence to "awake and shout for joy" is to do precisely the things that the physically dead cannot naturally do. However, there are no instances of sleeping and waking being used as a metaphor for the exile and national reconstitution.

Finally, v. 19f mentions the word רְפָאִים ("dead spirits, shades"). רְפָאִים in the HB is an obscure term. It is generally considered to denote one of the two entities – the mythological giants in antiquity appearing mainly in the Pentateuchal and Deuteronomistic History (Gen 14:5; 15:20; Deut 3:11; Josh 13:12), or the weakened dead denizens of Sheol who live a shadowy existence

---

96. Polaski, *Authorizing an End*, 240–241.

97. L. Wächter, "שְׁאוֹל šĕ'ōl," in *TDOT*, vol. 14, 246; Key, "Concept of Death," 241; Schmidt, "Memory as Immortality, 88; Hays, *Covenant with Death*, 328.

in the later prophets and the writings (Job 26:5; Ps 88:10, Isa. 14:9).[98] In both the cases, רְפָאִים does not indicate normal, living persons. In the context of chapter 26, רְפָאִים occurs twice, in v. 14 and v. 19. Hibbard, following Kaiser,[99] opines that the רְפָאִים in v. 14 refers to the community and its members who were oppressed by the "other lords" (Isaiah 26:13). Since he interprets "other lords" politically as foreign rulers, he also interprets רְפָאִים in v. 14 as well as in v. 19 as referring to the community, so designated, according to him, because they are suffering oppression.[100] However, the suggestion that רְפָאִים refers to living members of Israel's community is unattested in the HB. The term רְפָאִים was often considered a designation for the royal divinized dead,[101] which in the biblical traditions was probably democratized overtime to include dead common people. For instance, Stephen Cook thinks that רְפָאִים in v.19 is democratized; even so he also limits its application to the living dead.[102] So whether in its narrower or broader sense, רְפָאִים referred to the dead not the living. This collection of terms in v. 19 makes it difficult to discount the plausibility of a literal interpretation of resurrection in this passage.

In sum, the metaphorical interpretation suffers from a heavy dependence on the exilic setting that is still unsettled. The metaphorical reading also has a narrower nationalistic perspective compared to the more universalistic perspective of the book of Isaiah. Further, the use of several life-death phrases makes better sense when read literally. Thus, one can agree with Levenson who concludes that "minimally" resurrection in Isaiah 26: 19 is "less metaphorical" than in Ezekiel 37 and "maximally" it is closer to Daniel 12:1–3

---

98. Cf. Schmidt, "Memory as Immortality," 91 and Hays, *Covenant with Death*, 167.

99. Kaiser, *Isaiah 13–39*, 212.

100. See Hibbard, *Intertextuality in Isaiah*, 143-144, 148. Further, the appearance of *rephaim* in v. 19f is not well explained in some of the metaphorical readings of Isaiah 26:19. For instance, Wildberger and Johnson do not explain it; both Sweeny and Hays dwell very briefly on the significance of *rephaim* in this verse. Wildberger, *Isaiah 13–27*, 570; Johnson, *From Chaos*, 77, 80–81; Sweeny, *Isaiah 1–39*, 322; Hays, *Covenant with Death*, 331–332.

101. Although the precise identity of the Ugaritic *Rāpi'ūma* is contested, one of the suggestions is that they were divinized royals; cf. McAffee, "Rephaim, Whisperers," 78. In the biblical tradition, Isaiah 14:9 seem to reflect remnants of such an understanding that the רְפָאִים in Sheol were leaders of the earth. However, exclusion of the commoners cannot be deduced solely from silence of this one text on that matter.

102. Cook, "Deliverance as Fertility," 170–172; although it is difficult to find warrant for his reading of the *rephaim* as also a reference to Israel's founding fathers like Abraham, Jacob, and kings like Josiah. Schmidt similarly speaks of the democratization of רְפָאִים in the HB; Schmidt, "Memory as Immortality," 91.

indicating the resurrection of the dead.[103] The obscurity of the text of Isaiah 26:19 precludes a definite conclusion, nonetheless, a literal interpretation of the resurrection in v. 19 is still worthy of consideration.

If one considers the possibility that the resurrection refers to a literal resurrection of the dead, the question of interest to this study is what its implication is for the study of post-mortem divine retribution. Admittedly, the text is not primarily interested in post-mortem divine retribution and as such the results are not copious. The text is studied nonetheless to see if it can afford a glimpse in that direction even if only incidentally.

3.7. Basis and Aspect of Post-mortem Divine Retribution in Isaiah 26:19

In Isaiah 26:19 reward and punishment are not destinies one faces after resurrection. Instead, resurrection itself is the reward. For the righteous, the reward is no longer limited to a good, long life on earth before death; rather it now extends to the prospect of life even after death. The resurrection life that God will effect in the dead is one that rescues them from a shadowy existence in Sheol and makes them absolutely alive – they shout for joy! Several scholars posit that the idea of resurrection and divine retribution presented in Daniel 12:1–3 possibly alludes to Isaiah 26:19,[104] the question of the primacy of the texts being another matter. Consequently, it can be said that Yahweh's people are not left in the underworld to turn forever into dust but are raised to life again. However, apart from that there is little else in the text regarding what exactly constitutes a resurrection life. It is also not immediately clear if it speaks only of rewards or if there is any punishment discernible in this verse. Further, the basis of retribution needs to be examined. As such, the place to start is to identify who are the parties in the purview of this divine retribution.

Isaiah 26 speaks of two broad groups of people – the righteous and the wicked. However, the identities of interest to this study are not of the righteous and the wicked *per se*, but of those who rise from the dead and those who do

---

103. Levenson, *Resurrection and the Restoration*, 200.

104. Lester, *Daniel Evokes Isaiah*; Bailey, "Intertextual Relationship," 305–308; Nickelsburg, *Resurrection, Immortality*, 30–36; Lindenberger, "Daniel 12:1–4," 183–184; Goldingay, *Daniel*, 285.

not, and these two groups may or may not be identical with the righteous and the wicked. This contrast, between those who will rise and those who will not, is seen more clearly when vv. 14 and 19 of Isaiah 26 are studied together. The similarity in the languages of Isaiah 16:14 and Isaiah 26:19 is obvious and has been well noted.[105]

Isaiah 26:14	Isaiah 26:19
14a מֵתִים בַּל־יִחְיוּ (The dead ones, they will **not live**)	19a יִחְיוּ מֵתֶיךָ (Your dead ones will **live**)
14b רְפָאִים בַּל־יָקֻמוּ (the *rephaim*, they will not rise)	19b נְבֵלָתִי יְקוּמוּן (My corpse, they will **rise**)
	19f וְאֶרֶץ רְפָאִים תַּפִּיל (but the earth will cast down the ***rephaim***)

Both passages speak of some who are the dead and use the Qal participle form of the verb מות for the dead. They also share the same verbs, חיה ("to live") and קום ("to arise"). In v. 19 the dead are to live and arise, in v. 14 too both the verbs used, however, they are negated so that the dead ones remain dead. Further both verses speak of the רְפָאִים ("*rephaim*") although it is not evident if the *rephaim* in v. 14 and v. 19 function as parallels or as contrasts. The analysis of these two verses help unravel the question regarding the identities of the dead who rise and the dead who do not, which in turn can provide some indication of the basis of post-mortem divine retribution.

3.7.1. The Dead Who Rise

The parallelism in v. 19 suggests that מֵתֶיךָ ("your dead") and נְבֵלָתִי ("my corpse") refer to the same entity. If, as accepted earlier, the prophet utters the *Heilsorakel* in v. 19a-d on behalf of Yahweh, the addressee is the community, that is, the second masculine singular "your" in "your dead" denotes the community. Hence "your dead ones" refers to those from among the community of lamenters who have died. Yahweh then proceeds to call them "my corpse," identifying the dead ones as his own. This probably indicates, as Wildberger

---

105. For instance, Martin-Achard, *From Death to Life*, 135; Blenkinsopp, *Isaiah 1–39*, 371; Polaski, *Authorizing an End*, 240; Turner, *History of Hell*, 42; Levenson, *Resurrection*, 199; Krašovec, *Reward, Punishment*, 518.

states, that Yahweh is not undisturbed by the death of his people.[106] In this case, the dead who rise are part of the righteous, lamenting community and belong to Yahweh.

The righteous community represents a group with distinct interests that are in opposition to the wicked. First, verse 9 characterizes the righteous as learners. The righteous are the inhabitants of the world who לָמַד ("learn") righteousness from Yahweh's judgments, while the wicked neither learn nor acknowledge Yahweh even when shown favour and continue to act perversely (v. 10).[107] Secondly, the righteous are also characterized as trusting (בָּטַח "trust") in Yahweh. It may be recalled that v. 3 promises שָׁלוֹם ("shalom" or "well-being") to those who trust in Yahweh. Subsequently, the righteous community is portrayed as waiting for Yahweh (קִוִּינוּךָ "we wait for you" v. 8), which is an act of trust. The verb קוה translated "wait for" is used either to indicate awaiting an event or hoping in God. It is never used in the sense of placing confidence in other human beings.[108] Thus the community is presented as waiting and hoping for Yahweh's intervention, and the promised שָׁלוֹם is established for them (v.12), especially in the case of Yahweh's dead who receive the ultimate שָׁלוֹם in being raised back to life (v. 19).[109] Finally, the righteous are those who accept Yahweh's discipline. The righteous will be safe from Yahweh's wrath when he comes to punish the people of the earth (vv. 20–21). However, they are not altogether immune from Yahweh's punishments. Polaski views acceptance of discipline as a clear criterion for the righteous in Isaiah 26; according to him, the righteous are in fact formed by discipline. In v.16 they describe their distress as מוּסָר ("chastening"), and Polaski argues that it is by accepting discipline that they become righteous.[110] Hence, it may be inferred that the dead ones, and generally the righteous community, were those who learned from Yahweh's judgments, maintained an overall attitude of trust in Yahweh, and accepted Yahweh's discipline.

---

106. Wildberger, *Isaiah 13–27*, 567.

107. Polaski, *Authorizing an End*, 268. Polaski also draws an intertextual relationship between the portrayal of the righteous and the wicked in Isaiah 26 and Deuteronomy 32 (pp. 270–271).

108. Wildberger, *Isaiah 13–27*, 559; Waschke, "קוה," in *TDOT*, vol. 12, 569.

109. Polaski, "Politics of Prayer," 371. Blenkinsopp also says that the *Heilsorakel* is "an assurance of ultimate well-being" (v.19); Blenkinsopp, *Isaiah 1–39*, 368.

110. See Polaski, *Authorizing an End*, 267ff.

However, there is not enough to deduce whether the righteous are identified on moral as well as national lines or if it is purely moral. If righteousness is constructed as both moral and national, only the Israelites can qualify as righteous and there is a distinction within Israel between the righteous and the wicked. Conversely if righteousness is defined only on moral terms without any national or ethnic connotations, righteous individuals from both Israel and other nations would be within its purview. Isaiah's perspective is comparatively more universalistic vis-à-vis other prophetic literature;[111] however it still retains its nationalistic and corporate outlook.[112] The individual identity is still constructed in corporate terms; it is still embedded in the national identity. Hence it is possible that the distinction between national and moral is blurred, and righteousness entails not only religious allegiance to Yahweh but also implies a national identification with Israel.

Based on the above description of the righteous dead, it can be said that divine retribution in Isaiah 26:19 for those who resurrect exhibits the anthropocentric aspect of divine retribution according to which God responds to the deeds of human beings with either blessings or punishments, and is corporate in nature. This derives also from the sense of the "self" exhibited in the text in Isaiah 26, but also generally in Isaiah 24–27. Divine retribution is anthropocentric insofar as identity is defined chiefly in moral terms as righteous,[113] and characterized as malleable, trusting in Yahweh,[114] and willing to accept the yoke of discipline. Indeed, the fact that the community laments to Yahweh demonstrates that despite their sufferings they still trust in Yahweh to act on their behalf.[115] The lament in Isaiah 26:7–18, especially vv. 7–12, has a strong wisdom flavour that promises a good life for those who trust in Yahweh and walk in his ways. Wisdom literature presumes Yahweh's lordship over the destiny of individuals; similarly in the lament in Isaiah 26 such a lordship is presumed but for Israel as a whole.[116] Further,

---

111. For instance, Isaiah 56:3–7 promises inclusion and acceptance to foreigners who pledge themselves to Yahweh.

112. As universal as its perspective may be, the book of Isaiah still envisions a glorious age for Zion where other nations would be in service to Zion, for instance, Isaiah 60:5–14; 66:18–20.

113. So also, Wildberger, *Isaiah 13–27*, 559.

114. Redditt, "Isaiah 26," 195.

115. Redditt, 196.

116. Wildberger, *Isaiah 13–27*, 559; Redditt also thinks that v. 7 "sounds like a proverb"; Redditt, "Isaiah 26," 196.

the community claims innocence and fidelity to Yahweh in the face of other lords who present themselves as claimants of their allegiance (v. 13).[117] Thus, resurrection is Yahweh's response to and intervention on behalf of the community that trusts in him. Moreover, divine retribution is corporate in nature in that the agency lies with the community as a whole. The individual does not emerge in the text. The prophet does speak; however, he is perceived not as distinct from the community but as part of it, and when he speaks he does so on behalf of community. If there was any dissenting voice, any conflict or apostasy among the lamenting community, there is no hint of it in the lament. There is no critique of some in the community apart from the rest; and the community is chastised as a whole, rather than individually (v. 16).[118] Thus the community is taken together and presented as one. Additionally, the corporate nature of retribution shows the underlying influence of the theocentric aspect of divine retribution according to which God's action towards human beings is not dependent on their action but is motivated mainly by his own purposes. This can be traced back to the fact that the framework of the Torah was corporate. As such, that the community as a whole is perceived as either trusting or as failing Yahweh has its roots in the covenant that Yahweh made with Israel. This covenant was based not on Israel's merit but on Yahweh's divine purposes. Therefore, although the retributive aspect exhibited in Isaiah 26:19 is primarily anthropocentric, it is operational within the framework of the theocentric aspect, and expresses itself corporately.

3.7.2. The Dead Who Do Not Rise

The parallelism in v. 14 suggests that מֵתִים ("the dead ones") are the רְפָאִים ("*rephaim*"). However, the identity of the dead ones in v. 14 becomes clearer when v. 13 is taken in conjunction.[119] The antecedent of "the dead ones" can be found in v. 13 – the אֲדֹנִים ("lords") who, besides Yahweh, have ruled the community. The term אֲדֹנִים has been interpreted as foreign rulers who have

---

117. So also Redditt, 197.

118. Similarly, Johnson who rejects Plöger's reading that the text reflects division within the community between those who remain faithful to the covenant of Yahweh and those who fall away, especially in times of testing. Johnson, *From Chaos*, 75, 80.

119. Several scholars analyze verses 13 and 14 together. See McAffee, "Rephaim, Whisperers," 86. Wildberger, *Isaiah 13–27*, 564–565; Sweeney, *Isaiah 1–39*, 340; Blenkinsopp, *Isaiah 1–39*, 370; Polaski, *Authorizing an End*, 238–239; Cook, "Deliverance as Fertility," 173; Wieringen, "'I' and 'We,'" 244.

oppressed Judah and hence the identity of the אֲדֹנִים has been treated as purely political.[120] However, אֲדֹנִים here is likely referring to more than just the despotic foreign human rulers over Israel and there are good reasons to revise that understanding to include a more religious connotation of the term. This interpretation derives from the fact that, first, within the ANE royal ideology the rulers were not just political figures, but considered semi-divine. Hence, a purely political conception of אֲדֹנִים does not capture the whole essence of the identity of the rulers.[121] Second, אֲדֹנִים are contrasted with Yahweh[122] – the community says that other lords זוּלָתֶךָ ("besides you" i.e., Yahweh) have ruled over them. This prepositional phrase, זוּלָה, when used to draw a contrast with Yahweh usually occurs in contexts that affirm that there is no other God besides Yahweh,[123] as in 2 Samuel 7:22, thus placing the אֲדֹנִים in direct juxtaposition with Yahweh. Third, this view is corroborated by the choice of the verb בָּעַל (בְּעָלוּנוּ "they ruled over us") along with אֲדֹנִים in v. 13. The use of the verb בעל in the context of human rulers over Israel is extremely rare, occurring possibly only here and in 1 Chronicles 4:22. Instead, the most common use of בעל is in the context of marriage or in the context of referring to Yahweh as Israel's spouse.[124] Consequently, Hays argues that the אֲדֹנִים ("lords") in Isaiah 26:13 primarily denotes other gods.[125] Hence there is a strong possibility that the אֲדֹנִים are not merely political human rulers but their identity should also take into account both the religious overtones

---

120. For instance, Kaiser, *Isaiah 13-39*, 212; Hibbard, *Intertextuality in Isaiah*, 144. According to Hibbard, Yahweh punishes the foreign lords ("them" in v. 14) for oppressing the *rephaim* who he identifies as the community that cries out to Yahweh. While Edward Young likewise identifies the "lords" in political and human terms as tyrant who ruled Israel, he also views the rulers as synonymous with the *rephaim* and states that they are now shadows which "cannot arise again to trouble the people of God." In Robert's view, the other lords "clearly are political powers such as Egypt and Assyria," although he considers the possibility of a reference to "past idolatry." Roberts, *First Isaiah*, 331; See also Young, *Book of Isaiah*, 219-220; Oswalt, *Book of Isaiah*, 481; Wildberger, *Isaiah 13-27*, 564.

121. This view is also taken by Johnson who rightly critiques the failure of some scholars to take into account the religious nature of kingship in the ANE. He opts for a relatively more comprehensive understanding of אֲדֹנִים ("lords") as including "both the human rulers and their deities." See Johnson, *From Chaos*, 77.

122. McAffee, "Rephaim, Whisperers," 86.

123. Gordon, "Gods Must Die," 52-53.

124. Koopmans, "בעל," in NICOTTE, vol. 1. Also, observed by Gordon as well as Hays. Gordon, "Gods Must Die," 52-53; Hays, *Covenant with Death*, 325-326.

125. So Hays, 325-326.

provided by the ANE royal ideology that invested the kings with divine sanctions and the context of v. 13.

It can further be argued that the identity of the dead lords not only encompasses the political cum religious aspects of kingship, but goes a step further to imply that the lords were the dead divinized royals[126] who were among the *rephaim*, albeit used as a polemic in Isaiah 26:14,[127] which will be explained shortly. This identification of the dead ones as the *rephaim* is brought to the fore through the juxtapositioning of the concept of זכר ("to remember, mention, acknowledge") in vv. 13 and 14. Verse 13 not only sets up a contrast between Yahweh and the lords but also draws a contrast between Yahweh who is remembered (v. 13) and the *rephaim* whose remembrance is abolished (v. 14).

The *rephaim* in the HB is an obscure term and the Ugarit parallel *rpʾum* or *rāpiʾūma* is often cited to aid our understanding of the elusive *rephaim* scattered in the HB. Mark Shipp states that in the Ugaritic texts, although the precise identity of the *rephaim* is difficult to ascertain, they positively included the dead royals of the past.[128] There are two important Ugaritic text relating to the study of *rephaim* – the Ugaritic royal funerary ritual text KTU 1.161/RS 34.126 and the Ugaritic King List KTU 1.112/RS 24.257.[129] The remembrance or invocation of names in Isaiah 26:13–14 recalls the Ugaritic cults of commemoration or geneonymy, one of the components of which was the public recital of names. The Ugaritic King List KTU 1.112/RS 24.257 listed the names of the kings along with their dynastic personal god which were read out during the commemoration. This was done, among other reasons, to perpetuate the memory of the person and deeds of the deceased, and thus avoiding fading into oblivion – the ultimate "death after death."[130] The KTU

---

126. In Isaiah 14:9 too the *rephaim* appear in the context of dead royalty. Cf. Doak, "Last of the Rephaim," 266.

127. McAffee, "Rephaim, Whisperers," 87; Cook thinks that *rephaim* here is democratized and hence applies to all the living dead. However, he also accedes that it does recall the images of dead divinized kings and heroes of antiquity. See Cook, "Deliverance as Fertility," 171, 173.

128. Shipp, *Of Dead Kings*, 149.

129. Scholars refer to either both or one of the texts in their analysis of the *rephaim*. For instance, Shipp, *Of Dead Kings*; Levine and de Taragon, "Dead Kings and Rephaim," 653ff; Blenkinsopp, *Isaiah 1–39*, 287–288; Schmidt, "Afterlife Beliefs," 236–239; Wyatt, "Concept and Purpose," 161–184; McAffee, "Rephaim, Whisperers," 79; Doak, *Last of the Rephaim*, 246.

130. See, Schmidt, "Afterlife Beliefs," 237–238; and Cook, "Deliverance as Fertility," 173–174.

1.161 (= RS 34.126) is similar insofar as it commemorates the death of the newly deceased king. It calls upon the *rāpi'ūma* to accompany and welcome the newly dead king to the underworld[131] as well as to seek favours for those alive.[132] Matthew McAffee examines Isaiah 26:14 in light of the Ugarit ritual of summoning the *rāpi'ūma* recorded in the royal funerary ritual text KTU 1.161 (= RS 34.126) which seem to reflect the belief that upon death, kings were deified and they exerted power in the world of the living, intervening on behalf of the descendants and granting them favours.[133] It is possible that some among the Jews held similar beliefs.[134] In the HB the existence of the "powerful dead" and their ability to foretell is not denied, only that the Yahweh's people are forbidden to take recourse to them, since foretelling was Yahweh's prerogative.[135] While the official Yahwistic cult forbade consulting the dead, there are evidences, both textual[136] and material,[137] that the practice never died out completely. Given that possibility, remembering someone's name, as Rüdiger Liwak says, was not merely a mental exercise but a "dynamic encounter" without which the dead die a second death and the descendants lose access to the ancestor's ability to bless and intervene on their behalf.[138] As such McAffee is probably right in concluding that the reference in Isaiah 26:14 to *rephaim* who will not rise could be read as a polemic against similar

---

131. A similar picture is presented in Isaiah 14:9, except the idea is used polemically – Sheol is astir and the royal *rephaim* rise, but they do not welcome the newly dead king as expected, rather they taunt him. See Hays, *Covenant with Death*, 209–210; Wyatt, "Concept and Purpose," 171–172.

132. McAffee, "Rephaim, Whisperers," 81–82; Levine and Tarragon, "Dead Kings and Rephaim," 654; Heider, *Cult of the Molek*, 125. For an alternate opinion, cf. Schmidt who says that the *rephaim* did not exhibit any "benefic powers" for the living. Schmidt, *Israel's Beneficent Dead*, 91; also "Memory as Immortality," 238.

133. McAffee, "Rephaim, Whisperers," 87. Similarly, Cook, "Deliverance as Fertility," 171–172.

134. Johnston, *Shades of Sheol*, 129.

135. So also Key, "Concept of Death," 244.

136. Isaiah 8:19–20a; Jeremiah 9:20–21; Isaiah 28:15–18. Key states that the personification of death and Sheol evokes the images of gods of death and the underworld. Key, "Concept of Death," 244; for analysis of relevant passages in the prophetic literature, see Lewis, *Cults of the Dead*, 128ff.

137. Cf. Spronk, *Beatific Afterlife*; Lewis, *Cults of the Dead*; Bloch-Smith, "Cult of the Dead, 213–224. However, there are some scholars who deny that ancestor cult was practiced in Israel, for instance, de Vaux, *Ancient Israel*, 56–61.

138. Liwak, "רָאפִים," in *TWOT* 13, 607–11, cited in Cook, "Deliverance as Fertility," 172, n. 20.

beliefs among the Judeans who regard the dead royals as powerful from beyond the grave.[139] Thus, in v. 14, it is plausible the dead refer to the dead divinized royals who were often identified with the *rephaim*.

Therefore, although Isaiah 26 contrasts the righteous and the wicked, those who will not rise are not the wicked *per se* but the already dead and divinized rulers. The ability of the dead divinized royals to exert influence over the living was rejected in official Yahwism. However, their appearance here functions polemically – if there was any belief among the Jewish community that the dead kings were powerful and could be summoned for favour or intervention among the living, the passage posits Yahweh as superior, as arbiter of their ultimate fate. The *rephaim* are dead, even their memory is obliterated forever, thus in effect consigning them to death after death, the ultimate death wherein one fades into oblivion.

This study examines the different aspects of divine retribution operational within the divine-human interaction when projected to the afterlife. Consequently, the aspects of divine retribution established in chapter 2 cannot serve as a framework for evaluating Yahweh's judgment towards the *rephaim* since they are not human beings. Hence, the *rephaim* being the already dead divinized royals rather than human beings *per se*, do not qualify. However, they do make for an interesting study. The exact infraction of the dead divinized royals is not explicit in the text (vv. 14, 19). The term *rephaim* by itself does not carry moral connotations since generally in the HB it was a designation for the undifferentiated dead inhabitants of the underworld. Hence if at all there is a moral judgment to be made, it is the context that suggests it.[140] What the context in vv. 13–14 does indicate is that the main transgression of the *rephaim* was that they posited themselves as contenders for Israel's allegiance.[141] It is probable that the *rephaim* were seen as a "competing source of divine power and knowledge,"[142] a characteristic of the *rephaim*. As discussed above, the use of terms like זוּלָתֶךָ ("besides you") usually occurs in contexts that affirm that there is no other God besides Yahweh,[143] and בעל ("to rule")

---

139. McAffee, "Rephaim, Whisperers," 87.

140. Johnston, *Shades of Sheol*, 129

141. Hays, *Covenant with Death*, 326. Hays says that in the book of Isaiah the dead are presented clearly as in competition with Yahweh.

142. Hays, *Covenant with Death*, 326.

143. Gordon, "Gods Must Die," 52–53.

is a term used most frequently in the context of marriage or in the context of referring to Yahweh as Israel's spouse.[144] But in v. 13 both these terms are used for the other lords who ruled over the community and indicate that the *rephaim* were viewed, if not as being at par with Yahweh, at least functionally as powerful in matters of granting favours and intervening on behalf of the living descendants. Hence, they are condemned to complete annihilation with the abolition of the very thing that attributed them with supposed power, that is, the invocation of their memory (v. 14). Thus in v. 19 as in v. 14, the *rephaim* are condemned.

3.7.3. Differentiated Fates in Isaiah 26:19

The understanding of אֲדֹנִים ("lords") as the *rephaim* in vv. 13–14 has implications for the understanding of Isaiah 26:19f – וְאֶרֶץ רְפָאִים תַּפִּיל. The phrase in v. 19f also has its share of interpretive difficulties. Among exegetes it is common to read this occurrence of *rephaim* as Yahweh's dead people whom he will raise,[145] or as referring to Yahweh's community who will be restored.[146] This reading either requires the *rephaim* who were condemned to not rise again in v. 14 to rise from the dead in v. 19, or to argue that they are two completely different types of *rephaim*. However, an alternate reading is possible: v. 19 draws a contrast between Yahweh's dead who rise again and the *rephaim* who do not rise, so that the *rephaim* who do not rise in v. 14 do not rise in v. 19f as well.[147] Hence, there is no contradiction between the fate of the *rephaim* in vv. 14 and 19. This interpretation is derived by reinvestigating the phrase תַּפִּיל (lit. "it will cause to fall"). The phrase תַּפִּיל is ambiguous in the verse and does not make immediate sense. Most scholars take the meaning of תַּפִּיל to be "give birth."[148] However, the root verb נָפַל nowhere denotes giving birth in any of the verbal forms. This translation of נָפַל as "give birth"

---

144. Koopmans, "בעל," in NICOTTE, vol. 1. Also observed by Hays as well as Gordon. Gordon, "Gods Must Die," 52–53; Hays, *Covenant with Death*, 325–326.

145. For instance, Oswalt, *Book of Isaiah*, 488. Cook, "Deliverance as Fertility," 175; van der Woude, "Resurrection or Transformation," 160.

146. For instance, Hibbard, *Intertextuality in Isaiah*, 148, also 149, n. 146.

147. McAffee, "Rephaim, Whisperers," 87.

148. For instance, Martin-Achard, *From Death to Life*, 132–133; Kaiser, *Isaiah 13–39*, 215; Wildberger, *Isaiah 13–27*, 551; Blenkinsopp, *Isaiah 1–39*, 366; Johnson, *From Chaos*, 107; Polaski, *Authorizing an End*, 262; van der Woude, "Resurrection or Transformation," 161; Hibbard, *Intertextuality in Isaiah*, 148.

derives possibly from two factors – i) the noun נֵפֶל which means miscarriage, in that the infant "fell" or died before birth, for example, in Job 3:16,[149] and ii) the immediate preceding childbirth imagery in v. 17, which influences the understanding of נָפַל as "give birth" in v. 18, which itself is an ambiguous verse, as well as in v. 19.[150] However, the noun נֵפֶל, even though it is related to childbirth, does not have a positive meaning to warrant the translation "give birth."[151] Further, Mark Finney points out that it is never uses in the sense of "giving birth" in Isaiah.[152]

The verb נָפַל in v. 19f (as also in v.18[153]) can be translated with its primary meaning, "to fall," to make good sense in the verse. The "וּ" is translated as a waw-disjunctive, "but," and נָפַל in the Hiphil causative stem as "cast down." The feminine singular form of the verb תַּפִּיל also agrees with its feminine subject אֶרֶץ ("earth"). Further, אֶרֶץ often functions as one of the several parallel expressions for Sheol and can be translated as "the underworld."[154] אֶרֶץ by itself rarely means the underworld, but when placed close to other terms, as here in Isaiah 26:19 with *rephaim*, this sense is plausible. אֶרֶץ here can be understood as a double entendre signifying both the physical earth as well as the underworld. Thus, v. 19f can be translated as:

---

149. Hays, *Covenant with Death*, 326–327; Wieringen, "'I' and 'We,'" 248; McAffee, "Rephaim, Whisperers," 94.

150. Polaski takes the meaning of נָפַל to be "give birth" based on the preceding fertility imagery, although he says that its use elsewhere renders "thou wilt let it fall," as in KJV, a plausible translation. Polaski, *Authorizing*, 237, n. 91.

151. McAffee argues that the negative connotation of miscarriage does not allow one to make the "semantic leap to the overtly positive notion of giving birth." McAffee, "Rephaim, Whisperers," 94.

152. Finney, *Resurrection, Hell*, 30.

153. The last part of v. 18 can be translated as "and the inhabitants of the world have not fallen." So does RSV; Hays similarly translates נָפַל in v. 18, although with a causative force. See Hays, *Covenant with Death*, 324.

154. The possibility of the use of אֶרֶץ to mean the underworld was first proposed by Gunkel in 1895. Philip Johnston states that since Gunkel other scholars have followed his cue and researched along those lines, and while there is no consensus on which occurrences of אֶרֶץ in the HB is to be translated as the underworld, it remains within the viable semantic range of אֶרֶץ. Gunkel, cited in Johnston, *Shades of Sheol*, 99. See Wächter, "שְׁאוֹל šeʾōl," 243; Cf. also Doak refers to the double entendre of אֶרֶץ in Isaiah 14:9 as referring to both the physical earth as also the underworld. Doak, *Last of the Rephaim*, 266; Similarly, Hays also translates אֶרֶץ as "underworld," although he translates the rest of the phrase differently. Hays, *Covenant with Death*, 324; McAffee, "Rephaim, Whisperers," 93–94.

v. 19f וָאֶרֶץ רְפָאִים תַּפִּיל
"but the earth will cast down the *rephaim*."

This translation draws a contrast in v. 19 between the fate of Yahweh's dead who will rise up and live again, and the *rephaim* who, both here and in v. 14, are consistently condemned to a second death. The *rephaim* are cast down to never rise again;[155] never again can they be summoned to bless their descendants or intervene in the world of the living. Hence, v.19a–b is contrasted with 14a–b, but v. 19f is parallel to v. 14a–b.

Isaiah 26:14	Isaiah 26:19
14a מֵתִים בַּל־יִחְיוּ (The dead ones, they will not live)	19a יִחְיוּ מֵתֶיךָ (Your dead ones will live)
14b רְפָאִים בַּל־יָקֻמוּ (the *rephaim*, they will not rise)	19b נְבֵלָתִי יְקוּמוּן (My corpse, they will rise)
	19f וָאֶרֶץ רְפָאִים תַּפִּיל ("but the earth will cast down the *rephaim*")

The foregoing discussion demonstrates that it is possible to argue for the presence of the concept of a post-mortem divine retribution in Isaiah 26:19. This differentiation of fates between God's dead and the *rephaim* becomes clearer when vv. 14 and 19 are studied together. They highlight the possibility that, as Robert Martin-Achard states, the distinction between God's people and God's enemies does not end in this life. Death becomes a transitional phase for God's people, but for those punished by God it is their eternal state.[156] Admittedly, details relating to the concept of post-mortem retribution are not as well developed at this point as they are in some other Jewish literature. Whether that is because the theology of a beatific afterlife was not the focus of the text, or because an afterlife concept had generally not yet entirely developed among the Jews is hard to say. In any case, in Isaiah 26 the concept of divine retribution moves a step further from being focused on the present life to the realization of divine retribution in the post-mortem realm. Immortality

---

155. McAffee, 94.

156. Martin-Achard, *From Death to Life*, 134–135. Martin-Achard identifies the righteous dead with the Hasidim martyrs during the time of Alexander's campaign, fourth century BCE, and those consigned to eternal death as "foreign tyrants" and the "renegade Jews."

and resurrection as categories of thinking about Yahweh's potentiality were already available to the people from the very start.[157] However, in Isaiah 26 resurrection is spoken of not only as something Yahweh can do, but also as something Yahweh will accomplish; the temporal orientation is still future, but it is more concrete.

Thus, resurrection in Isaiah 26:19 is the reward for the righteous, while the punishment for the *rephaim* is not simply non-resurrection but abolition of remembrance. In the HB, generally, the consequences and punishment for evil were to be met in the present life, with a bad death being the ultimate punishment. Death is classified as bad when it is untimely, violent or shameful, or when the corpse is not given a proper burial, or when one dies without an heir, or in a foreign land.[158] In Isaiah 26, however, the idea of death is intensified by the obliteration of all memory of the *rephaim* in the underworld. This is perhaps not much of a punishment to today's readers, but in a context where the significance of commemoration cult was understood this judgment brought about a final ruin. Remembrance or commemoration cult was a way of perpetuating one's existence among the living even after death.[159] But for Yahweh's dead enemies, such a remembrance is banned. There is to be no memorial for them. This implies that one dies when he physically dies, and he dies a second time when the invocation of the name ceases or is prohibited. So, the abolition of remembrance of the rulers is the ultimate death – the death after death. This ensures that the dead are now consigned to oblivion. Thus, the elimination of the possibility of their names being remembered is their dreaded and ultimate punishment.

As for the righteous, remembrance alone could have been enough reward but as Cook says Isaiah 26 presents an "extreme" contrast by positing the reward for Yahweh's dead ones as not limited to a "mere ongoing remembrance and communion beyond the grave" but that the "dead will rise reembodied on God's coming day."[160] The resurrection life does not merely enable the resur-

---

157. The Creation and the Fall narratives in Genesis 1–3 portray immortality as inbuilt in humankind although lost at the Fall; in the historical narratives, the great prophet Elijah (1 Kgs 17:21–22) and Elisha (2 Kgs 4:32–35; 13:21) revive people who were already declared dead. Further stories of Enoch assumption and Elijah's ascension added to repository of these ideas.

158. Spronk, "Good Death," 10–13; Key, "Concept of Death," 246.

159. Schimdt, "Memory as Immortality," 238.

160. Cook, "Deliverance as Fertility," 176.

rected to occasionally visit the world of the living, as did the *rephaim* when called upon, but it restores them to a full life. Unlike in the underworld where the inhabitants live "a joyless existence,"[161] it will be a life marked by vitality. Further, this implies that resurrection in Isaiah 26:19 is not universal since resurrection is a reward reserved only for those who belong to Yahweh. As such, in Isaiah 26:14 and 19 life-after-death and death-after-death constitute the reward and the punishment.

Additionally, at this point a possible shift in the concept of Sheol is emerging. Sheol is usually portrayed as a place of undifferentiated dead.[162] All the dead, whether righteous or wicked, are said to go down to Sheol at the end. Sheol is also a place of no return; there are gates with bars to keep its inhabitants from escaping (Job 16:22; Isaiah 38:10; Jonah 2:6).[163] The dead occasionally leave the underworld when summoned using necromantic rituals, or become malevolent upon neglect and disrupt the world of the living but can never completely leave Sheol to return to the world of the living.[164] However, in Isaiah 26 Sheol is no longer a place of undifferentiated dead, but a place of punishment for the wicked and the enemies of God.[165] Thus it can be said that a detectable moral distinction is slowly emerging in the conception of Sheol, and the righteous, those who belong to Yahweh's community, do not remain in the underworld. They are revivified and Sheol no longer contains them.

3.8. Conclusion

Isaiah 26:19 is a difficult passage to interpret. In whichever manner one interprets it, it must be conceded that no interpretation has the final say, at least not yet. This however also means that the reading of the passage as denoting a literal resurrection of the dead is possible, and the foregoing examination demonstrates it. Nonetheless, the concept of the resurrection of the dead appears only as a glimpse in Isaiah 26:19. It is mentioned so briefly, and in a context so ambivalent that the result is quite modest.

---

161. Keller, "Hebrew Thoughts on Immortality," 16.
162. Russell, *Method and Message*, 335.
163. Finney, *Resurrection, Hell*, 26, 27.
164. Schmidt, "Memory as Immortality," 89.
165. Lewis Bayles Paton states that Sheol in Isaiah 24–27 is not a common fate for everyone but only the fate of the wicked. Paton, "Hebrew Idea," 346.

There are indications of both positive and negative post-mortem divine retribution in Isaiah 26:19. Positively, resurrection in Isaiah 26:19 is presented as the end. It is the reward for Yahweh's righteous dead, rather than the means through which one is brought to face Yahweh's post-mortem judgment. The reading also points towards an anthropocentric aspect of divine retribution based on the community's willingness to learn, trust in Yahweh, and willingness to accept Yahweh's discipline. Further, divine retribution is corporate in nature and the individual is deeply embedded in the corporate. There is no individuation of retribution; there is no tension visible within the community. This corporate outlook can in turn be traced back to the corporate perspective of the covenant and hence the anthropocentric aspect of divine retribution operates within an overall theocentric framework. Therefore, it can be said that the dead who rise are characterized as Yahweh's righteous and are promised salvation as a community. When Yahweh comes to judge, Yahweh's dead ones can expect the ultimate reward – being raised from the dead.

Negatively, Yahweh's retribution is experienced by the *rephaim*. The study identifies them as dead divinized kings, which harmonizes the reference to *rephaim* in both vv. 14 and 19 by consigning them to death by oblivion. However, as non-human entities their post-mortem retribution does not come exactly within the purview of the aspects of divine retribution that this dissertation examines. Nonetheless, the presence of *rephaim* in v. 19 provides a foil for contrasting the fate of Yahweh's enemies with the fate of the righteous by juxtaposing death-after-death with life-after-death. Lastly, it is observed that in v. 19 the concept of Sheol was possibly taking its first step of transforming from a place of undifferentiated dead to a place of punishment for Yahweh's enemies.

CHAPTER 4

Post-mortem Divine Retribution in Daniel 12:1–3

4.1. Introduction

Daniel 12:1–3 is one instance of a passage in the HB that has achieved near consensus status among scholars regarding its witness to the concept of resurrection, albeit varying opinions on the particulars. The apocalyptic section of the book of Daniel (chs. 7–12) consists of four visions of end times, Daniel 7, 8, 9, and 10–12, climaxing in Daniel 12:1–3. These visions oscillate between scenes of battle in heaven and battles on earth culminating in a promise of deliverance and vindication. Chapters 10–12 record a single vision, more auditory than visual, in which a majestic heavenly being presents history as a succession of reigns. It provides a two tiered perspective on the world with human events mirrored by cosmic realities. The heavenly being reveals the final aftermath of the conflict between the faithful who remain unswerving in their faith and those who oppose them – the resurrection of the dead followed by judgment. Thus, Daniel 12:1–3 forms the climax of the long and final vision taking the perspective beyond time, encompassing both the human and the cosmic spheres, and expressing a powerful hope unparalleled in the HB.

This chapter is driven by its interest in examining the nature of post-mortem divine retribution as presented in Daniel 12:1–3. Two issues need to be addressed before investigating the nature of divine retribution in the passage. First is the date of Daniel. The interpretation of the text of Daniel, in some passages more than others, is driven by the date assigned to its composition or final redaction. Hence, before delving into the book's perspective on resurrection and post-mortem divine retribution, an examination of the issues involved in dating it is dealt with. The second question pertinent to understanding the nature of post-mortem divine retribution in Daniel 12:1–3 is whether the resurrection image is used literally or metaphorically. Hence, this chapter begins by discussing these two questions that influence the interpretation of the passage. It then proceeds to examine the function of resurrection in relation to post-mortem divine retribution. This is followed by an examination of the basis and aspect of post-mortem divine retribution and whether divine retribution in Daniel is corporate or individual in nature from the perspective of the aspects and nature of divine retribution as seen in Deuteronomy.

4.2. Date of the Book of Daniel

That the dating of a book influences its interpretation is possibly truer of Daniel than the other books of the HB, and as such it is necessary to set out how this chapter will navigate the issue. The setting of the book in the Neo-Babylonian era and early years of the Persian era was assumed to be its date of composition as well. As such, it was traditionally dated to circa sixth century BCE and a single Jewish writer, possibly Daniel himself, was assumed to be its author. This date gained wide acceptance, with the exception of a challenge from Neo-Platonist philosoper Porphyry. In the third century AD he contested this date in his polemical work, *Against the Christians*, and proposed instead a second century BCE date for the Book of Daniel. The church was quick to condemn it; and his work was subsequently lost. Porphyry's view, however, remains recorded in Jerome's Daniel commentary, which along with works from other Christian scholars provided a rebuttal to Porphyry.[1] Engagement from scholars concerning Porphyry's view regardless, the sixth-century date continued to be assigned to the Book of Daniel, until around the nineteenth century when the second-century BCE date gained currency in German critical scholarship.[2] Their serious reconsideration of the late date

---

1. McCollough, "Introduction to Daniel," 151–152; Miller, *Daniel*, , 23–24; Waltke, "Date of the Book," 319.

2. Miller, *Daniel*, 23–24; Waltke, "Date of the Book," 319; Goldingay, *Daniel*, xxxvi.

opened the debate for the dating of Daniel, and scholars soon became polarized into two camps: those who date the book to the sixth century BCE with Daniel as the author, and those who date the book to the second century BCE, at least in its final form, written pseudonymously, and as a *vaticinium ex eventu* (prophecy after the event).[3] There also emerged a third group of scholars who take a more eclectic approach. They perceive the text of Daniel as spanning two eras, generally identifying the narratives as from the early period and the visions as bearing a Hellenistic hallmark.[4]

Much has been said regarding the details on both sides of the debate, and fresh arguments have been made based on newer studies and findings, which need not be reiterated here.[5] However, a resolution is unlikely anytime soon. What further impedes the attempts to arrive at a consensus is that the date of Daniel is seen as having larger implication on issues of veracity of the Scriptures. As such, it is not uncommon for scholars to argue from an underlying priori position – early-date advocates see the veracity and reliability of the Bible, and on faith as a whole, riding on this issue. Bruce Waltke, for instance, states that the sovereignty of God, the Bible's divine inspiration, and the "understanding of the nature of Jesus Christ" are at stake in this debate.[6] The assumption on the part of those favouring the late date is often that of the improbability of predictive prophecy in the HB, or at least that is the

---

3. Scholars who espouse the late date come to varying conclusions regarding the precise dating and the stages of composition.

4. For instance, Von Rad, *Theologie des Alten Testaments*, 316–331; Childs, *Introduction*, 15.

5. Points of contention in this debate include linguistic evidence, manuscript evidence, historical accuracy, placement of Daniel in the canon, theological themes, among others. It may be pointed out that earlier the presence of four different languages in the Book of Daniel – Hebrew, Aramaic, Persian, and Greek – was taken as irrefutable evidence of its late composition. However, reinvestigations of the linguistic features of Daniel have cast a shadow over such confidence, and late date reasoning on linguistic ground needs to be reassessed. One such significant study on the languages used in Daniel was that of Kenneth Kitchen; Kitchen, "Aramaic of Daniel," 31–79. For arguments in favor of an early date see Zöckler, *Book of the Prophet Daniel*, 20–41; Young, *Daniel*, 19–26; Harrison, *Introduction to Old Testament*, 1105–1134; Baldwin, *Daniel: An Introduction and Commentary*, 21–38; Miller, *Daniel*, 24–43; Waltke, "Date of the Book," 319–329; Yamauchi, "Archeological Background of Daniel," 3–16; Finley, "Book of Daniel," 195–208; For late-date arguments, whether in its entirety or in its final form, see Anderson, *Understanding the Old Testament*, 618ff; Goldingay, *Daniel*, 281–86, 304–6; Redditt, *Daniel*, 1–20; Collins, *Daniel*, 1–38; Lucas, *Daniel*, 306–312.

6. Waltke, "Date of the Book," 320.

priori reasoning imputed to them for arguing for *vaticium ex eventu*.[7] This, Ernest Lucas admits, is probably true of some critical scholars.[8] However, the issue is deeper than one's view on the possibility of predictive prophecy, as briefly explained below.

There are three aspects that need to be addressed in considering whether Daniel is prophecy or quasi-prophecy: philosophical, theological, and literary or formal questions. John Goldingay and Lucas explain the issue in the following manner. From a philosophical standpoint the question is, "Can God reveal something of the distant future?" Most scholars have no problem answering that question in the affirmative.[9] However, what drives those who accept the philosophical possibility of predictive prophecy to still contend for a second-century date are the other two underlying considerations – as Lucas puts them, a theological question, "Would God do it?" and a literary-critical question, "Did God do it?"[10] Daniel 10–12, especially chapter 11, is a highly detailed vision or audition. Stephen Miller himself states that the historical details are "astounding."[11] Theologically, Goldingay asserts, God as characteristically revealed in the Bible calls people to a life of faith, and such a detailed prediction is neither consistent with the picture of God in the Bible, nor typical of biblical prophecy. God does reveal "key truths" whenever there are prophecies about the end times, but they are more general and usually have implications for the present.[12] Thus, although God could reveal events of the distant future, this theological consideration precludes some late-date advocates from assuming he has conclusively done so in Daniel. Hence, as Lucas states, even those who disagree with the views of the late-date

---

7. Waltke, 329.
8. Lucas, *Daniel*, 308.
9. Goldingay, *Daniel*, 321; Lucas, *Daniel*, 308.
10. Lucas, *Daniel*, 308.
11. Miller, *Daniel*, 290.
12. Goldingay, *Daniel*, 321. The HB does not generally deny the efficacy of supernatural powers, only that it forbids the Israelites from practicing it. They were to depend on Yahweh, not on foreknowledge. For instance, when Saul resorts to consulting a necromancer, it is Saul who is cast in a poor light. The text does not show the ineffectiveness of necromancy; in fact, it shows that the prediction came to pass. Also cf., Key, "Concept of Death," 244; Hays, *Covenant with Death*, 169.

supporters need to acknowledge that "there is theological integrity on both sides of the argument."[13]

Further, regarding the literary-formal question, "Did God do it?" there are no parallels in the HB to the visions recorded in Daniel. There are a few similar extrabiblical prophecies from Mesopotamia, Egypt, and Greece,[14] however, they are all pseudonymous, "extensive quasi-prophecy of events before the writer's day with more limited actual prophecy of events still to come."[15] As such, Daniel as a pseudonymous quasi-prophecy would fit comfortably with these other ANE texts, and this has been taken as a support for the late date.[16] Furthermore, in terms of serving as evidence for dating Daniel, it is ambiguous. The period during which this form was prevalent ranges from the late second millennium, the Marduk prophetic speech from the time of Nebuchadnezzar I (1126–1105 BCE), to the Hellenistic period.[17] Hence, even an appeal to parallels from extrabiblical sources does not tilt the balance decisively to one side of the date debate.[18] As such, even when scholars agree on the philosophical possibility of predictive prophecy, the theological and literary-formal aspects of the matter continue to pose a problem.

Additionally, significant to the present study is Daniel 11 – not only does Daniel 12:1–3 flow from it, but it also happens to be at the centre of the date debate.[19] As Joyce Baldwin notes: "Though several arguments are adduced with the intention of giving cumulative force to a second-century date, there is basically one reason for the tenaciously-held opinion, and that is the content

---

13. Lucas, *Daniel*, 309.

14. Goldingay, *Daniel*, 282; also Edwin M. Yamauchi, "Hermeneutical Issues"; Collins, *Daniel*, 99–100. There are also Jewish and Christian quasi-apocalypses from ca. 200 BCE to 200 CE; Lucas, *Daniel*, 271–271.

15. Goldingay, *Daniel*, 282, 321.

16. For instance, Goldingay says in considering the visions in Daniel in its ANE context, it is more natural to think that the author used the familiar quasi-prophecy form than to say "that the author has turned a familiar way of giving quasi-prophecies into a way of giving actual prophecies" and Collins, who examines Daniel in the context of Jewish apocalypse, similarly says "those who wish to argue that Daniel is different from the other examples of the genre" must bear the burden of proof. Goldingay, *Daniel*, 282; Collins, *Daniel*, 33–34.

17. Yamauchi, "Hermeneutical Issues," 15; Goldingay, *Daniel*, 282.

18. However, see Collins who argues for a late date of Daniel based on The Dream Visions (1 Enoch 83–90). The Dream Vision is the closest parallel to the genre of visions in Daniel 7–12, presenting precise predictive prophesies, and is dated to second to first century BCE; Collins, *Apocalyptic Imagination*, 88.

19. Meadowcroft, "History and Eschatology, 243.

of chapter 11."[20] While this is in fact the case, both late-date and early-date scholars largely agree on one thing, that is, the events in Daniel 11:1–35 "correspond [. . .] remarkably" to the Seleucid period, especially the reign of Antiochus IV.[21] The vision in chapter 11 evinces a close acquaintance with the political events from the time of Alexander to Antiochus IV. Although it is impossible to say with certitude, the references do line up well with events during that period, especially as it concerns Antiochus IV.

However, this agreement ends in verse 35. Hereafter the two diverge again. The question here is, should Daniel 11:36–45 be interpreted historically or eschatologically? In general, the late-date view is that the verses in Daniel 11:36–12:3 continue to refer to the time of Antiochus IV but erroneously predict his death.[22] The dominant early-date view, by contrast, is that Daniel 11:36–12:3 refer to the end times. Thus, the "king" in verses 36–39 is identified as the eschatological figure, the Antichrist, and the following events are considered a description of his defeat (Dan 11:40–45), the tribulation (the one Jesus predicted in Matthew 24:21), and the final resurrection (Dan 12:1–3).[23]

Such discrepancy among scholars in assigning a referent to the events described in Daniel 11:36–45 stems partly from methodological difficulties. Paul J. Alexander and Lorenzo DiTommaso shed some light on this matter.[24] Although the cited works of both these scholars focus on pseudonymous *ex eventu* apocalypse, some of their insights can illuminate the problem at hand. Apocalypse[25] as a genre intertwines "historical facts and eschatological

---

20. Baldwin, *Daniel*, 41.

21. Yamauchi, "Hermeneutical Issues," 16; Tanner, "Daniel's King," 316.

22. Montgomery, *Critical and Exegetical Commentary*, 460; Clifford, "History and Myth, 23–26; Hamner, *Book of Daniel*, 114; Hartman and Di Lella, *Book of Daniel*, 301; Porteous, *Daniel*, 169; Anderson, *Signs and Wonders*, 141; DiTomasso, "Deliverance and Justice," 79.

23. So also Jerome; see Stevenson and Glerup, eds., *Ezekiel, Daniel*, 298–303; Keil, *Ezekiel, Daniel*, 461; Miller, *Daniel*, 304–320; Steinmann, "Is the Antichrist," 195–209. A third view, held by a few scholars, is to see Daniel 11:36–45 as referring both to Antiochus IV and to Antichrist, for instance, Baldwin, *Daniel*, 199–203. A similar double-reference interpretation, though not precisely the same, was held by John Calvin, *Commentaries on the Book*, 339–377, and is followed by Parry, "Desolation of the Temple," 485–526.

24. Alexander, "Medieval Apocalypses," 997–1018; DiTommaso, *Book of Daniel*, 104–107.

25. The genre of Daniel is another area of animated discussion. It is often considered not characteristically an apocalypse, however, many attribute to it the status of proto-apocalypse or the earliest form of Jewish apocalypse. Within the genre of apocalypse, Daniel falls into one of two broad categories – one that includes historical reviews, the other that includes other

prophecy,"²⁶ and it is not unusual to witness a leap forward from history to eschatology²⁷ in a matter of a single verse.²⁸ DiTommaso states, such a shift from history to eschatology can be ascertained by considering two elements: i) in chronological terms, historical review covers a long period while prophecy regarding the future does not "extend too far from the author's own time,"²⁹ and ii) data in historical review are much more detailed while the shift to prophecy is characterized by broader strokes; they are more general and vague. However, he is quick to add that where it becomes problematic is in ascertaining when exactly historical review shifts to eschatological prophecy.³⁰ This task of drawing a line between historical review and prophecy is often not as simple as it appears, an example being Daniel, which he states contains "a battalion of cryptic details" that resists "attempts to draw the line between history and prophecy."³¹ This difficulty in locating precisely when the shift from history to prophecy happens in an apocalypse provides a glimpse of the

---

worldly journeys. Lucas quotes Collins' definition for the seminar of the Society of Biblical Literature, cited in Lucas, *Daniel*, 310.

26. Alexander, "Medieval Apocalypses," 998.

27. Eschatology (from the Greek word ἔσχατος meaning "last" in time or in place) refers to the concept and teachings about the last things. However, because biblical scholarship distinguishes between the present age and the age to come, eschatology sometimes is ambiguous as to its temporal perspective. Some distinguish between two types of eschatology: prophetic and apocalyptic. The purview of prophetic eschatology is this-worldly, and includes all of God's future interventions in space and time history for the sake of Israel and the nations. The apocalyptic eschatology alternatively extends to an other-worldly reality. Here eschatology is used in the second sense as referring to events that are expected to take place in the age to come. However, Stephen Cook is right in saying that the distinction should not be overemphasized. See Wielenga, "Eschatology in Malachi," 1; Collins, "Eschatology of Zechariah," 74–84; Cook, *Apocalyptic Literature*; Hiers, "Eschatology," 302–305; Evans and Flint, "Introduction," 2; Noble, Eschatology," 296–299.

28. Tanner, "Daniel's King," 317.

29. For instance, Goldingay states that in the "Dynastic Prophecy" from the Hellenistic period the historical review covers history from the "Assyrian, Babylonian, Persian, and Hellenistic empires" and ends with a prophecy of "the fall of the Seleucid empire and a rubric regarding keeping the prophecy secret." Goldingay, *Daniel*, 282.

30. In discussing the difficulty of discerning the point where history ends and prophecy begins, both Alexander and DiTommaso are primarily interested in how that affects the debate on date of composition of apocalyptic texts that are generally pseudonymous and *ex eventu*. Alexander, "Medieval Apocalypses," 999–1000; DiTommaso, *Book of Daniel*, 104–107.

31. DiTommaso also discusses maximalist and minimalist approaches to determining the end of history and beginning of eschatology. Cf. DiTommaso, *Book of Daniel*, 104–107. Alexander also hints towards this complication when is notes that it is often unclear as to which exactly is the latest historical event an apocalypse in the context of determining where history ends and prophecy begins. Alexander, "Medieval Apocalypses," 1001, n. 13.

difficult task that faces exegetes of Daniel 11. The early-date scholars generally identify the change from historical prophecy to eschatological prophecy in verse 36, but the late-date scholars do not see any movement towards eschatology in Daniel 11. They view it instead as a continuation of the Antiochus narrative, and if there is a shift it is from historical review or quasi-prophecy to historical prophecy about Antiochus VI's death, with some identifying this movement in verse 36 and others in verse 40.[32] This disagreement over the interpretation of the final verses of chapter 11 impacts the interpretation of Daniel 12:1–3 as will be seen shortly.

In dating Daniel, evidence from linguistics, manuscriptal, or historical accuracy points of view may have benefited from newer discoveries and studies, and may favour one position over the other. Further, scholars from both side of the debate may agree that predictive prophecy is a real possibility. Nevertheless, the theological, literary-formal, and methodological considerations briefly discussed above still hang on the balance of probability. Thus, it should not be surprising that scholars on both positions are yet to arrive at a consensus, and that some on the same side of the date-debate often disagree on other details. With this discussion in view, the text of Daniel 12:1–3 will be examined and wherever applicable both perspectives, that is, 12:1–3 as an eschatological prophecy and as a prophecy concerning Antiochus IV's expected end, will be presented.

The text central to the present examination is Daniel 12:1–3:

¹וּבָעֵת הַהִיא יַעֲמֹד מִיכָאֵל הַשַּׂר הַגָּדוֹל הָעֹמֵד עַל־בְּנֵי עַמֶּךָ וְהָיְתָה עֵת צָרָה אֲשֶׁר לֹא־נִהְיְתָה מִהְיוֹת גּוֹי עַד הָעֵת הַהִיא וּבָעֵת הַהִיא יִמָּלֵט עַמְּךָ כָּל־הַנִּמְצָא כָּתוּב בַּסֵּפֶר׃
²וְרַבִּים מִיְּשֵׁנֵי אַדְמַת־עָפָר יָקִיצוּ אֵלֶּה לְחַיֵּי עוֹלָם וְאֵלֶּה לַחֲרָפוֹת לְדִרְאוֹן עוֹלָם׃
³וְהַמַּשְׂכִּלִים יַזְהִרוּ כְּזֹהַר הָרָקִיעַ וּמַצְדִּיקֵי הָרַבִּים כַּכּוֹכָבִים לְעוֹלָם וָעֶד׃

---

32. Not all late-date scholars agree on where precisely the "quasi-prophecy" ends and where actual prophecy begins. For instance, in Goldingay's opinion the "quasi-prophecy" ends in verse 35, Goldingay, *Daniel*, 321; Clifford posits that in verse 36–45 the author of Daniel, no longer restricted by the contemporaneous historical events, reuses the traditions of the HB and Canaanite mythic materials to portray Antiochus IV, see Clifford, "History and Myth," 25–26; while Di Lella posits that "quasi-prophecy" ends in verse 39 and considers only 40–45 as prophecy, Hartman and Di Lella, *Book of Daniel*, 303; so also Towner, *Daniel*.

While there are several issues in this text, the following section will examine those that have a bearing on the concept of post-mortem divine retribution. It is generally accepted that Daniel 12:2 makes an unequivocal statement on literal resurrection of the dead. Philip Johnston, after examining dozens of texts in the HB relating to death and afterlife, breathes a sigh of relief in speaking of Daniel 12:2: "Finally, one text speaks unmistakably and unambiguously of personal resurrection."[33] There are nonetheless some dissenting voices; hence this section will first examine if resurrection in Daniel is used in a metaphorical or literal sense. Based on the conclusion on that matter three other aspects emerge: i) resurrection leading to post-mortem divine retribution, ii) emphasis on the anthropocentric aspect of divine retribution in Daniel's post-mortem retribution and, iii) emphasis on the individual nature of divine retribution. But first, we examine whether resurrection in Daniel 12:2 is used metaphorically or literally.

4.3. Resurrection: Literal or Metaphorical

The writer of Daniel employs the language of sleeping and waking – ישן ("to sleep") and קיץ ("to awake") – when referring to dying and revivification, a practice common among the writers of HB.[34] The question is whether this revivification in Daniel 12:2 is a literal, corporeal resurrection of people or a metaphorical one denoting the restoration of Israel.

4.3.1. Literal Interpretation

Interpreting Daniel 12:2 as referring to literal resurrection of individuals has wide support.[35] Leonard Greenspoon concludes that the author of Daniel 12:2 conceived of a bodily resurrection of some of those who have died.[36] Johnston sees this as a clear reference to "personal, individual resurrection"

---

33. Johnston, *Shades of Sheol*, 225.
34. For instance, 2 Kgs 4:31; Jer 51:39, 57; Job 3:13, 14:12. Cf. Nickelsburg, *Resurrection, Immortality*, 30; Goldingay, *Daniel*, 307.
35. Young, *Daniel*, 256–257; Cavallin, *Life After Death*, 26–27; Collins, *Daniel, 1–2 Maccabees*, 110–111; Miller, *Daniel*, 316; Segal, *Life After Death*, 261–262; Lucas, *Daniel*, 294; Nickelsburg, *Resurrection, Immortality*, 23, 38.
36. Greenspoon, "Origin of the Idea," 284.

even if it does not envision a universal resurrection.[37] Ernest Lucas is more cautious about deeming it to be a reference to bodily resurrection though he suspects that it is presumed.[38] However, in the past, a few scholars like John Nelson Darby have argued that the language of resurrection functions metaphorically and its application is specifically to the restoration of the nation or remnant of Israel,[39] and others have contended that it is a metaphor for spiritual awakening.[40] There are instances in the HB of the metaphorical use of the reawakening of the dead to denote the reconstitution and restoration of Israel. Its potent imagery speaks hope into a hopeless situation. Such an interpretation makes for a compelling case for texts like Ezekiel 37, especially since the text itself elaborates its metaphorical usage explicitly (Ezek 37:11–14). However, resurrection as a metaphorical reference to the restoration of Israel becomes problematic when applied to Daniel 12:1–3 for at least three reasons discussed below.

4.3.2. Problems of Metaphorical Interpretation

First, ישן ("to sleep") as a metaphor for an exile or a national distress is unattested in the HB. As mentioned earlier, ישן ("to sleep") and קיץ ("to awake") are usual metaphors for dying and revivification, and exile has been compared to death (Ezek 37).[41] However, there is no instance of sleep being used as a

---

37. Johnston, *Shades of Sheol*, 226.

38. Lucas, *Daniel*, 304.

39. Darby, *Studies*, 113; Ironside, *Lectures on Daniel*, 231; Gaebelein, *Prophet Daniel*, 200 and Kelly, *Notes on the Book*, 255ff, both cited in Walvoord, "Resurrection of Israel," 6.

40. Carl Armerding, "Asleep in the Dust," 156. Armerding reasons that the word "awake" occurs about twenty-one times in the HB in the same mood as in Daniel 12:2 and that in several of those instances it means other than to wake from sleep or physical resurrection; for instance in Ps 35:23 he argues that it means to stir up. Further, according to him the occurrence of the same word in Isa 26:19 in the context of the dweller of the dust being called upon to wake up proves that it is not speaking of resurrection as the "Scripture never speaks of the physical dead as dwelling in the dust." Hence according to him, Daniel 12:2 is speaking of a spiritual awakening. However, the interpretation of Isaiah 26:19 is far from settled, and the HB does not speak of the spiritual as distinct from the physical (see Russell, *Method and Message*, 140, 153). Further, Gen 3:19 sets the paradigm for physical death in the HB and uses the language of dust – at death human beings will return to עָפָר ("dust"). Thus, returning to dust is the typical metaphor for physical death. Gen 3:19 in turn alludes to God's creation of humans using עָפָר מִן־הָאֲדָמָה "dust from the ground" (Gen 2:7).

41. Mitchell Chase observes that death as denoting exile goes back to Genesis 3. In Genesis God pronounces the penalty for eating the fruit from the forbidden tree as death, but upon eating from it, Adam and Eve are not met with immediate physical death; rather they are exiled

metaphor for exile or persecution. Further, Artur Stele states, "sleep" is too "peaceful and restful a state" to be a metaphor for national distress.[42] Hence sleeping and waking as a metaphor for the exile and restoration of Israel is contrived.

Secondly, restoration for a nation to חַיֵּי עוֹלָם ("eternal life" 12:2) is difficult to explain. The expression חַיֵּי עוֹלָם is unique in the Hebrew Bible.[43] It is a compound of two common words, but their combination to express an idea is singular. How is חַיֵּי עוֹלָם to be interpreted in relation to the nation? Where resurrection of the dead is used as a metaphor to indicate the restoration of Israel, none of the texts use חַיֵּי עוֹלָם. Moreover, the word חַי ("life") alone expresses the idea of revivification of a nation sufficiently in context. For instance, in Ezekiel 37 God commands Ezekiel to command the winds to breathe into the slain וְיִחְיוּ ("so that they may live"), and at once breath enters the slain וַיִּחְיוּ ("and they came to life") (Ezek 37:9, 10, also in v.14). As such, the addition of עוֹלָם piques one's interest and suggests that something else is intended.

Admittedly, "eternity" in the philosophical sense, as commonly used in English to denote something "unbounded by time" or "eternal timelessness," is neither the most common nor the basic meaning of עוֹלָם in the HB. The basic meaning is linked to occurrences of events in the "distant past or future,"[44] and contextually it could mean either a lifetime, or ancient, or an era, or a long

---

from Eden. He states that the author of Genesis viewed death dynamically and that the exile "was a kind of death." Chase, "'From Dust You Shall Arise,'" 21–22.

42. Stele, "Resurrection in Daniel 12."

43. Collins, *Daniel*, 392; Miller, *Daniel*, 317; Lucas, *Daniel*, 295; Levenson, *Resurrection and the Restoration*, 187. In the Hebrew Bible, the assumptions of Enoch (Gen 5:24) and Elijah (2 Kgs 2:11) may be considered as precedents for the concept of everlasting life; however one could also argue that since they did not experience death they make better cases for immortality or deathlessness rather than resurrection unto everlasting life. For the distinction between the concepts of resurrection and immortality see, Moore, "Resurrection and Immortality," 34. Further, even in the case of Elijah resuscitating the son of the widow of Zarephath (1 Kgs 17:17–24) and the Shunammite woman's son whom Elisha resurrected from the dead (2 Kgs 4:32–37), their revivification is not described in this language and there is no reason to assume that the two boys lived eternally. In the bizarre story of the resurrection of a corpse on contact with Elisha's bones (2 Kgs 13:21) the focus is more on Elisha – understood variously as indicating Elisha's restorative power, a demonstration of his owning a double portion of Elijah's spirit, Elisha's hagiology, or a hyperbolic description of his power as preserved in tradition – than on the dead man's resurrection *per se*. Gray, *1 and 2 Kings*, 600; Fritz, *1 and 2 Kings*, 312. However, as Jephet Ibn Ali observes, the cases of revivification set a precedence so that resurrection of the dead of Israel is no longer an impossibility; Ali, *Commentary*, 76.

44. Tomasino, "עוֹלָם," in *NIDOTTE*, vol. 3, 346.

period.⁴⁵ However, there are instances when the idea of eternity or something very close to it is expressed. For instance, when God banishes humans from Eden and makes inaccessible the tree of life to humans so that they would not וָחַי לְעֹלָם ("live forever" Gen 3:22). It is significant that וָחַי לְעֹלָם ("live forever") in Genesis 3:22 is the closest parallel to לְחַיֵּי עוֹלָם ("to eternal life") of Daniel 12:2, and increases the plausibility that in both the Genesis and Daniel passages, life is being conceived of in the same sense – that of living forever.

Other instances of עוֹלָם expressing the idea of eternity include the description of the temple as God's dwelling place forever (1 Kgs 8:13), which as Anthony Tomasino argues is not invalidated by the temple's destruction. The description of Zion as established forever (Ps 48:8[9]), or of God as the eternal light of his people (Isa 60:19–20) are other cases of similar usages.⁴⁶ Thus, in Daniel 12:2 חַיֵּי עוֹלָם perhaps indicates, as Lindenberger says, "a new life stretching as far into the future as one can see."⁴⁷ Levenson also explains חַיֵּי עוֹלָם as an "irreversible triumph of life," the absence of a "second death," and as comparable to Daniel 2:44 which speaks of God establishing his kingdom that would stand forever.⁴⁸ John Collins states that modern scholars are "virtually unanimous" that this passage is speaking of actual resurrection of people "because of the explicit language of eternal life."⁴⁹ And although John Goldingay postulates that the sleeping and waking imagery has a "this-worldly connotation," he finds the expression חַיֵּי עוֹלָם sitting uneasy with his interpretation. He acknowledges that using חַיֵּי עוֹלָם to express the idea of reviving of the dead "suggests more than that."⁵⁰ Thus, the fact that חַי is paired with עוֹלָם in this resurrection text, and not in other texts where the idea of resurrection is clearly used as a metaphor, and has a close parallel in Genesis 3:22 which speaks of the loss of access to possible immortality, is exceptional and raises a question for the metaphorical interpretation of this passage. It is conceivable that in speaking of a literal resurrection of individuals the author

---

45. Preuss, עוֹלָם, 'ôlām; עָלַם 'ālam in *TDOT*, vol. 10, 534; Tomasino, עוֹלָם, 346–348.
46. Tomasino, עוֹלָם, 348–349.
47. Lindenberger, "Daniel 12:1–4," 183. Tzomasino also understands עוֹלָם in Dan 12:2 as referring to perpetuity; Tomasino, עֹלָם, 348.
48. Levenson, *Resurrection and the Restoration*, 187; Cogan and Tadmor, *2 Kings*, 150; Barnes, *1-2 Kings*, 288.
49. Collins, *Daniel*, 392.
50. Goldingay, *Daniel*, 307, 308.

uses חַיֵּי עוֹלָם to express the idea in a distinct and emphatic manner rather than to signify the restoration of Israel.

Thirdly, and lastly, explanation for a metaphorical resurrection to לַחֲרָפוֹת לְדִרְאוֹן עוֹלָם "reproach and eternal contempt" is problematic. If one argues that the reawakening to life is a metaphor for the restoration of the nation of Israel, the question arises as to who or what those awakened to "reproach and eternal contempt" represent.[51] This poses a problem to the metaphorical interpretation of resurrection and those who maintain the metaphorical interpretation of resurrection seemingly do not deal with this question.[52] But this is explained with relative ease if resurrection is understood as literal.

4.3.3. Section Conclusion

Thus, it seems reasonable to view Daniel 12:1–3 as speaking of an actual, corporeal resurrection as it explains the metaphors of sleeping and waking, the term "eternal life," and the resurrection of others to condemnation. But there are two caveats. First, while this verse is a good case of literal resurrection in the HB and has been influential in the development of Jewish and Christian belief of the doctrine of resurrection, this text is not precisely a statement of a theology of resurrection or formulating a doctrine. Second, one must admit there is little in this text concerning the fates of the resurrected ones. Nevertheless, if Daniel 12:1–3 is indeed speaking of a literal resurrection, three questions relevant to this study emerge: i) Is there a discernible post-mortem divine retribution in Daniel 12:1–3? ii) What is the basis of retribution and which aspect(s) of divine retribution is in focus? iii) Is divine retribution in Daniel 12:1–3 individual or corporate?

4.4. Resurrection and Post-mortem Divine Retribution in Daniel 12:1–3

The first question is whether a post-mortem divine retribution is discernible in Daniel 12:1–3. Daniel 12:1–3 presents resurrection not as an end in itself

---

51. Walvoord, makes the same argument though he uses it to make a slightly different point. Cf. Walvoord, "Resurrection of Israel," 7.

52. For instance, Darby interprets resurrection as the national restoration of Israel but does not deal with the question of those raised to contempt. Darby, *Studies*, 110–113.

but as a means to an end, the divine retribution of the righteous and the wicked being one of them.[53] Sibley Towner argues that the *eschaton* in the Daniel 7–12 is concerned not with divine retribution of the righteous and the wicked, but centres rather on the "nearness of the Kingdom of God," on "divine self-vindication" by ending evil as promised, and on the "interim posture of the saint."[54] Towner is right, in as much as it concerns the whole of Daniel 7–12, the theme of divine retribution as it affects the fate of the righteous and the evildoers is not the primary focus. However, in the context of the last vision, Daniel 10–12, it would be amiss to say that divine retribution does not form a part of the hope that it offers. The nearness of God's Kingdom brings hope also because it firmly establishes divine retributive justice, and the envisaged final resolution is retributive. The retributional aspect of the hope of Daniel 12:1–3 has been recognized by several scholars:[55] Michael Moore states that Daniel 12:2 delivers an "even stronger retributional promise" than do other passages in the HB by positing the fate not only of the righteous but also of the wicked.[56] George Nickelsburg states, "For Daniel, resurrection had a judicial function," while Andrew Chester says resurrection specifically results in retribution.[57] According to Goldingay, the awakening from death is not an end in itself but "as part of and as a means to vindication."[58] He sums it up when he says that in this Danielic text "the prophetic eschatological hope and its stress on the realization of God's sovereignty in relation to Israel as a whole" and "a concern for the destiny of the individual characteristic of

---

53. Other proposals regarding the purpose of resurrection in Daniel 12:1–3 include reconstitution of Israel as a nation, encouragement of the Jews, demonstration of God's sovereignty and glory. However, there is no reason to presume that these are mutually exclusive; it is possible for the book to be serving more than one main purpose. For a brief description of each, refer Stele, "Resurrection in Daniel 12," 66–75.

54. Towner, "Retributional Theology," 206.

55. Spronk states that Dan 12:2–3 answers "the problem of the untimely death of faithful Jews." Spronk, *Beatific Afterlife*, 305; Casey Elledge states that by speaking of retribution for the righteous as well as the wicked the author "reveals his concern" for justice. Elledge, "Resurrection of the Dead, 28; Routledge says that the emphasis is on vindication. Routledge, "Death and Afterlife," 28; DiTommaso states that in the Book of Daniel, salvation portrayed in the visions "equates with justice." DiTommaso, "Deliverance and Justice," 81.

56. Moore, "Resurrection and Immortality," 31.

57. Chester, "Resurrection and Transformation," 60.

58. However, Goldingay argues the author's concern is limited to the crisis facing his people as described in Daniel 11:21–12:3 and hence it is not concerned with the eschatological restoration of Israel nor with "the transcendence of death"; Goldingay, *Daniel*, 307–308.

the wisdom tradition and Psalms" all come together.[59] Hence, post-mortem divine retribution constitutes a vital part in the hope that the text presents its readers, and is presented as the fate of both the righteous and the wicked.

4.4.1. Double Resurrection

This text is not the only one in the HB to speak of post-mortem divine retribution. The case in Isaiah 26:14, 19 has been examined above, but is distinct in not positing the resurrection of both the righteous and the wicked. In Isaiah 26 retribution is envisaged as the resurrection of God's people alone (Isa 26:19), while the foreign overlords who oppressed Israel remain dead; they do not rise up (Isa 26:14). As such, in Isaiah 26 resurrection is an end in itself; it is the reward. Nicklesburg, assuming a late date for the final form of Daniel, observes that Daniel 12 pushes the boundary of Isa 26:19[60] a little further by positing "a double resurrection" whereby both the righteous and the wicked resurrect but to different fates.[61] In any case, regardless of primacy of the texts in terms of date, it remains that while Isaiah 26:19 postulates resurrection as a reward for God's people, Daniel envisions double resurrection as a means to reward or punishment. Thus, resurrection becomes a means for retribution in Daniel 12.

According to those who assign an early date to Daniel, resurrection in this passage alludes to the final resurrection at the second coming of Jesus, as mentioned in Revelation 20:4–6, when the believers in Christ or the elect will receive eternal life and the unbelievers or ungodly, because they rejected Christ, will be doomed to "eternal disgrace and condemnation."[62] On the other hand, if the Antiochene persecution of 167 BCE is taken as the historical context from which this Danielic text derives, resurrection is perceived as the solution to the theological problem raised by the persecution – the Jews who faced persecution and death did so precisely because of their fidelity to the Torah, while the Hellenizing Jews escaped persecution because

---

59. Goldingay, *Daniel*, 307–308.
60. Several scholars have noted in Daniel an allusion, if not dependence, to Isaiah 26:19 and 56–66. Lester, *Daniel Evokes Isaiah*; Bailey, "Intertextual Relationship," 305–308; Nickelsburg, *Resurrection, Immortality*, 30–36; Engnell, "'Ebed Yahweh Song," 77, cited in Lester, *Daniel Evokes Isaiah*, 2; Lindenberger, *Daniel 12:1–4*, 183–184; Goldingay, *Daniel*, 285.
61. Nickelsburg, *Resurrection, Immortality*, 33.
62. So John Calvin, *Daniel 7–12*, 373–375; Young, *Daniel*, 256; Miller, *Daniel*, 316.

they were willing to contravene the Torah stipulations. Late date scholars do not agree as to when this resurrection will take place.[63] Regardless of the disagreement as to when the resurrection will take place, in the face of a reality in which the righteous suffer, the belief in God's deliverance from mortal danger (espoused by some of the Jewish traditional teachings as well as the court tales in Daniel 1–6), could not go unchallenged. If the book of Job wrestles with this problem at an individual level, the persecution of the faithful Jews escalates it to a national level. Resolution is found in a double resurrection of the dead, arising from the belief that Yahweh will not let it go unaccounted.[64] Hence, not only do the righteous resurrect but the wicked too are resurrected, albeit to a different fate.

Having said that resurrection leads to divine retribution, there is little else in the text in terms of details relating to it. The fates of the two groups of the resurrected are described neither elaborately nor plainly. It is not clear what constitutes the damnation of the wicked. The text uses the words

---

63. For example, Di Lella and Goldingay take the phrase "At that time," in v. 1 as an indication that the events described in Daniel 12:1–3 form a continuity with the events of chapter 11, which according to them refer to Antiochus IV, and not as referring to some events in the distant future. Di Lella posits the author of Daniel expected God's intervention following the death of Antiochus. Hartman and Di Lella, *Book of Daniel*, 306; Goldingay, *Daniel*, 306. Sibley Towner, on the other hand, views Daniel 12:1–3 as a movement towards "eschaton itself" although he acknowledges that it is "also identical with the historical moment" of Antiochus' death. Towner, *Daniel*, 166.

64. Nickelsburg argues that this was a development arising from the belief of the Jews that God would keep his promise. Third Isaiah had envisioned retribution of the righteous and the wicked. However, to the writer of Daniel, as a Jew reading the prophet Isaiah in a situation of acute distress brought on by the Antiochene persecution, where the Hasidic Jews were being persecuted while the Hellenizers escaped and even in death their bodies were not lying exposed in the Valley of Hinnom as promised in Isaiah 66:24, prophet Isaiah's words did not fit. So if the Isaianic vision of retribution was to be realized, the dead needed to be revived. Consequently, the writer of Daniel develops the Isaianic concept further to that of "a double resurrection" thus vindicating the righteous and establishing divine justice. Nickelsburg, *Resurrection, Immortality*, 32–37. However, it would be simplistic to attribute the concept of a double resurrection purely to a historical crisis at one point in time, although it is likely that the Antiochene persecution and the Hasidic-Hellenizers controversy proved catalytic. Collins posits that there were movements towards a belief in resurrection before its enunciation in Daniel – one of such movements can be traced in Psalms where the psalmist expresses confidence that even death cannot end his relationship with God (e.g. Ps 16:9–1). The second movement towards resurrection belief is seem in the use of resurrection language to express the idea of national restoration (e.g. Hos 6:2). Lucas adds a third instance – these are found in books like Job and Isaiah. Job wants his case to be recorded so that even after he dies a vindicator can acquit him (e.g., Job 19:23–27). Isaiah 53:9–12 seems to point towards the continuation of life beyond the grave. Collins, *Daniel*, 394–396; Lucas, *Daniel*, 302–303.

חֶרְפָּה ("reproach") and דְּרָאוֹן עוֹלָם ("eternal "abhorrence"") to describe the punishment (Dan 12:2). They are the antitheses to חַיֵּי עוֹלָם ("eternal life"), which was examined above. Anne Gardner examines the instances of חֶרְפָּה ("reproach") in the HB and finds that it is often borne by the innocent,[65] but is also something that God brings upon the wicked.[66] In the prophets, within Israel חֶרְפָּה ("reproach") is God's punishment on his people for violation of the covenant stipulations.[67] She concludes, "contravention of the Torah is the main reason for such punishment."[68]

The other word used to describe the punishment of the wicked, דְּרָאוֹן ("abhorrence" Dan 12:2), is rare, occurring elsewhere only in Isaiah 66:24. Although Nickelsburg excises this word as a gloss, he does note that דְּרָאוֹן ("abhorrence") has also never appeared in any of the Qumran material to date.[69] Even if verse 24 were indeed a later interpolation, in its final form, apart from necessitating an analysis, it also links Daniel 12:2 and Isaiah 66:24. It is interesting that in both occurrences of this term the context is that of the punishment of the wicked. This has attracted scholarly attention. Both Greenspoon[70] and James Lindenberger,[71] who assume the primacy of the Isaianic text, note that the use of דְּרָאוֹן ("abhorrence") in Daniel 12:2 is intentional and meant to evoke the imagery in Isaiah 66:24 of the fate of those who rebelled against the LORD. Compositional primacy of the texts notwithstanding, דְּרָאוֹן ("abhorrence") in Isaiah 66:24 provides a significant parallel with which to read Daniel 12:2.

In Isaiah 66, the rebels are not raised from the dead; rather their bodies lie exposed, eternally consumed by worms and fire. The words in Isaiah 66:24, תּוֹלַעְתָּם לֹא תָמוּת וְאִשָּׁם לֹא תִכְבֶּה ("their worm will not die, their fire will not be quenched"), which was examined in the introduction chapter, indicate that their abhorrent state is perpetual. Claus Westermann states that this

---

65. For instance, Job 19:5; Jer 15:5.
66. As in Ps 78:66; Prov 6:33.
67. For instance, in Jer 24:9; 29:28; 32:40 and Ezek 5:8, 14; 22:4–12.
68. Gardner, "Way to Eternal Life," 11, n. 16.
69. Nickelsburg, *Resurrection, Immortality*, 33, n 51. For Nickelsburg this is one of the reasons why דְּרָאוֹן is likely to be a gloss. However, even if one considers it as a later addition, rejecting it does not help explain the final form of the text.
70. Greenspoon, "Origin of the Idea," 284.
71. Lindenberger, "Daniel 12:1–4," 183–184.

verse contains "the earliest idea of hell," a destination for those who rebelled against the LORD. He notes that the "everlasting annihilation" in the valley of Hinnom[72] was the counterpart of the "everlasting worship" in the temple. History and its activities thus become focused on these two localities – the valley of Hinnom and the Temple – and those who go to the temple to worship see "the dead bodies of men whose annihilation is forever," a state that is דֵרָאוֹן (an "abhorrence") to all flesh. He states, "this means seeing the confirmation of God's victory over all his enemies."[73] It is worth noting that the Valley of Hinnom, *gēhinnom* (Aramaic), later transliterated as γέεννα ("Gehenna") in the Septuagint and usually translated as "hell" in English translations, earned its notoriety as the place of torment from the incident recorded in 2 Kings 16:3 – King Ahaz takes his apostasy to the extreme by sacrificing his son to Molech, presumably at the Valley of Hinnom (cf. 2 Kgs 23:10). In the NT Jesus links Gehenna with Isaiah 66:24 when he uses the language of the verse to describe Gehenna as the eventual place for those who do not disassociate from sin (Mark 9:47–48).[74] Later Jewish writings also allude to Isaiah 66:24 in expressing the idea of condemnation, for instance fire and worm are the punishment for those who do not humble themselves (Sirach 7:17), and the means of God's vengeance upon those nations who rise up against God's people (Judith 16:17).[75] Consequently, as Bernstein states, burning, shame, wickedness, and death became associated with the Valley of Hinnom and the valley became "ripe for metaphorical extension into a place of torment,"[76] eventually taking on the characteristics of and becoming synonymous with the underworld.[77] Hence, the word דֵרָאוֹן ("abhorrence") as depicted in Daniel 12:2 and Isaiah 66:24 recalls the awful punishment awaiting the unfaithful.

---

72. The valley of Hinnom was located south of Jerusalem, and at the center of the valley of Hinnom was Topheth, a high place. Josiah would later destroy the altar at Topheth in Hinnom to prevent child sacrifices to Molech as part of his religious reform (2 Kgs 23:10).

73. Westermann, *Isaiah 40–66*, 428.

74. Evans, *Mark 8:27–16:20*, 71–72; Mann, *Mark: A New Translation*, 383; McKenzie, *Second Isaiah*, 208. It must be noted that not all scholars think that the NT references to Gehenna imply eternal punishment. For instance, see Albright and Mann, *Matthew: A New Translation*, 61–62.

75. Evans, *Mark 8:27–16:20*, 71–72.

76. Bernstein, *Formation of Hell*, 168–169.

77. Bailey, "Gehenna: Topography of Hell," 187.

It is unclear what exactly this state of abhorrence and everlasting shame of the wicked in Dan 12:2 entails and, as Lucas observes, there is no indication that it includes eternal suffering.[78] However, both Collins and Lucas state that Daniel 12:2 suggests the wicked will be resurrected to experience this shame consciously.[79] Further, as mentioned earlier, the text posits the righteous being rewarded with חַיֵּי עוֹלָם ("eternal life") is an antithesis to the fate of the wicked. As Jon Levenson explains, if חַיֵּי עוֹלָם ("eternal life") is understood as in terms of duration, the implication for the wicked would be that they are raised only to be humiliated and die a second death after it. However, alternatively, חַיֵּי עוֹלָם ("eternal life") could also be understood in terms of quality; in which case, the righteous survive in perpetual bliss and vindication, the wicked survive also in perpetuity but in disgrace.[80] Moreover, if Daniel 12:2 goes beyond Isaiah 26:19's resurrection of God's people alone to envisage a double resurrection, a postulation emanating from dating Daniel to second century BCE, it is reasonable to surmise that here too the author of Daniel goes beyond Isaiah 66:24 – where the rebels seem to endure their abhorrence in perpetuity as unburied corpses – to envisage resurrected wicked who experience their disgrace not just perpetually but also consciously. Whatever the precise nature of their punishment it is likely that it was conceived as worse than shadowy existence in Sheol. As described by both Venn Pilcher and Lindenberger, the wicked are resurrected because "the neutral oblivion of Sheol"[81] was deemed "inadequate for their crimes."[82]

4.4.2. Section Conclusion

Resurrection in Daniel 12:1–3 is not the end in itself but functions as a means through which post-mortem divine retribution is affected. By positing a double resurrection, the Daniel passage goes one step further than the conception of resurrection in Isaiah 26 where resurrection was only for the righteous and functioned as the reward itself. Resurrection of the wicked along with the righteous highlights the vindication of the righteous by the

---

78. Lucas, *Daniel*, 295, 304.
79. Lucas, 295, 304.
80. Levenson, *Resurrection and the Restoration*, 190. This view of eternal life being qualitative rather than just duration is also expressed by Davies, *Daniel*, 116.
81. Lindenberger, "Daniel 12:1–4," 183.
82. Pilcher, *Hereafter in Jewish*, 142, cited in Stele, *Resurrection in Daniel 12*, 58.

stark contrast between the fates of the groups. The righteous rise from the dust to a glorious existence; the wicked rise, also from the dust, but become an abhorrence, perhaps a loathsome sight to all who see them, to use the words of Isaiah 66:24. Thus, however brief and elusive the imagery may be, there is no doubt that there is post-mortem divine retribution in Daniel 12:2–3, and the contrast between the post-mortem fates of the righteous and the wicked highlights the fact.

4.5. Basis and Aspect of Post-mortem Divine Retribution

Having examined the function of resurrection in post-mortem divine retribution, the question arises as to what the basis for the retribution is, the answer to which would further help identify the aspect of divine retribution emphasized here. To begin with, a better understanding of the basis of retribution post resurrection rests on the identification of the resurrected ones, the רַבִּים ("many") who wake up from sleep in Dan 12:2. There is a myriad of interpretations among scholars regarding the identity of the רַבִּים in Daniel 12:2. For the purpose of discerning the basis of divine retribution they can be broadly classified as two lines of interpretation, although there are several nuanced positions within each one.[83]

4.5.1. "Many" As "All"

The first line of interpretation is one that views resurrection in Daniel 12:2 as referring to the final resurrection at the coming of Christ. Scholars who favour this understanding of the text often read רַבִּים as "all" – inclusive of Israel as well as other nations. Augustine espouses this view in his *City of God* when he states that there is no real contradiction in reading "many" in Daniel as "all" in the same manner as used by John the apostle when he says, "all who are in the tombs" (Jn 5:28).[84] This interpretation often takes into account the Semitic range of possible meanings of רַבִּים that includes "all."[85] Di Lelle, although he

---

[83]. For a quick overview of the different views and the authors associated with each view, see Stele, *Resurrection in Daniel 12*, 38–66.

[84]. Stevenson and Glerup, *Ezekiel, Daniel*, 304.

[85]. Baldwin, *Daniel*, 204; also, cf. Di Lella who considers "all" as a possible interpretation for רַבִּים in this verse since "all" is within the Semitic range of meanings for רַבִּים; however,

eventually decides against it, states that reading רַבִּים as "all" finds corroboration in Isaiah 52:14, 53:12 and some Qumran texts where רַבִּים ("many") or הָרַבִּים ("the many") are used to express the idea of "the multitude, the community, the totality."[86] However, this line of interpretation has a few problems. To make a case for רַבִּים as "all" in this passage also grammatically requires the preposition מִן in רַבִּים מִיְשֵׁן (v. 2), to be explicative – as in "many, *that is*, those who sleep." As Goswell points out, the explicative usage for מִן is rare,[87] and מִן is "most naturally taken in its partitive sense,"[88] indicating that only a part of the whole is referred to here. Hence, the more likely reading would be "some *from among* those who sleep" will wake up while others will not.

However, even though some commentators do not accept reading רַבִּים as "all," they still contend that resurrection of all is implicit in this passage. An example of such an interpretation is that of Carl Friedrich Keil who argues that Jesus makes explicit in John 5:28f what is implicit in Daniel 12:2. Keil recognizes that the text speaks of the people of Daniel which in context is Israel. Nevertheless, according to him Israel at the end of times "consists not merely of Jews or Jewish Christians, but embraces all peoples who belong to God's kingdom of the New Covenant founded by Christ."[89] Scholars like Otto Zöckler[90] and Miller have similar views, although Miller prefers the word "multitude" for רַבִּים, and argues for a time gap of "a thousand years" separating the resurrection of the righteous and the resurrection of the wicked.[91] Generally, this line of interpretation that understands the resurrection

---

he eventually dismisses it. Hartman and Di Lella, *Book of Daniel*, 307. Young considers the interpretation of רַבִּים in the sense of "all" in Daniel as "forced and unnatural." However, he states general resurrection is implied in this passage. He explains this apparent contradiction in his interpretation by arguing that רַבִּים refers to "those who died during the tribulation." According to him, the passage does "not exclude general resurrection" but the focus of the text is to emphasize that salvation "extend[s] also to those who had lost their lives" during the tribulation and hence uses רַבִּים "many." Young, *Daniel*, 256.

86. Hartman and Di Lella, *Book of Daniel*, 30.

87. Goswell, "Resurrection in the Book," 150; Collins, *Apocalyptic Imagination*, 392; Goldingay, *Daniel*, 281.

88. Lucas, *Daniel*, 295; Goswell, "Resurrection in the Book," 150. Parry agrees that מִן is partitive but as limiting the resurrection to "a subset of those who are dead." According to him "many of the dead" include "all of the deceased members of ethnic Israel," leaving unaddressed the question of inclusion or exclusion of the gentiles. Parry, "Desolation of the Temple," 522.

89. Keil, *Biblical Commentary*, 481–483.

90. Zöckler, *Book of the Prophet Daniel*, 262.

91. Miller, *Daniel*, 316–318.

in Daniel 12:1–3 as the final resurrection at the advent of Christ is a reading of the text through a NT lens. One of the reasons Keil, for example, rejects the partial resurrection view for this text is because it contradicts the NT.[92] Likewise, Miller explicitly states that his argument for two separate resurrections is based on other passages like Revelation 20:4–6.[93]

Assuming this interpretation, it follows that the basis of retribution in Daniel 12:2 is whether or not an individual is part of God's kingdom. Miller is more forthcoming on this matter. He states that those who resurrect and are rewarded with eternal life are believers, who in their "new bodies . . . reign with Christ," while those assigned to reproach and eternal contempt are unbelievers, whose foremost sin is that of rejecting the Messiah.[94] Post-mortem divine retribution in this view is not based on human deeds *per se*, since the primary criterion is faith in Christ. This seems to indicate that the aspect of divine retribution at work here is more in line with the theocentric aspect of divine retribution that emphasizes God initiating acts of grace on behalf of humanity and to fulfil his purposes. Nonetheless it is also anthropocentric in as much as the post-mortem divine retribution, according to this interpretation, is a consequence of the human act of choosing whether or not to believe in Christ. Miller upholds human, individual responsibility in post-mortem divine retribution when he states that each person "decides his or her destiny by accepting Christ or rejecting him."[95] According to this interpretation, all persons, whether believers or unbelievers, will be raised from the dead at the end of time. Those who belong to God's kingdom by virtue of believing in Christ will receive eternal life, but the unbelievers who reject Christ are destined for eternal contempt.

4.5.2. "Many" As "Some, Not All"

The second interpretation takes רַבִּים as "many" in the sense of "some, not all," and hence resurrection is partial. רַבִּים is therefore exclusive rather than inclusive, and the preposition מִן functions in its partitive sense of "out of," thus reading "many from among those who sleep." More of interest to the purpose

---

92. Keil, *Biblical Commentary*, 482.
93. Miller, *Daniel*, 318.
94. Miller, 316–317.
95. Miller, 317.

of this dissertation is the interpretation that understands רַבִּים as having only Israel in its purview.⁹⁶ This view is also not without difficulties. It raises the question, "Who are included or excluded in the partial resurrection?" Scholars espousing the partial resurrection view are divided on this question. Some posit that רַבִּים ("many") refers to all Israel, past and present, to the exclusion of other nations.⁹⁷ Gardner, who espouses this view, examines the use of the term רַבִּים in the HB and argues that the Israelites are referred to as רַבִּים and רַב in several occasions.⁹⁸ She also notes that at Qumran "The Many" was used to designate "the community which saw itself as the true Israel,"⁹⁹ and contends that if Daniel were concerned about God's justice it would imply that all Israelites who lived before the persecution were also in view.¹⁰⁰

Other scholars identify the resurrected רַבִּים ("many") as referring only to the Jews of the Antiochene persecution.¹⁰¹ This interpretation of רַבִּים derives support from two considerations. First, the distress that precedes the resurrection in Daniel 12 is described as one that has no precedence in history (Dan 12:1). This makes it unique. Hence, the solution is also designed to address the author and his people who find themselves in this unique situation without necessarily taking all the Israelites from the past into purview.

---

96. A further nuanced position in the partial resurrection view is that only the righteous will be resurrected. This view reads the second occurrence of אֵלֶּה in Daniel 12:2 (lit. "these," translated as "some" in EVs) as not part of the "many" who awake, but rather they are those who do not rise up and are doomed to shame and eternal contempt. Here too, one opinion is that the righteous in general will rise; for example, Tregelles, *Remarks on the Prophetic*, 136, while the other interpretation is that only the righteous Jews are in view; for instance, Kaiser, *More Hard Sayings*, 247.

97. Bevan, *Short Commentary*, 201; Davidson, *Theology of Old Testament*, 528; Gardner, "Way to Eternal Life," 8–9; Sutcliffe, *Old Testament*, 138.

98. For instance, "Pharaoh continued, "Now they are רַבִּים than the people of the land and yet you want them to stop working!" (Exod 5:5), or "Judah and Israel were as רַבִּים as the sand by the sea; they ate and drank and were happy" (1 Kgs 4:20). Gardner, "Way to Eternal Life," 8–9, See also 1 Kgs 3:8; 1 Chr 1:9.

99. Gardner, 9, n. 19.

100. Gardner, 7, n. 16.

101. Martin-Achard, *From Death to Life*, 144; Collins, *Daniel*, 391–392; Elledge, "Resurrection of the Dead," 27; Nickelsburg, *Resurrection, Immortality*, 29–30, 37; DiTommaso, "Deliverance and Justice," 80; Goldingay, *Daniel*, 308. Lucas, *Daniel*, 295; Routledge, "Death and Afterlife," 28. Porteous' understanding is that only the most righteous martyrs will experience resurrection; Porteous, *Daniel*, 170; Spronk views the resurrection as limited to those who did not receive their due compensation before; however, he does not state explicitly whether it is limited only to the Jews or includes individuals from other nations as well. Spronk, *Beatific Afterlife*, 340–341.

Secondly, the perspective in the book of Daniel does not have the history of Israel or its people from the nation's very inception in its purview.[102] The visions consistently engage with the present and future of Israel rather than with the past. Daniel's vision can thus be seen as an attempt to grapple with contemporaneous politics as it affects the fate of his people and the theological issue raised by the persecution of the faithful, and resurrection as a means to bring about divine post-mortem retributive justice.[103] Thus the interpretation of רַבִּים as referring to Jews of a particular period, probably from the author's immediate context (rather than to Jews of all time) is also tenable. Regardless of these differences in opinion, the exclusive view understands רַבִּים as referring only to Israelites. Such a reading brings into sharper focus the contrast, and possible conflict, between faithful Jews and apostates within the covenant community.

4.5.3. Section Conclusion

The two views disagree especially on the time frame of the resurrection presented in Daniel 12:1–3. One sees it as happening at the end times at the second coming of Christ and consequently interpret "many" as referring to all persons. Thus everyone, whether believers or unbelievers, will be raised from the dead at the end of time to face post-mortem divine retribution. The other sees resurrection as imminent during the persecution, and although varying in detail, limits the "many" to Israelites; consequently the righteous and the wicked both stem from this particular community. Nonetheless, both views agree that following resurrection there will be post-mortem retribution for the righteous as well as the wicked. Further, there appears to be a

---

102. Except perhaps in the prayer recorded in Daniel 9:4–19 where he repents for the sins of the forefathers. However, in this instance too the past comes into view because it is seen as affecting the lot of the present Jews (for instance, 9:7–8, 17–18), and some scholars suspect that the prayer is a later interpolation; for instance, Hartman and Di Lella, *Book of Daniel*, 12; Van Deventer, "End of the End," 62–75.

103. The "when" of the resurrection of Daniel 12:2 is also debated. There are three main views: i) resurrection was to take place after Antiochus IV's death and is a failed prophesy, e.g., Collins, *Daniel*, 104, and Towner, *Daniel*, 178; ii) resurrection has already taken place; and iii) resurrection will take place at the end of the world. This issue is not dealt with here because it does not impact the analysis of the basis of post-mortem divine retribution. Some scholars discuss the passage without any specific temporal reference; e.g., Montgomery, *Critical and Exegetical Commentary*, 471.

sub-group among the righteous who receive distinct recognition, and this is examined next.

4.5.4. Post-mortem Reward for the "Wise One"

Among the righteous raised to eternal life, there seems to be another group – the מַשְׂכִּלִים ("wise ones") – who are singled out for special attention. The precise identity of the wise ones is debatable. Opinion is divided on whether the רַבִּים ("many," Dan 12:2) and the מַשְׂכִּלִים are the same or if the מַשְׂכִּלִים refers to a distinct group within the righteous. Scholars like Baldwin, Lucas and Di Lella,[104] identify the wise ones with the righteous who were resurrected to eternal life. They argue that the wise ones are the "true believers," and "not a special class of saints."[105] Baldwin reasons that the wise in bringing others to righteousness are exercising their faith and encouraging others to faith and "this the humblest believer can do."[106] Other scholars consider the מַשְׂכִּלִים as signifying distinguished leaders or teachers among the righteous of the community resurrected in Daniel 12:2.[107] This interpretation of the מַשְׂכִּלִים as denoting a separate group within the righteous has some merit.

First, the term מַשְׂכִּלִים derives from the root verb שׂכל ("to be wise or have insight"), which in the book of Daniel is consistently used in the context of Daniel and his friends. In various forms, the root שׂכל occurs ten times in the book of Daniel, out of which nine times the reference is to Daniel and his friends.[108] This connection between הַמַּשְׂכִּלִים and the use of the root verb שׂכל in the narrative section of Daniel has also been observed by Gregory Goswell, who argues that the wise refers to an elite group rather than to the Israelites in general.[109] It is illuminating to note that this root is never used for the Babylonian wise men in the king's court; they are referred to by the noun חַכִּים ("wise man"). Further, even though there were most probably other

---

104. Hartman and Di Lella, *Book of Daniel*, 309.

105. Lucas, *Daniel*, 302, 319. He does admit that it is possible to interpret מַשְׂכִּלִים in 11:33 as "teachers," distinct from the faithful.

106. Baldwin, *Daniel*, 206.

107. Young, *Daniel*, 257; Nicklesburg, *Resurrection, Immortality*, 38; Spronk, *Beatific Afterlife*, 341; Levenson, *Resurrection and the Restoration*, 182; Goldingay, *Daniel*, 308.

108. Moore, "Resurrection and Immortality," 31.

109. Goswell, "Resurrection in the Book," 148. In Goswell's view, the deliverance in Daniel 6 and 3 of Daniel and his friends respectively, who are described with the root שׂכל, foreshadows the resurrection of הַמַּשְׂכִּלִים in Daniel 12.

Jewish exiles serving in the king's court, Daniel and his friends were highlighted as a special group even among the exiles and quickly distinguished themselves above others. Hence it is probable that the term מַשְׂכִּלִים is being used in a distinctive manner here as well.

Secondly, the language here is strongly reminiscent of Isaiah's description of the Servant[110] who is,

1. referred to with the same root verb שׂכל – הִנֵּה יַשְׂכִּיל עַבְדִּי ("Behold, my Servant will prosper/act wisely" Isa 52:13) and
2. the Servant's work is described as יַצְדִּיק צַדִּיק עַבְדִּי לָרַבִּים ("the righteous one, my servant, will make many righteous" Isa 53:11).

The description of the wise in Daniel 12:3 connects them with the language used for the in Isaiah 53:11.[111] The Servant in Isaiah is no ordinary person but Yahweh's Servant who by his suffering brings many to righteousness, a task that Israel failed to fulfill, and is "vindicated and exalted after death."[112] If the author of Daniel is alluding to or drawing from Isaiah's Servant image, it is possible that, while pluralizing Isaiah's wise one by applying the designation ("wise") and the description of the Servant ("make many righteous") to a group, the מַשְׂכִּלִים, the author of Daniel was at the same time expressing with it the idea of something more distinctive, something not entirely democratized. Even if the author of Daniel did not draw from Isaiah, this verbal and thematic connection, in terms of designation and description, with Isaiah's Servant nevertheless renders it a possible reading: that the wise in Daniel are like the Servant both in their suffering, later vindication and even exaltation, and also in being distinct from the whole righteous community to which they belong.

Finally, the author uses parallelism to describe the מַשְׂכִּלִים – וּמַצְדִּיקֵי הָרַבִּים, literally "those who make many righteous" (Dan 12:3). The term מַצְדִּיקֵי is the *hipihil* form of the verb צדק ("to be right or just") and means "to justify." However, in this context it is not referring to justification in the forensic sense

---

110. This Isaianic reference has been recognized by several scholars: Ginsberg, "Oldest Interpretation," 400–404; Collins, *Daniel*, 393; Levenson, *Resurrection and the Restoration*, 188–189; Lindenberger, "Daniel 12:1–4," 184; Spronk, *Beatific Afterlife*, 341; Nickelsburg, *Resurrection, Immortality*, 39; Goswell, "Resurrection in the Book," 148; Goldingay, *Daniel*, 308, Engnell, "'Ebed Yahweh Song," 77, cited in Lester, *Daniel Evokes Isaiah*, 2.

111. Lindenberger, "Daniel 12:1–4," 183.

112. Levenson, *Resurrection and the Restoration*, 189.

but in the sense of making others righteous.¹¹³ Thus, the מַשְׂכִּלִים are teachers and leaders of the community who led others in the way of righteousness, and thus form a distinct subset of the righteous who resurrect to eternal life. Their glorified existence is conveyed through two similes – יַזְהִרוּ כְּזֹהַר הָרָקִיעַ ("they shall shine like the brightness of the sky") and כַּכּוֹכָבִים לְעוֹלָם וָעֶד ("like stars forever and ever"). The precise meaning and implication of the phrases "shining like the brightness of the sky" and "like the stars" has been variously interpreted.

The reward for these מַשְׂכִּלִים ("wise ones") is also distinct. One view is that the resurrected wise ones who are compared to the stars will come back to live in this world with those who have not died.¹¹⁴ However, as Klaas Spronk points out, there is no textual support for the return of the מַשְׂכִּלִים to the earth to continue their earthly life.¹¹⁵ The other view is that the wise achieve an astral afterlife or angelification.¹¹⁶ According to this view the מַשְׂכִּלִים (will be "lifted up high and be like a star high up in heaven,"¹¹⁷ or that upon resurrection the wise will join the angelic host in heaven¹¹⁸ as stars were often identified as angels. Some of the scholars espousing this view see in Daniel 12:3 an influence of the Egyptian and Ugaritic beliefs that the beatific dead become stars. For instance, De Savignac posits that the belief in the glorification of the resurrected probably shows influences of "the Egyptian identification of the beatific dead with the stars."¹¹⁹ Spronk argues for influence from the Ugaritic literature according to which "the deified spirits of the dead" can become like stars, taking their place among the heavenly host.¹²⁰ The extent of Egyptian and Ugaritic influence on this Danielic text is impossible to determine, and by itself is insufficient to make a case for this view.

However, there is potential textual support for this view from the book of Daniel, some Jewish intertestamental texts, and NT texts. Daniel 8:10 states

---

113. Young, *Daniel*, 257.

114. Manson, "Bible and Personal Immortality," 123–124; Sternberger, (1972), 277; Plager, *Das Buch Daniel*, 171; and Lebram, *Das Buch Daniel*, 135; cited in Spronk, *Beatific Afterlife*, 342.

115. Spronk, *Beatific Afterlife*, 342.

116. Thiessen, "Buried Pentateuchal Allusion," 282ff.

117. Spronk, *Beatific Afterlife*, 342.

118. Collins, *Apocalyptic Imagination*, 90–91; DiTommaso also states that the wise will become angels; DiTommaso, "Deliverance and Justice," 80.

119. de Savignac, "L'immortalité de l'âme," 196–204, cited in Spronk, *Beatific Afterlife*, 56.

120. Spronk, 342.

that the small horn exalted itself and attacked צְבָא הַשָּׁמַיִם ("the heavenly host"), causing some of the hosts to fall to the earth, which included some of הַכּוֹכָבִים ("the stars"), and the small horn trampled them. Here צְבָא denotes the heavenly army of which the stars were a part. Also, there are indications that the ancient Israelites and ANE people often identified and worshipped stars as celestial beings.[121] As such the stars are understood to be angelic beings and the passage in Daniel as referring to the astralization or angelification of the wise.[122] The Book of Enoch, an intertestamental Jewish text, for instance, promises that the righteous will "shine like the lights of heaven" (104:2), and in the NT, Jesus states that at resurrection there is no marriage but rather people "are like angels in heaven" (Matt 22:30).[123] Further, Matthew Thiessen notes that early interpreters, both Jewish and Christian, for instance Philo and Irenaeus, understood Yahweh's promise to Abraham comparing his descendants to the stars (Gen 15:5; 22:17; 26:3–4) not only quantitatively but also qualitatively as a promise of the exaltation of Abraham's descendants.[124] This pushes back the argument for understanding the resurrected wise ones as achieving an astral afterlife back into the time of the patriarchs. All these bear out Cavallin's view that the comparison to stars was deliberate and that the angels and stars not only often appear together but are also sometimes identified as being the same.[125] Hence, the view that the resurrected wise ones of Israel become part of the angelic host is not easily dismissed.

One difficulty with this view remains, however. That stars were identified or associated with angelic beings does not conclusively prove that the resurrected in Daniel 12:3 become angels because the text only compares

---

121. Stars were sometimes considered personalized objects of worship (Deut 4:19; 17:3–5), or as Yahweh's servants who fight on behalf of Israel (Judg 5:20), other times the Israelites were forbidden from worshipping the stars who were thought to be divine beings (Jer 19:13). Further, among the peoples of the ANE, Ishtar/Inanna was identified as Venus, and Venus was in turn was believed to be not a planet but one of the brightest stars. Cf. Thiessen, "Buried Pentateuchal Allusion," 283.

122. Thiessen, 278; Goldingay, *Daniel*, 210; Lucas, *Daniel*, 215–216. Dale Allison, in writing about the star that led the wise men to the Jesus, has argued that Jews believed stars were angels. Allison, *Studies in Matthew*, 17–41.

123. Spronk, *Beatific Afterlife*, 342. 2 Baruch 51:10 also says that God's vindicated people will be like angels, equal to stars.

124. Behr, *On the Apostolic Preaching* cited in Thiessen, "Buried Pentateuchal Allusion," 284–287.

125. Cavallin, *Life After Death*, 27.

the מַשְׂכִּלִים to stars rather than state that they become stars.[126] This taking of the language of comparison to imply identification is contested by scholars who do not agree with both the views presented above. The text uses the "כ" particle of comparison to express the state of the wise ones in terms of similes: כְּזֹהַר הָרָקִיעַ ("like the brightness of the sky") and כַּכּוֹכָבִים ("like the stars"). A simile is typically a language of comparison using one thing to describe another, and the two things compared are not one and the same. This is similar to the author's use of the "כ" particle to describe other things he sees in his visions, for instance, his description of the angel in Daniel 10:6

וּגְוִיָּתוֹ כְתַרְשִׁישׁ וּפָנָיו כְּמַרְאֵה בָרָק וְעֵינָיו כְּלַפִּידֵי אֵשׁ וּזְרֹעֹתָיו וּמַרְגְּלֹתָיו כְּעֵין נְחֹשֶׁת קָלָל וְקוֹל דְּבָרָיו כְּקוֹל הָמוֹן:

("His body was like beryl, his face like lightning, his eyes like flaming torches, his arms and legs like the gleam of burnished bronze, and the sound of his words like the roar of a multitude," NRSV).[127] These are understood as comparisons, not literal descriptions of the heavenly being, and there is no indication that the "כ" particle in Daniel 12:3 is used in a different manner.

A further constraint to the literal interpretation is set by the fact that the idea is expressed not just as a simile, but as a poetic simile. As Casey Elledge states, the imagery is used in Daniel 12:3 with a certain "restraint" and its use within a poetic simile in the verse "lacks a more direct equivalence" between the resurrected wise and the stars as is the case in Greek cosmology.[128] It is likely that the author is using known categories to conceptualize and express the yet unknown. Similarly, the language from the passages in Enoch and Matthew also point towards comparison. Jesus' statement on people becoming like angels is to be understood primarily with respect to marriage, an aspect of human life that does not apply to the angels, and which served as the original problem on which the Sadducees based their question on resurrection. It does not necessarily mean that people become angels.[129] Hence, a literal interpretation has its own problem.

---

126. Ollenburger, "If Mortals Die," 33; Levenson, *Resurrection and the Restoration*, 190; Goldingay, *Daniel*, 308; Lucas, *Daniel*, 296; Elledge, *Resurrection of the Dead*, 22.

127. Also in Daniel 7:4, 6.

128. Elledge, *Resurrection of the Dead*, 22.

129. Hanger, *Matthew 14–28*, 641.

What the text does seem to indicate is that the wise partake in some kind of glory and that their exaltation is something to be desired. Levenson may have a point when he argues that at resurrection the body is transformed so that it is "both like and unlike" anything we know;[130] or as Elledge describes it, "a glorified human embodiment."[131] Moreover, to say that they ascend to the heavens and become part of the heavenly host or that they return to the earth to live with those who are still alive is to attempt to say definitely what the text itself expresses only through imagery. As Lorenzo DiTommaso says, the location of the resurrection and the transformation affected thereafter seems less important than the fact of its otherworldliness.[132] The point in Daniel 12:2–3 is the vindication of the righteous and divine justice.[133] This vindication of the wise further emphasizes the anthropocentric aspect of divine retribution by postulating greater reward for those who exhibited a greater degree of faithfulness.

Hence, if the רַבִּים who resurrect refer only to the Jews, and the מַשְׂכִּלִים are a distinct group among the righteous, the following criteria of retribution are discernible: first, if those resurrected are Jews but some are designated for eternal life and others for eternal contempt, it implies that post-mortem divine retribution is not solely based on membership of the covenant community. Being a member of the covenant does not automatically elect the Jews for reward. Thus, the criterion for post-mortem retribution lies somewhere other than membership of the covenant.

Second, if as discussed above, רַבִּים ("many") in Daniel 12:2 consists of some Jews during the Antiochene persecution, rather than all Israel, then those who are raised to eternal life could be said to consist of the faithful Jews, some of whom lost their lives (Dan 11:33), and those who receive eternal

---

130. Levenson, *Resurrection and the Restoration*, 189. Elledge similarly expresses the possibility of the resurrection affecting a transformation of the body. Although, unlike Levenson, he considers the possibility of the "transformation into angelic beings," Elledge, "Resurrection of the Dead," 28. Another issue regarding resurrection concerns if what is resurrected is the body or the soul. The case for the resurrection of the soul seems untenable in the light of the fact that the division of a person into body and soul is not typically a Hebraic category. Moreover, the text does not address the form of the resurrected ones, as Collins says; Collins, *Daniel*, 392. Further, we have argued for a literal resurrection, as opposed to a metaphorical and spiritual one, and it suffices that there is resurrection, and resurrection for retribution at that.

131. Elledge, *Resurrection of the Dead*, 23.

132. DiTommaso, "Deliverance and Justice," 80.

133. So also Levenson, *Resurrection and the Restoration*, 190.

damnation could refer to the Hellenizers, the covenant breakers mentioned in Daniel 11:32, who escaped persecution.[134] This could also apply to Jews in the past since a suffering-righteous and a prosperous-wicked are not unknown categories. As such, though members of the same covenant community, the righteous and the wicked are differentiated by their faithfulness (or unfaithfulness) to Yahweh. More specifically, their adherence to the Torah stipulations becomes the major criterion for post-mortem divine retribution. This – God responding to human deeds with blessing or punishment within the framework of the covenant between Yahweh and Israel – is characteristic of the anthropocentric aspect of divine retribution.

Third, it was also observed that among the righteous raised to eternal life was a distinct group, whom the author calls הַמַּשְׂכִּלִים ("the wise"), who were singled out for special glory (Dan 12:3). Those who risked their lives and led others to righteousness are rewarded with a glorious life. This special reward for the high-risk takers further emphasizes the anthropocentric aspect of the post-mortem divine retribution.

This analysis on post-mortem divine retribution as characteristically anthropocentric is echoed by a few other scholars as well, albeit without using the same terminology. According to Gardner, who views רַבִּים as denoting all Israel, past and present, Israel's covenant with Yahweh meant their fidelity or infidelity became the "yardstick for reward or punishment."[135] She examines the HB to identify what constitutes the ways leading to life and to reproach, and explains the criterion for retribution as "adherence to the covenant, humility or fear of the Lord, following the path of wisdom and association with a righteous one."[136] Levenson rightly points out that covenant membership is both "ascribed" as well as "achieved." Hence by breaking the covenant and refusing to live by its stipulations (Dan 11:32) the wicked reject their "national identity," disqualifying themselves from a share in the fate of the faithful who rise to eternal life for their unwavering faith and adherence to the Torah.[137]

---

134. Nicklesburg, *Resurrection, Immortality*, 36–38; Levenson, *Resurrection and the Restoration*, 184.

135. Gardner, "Way to Eternal Life," 9.

136. Gardner, 19. Gardner, as mentioned earlier, understands רַבִּים ("many") as all Israel, which is a slightly different stance from the one adopted in this dissertation (that is, רַבִּים as referring to some Israelites, not all); however, her conclusion on what constitutes the basis of retribution applies here nonetheless.

137. Levenson, *Resurrection and the Restoration*, 184.

That the deeds of the people during their lifetime are the basis of their post-mortem retribution also finds resonance in DiTommaso's statement, "The martyrs' deaths in the present have an effect on their lives in the future" (ref. Dan 11:35).[138] The wise, who were once persecuted and found themselves in mortal danger for the sake of their faith and Torah obedience (Dan 11:35), now find their fortunes reversed and they receive the highest glory.[139]

4.5.5. Section Conclusion

The post-mortem divine retribution in Daniel 12:1–3 exhibits both a deeds-based and grace-based retribution. The perspective from the HB emphasizes individual faithfulness as the basis of retribution and hence evinces a stronger emphasis on the anthropocentric aspect of divine retribution. The NT perspective alternatively brings with it an emphasis on salvation by faith in Christ and therefore lends post-mortem divine retribution its more theocentric slant, although there are also instances of an anthropocentric aspect. Nevertheless, whether it is in the old covenant or the new, while still operating within the framework of the covenant that God initiated, and thereby under God's grace, his people are bound by the covenant and are judged based on their deeds. The deed may be the act of choosing to place one's faith in Christ and living accordingly, or their fidelity to the Torah stipulations and way of life. At resurrection, each receives the consequences of his or her own choice and deeds. The reward for the wise for going above and beyond the call of individual faithfulness in leading others also to righteousness further emphasizes the anthropocentric aspect of post-mortem divine retribution. Hence post-mortem divine retribution in Daniel 12:1–3 exhibits the characteristic of the anthropocentric aspect that emphasizes God's response to human deeds within a theocratic framework.

4.6. Nature of Divine Retribution: An Emphasis on Individuals

The nature of divine retribution in Daniel 12:1–3 evinces a greater emphasis on individual responsibility. The analysis in the above section has brought

---

138. DiTommaso, "Deliverance and Justice," 86.
139. Willis, *Dissonance and the Drama*, 170.

out much of the individual emphasis of post-mortem divine retribution in Daniel. As discussed above, post-mortem retributive justice in Daniel 12:1–3 is individuated with each one receiving their due recompense based on their actions during their lifetime. If one considers resurrection as restricted to only Israel, the individual nature of divine retribution comes into play in that it is the person's fidelity or infidelity to the covenant, and not mere membership in the covenant community, that determines his or her post-mortem fate. Such a differentiated fate among the covenant people highlights an interest in the individual nature of divine retribution.[140]

Alternatively, if the resurrection in view is the final resurrection at the end of time, the individual nature of divine retribution is seen in that each person during his or her lifetime makes the choice of believing in Jesus or rejecting him. Jerome similarly understands that the fate of the resurrected is "in accordance with the merits of each."[141] Further, the fate of the resurrected wise, as distinct from the righteous ones, underlines this individual and anthropocentric aspect of retribution. As DiTomasso surmises, there is perhaps "a measure of personal choice on the part of individuals."[142] The "wise" risk much and in turn are rewarded with special distinction over and above the general righteous in the community.

This individual emphasis is different from the corporate emphasis; however, as Collins says, it is not necessarily opposed to it.[143] For those who see the resurrected ones as restricted to Israel, first, retribution of the resurrected ones is still within the context of the covenant between God and his people. It is the covenant that sets the paradigms for obedience and disobedience and delineates the consequences for each.[144] Hence, the interest in individuals and the standard by which their deeds are measured is defined by and within the bounds of the covenant with the community. Secondly, although Daniel 12:1–3 does not state explicitly its interest in the corporate nature of retribution, the book as a whole evinces concern for the fate of the nation Israel. It exhibits two levels of conflict – an ongoing, primary conflict between the

---

140. DiTommaso, "Deliverance and Justice," 86.
141. Stevenson and Glerup, *Ezekiel, Daniel*, 306.
142. DiTommaso, "Deliverance and Justice," 85.
143. Collins, *Daniel*, 386.
144. Gardner, "Way to Eternal Life," 9.

foreign nations and the Jews as a whole, and a conflict of interest among the Jews themselves, between the faithful and the unfaithful, or between those who collaborate with foreign elements and those who resist. The internal conflict finds its resolution in Daniel 12:1–3 in the individuated retributive justice that results in the triumph of the faithful and the damnation of the wicked. It can be argued that this individuated post-mortem retribution in turn leads to the triumph of Israel as a nation: if as argued earlier, the wicked, by collaborating with foreign interests and rejecting the Torah, excluded themselves from their Jewish identity, then the faithful who received eternal life and exaltation now constitute the real Israel.[145] Such being the case, the wicked, and along with them the interest of the foreign nations, are defeated in a final and ultimate reversal of fate at the resurrection and exaltation of the righteous and the wise ones, and the nation of Israel once again emerges triumphant. Therefore, while the divine retribution in Daniel 12:1–3 is individuated, it ultimately leads the reconstitution and triumph of the corporate expression of God's people.

4.7. Conclusion

The significance of Daniel 12:1–3 derives from its singular expression of the hope of resurrection. There are numerous issues in this short text, and they may continue to be contentious. The date of the book, so determinative for its interpretation, has persistently evaded definitive conclusion and consequently scholars remain divided on several crucial questions raised by the book. As such, this chapter presented the interpretation of the passage, wherever applicable, from both perspectives, that is, 12:1–3 as an eschatological prophecy (early date view) and as a prophecy concerning Antiochus IV's expected end (late date view).

This brief examination of the passage demonstrates that resurrection as portrayed in Daniel 12:1–3 leads to a post-mortem retribution for the righteous as well as the wicked – a rare statement in the HB, although it is neither as explicit nor as elaborate as one would have liked. Resurrection functions not as a reward, but as the means through which divine retribution, whether reward or punishment, was achieved. The passage also portrays a more

---

145. Similarly, Levenson, *Resurrection and the Restoration*, 184.

anthropocentric and individualized aspect of divine retribution by portraying human deeds committed during one's lifetime as the basis for post-mortem divine retribution. The two groups of people, the wicked and the faithful, with the wise as a subset of the faithful, are adjudicated to inversely corresponding post-mortem fates in relation to their earthly lives. This inversion of the post-mortem fates affects divine justice – those who unjustly suffered the most receiving the highest glory and those who prospered while alive by being disloyal to the covenant being exposed to reproach and eternal contempt.

Further, the resurrection and subsequent retribution may be individuated, but viewed in its larger context of the book of Daniel, victory for God's people emerges. The wicked, having been identified more with foreign elements than with the covenant way of life are defeated, whereas the faithful who are essentially the real people of God receive the gifts of eternal life and glory. Hence, within the larger context of the book of Daniel the resurrection text betrays its corporate interest as well.

CHAPTER 5

Post-mortem Divine Retribution in the Book of Watchers 22

5.1. Introduction

The last two chapters examined the concept of post-mortem divine retribution in the HB as evinced in Isaiah 26:14, 19 and Daniel 12:1–3. The picture that emerged was rather indistinct and far from comprehensive. Nonetheless, a few definite developments and metamorphoses in the concept of post-mortem retribution were traceable in these two texts: emergence of a moral distinction of the inhabitants of Sheol as righteous or wicked, the development of the notion of post-mortem divine retribution, and a relatively clearer expression of the idea of resurrection, which serves either as the reward itself (Isaiah 26) or as a means through which retribution is achieved (Daniel 12). We also observed some elements of continuity between divine retribution in Deuteronomy and divine retribution in these two texts.

The following two chapters will examine selected texts from the extra-biblical Jewish literature of the Second Temple period (STP) – the Book of Watchers (BW) 22, and 2 Maccabees 7 – to observe the formulations of post-mortem divine retribution during the STP and to see if there is any continuity with patterns of divine retribution in Deuteronomy. In general, the extra-biblical literature exhibits more drastic changes in the conception of the nature of afterlife as compared to the HB,[1] and the presentation of ideas

---

1. Russell, *Method and Message*, 359.

is significantly more detailed. The typical presentation of the afterlife in the HB as undifferentiated shades eking out an existence in dark and dusty Sheol is replaced by clearer expectations of retribution in the afterlife, albeit with astounding variations. For instance, sometimes the afterlife is experienced by the discarnate souls or spirits of individuals who "survive as individual conscious beings,"[2] as will be seen in BW, and at other times the expectation is of a resurrection and physical reconstitution, as will be evident in 2 Maccabees. At any rate, the afterlife fates envisioned in these extra-biblical texts are complex and go much beyond the baby steps taken in the HB.

The Second Temple section of the dissertation begins with BW 22 which has the distinction of being unparalleled among early Jewish traditions in presenting not only a differentiation of fates between the righteous and sinners but also a sub-categorization of sinners for different post-mortem fates.[3] The BW is part of the collection known variously as the Book of Enoch, 1 Enoch, or Ethiopic Enoch. 1 Enoch is not so much a book as it is a collection of writings, consisting of five books with two small appendices.[4] These books are bound together by their reference to Enoch, and shared motifs and allusions.[5] It derives its authority from the pseudonymous claim to the biblical character Enoch, the son of Seth, described briefly in Genesis 5:18–24, who is presented as having received the heavenly mysteries contained in 1 Enoch. At the narrative level this anchors the book in antediluvian times, the very beginning of the biblical period, and makes Enoch the first of the prophets of Yahweh.

This chapter begins by locating the BW in the Enochic corpus and by presenting a brief overview of the contents of the BW to provide a context for BW 22. It then examines the view that the collection of 1 Enoch espouses

---

2. Russell, 357–358.

3. Collins, "Afterlife in Apocalyptic Literature," 121–122.

4. Nicklesburg views the collection as a literary unity that grew overtime, cf. Nicklesburg, *1 Enoch 1*, 25–26. However, others see it more as a loose collection of books as no fragment of the Book of Parables was found at Qumran where Aramaic ms. fragments for the four other booklets were found; and the Astronomical Book was attested among the Qumran finds of 1 Enoch but seemed to have circulated as an independent entity as it was always found on a separate scroll from the other three which were found together in one scroll. Further, that three parts were found together in a single scroll in Aramaic does not prove that they form a unity. The Greek mss. show that the Book of the Watchers and the Epistle of Enoch circulated independently for a long time. See Tiller, "George Nickelsburg's '1 Enoch,'" 367–368, and Collins, "An Enochic Testament," 366–377; Bauckham, "Apocalypses," 135–136; Knibb, "Book of Enoch," 35; Macaskill, *Revealed Wisdom*.

5. See Collins, "How Distinctive was Enochic," 18.

a distinct and competing strand of Judaism called Enochic Judaism. The rationale for discussing this view is also stated below. In examining texts from the HB, arguments had to be made for reading the texts as referring to post-mortem retribution. In contrast, BW 22 is explicit in its reference to post-mortem divine retribution. As such, the chapter looks instead at the various elements in the BW 22 that showcase this interest. This is followed by an examination of the basis and aspect of post-mortem divine retribution in BW 22 in relation to the aspects of divine retribution in Deuteronomy. The chapter concludes with an investigation that seeks to answer whether post-mortem divine retribution in the BW 22 operates on the individual or corporate level.

To begin, a quick look at its composite nature, the location of the BW within the Enochic corpus, and a brief overview of the content of the BW to facilitate an understanding of the larger context of BW 22.

5.2. 1 Enoch

The books comprising the collection of 1 Enoch are generally considered to have been composed between the third century BCE and the turn of the millennium:[6]

> The Book of the Watchers (chs. 1–36; third century BCE)[7]
> The Book of the Parables or the Similitudes
>   (chs. 37–71; first century BCE)
> The Astronomical Book or Book of the Luminaries
>   (chs. 72–82; third century BCE)
> The Book of Dream Visions or Book of Dreams
>   (chs. 83–90; second century BCE)
> The Epistle of Enoch (chs. 91–105; second century BCE)[8]
>   The Birth of Noah (chs. 106–107)
>   Another Book of Enoch (ch. 108)

---

6. Nickelsburg, *1 Enoch 1*, 1.

7. Beckwith, "Earliest Enoch Literature," 371.

8. The dates assigned to each part are the generally accepted dates. See Reed, "Textual Identity, 284.

Another probable literary unit of 1 Enoch is called the Book of Giants, fragments of which were discovered among the Qumran Aramaic mss.[9] Before this discovery the Book of Giants was only known because the Manichaeans preserved it[10] in the third century AD.[11] Except perhaps for the unit known as the Book of Parables (chs. 37–71) and chapter 108,[12] the rest of 1 Enoch is considered to be of Semitic origin, Aramaic or even Hebrew.[13] However, the complete text of 1 Enoch is extant only in the Ethiopic version in the Ge'ez language, discovered in 1773, which is generally considered to be a translation of a Greek *Vorlage*. The fragments of Greek manuscript[14] constitute about a third of 1 Enoch and is in turn a rendering from an Aramaic version or Semitic text.[15] The Aramaic fragments of 1 Enoch consist of a mere 5 percent of the Ethiopic version[16] and were discovered at Qumran.

This chapter examines chapter 22 from the Book of the Watchers (1 Enoch 1–36). The BW is also a composite work[17] and is variously subdivided, but a broad five parts division can be made as follows:

---

9. Milik, ed., with Black, *Books of Enoch*, 4.

10. Manichaeism was a religious movement founded in the third century CE by the prophet Mani (216–276 CE) in the Sasanian Empire, the last pre-Islamic Persian Empire. Manichaeism was for a time misunderstood as a Christian heresy. Baker-Brian, *Manichaeism*, 1–2; "Manichaeism: Ancient Religious Movement."

11. Milik says that the Manichaeans "canonized" the Book of Giants. Milik, *Books of Enoch*, 4; Nickelsburg, *1 Enoch 1*, 8.

12. Among the many Aramaic fragments of 1 Enoch discovered in Qumran there was none that corresponded to the Book of Parables. See Milik, *Books of Enoch*, 4; Nickelsburg, *1 Enoch 1*, 9.

13. Milki considers Aramaic to be the original language, cf. Milik, *Books of Enoch*. But others like Charles argue for a Hebrew original in chapters 37–71, still others like Matthew Black, Knibb and Nickelsburg leave open the question of the possibility of a Hebrew original. cf. Charles, *Book of Enoch*, lxi–lxviii; Black, *Book of Enoch*, 3;. Davidson, *Angels at Qumran*, 18; Nickelsburg, *1 Enoch 1*, 9; Knibb, "Book of Enoch," 21ff.

14. The Greek manuscript found at Akhmim in 1886–1887 is called Codex Panopolitanus or Akhmim, Gk^a.

15. For a more nuanced argument on "translation" of the text from one language to the other refer to Knibb who argues that the Ge'ez and Greek texts are not straight translations but that these versions underwent revisions at different stages of development and differ in literary and historical context, i.e., from a Jewish context to a Christian one. Knibb, "Book of Enoch," 21–40.

16. Black, *Book of Enoch*, 1, 3–4; Nickelsburg, *1 Enoch 1*, 1.

17. Collins, "Apocalyptic Technique," 95; VanderKam, *From Revelation to Canon*, 281; Wright, *Origin of Evil Spirits*, 15; Macaskill, *Revealed Wisdom*, 30.

Chapters 1–5	Introduction[18]
Chapters 6–11	Descent of the Watchers
Chapters 12–16	Enoch's interaction with the Watchers and commission to announce God's judgment on them
Chapters 17–19	Enoch's first guided heavenly journey
Chapters 20–36	Enoch's second guided heavenly journey

One of the primary concerns of the BW is God's coming judgment on the whole world.[19] This coming judgment is portrayed in a series of otherworldly journeys that Enoch embarks on (1 Enoch 17–36).[20] These journeys take Enoch to the places of final judgment prepared for the fallen angels or Watchers,[21] the disobedient stars, and humanity.

The sins and evil doings resulting in the divine judgments are narrated in BW 6–16 which traces the origin of evil and the spread of impurity on earth to the fallen angels. In cohabiting with mortal women (12:4; 15:3) the Watchers violate the divinely designated boundary between that which belongs to the realm of the heavens and that which belongs to the earthly realm.[22] The spiritual, eternal, and immortal (15:6) commingled with the material, finite, and eradicable, resulting in the birth of the giants (7: 2; 15:8). The dual nature of the giants meant that their flesh would die but their spirits would be eternal.[23] Upon death, the giants' evil spirits were released on earth creating a realm of demons, responsible for evil in the world, and afflicting humanity (15:8–11)

---

18. Earlier 1 Enoch 1–5 was considered to be an introduction not only to the Book of the Watchers, but to the whole Enochic corpus written by a later redactor or editor. However, this assumption has been overturned by the discovery of Aramaic fragments of chapter 1–5 indicating that they were written early. See Milik, *The Books of Enoch*, 144; Wright, *Origin*, 15–16. So, although BW 1–5 are still considered as introduction to 1 Enoch by some, it should be noted that it was part of the BW before 1 Enoch reached its final form.

19. The coming divine judgment as the central motif of the Enochic corpus is a view held by scholars like Nickelsburg, *1 Enoch 1*, 37–56; Collins, "How Distinctive," 19; and Paul Heger, *Challenges to Conventional*, 127–130. Also see Young Namgung on the hermeneutical importance of introductions (here, BW 1–5 an oracle of judgment), as well as conclusions for the interpretation of any text. Namgung, "Sin and Human Accountability," 97.

20. Unless otherwise stated, all citations of 1 Enoch are from Nickelsburg and VanderKam, *1 Enoch*.

21. The Watchers were possibly a class of angels who had the responsibility of keeping watch (20:1). See Wright, *Origin*, 98–100.

22. Nickelsburg, *1 Enoch 1*, 229.

23. Nickelsburg, *1 Enoch 1*, 229.

until the end when all these will be called into account (16:1). Enoch is commissioned to announce the divine judgment to the Watchers – the Watchers will be imprisoned, the giants will be killed, and the earth will be inundated, and resolution to all sin and impurity on earth will come at the final judgment (10:4–11:2). and Enoch's journeys (1 Enoch 17–36) are presumably designed to enable him to better grasp the extensiveness of Yahweh's coming judgment.[24] It is in one of these journeys that 1 Enoch 22 describes. In this journey, Enoch visits a mountain that serves as an intermediate repository for the souls of the dead and the sights he sees are explained by the accompanying angel, Raphael.

However, before getting into the text of BW 22, a brief detour discussing a particular aspect of the reception history of 1 Enoch is necessary. Enochian scholars have proposed that 1 Enoch presents a distinct strand of Judaism called Enochic Judaism, the details of which will be discussed shortly.[25] It is uncertain if the BW, which is dated to the third century BCE, was read as espousing a different kind of Judaism before it became a part of 1 Enoch, which came together sometime in the CE.[26] But within the collection of 1 Enoch as it now stands, the contents of the BW have been interpreted in this manner and to this we briefly turn.

5.3. Enochic Judaism

Some scholars have perceived 1 Enoch as espousing a Judaism whose distinctiveness warrants its being spoken of as an alternative to mainstream Torah-centred Judaism.[27] For instance, Corrado Martone perceives the theology of the Enochic corpus to be so divergent from the Torah that he deems it

---

24. Venter, "Allotted Place," 675.

25. Since the approach adopted in this thesis is a reception-centred intertextuality, this claim does not preclude studying the BW 22 intertextually with a Mosaic text, in this case Deuteronomy. Whether these claims hold out or not, the results of an intertextual study will be gainful. If the Enochic Judaism claims are not sustainable, the investigation would proceed as did the previous chapters. If it holds out, it would be interesting to see how different or similar is the conception of the divine retribution in Mosaic and non-Mosaic traditions.

26. Kiel, *"Whole Truth"*, 101; Knibb, "Book of Enoch"; Stuckenbruck, "Book of Enoch," 8–9.

27. Scholars espousing this view include Boccaccini, *Beyond the Essene Hypothesis*; Collins, "How Distinctive," 17–34; Nickelsburg, *1 Enoch 1*, 50; Kvanvig, "Enoch – From Sage," 48–51. Martone, "Enochic Tradition," 51–55; See Bedenbender, "Place of the Torah"; Suter, "Fallen Angel, Fallen Priest," 115–35; Macaskill, *Revealed Wisdom*, see especially 47.

necessary to question the accuracy of "Jewish" as an epithet for it.[28] Gabriele Boccaccini, one of the staunch proponents of this view, coined the term "Enochic Judaism"[29] as a designation for this Judaism evinced in the Enochic writings. The question that arises is: is 1 Enoch distinctive enough to warrant discussion as an alternative to the Torah-centred Judaism?

Proposing a different strand of Judaism is not new. Some scholars consider it more accurately reflective of the reality of STP Judaism to speak of diversity of Judaism, "Judaisms," or distinctive movements within Judaism, rather than a monotonic Judaism because of the varying emphases of the different strands of Judaism during this period,[30] perhaps something akin to the many denominations under the umbrella called Protestant Christianity. However, some proponents of Enochic Judaism pose Enoch and Moses as ideological opponents, presenting competing perspectives on understanding the world. This strand of thought probably has its roots in G. H. Dix who spoke of an Enochic Pentateuch as early as in 1926.[31] This proposition of an Enochic Judaism as an alternative to Torah-centred Judaism is based on two principal observations: i) 1 Enoch's reticence on certain markers of Torah Judaism – Moses, Torah, Sinai covenant, and ii) 1 Enoch's explanation of sin as originating from the misdeeds of the Watchers. While the argument for Enochic Judaism takes the whole of 1 Enoch into its purview, the following discussion will concentrate primarily, although not exclusively, on the BW for the following reasons: i) the mythic core constituting 1 Enoch's version of the origin of sin is in the BW, ii) each part of the Enochic corpus "has its own emphasis" regarding evil and sin,[32] iii) the BW has often been characterized as strongly non-Mosaic or anti-Mosaic more than the other books of 1 Enoch,[33] and iv) the Enochic passage of interest for the present study, 1 Enoch 22, is in the BW.

---

28. Martone, "Enochic Tradition," 51–55 (53).

29. Boccaccini, *Beyond the Essene*, xv. According to Boccaccini the Enochic Judaism and the Essene Judaism are the same mainstream group (165ff).

30. Neusner, "Comparing Judaisms," 177–191; Michael L. Satlow suggests that Judaism is best seen as a "family of tradition." See Satlow, *Creating Judaism*, 5–7.

31. Dix, "Enochic Pentateuch," 29–42. Later Milik also proposed the existence at some point of an Enochic Pentateuch. Milik, "Problèmes de la Littérature," 333–378. Milik's theory are cited and critiqued by Greenfield and Stone, "Enochic Pentateuch," 51–65.

32. Nickelsburg, *1 Enoch 1*, 46.

33. Bachmann, "Book of the Watchers," 6.

5.3.1. Insignificance of Moses and Torah in 1 Enoch

The absence of figures and institutions central to Mosaic Judaism, like Moses, Sinai covenant, Torah,[34] in the Enochic literature raise questions regarding their significance and is cited as evidence of their displacement in Enochic Judaism. For instance, Boccaccini states, "The Enochians completely ignore the Mosaic Torah and the Jerusalem temple."[35] George Nicklesburg states that the Mosaic Law and covenant were not of "central importance" to the authors of 1 Enoch.[36] Instead, Enoch was revered as the revealer of wisdom or mysteries,[37] and the knowledge of right and wrong, the "law and its interpretation," on which divine retribution is based, is embodied in "revealed wisdom," which Enoch received upon ascending to heaven (81:1–83:3; 104:12–13).[38] As such, revealed wisdom replaces the Torah[39] and becomes the source and criterion for divine judgment of human conduct. However, this argument needs to be considered in light of the following reasons.

First, methodologically, Enochic Judaism and community is a hypothesis based on the silence of 1 Enoch regarding Mosaic elements rather than on positive evidence. As Paul Heger[40] rightly points out, an argument from silence can hardly be sustained, especially for an idea as radical as a rejection of or rivalry to the Mosaic Torah. He observes that no other source points towards the existence of an Enochic Judaism, neither positively nor as a reaction.[41] In the absence of any positive evidence, Enochic Judaism is more likely a scholarly construct.

---

34. 1 Enoch 93:6 contains the only explicit reference to the Mosaic covenant or Torah in the Enochic literature, with possible allusions to it in 99:2, "everlasting covenant," and 106:13, "the covenant of heaven." Nickelsburg, *1 Enoch 1*, 446. However, since the Ethiopic term *sher'ata* can be translated as "covenant" as well as "law," Bedenberder states that even the term *sher'ata* in 93:6 is more appropriately translated as "law" rather than as "covenant." See Bedenbender, "Place of the Torah," 75.

35. Boccaccini, *Beyond the Essene*, 74.
36. Nickelsburg, *1 Enoch 1*, 50.
37. Collins, "How Distinctive," 33.
38. Nickelsburg, *1 Enoch 1*, 52.
39. See Nickelsburg, "Enochic Wisdom," 124.
40. Paul Heger deconstructs the arguments for Enochic Judaism, and posits instead that 1 Enoch assumes the Torah. For a detailed argument against Enochic Judaism based on the absence of Moses and the Torah in 1 Enoch see Heger, "1 Enoch," 29–62.
41. Heger, "1 Enoch," 32–33.

Secondly, the absence of reference to Moses and the Sinai covenant is amplified as evidence for 1 Enoch's anti-Mosaic stance. However, as both Heger and Martha Himmelfarb point out, the omission of references to Moses and the Torah is necessary considering the need to keep up the myth of 1 Enoch as predating Moses.[42] It would be anachronistic for 1 Enoch to speak of Moses and the Sinai covenant. The figure of Enoch is not chosen because he predated Moses or the formation of Israel, as Collins argues,[43] if those were the only criteria other figures could have served just as well, like Methuselah whose longevity could be considered a blessing, or Noah who is described as righteous and blameless. But Enoch is the choice of pseudonym because he had the unique distinction of being remembered as one who was simply taken away (לָקַח) by God. This makes him the ideal candidate for heavenly access and cosmic tours. As such, the silence of 1 Enoch regarding Moses and Torah is more naturally explained as part of the essential authorial façade and claim to authority than as an evidence of anti-Mosaic sentiments of a hypothetical community (see below for more on the Enochian community).

Thirdly, 1 Enoch is not the only book that does not mention Moses or Sinai covenant. Several other books in the HB do not to refer to Moses or the Sinai covenant as well, for instance, the Book of the Covenant (Exod 20:22–23:19) itself does not contain the word "covenant"; the book of Joshua does not mention the Sinai covenant; some prophets mention neither Moses nor Sinai.[44] However, none of the books are perceived as presenting distinct or competing ideology with the Mosaic tradition or forming a different group.[45] Hence lack of mention of Moses and the Torah is not convincing as an argument for 1 Enoch being anti-Mosaic.

The paucity of reference to Mosaic elements in 1 Enoch is indeed curious, and may point to 1 Enoch's divergent emphasis. However, it is not a strong enough basis to make a compelling case for an anti-Mosaic stance in 1 Enoch. Further, despite the rarity of direct Mosaic related references in 1 Enoch,

---

42. Heger, "1 Enoch," 37; Himmelfarb states, "reticence about the laws of the Torah is a function of genre, not of distance or discomfort." Himmelfarb, *Kingdom of Priests*, 41.

43. Collins, "How Distinctive," 32.

44. For instance, Moses' name is mentioned only five times among the prophets: Isa 63:11–12; Jer 15:1; Mic 6:4; and Mal 3:22 (Heb.). Heger, "1 Enoch," 35.

45. Heger, 34.

several implicit references and allusions to the Torah can be detected, as the brief discussion below shows.

5.3.2. Torah and 1 Enoch

Several Enochic Judaism proponents themselves have noted that there are parallels, allusions, and quotations in 1 Enoch from the Torah and the prophets. For instance, Hartman observes the similarity between the pronouncement of curses (BW 5:4–6) and blessings (BW 5:7–10) and Deuteronomy 28, while Nickelsburg finds it resonant with Isaiah 65–66.[46] Nickelsburg further states that the Torah serves as a basis for the judgment announced in BW 1:4.[47] Grant Macaskill states as well that there are "frequent allusions to the Torah" in chapters 1–5.[48] Despite such admissions, these scholars downplay the relationship between the Torah and 1 Enoch because it is not made explicit.[49] Roger Beckwith observes that at several crucial points the BW presupposes familiarity with the book of Genesis. For instance, Enoch is chosen to receive revelation because he is known to have walked with God (Gen 5:22, 24), condemnation of eating flesh (BW 7:4–6) reflects knowledge of Genesis 1:29; 9:3, and reference to the fall of Adam and Eve (BW 32:2–6) and to Abel's murder (BW 22: 6–7) assumes knowledge of Genesis 2–4.[50] Young Namgung also notes that BW 1:3–9, which speaks of God coming forth from his dwelling and marching up to Mt. Sinai to execute his judgment, is an allusion to Deuteronomy 33:2, which is in the context of Yahweh coming from Sinai and giving the law to Israel through Moses. He concludes that despite the absence of an explicit mention of the Sinai covenant and the Mosaic law, such an allusion, and that too in the introduction to the book, could imply "that the Law (the Sinai covenant) will play a directive role in discerning what is good and what is evil."[51] As such there seem to be ample reasons to assume a connection between the Torah and 1 Enoch.

However, scholars of Enochic Judaism instead claim that Torah is replaced by "revealed wisdom," and this wisdom ($\sigma o\phi i\alpha$) is 1 Enoch (81:1–83:3;

---

46. Hartman, *Asking for a Meaning*, 44; Nickelsburg, *1 Enoch 1*, 160.
47. Nickelsburg, *1 Enoch 1*, 52.
48. Macaskill, *Revealed Wisdom*, 46.
49. For instance, see Nickelsburg, *1 Enoch 1*, 50; Bedenbender, "Place of the Torah," 65.
50. For more details see, Beckwith, "Earliest Enoch Literature, 371.
51. Namgung, "Sin and Human," 100.

104:12–13).⁵² However, as Bachmann rightly states, the BW does not make any explicit claim about conveying wisdom.⁵³ Wisdom, in the BW, is presented in its traditional garb of welfare for the righteous (BW 5:8–9). This paradigm of good-for-the-righteous is presently dysfunctional only because the world has been steeped in disorder by the sin of the Watchers. But God will restore the earth to its original state and order will be established, and wisdom will be given to the chosen as an eschatological gift (BW 1–2).⁵⁴ Hence, wisdom will be given in the future. Meanwhile the Watchers have corrupted the world by transmitting forbidden or bad knowledge. This can be countered by good knowledge that is not bound to a future time and is available to the people, but 1 Enoch does not elaborate what this good knowledge is. Heger⁵⁵ and Bachmann detect in 1 Enoch a call to repentance or to the Jewish way of life (1 Enoch 91:4), and both suggest that the good knowledge is never explained, perhaps because it is already known to its readers – the Torah or the Jewish heritage.⁵⁶

Moreover, despite the centrality of the concept of judgment in 1 Enoch scholars are also compelled to admit there are no parallels in 1 Enoch to formal specific laws found in the Torah. For instance, God accuses humanity of not standing firm "according to his commandments" (BW 5:4), but it does not specify what those commandments are. Nickelsburg for example states 1 Enoch exhibits a "sense of cosmic order," and that it expresses "concern for the violation of divine law." He however acknowledges, "one looks in vain for formal parallels to the specific laws and commandments found in the Mosaic Pentateuch."⁵⁷ Collins explains this vacuum by proposing that "the law of the Lord" mentioned in BW 5:4 is "the law of creation, or of nature."⁵⁸ However,

---

52. Nickelsburg, *1 Enoch 1*, 52, followed by Bedenbender, "Place of Torah," 71.
53. Bachmann, "Book of the Watchers," 17.
54. Bachmann, 17; Eibert Tigchelaar, "Wisdom and Counter-Wisdom," 184.
55. Heger rightly sees the categorization of people into righteous and sinners as similar to the prophets' view of people in their call to repentance, rather than as indicating an ideological division based on whether one follows Enoch or not. Heger, *Challenges*, 198.
56. Heger, "1 Enoch," 54; Bachmann, "1 Enoch 1–36," 18.
57. He also states, "The specific laws and commandments that are the criteria for this judgment are not explicated by the authors, Nickelsburg, *1 Enoch 1*, 51, 53.
58. Collins concedes that this "law of creation" may even be the same as the Mosaic Torah but denies that it is a reference to the Torah because the does not explicitly designate it as Mosaic law. Collins, How Distinctive," 30–31. "Law of nature" is probably a reference to natural law, see Heger, "1 Enoch," 46–47.

neither of their proposals explains how human beings were to deduce, from a "sense of cosmic order" or "the law of creation," that actions such as pride (BW 5:8), or drinking blood (BW 7:5) constitute sin.[59] Therefore it is reasonable to conclud with scholars like Eibert Tigchelaar, Heinrich Hoffmann, Heger, and Young Namgung that even though there is no explicit reference to the Mosaic figure and institution, the Mosaic law could have been implicitly expected to be the criteria for discerning good and evil.[60]

Thus, although there has been much discussion regarding 1 Enoch's lack of explicit reference to Mosaic figure and institutions, there are ample instances and occasions to suggest that 1 Enoch was not non- or anti-Mosaic. It probably assumed the Mosaic Law in its announcement of the coming judgment and hence viewed itself as complementary to the Torah rather than as vying with it for followers.

5.3.3. Distinct Explanation of the Origin of Evil

The second principal reason for postulating Enochic Judaism is the distinct explanation of the origin of evil found mainly in the BW. The idea that the BW addresses the issue of the origin of evil was initially proposed by Paolo Sacchi,[61] and later built upon by Boccaccini. This idea of the supernatural origin of sin in the BW, according to Boccaccini, is the "generative idea" behind early Enochic literature and Judaism.[62] This is one crucial aspect that sets Enochic Judaism apart from the Mosaic Judaism.[63] The Enochic location of the origin of evil in the sin of the Watchers is indeed distinct from the explanation of the origin of evil in the Torah, the Fall narrative in Genesis 3. Generally speaking, in the Enochic narrative the ultimate responsibility for the origin of sin is placed on the Watchers. The Watchers[64] cohabit with human women (BW

---

59. Heger, "1 Enoch," 47, fn. 64.
60. Eibert Tigchelaar, "Balaam and Enoch," 94; Hoffmann, *Das Gesetz*, both cited in Namgang, "Sin and Human Accountability," 100–101; Heger, "1 Enoch," 54.
61. Sacchi, "Riflessioni sull'Essenza," 59–60, cited in Heger, *Challenges*, 103; Sacchi, *Jewish Apocalyptic*; Sacchi, "Book of the Watchers," 9–26.
62. Boccaccini, *Beyond the Essene*, 170, 185.
63. Boccaccini, 78; Boccaccini, *Roots of Rabbinic Judaism*, 90–91, 95; Bedenbender, "Place of the Torah," 68.
64. Led by Shemihazah, who led his followers into taking wives for themselves from the daughters of men and teaching spells (6:3–6; 7:1; 8:3) and Asael/Azazel, another chief angel, who follows Shemihazah in mating with humans (6:7) and was primarily responsible for imparting knowledge to human beings (8:1). It is generally considered that the Watchers story

7:1; 9:8; 10:11; 12:4; 15:3–4) and thereby, in effect, trespass the cosmic boundary established by Yahweh between celestial and earthly beings, between the immortal and the mortal. They also impart forbidden knowledge to human beings (BW 8). Such an explanation, argues Boaccaccini, exonerates Yahweh "from being the source of evil" in the context of STP Jewish monotheism.[65]

The BW presents the story of the fallen angels in a different and elaborate manner from the version in the Torah (Gen 6:1–4). In the Torah, the story of the fallen angels is an episode that is resolved in the Flood (Gen 6–8) and exerts no deep, long-lasting effect. Sin continues after the great deluge, but it is explained as deriving from human nature – the evil inclination of men's heart (Gen 8:21). But in 1 Enoch the story of the fallen angels constitutes the mythic core and becomes, as Boccaccini puts it, the "mother of all sins."[66] After they mate with human women, Yahweh brings judgment upon the rebel angels and the earth. The Watchers are confined in a pit in the wilderness awaiting the final judgment (BW 10:4–6, 11–12) and their offspring, the giants, are destroyed (BW 10:9–10) perhaps through the Flood,[67] but they become evil spirits and spread evil and impurity on earth (BW 15:8–10). The world is now steeped in disorder and only the divine final judgment can restore it back to order. The story of the fallen angels is thus employed to place the ultimate responsibility of sin in the world on the Watchers. Hence from the perspective of Enochic Judaism, evil on earth springs originally from the trespassing of the divine boundary by the Watchers and is carried on by evil spirits and humans.

However, not all proponents of Enochic Judaism agree that the Watchers narrative is paradigmatic for origin of evil and the generative idea for the Enochic tradition. For instance, Collins considers it as just one of the several motifs in the corpus rather than an Enochic paradigm of the origin of evil,[68] while Pierluigi Piovanelli suggests that the book is actually an attempt to explain the magical or supernatural dimension of the universe.[69] Further,

---

in BW 6–11 weaves together two traditions – the Shemihazah tradition and the Asael tradition. See Nickelsburg, "Apocalyptic and Myth," 383–405; Hanson, "Rebellion in Heaven," 197–233.

65. Boccaccini, *Roots of Rabbinic*, 95.
66. Boccaccini, *Roots of Rabbinic*, 91.
67. See Stuckenbruck, *Myth of Rebellious Angels*, 15.
68. Collins, "How Distinctive," 19, 34.
69. Piovanelli, "Theology of the Supernatural," 90, cited in Heger, *Challenges*, 108.

while the Enochic treatment of Watchers story diverges from the Torah's presentation, there are points to the contrary that need to be considered in positing the sins of the Watchers as the generative core of the whole corpus.

5.3.3.1. *The BW Is Ambivalent*

Proponents of Enochic Judaism assert that in 1 Enoch culpability for the origin of sin lies solely with the Watchers and human beings are portrayed as without agency. For instance, Boccaccini states human beings are victims and "cannot control the spread of evil and impurity."[70] However, the BW is not as clear as they make it out to be. While the text focuses predominantly on the misconduct of the Watchers, human beings are not completely absolved. This can be deduced from both the text and structure of the BW.

At the textual level, there are two aspects to be considered regarding the ambivalence: first, the text itself presents a mixed picture regarding human culpability – they are sometimes portrayed as victims of the deeds of the angels. For instance, God commands the destruction of the giants and the evil spirits "because they have wronged men" (BW 10:15; or BW 10:7). However, there are other instances where human beings are blamed for the corruption of the world.[71] For example, after learning metallurgy and the art of beautification from the Watcher Asael, men made weapons of war, cosmetics, and jewellery for themselves and for their daughters, "and they transgressed and led the holy ones astray"[72] (BW 8:1). Thus, the BW also states that human beings used knowledge for their own corruption, proving human culpability and hence deserving of divine judgment. It must be noted here that the above quoted sentence of BW 8:1 is attested in Gk^s, the version preserved by George Synkellos/Syncellus dating to the ninth century CE,[73] but missing in some mss. The Ge'ez (Ethiopic) and the Panopolitanus or Akhmim (Gk^a) texts preserve a shorter version. Kelly C. Bautch compares the Panopolatinus and Synkellos texts to the Aramaic fragment (4QEn^b)[74] which is considered older, and concludes that there are indications Synkellos is an authentic variant of

---

70. Boccaccini, *Beyond the Essene*, 73–78.

71. See also Wright, *Origin*, 18.

72. Holy ones "refer to the good angels, messengers of God, the guardians and the guides of just men." Milik, *Books of Enoch*, 144.

73. Knibb, "Christian Adoption," 402.

74. 4QEn^{a-g} are Aramaic fragments of 1 Enoch of Qumran Cave 4. Milik, *Books of Enoch*, 4.

the Semitic version rather than a motivated later addition.[75] Hence the text seems to view the angels and human beings as sharing the responsibility of sin; this point is discussed further in the succeeding paragraphs.

The second aspect that should be considered regarding the text's ambivalence about the Watcher's total culpability for the origin of sin is that the BW alludes to Adam and Eve briefly with reference to the tree of wisdom (BW 32:6). Interestingly, despite this clear allusion to the Genesis story in the BW, it significantly does not have anything to say regarding "the *total* absence of sin prior to" the sin of the Watchers;[76] it is simply assumed by the readers. Macaskill in fact opines that the allusion to Adam and Eve serves to draw a contrast between Enoch's reception of wisdom from angels who ate from the tree and Adam and Eve's reception of wisdom directly from the tree that resulted in their being cast away from paradise.[77] If Macaskill's reading is plausible, then 1 Enoch is not silent but attests to the presence of sin before the Watchers' descent. Additionally, Animal Apocalypse (1 Enoch 85-90), which belongs to the Dream Visions in the Enochic corpus, like the BW does not include the Fall narrative of Genesis 3. However, the first sin in Animal Apocalypse is still committed by human beings, that of fratricide, and those from the line of Cain are complicit in the spread of corruption in the world.[78] Similarly, the Epistle of Enoch (1 Enoch 91–105) places the blame for sin and corruption in the world on human beings: "Thus lawlessness was not sent upon the earth; but men created it by themselves. . . ." (1 Enoch 98:4). Therefore, it is unlikely, as Heger says,[79] that writers of 1 Enoch, who were also readers of the BW, and living closer to the time of the writing of BW would have missed the (supposed) distinctive, paradigmatic theology of the BW

---

75. Some of the reasons are: i) Synkellos of 1 Enoch 8:1 preserves the Semitic expression, "sons of men" against Panopolitanus' "men" or "women." ii) In 1 Enoch 8:2 Panopolitanus contains the verb in the passive form, "were led astray," while Synkellos' active rendering, "they went astray" is attested in Ge'ez. The active verb form is similar to Genesis 6:12 כִּי־הִשְׁחִית כָּל־בָּשָׂר אֶת־דַּרְכּוֹ ("for all flesh had corrupted their way"), iii) Similarity between the longer version of 1 Enoch 8:1 and the description of Asael tradition in Animal Apocalypse (1 Enoch 86:1-6). For further details of the argument, see Bautch, "Decoration, Destruction and Debauchery," 79–95.

76. Adams, *Wisdom in Transition*, 192.

77. Macaskill, *Revealed Wisdom*, 35.

78. VanderKam, *Enoch: A Man*, 74; Bautch states, "The onus does not fall solely upon Asael or upon the Watchers." Bautch, "Decoration," 92.

79. See Heger's argument on this, though he approaches from a slightly different angle. Heger, *Challenges*, 112–113.

regarding the origin of evil. And if the Watchers story as the paradigm of the origin of sin is a distinctive of Enochic Judaism, this contradiction whether within the BW itself (between BW 10:7 and BW 8:1), or within the Enochic corpus (between BW 10:7 and Epistle of Enoch 98:4), is a major discrepancy that is not easily explained.

Further, at the structural level, introductions and conclusions can be considered as providing "a hermeneutical key to understanding the body of any text" and hence is crucial for understanding the intent of the author or redactor.[80] The introduction to the BW,[81] and to 1 Enoch as well, is an oracle of judgment (BW 1–5) and focuses on the sin of humanity. It describes a theophany of the final judgment to come (BW 1:3c–9), and compares the obedience of the natural order to God's ordained ways and humanity's disobedience to God's commandments (BW 2:1–5:3). There is a succession of imperatives that call its readers to observe how the various phenomena of nature, both earthly and cosmic, have not deviated from their divinely designated paths and functions (BW 2:1–5:3). The introductory oracle then concludes by contrasting the constancy and obedience of this created order with an accusation that humanity has in contrast not acted according to his commandments (BW 5:4), and thus declares calamity (BW 5: 4–6: 7c) for the wicked and salvation to the chosen (BW 5: 7a–b: 8–9).[82] Thus the introduction of the BW with its focus on the coming judgment on humanity balances the Watchers' descent narrative – both humanity and the Watchers have deviated from God's commands, they have "changed and transgressed the created order."[83] In fact, the judgment scenes towards the end of the book dedicate only one chapter to the description of the place of judgment for the Watchers and the disobedient stars (BW 21). The rest of the chapters, 22–32, are taken up by the description of the spaces allocated for the judgment of human beings. As such, human culpability is not a minor issue in the BW.

---

80. Namgung, "Sin and Human," 97.

81. One might say the introduction was added by a later editor who was favourable to the Torah, but as has been pointed out, Aramaic fragments of the introduction among 4QEnª, discovered in Qumran cave 4, proves it was composed quite early, before 1 Enoch came to its final form. See Milik, *Books of Enoch*, 139–140; Wright, *Origin*, 15–16.

82. See Namgung, "Sin and Human," 101–102.

83. Namgung, 102.

Additionally, other traditions like Jubilees, which is dependent on Enochic literature,[84] also contain the Watchers tradition. However, in Jubilees the Watchers do not alone bear the onus of introducing sin into the world.[85] Textual ambivalence remain in Jubilees as well regarding the Watchers' and human culpability: the watchers' misdeed with human women is said to be the beginning of uncleanness and much corruption in the world (Jub 7:21ff), quite similar to the description of the Watchers in the BW. However, human beings are also blamed. For instance, Kainan, son of Elam, chances upon and learns heavenly signs and sins by practicing them (Jub 8:2-3). Hence blaming the Watchers is not unique to 1 Enoch. The representation of the Watchers is similar in Jubilees, but Jubilees is not cited as espousing Enochic Judaism, and there is no reason to dismiss the textual instances in BW that do describe human culpability. Hence, there are indications in the text and the structure of BW, and in other texts within and outside 1 Enoch that the Watchers were not considered the sole originators of sin.

5.3.3.2. Punishment Assumes Human Culpability

The BW clearly depicts the time of eschatological judgment when the righteous and the wicked among human beings will be separated and rewarded or punished (BW 22, 25, 27). Boccaccini states, "Human beings are still held accountable for their actions, but they are victims of an evil that they have not caused and cannot resist."[86] This statement is illogical and inexplicable within the context of Judaism. Blaming the origin of sin on the Watchers may exonerate God from being the source of evil, but culminating in the punishment of human beings, who themselves are victims, paints God as an arbitrary, unreasonable entity. Nickelsburg likewise views human beings as "prey of evil spirits who oppose God."[87] Responsibility for sin is logical only under the assumption of choice and consequent culpability. That there is a righteous one, like Noah, who is warned of the flood (BW 10:3), implies

---

84. See VanderKam, "Enoch Traditions in Jubilees," 228–251.

85. Although Boccaccini takes Jubilees as evidence that in the post-Maccabean revolt some Enochians appropriated Zadokite ideology. Boccaccini, *Beyond the Essene*, 114. However, as Hindy Najman states, to accept this was the case it must be proven there was an ideological schism in the first place. Najman, "Review: Gabriele Boccaccini," 353.

86. Boccaccini, *Beyond the Essene*, 73.

87. Nickelsburg, *1 Enoch 1*, 41.

human decision or wilfulness in their participation or non-participation in the sin of the Watchers. Boccaccini's argument that human resistance to evil might have "weakened"[88] does not completely exonerate human beings from their role in corrupting the world with sin,[89] and is made suspect by 1 Enoch's reference to Noah. In the BW, the Watchers are held more culpable than their human counterparts. Consequently, the Watchers are refused forgiveness despite mediation through Enoch (BW 14:4–7; 13:4–7; 15) and assigned for certain doom and destruction. Alternatively, human beings are less culpable, therefore the possibility of attaining paradise remains for them.[90] However, human beings do not simply go scot-free and the wicked are liable to be penalized at the final judgment.

5.3.3.3. Ideological Reading is Suspect

One of the reasons the Watchers story as a paradigm of the origin of sin is presented as typifying Enochic Judaism is because the Watchers story is seen as functioning polemically against the Zadokite priests by the dissenting Enochian priests.[91] Boccaccini hypothesizes that during the Persian period, Judaism was divided into three competing Jewish ideologies or "system of thoughts": i) Zadokite Judaism, which according to him, eventually became Rabbinic Judaism, ii) Enochic Judaism, from which emerged Christianity,[92] and iii) Sapiental Judaism, which was eventually subsumed into Zadokite Judaism.[93] The chaos resulting from the sin of the Watchers is central to Bocccaccini's ideological reading of the text. It posits that the Enochians

---

88. Boccaccini, *Beyond the Essene*, 73.

89. Matthew Goff states the introduction (chs. 1–5) "stresses the sinfulness of humans and the inevitability of judgment," and the certainty of the coming punishment of the wicked is maintained throughout the book. Goff, "1 Enoch," 226; Bachmann notes that despite centering on the sin of the Watchers, 1 Enoch also mentions the wrongdoings of human beings in "every of its literary parts." Bachmann, "Book of the Watchers," 16, n. 42.

90. Bachmann, 16–17. Bachmann says, "[T]he BW insinuates that returning to a decent way of life still pays off for humans," 16.

91. Some of the scholars espousing this view are Himmelfarb, "Temple and Priests," 219–235; Bedenbender, "Place of Torah," 71; Macaskill, "Priestly Purity," 67–89; Suter, "Temples and the Temple," 195–218; Kvanvig, "Enochic Judaism," 163–77.

92. Also see Boccaccini, *Beyond the Essene*, 159, 188–191.

93. Boccaccini, *Roots of Rabbinic*, 31, 35–37, 207f. Zadokite Judaism – captured power and office high priests, represented by Mosaic Torah; Enochic Judaism – priests but marginalized, represented by 1 Enoch; Sapiential Judaism – lay scribal traditions, represented by Job and Qohelet.

belonged to the disenfranchised Levitical families and took a stand against the Zadokite, who were the guardians of the Mosaic Torah. According to him, the Enochic Judaism worldview presented the world as in a state of disorder after the sin of the Watchers and the Flood, and redeemable only through re-creation after the final judgment. This was at odds with Zadokite Judaism, which maintained power by presenting the world as stable and orderly post Flood, and as so maintained through the temple rituals.[94]

Boccaccini presents this historical reconstruction of an Enochian community in a tone that conveys certainty. However, he often overstates his case; there is no evidence – whether concrete, a hint, or an allusion – to prove his reconstruction of history or of the said schism between the groups. By Boccaccini's self-admission, "A major problem is given by the absence in Enochic literature of any detailed reference to the communal life of the Enochians."[95] It may be added that reference to the communal life of the Enochians is not only absent in Enochic literature but also outside it. Further, as Richard Bauckham argues, 1 Enoch is generally classified as an apocalypse and it is misleading to speak of an apocalypse as propagating a different Judaism, as "apocalyptic is not an ideology but a genre."[96] Thus the ideological reading that necessitates a historical reconstruction goes beyond available evidence, and many reviewers of his work have noted the hypothetical nature of his Enochic community.[97] In other words, there is no evidence for the existence of Enochic community and the centrality of the superhuman origin of sin is overplayed to make a case for an ideological reading of the text that has not yet been attested elsewhere.

5.3.3.4. Section Conclusion

In sum, the proposition for Enochic Judaism is a fascinating one and several scholars have pursued it vigorously. However, both of the principal aspects briefly discussed above have been built on silence: in one, silence has been used to say what it is not – not Mosaic Judaism; in the other, silence has been

---

94. See, Boccaccini, *Roots of Rabbinic*, 43–44; Bedenbender, "Place of the Torah," 69–71.
95. Boccaccini, *Beyond the Essene*, 166.
96. Bauckham, 'Apocalypses," 135.
97. See reviews of Boccaccini's work by Schnabel, "Review: Gabriele Boccaccini," 372–373; Najman, "Review: Gabriele Boccaccini," 352–354; Kaminsky, "Review: Roots of Rabbinic," 289–292; Fonrobert, "Review: Roots of Rabbinic," 156–159.

used to say what it is – that there was Enochic Judaism, Enochians, and schism between various groups. There is no external evidence yet to substantiate the claims for an anti-Mosaic outlook in 1 Enoch, the existence of an Enochic Judaism or community, or the schism among the religious groups. As such, Enochic Judaism seems to remain largely conjectural in nature, and until there is some positive evidence it is difficult to enthusiastically join in the discussion no matter how interesting the discussion or how distinguished the scholars representing it. This is not to discount the different perspective that BW or 1 Enoch brings in the study of Judaism. 1 Enoch does provide a sampling of the variety of perspectives in STP Judaism and adds to its many voices. However, to state that 1 Enoch evinces a distinct Enochic Judaism as an alternative to the Mosaic Judaism, that it points to an Enochian community and ideological conflicts between groups that are otherwise unattested elsewhere, is perhaps overstating it. With that in view, the study proceeds to examine BW 22 and its perspective on the post-mortem divine retribution.

5.4. Post-mortem Divine Retribution in BW 22

In BW 22[98] interest in post-mortem divine retribution is evident. Unlike in the texts in the HB there is no ambiguity about the fates of the dead in the afterlife. It exhibits interest in expounding the sins of the created beings and the consequent divine retribution.[99] As mentioned earlier, BW 17–36 describe Enoch's otherworldly journeys. In BW 21 Enoch begins his eastward journey where he makes his first stop and sees two fiery places – one where the transgressing stars were being punished and the other for the rebel angels. BW 22 describes Enoch's second stop where he visits another place of punishment, but this time, the objects of punishment are dead human beings. It depicts an unusual afterlife scene – a categorized repository for the dead human souls

---

98. The Greek text of BW 22 mainly used for this study is the Codex Panopolitanus (Cairo Papyrus 10759), also called Codex Gizeh or Akhmim fragments recovered from Akhmim in Egypt and published five years later, in 1892. This codex consists of fragments of two late fifth – sixth century papyri containing portions of chapters 1–32. "Book 1 of Enoch: Chapters 17–32," http://www.textexcavation.com/greek1enoch17-32.html; Knibb, "Book of Enoch," 33. Brief extracts of Greek text of 1 Enoch are also preserved in at least three other groups of fragments, and there are also fragments of Aramaic BW 22 in 4Q205 and 4Q206.

99. Bedenbender, "Place of Torah," 67; Macaskill, *Revealed Wisdom*, 31–35.

awaiting their final judgment.[100] BW 22 also serves as a hinge between the preceding and succeeding chapters. BW 21 described the awful fate of the Watchers and disobedient stars, while chapter 22 portrays the dual character of post-mortem divine retribution by bringing together and contrasting the fates of the wicked and the righteous. Enoch's journey eastward from BW 22 on grows increasingly positive[101] as BW 24–36 predominantly describe the fate of the righteous. BW 22 lends a fascinating glimpse into the Jewish conception of post-mortem divine retribution, preserving perhaps one of the earliest[102] Jewish textual records on this subject. As discussed earlier, the BW focuses on the superhuman origin of sin and the ensuing judgment. However, human beings are also held responsible and therefore subject to retribution, which is the theme of chapter 22. The following elements in BW 22 highlight its interest in post-mortem divine retribution:

5.4.1. The Spirits of the Souls of the Dead

Divine retribution in BW 22 is clearly post-mortem as indicated by the phrase τὰ πνεύματα τῶν ψυχῶν τῶν νεκρῶν[103] ("the spirits of the souls of the dead" 22:3). The nouns τὰ πνεύματα τῶν ψυχῶν τῶν νεκρῶν are in the type of appositional relationship called genitives of apposition or epexegetical apposition, and τῶν νεκρῶν (the dead) modifies the words πνεῦμα ("spirit") as well as ψυχῶν ("soul") specifying that these are the spirits of the dead and not of the living. Although πνεῦμα as well as ψυχῶν have their Hebrew counterparts in רוּחַ ("spirit") and נֶפֶשׁ ("soul") respectively,[104] these Greek

---

100. See Macaskill for "final judgment." Macaskill, *Revealed Wisdom*, 33.

101. So also, Venter, "Allotted Place," 674.

102. Several authors propose a third century BCE date, while traditions in the BW could have originated much earlier. See Milik, *Books of Enoch*, 24–28; Nickelsburg, *1 Enoch 1*, 230, 304; Hanson, "Rebellion in Heaven," 197, 219–220; Stone, "Book of Enoch," 484; Knibb, *Essay on the Book*, 18.

103. The phrase in verse 3 could be an intentional construction. However, this chapter also exhibits signs of conflation; for instance, the text switches between referring to the inhabitants of the pit as simply "souls" (22:5–7) at times and as "spirits" in other instances (22:8–13). Such discrepancy has also been detected by some scholars in its reference to the number of compartments: four compartments in 22:2 and three in 22:9a. It could also be a result of conflation of different versions of the text with which the author or editor was working. See also Nickelsburg, who surmises that this is possibly due to the growth of the tradition over time; Nickelsburg, *1 Enoch 1*, 305.

104. The Greek ψυχή is multivalent, with meanings ranging from earthly life (Acts 15:26), self, or the center of inner life as it relates to emotions and desires (Mark 13:34). The Hebrew

terms are used distinctively from the Hebrew counterparts. Both πνεῦμα and ψυχῶν are used to designate discarnate souls of the dead that are presented as "individual conscious beings," and came to be used synonymously in the apocalyptic writings "to describe the form of a man's survival immediately after death."[105] Such a notion is attested neither for רוּחַ nor for נֶפֶשׁ. In the HB, the departed who inhabit Sheol are instead called "shades" or *rephaim*. The shades were the shadowy disembodied forms of their former selves, and at death, as D. S. Russell says, although consciousness may have survived to some extent, a person's personal existence came to an end. The conception of afterlife existence in writings like BW 22 departs radically from that which is typical in the HB. It seems to present a "continuity" between earthly life and post-mortem existence so that the deceased retains personal consciousness and identity in the underworld. This is seen especially in the case of Abel who brings a case against his brother Cain (BW 22:7) and is apparently even able to communicate with God.[106] Nickelsburg notes that Abel is perhaps presented as a type of those who suffered violent unjust death.[107] Thus the souls in the compartments are conscious individual beings who are awaiting their final fate.

5.4.2. The Differentiated Dead

The dead in BW 22 are differentiated on the basis of morals, indicating its interest in post-mortem retribution. The souls of the dead are designated as "righteous" and "sinners." Unlike Sheol where there was no moral distinction between the righteous and the sinners, in these hollow places the souls of the dead were further segregated depending on whether they had received their appropriate retribution in their lifetime (BW 22:9–13). As such the first compartment belonged to the righteous, the second contained the spirits of sinners who escaped unpunished in their lifetime, the third was occupied by

---

counterpart of ψυχή is the word נֶפֶשׁ, which also has a similar range of meanings. Πνεῦμα on the other hand means wind, breath, spirit or Spirit, with רוּחַ as its Hebrew counterpart. By extension πνεῦμα can sometimes denote heart, mind, seat of emotions, the immaterial part of the inner person that can respond to God. Some nuances of the two words may overlap but unlike πνεῦμα, ψυχή does not mean breath or wind and is not used to refer to the Spirit.

105. Russell, *Method and Message*, 357–358.
106. Russell, 359.
107. Nickelsburg, *1 Enoch 1*, 306.

souls who met unjust violent deaths,[108] and the fourth compartment hosted those sinners who received their due punishments while alive and hence would not be judged anymore (BW 22:13). Such a detailed segregation of the souls is perceived as not only ensuring appropriate reward and punishment to all but also as reflecting God's righteous judgments,[109] which consequently Enoch praises (BW 22:14). This meticulous division between the souls of the dead is quite unparalleled and demonstrates BW's interest in post-mortem divine retribution.

5.4.3. Foretaste of Final Retribution

Not only is a distinction maintained between the souls of the dead righteous and sinners, but the hollow places are so designed that the souls of the dead already experience a foretaste of their ultimate fate even as they await the day of judgment.[110] For instance, the compartment of the righteous is illuminated as well as supplied with a "bright fountain of water" (BW 22:2, 9). Light as an imagery could be suggestive of divine presence, while water is referred to here for its life-giving characteristic. Elsewhere in the BW water is associated with life-giving qualities in the paradise of the righteous[111] (BW 28:2; 30:1; also 17:4). As Nickelsburg points out, to a Jewish reader this combination of light and water would probably recall Psalm 36:10 (9) in which the two elements appear together – כִּי־עִמְּךָ מְקוֹר חַיִּים בְּאוֹרְךָ נִרְאֶה־אוֹר ("For with you is the fountain of life; in your light we see light," NRSV).[112] As such BW 22 portrays the righteous souls as already experiencing the reward of renewed life that they will eventually receive in full (BW 24:4; 25:4–6).

The compartments of the wicked by contrast are said to be dark (BW 22:2), reminiscent of Sheol. The second compartment has been created for the souls of the sinners who did not receive their due punishments in their lifetime. These souls whose sins were previously unaccounted for are now subjected to torments in their compartments even though they will be judged at the

---

108. The moral status of this category of souls is discussed below.
109. Nickelsburg, *1 Enoch 1*, 309.
110. So also Russell, *Method and Message*, 361, 364.
111. Living water generally refers to flowing water body, however in the context of paradise it could refer to its life-giving qualities or refer metaphorically to life itself. See Nickelsburg, *1 Enoch 1*, 282.
112. Nickelsburg, *1 Enoch 1*, 307.

final judgment (BW 22:10–11). Hence, they too get a foretaste of their final fate. The angel Raphael, Enoch's guide, assures him they will eventually be bound "there" forever. The text itself is not clear about where the final "there" is. Russell connects "there" to the accursed valley in BW 27:1 and states that is a reference to the Valley of Hinnom or *Ge Hinnom*.[113] Hence he takes this as "the first reference in apocalyptic writing to the idea of hell as a place of torment."[114] Nicklesburg however connects the place of the future judgment ("there") to the fiery abyss, the destination for all the rebel angels and the sinners in BW 10:13–14 and 21:7–10.[115] Regardless of where this final destination is, perpetual suffering is envisioned as the fate of sinners both while in the hollow place and where they will eventually be taken and bound to experience the full extent of their judgment.

5.4.4. Coming Final Judgment

The expected coming judgment is one that is still in the future but when it does come it will be final. The word κρίσις means "judgment, administration of justice, reward, punishment." It occurs five times (vv. 4 (2x), 10, 11, 13) and is frequently used with ἡμέρα, "day," and hence refers to the Day of Judgment (vv. 11, 13, similar sense in v.4). It is also used in the sense of punishment, that the sinners in a particular pit were not judged or punished during their lifetime (v. 10). The repetition of the word reinforces a sense of finality and of justice and recompense for the dead. This final judgment in the BW is not described as imminent but it suffices "that there is an eventual judgment" and that the locations for punishment are already in place.[116] To Macaskill such a future orientation that looks to the coming judgment upon the Watchers and fallen humanity is "clear almost immediately" in the BW.[117] In BW 22 itself,

---

113. The Valley of Hinnom, also called Topheth, was a valley west of Jerusalem, and had gained notoriety during the reigns of Ahaz and Manasseh as the place for human sacrifice to Molech, the Ammonite god (2 Kgs 16:3; 2 Chron 28:3; Jer 7:31). This place was desecrated during Josiah's reform (2 Kgs 23:10) and became a garbage incinerator but retained its evil reputation. This later transformed into an imagery signifying a place of punishment of those who rebel against Yahweh (Isa 66:24) and eventually came to be the designation for Hell. See Prusak, "Heaven and Hell," 479; Bailey, "Gehenna," 188; Milikowsky, "Which Gehenna," 238.

114. Russell, *Method and Message*, 365; Peterson, *Hell on Trial*, 31.

115. Nicklesburg, *1 Enoch 1*, 308.

116. Collins, "Apocalyptic Technique," 109.

117. Macaskill, *Revealed Wisdom*, 31.

the hollow places are intermediary receptacles for the souls and not the final destination; they confine the souls "until the time of the day of the end of the great judgment that will be exacted from them" (BW 22:4). And although the souls of the dead experience a foretaste of their final fate, they are still to expect the "final and full"[118] retribution, which is still in a time to come. This concentration of the BW on the final eschatological judgment is consonant with the focus of the whole book of 1 Enoch.[119] Hence in BW 22, post-mortem divine retribution is already in effect in the hollow places but will be executed in its full extent in a future time when there will be a dispensing of rewards for the righteous and punishments for the sinners. Sin and impurity will be obliterated, and creation will be restored to its pristine state.

Thus, in BW 22 the concept of post-mortem divine retribution is presented in a clear and comprehensive way, and its interest in divine justice is apparent. Divine retribution is transposed to the afterlife so that even after death, reward and punishment remain viable fates of individuals. Death no longer poses a barrier to retribution; rather life and death are perceived as a continuum in which divine retribution remains actionable regardless. As such, there is no escape for human beings from the coming judgment. This leads to the question, what exactly are human beings held accountable for? This question is explored in the following discussion.

5.5. Basis and Aspect of Post-mortem Divine Retribution

Divine retribution in BW 22 is neither something that unfolds as a natural consequence of the deeds committed, nor as God using sufferings and blessings for pedagogical purposes. At a glance, post-mortem divine retribution in BW 22 exhibits the characteristics of both the theocentric and anthropocentric aspects of retribution.

---

118. Nickelsburg, *1 Enoch 1*, 308.

119. Nickelsburg views the final judgment as central to 1 Enoch, one that is not imposed from the outside but woven into the very structure and core narrative of the book. For an argument on the whole of 1 Enoch as centering on the theme of coming divine judgment, see Nickelsburg, *1 Enoch 1*, 37. See also Heger, *Challenges*, 127–130; Elledge, *Life and Death*, 7.

5.5.1. The Theocentric Aspect

The theocentric aspect can be explained briefly since the reasons for assuming a Torah background have been explained above in the section "Torah and 1 Enoch." The laws or commandments necessary for following in the right path, and for judging right and wrong actions are given or revealed by God. Hence it exhibits the theocratic aspect of retribution in which God is the initiator; his actions are directed to achieving his own purposes and are not dependent on the deeds of human beings. God has given his law or wisdom for the benefit of humanity so that they may act according to his commandments (BW 5:4), and so that all humanity may become righteous. Thus, rooting divine judgment in the law given to human beings shows God's initiative and hence exhibits the theocentric aspect of divine retribution.

5.5.2. The Anthropocentric Aspect

The anthropocentric aspect is seen in that retribution is God's response to human action. However, BW 22 itself does not specify the sin, only that they were sinners. This forces us to seek the answer to the basis of retribution elsewhere in the BW. As mentioned earlier, there is an instance in the BW where human beings are implicated for sin. It is generally accepted that the Watchers story in BW 6–11 weaves together two strands of tradition, the Shemihazah tradition and the Asael/Azazel tradition. Scholarly opinions vary regarding the origin of the independent units, the reason behind and the process of redaction in the BW,[120] and the function of the redacted text, but most[121] recognize that distinct strands have been edited into the form that we now have.[122] In the Shemihazah tradition, the Watcher Shemihazah and his followers were guilty mainly of taking human wives (e.g., 6:3–6)

---

120. For reasons behind incorporating Asael tradition into the narrative, Nickelsburg states that there is no consensus opinion among scholars, Newsom see no clear reason, while Kiel argues that although the Asael tradition offered a divergent perspective on the origin of evil, its assimilation into the narrative was done in such a way as to diminish human culpability. Nickelsburg, *1 Enoch 1*, 190; Newsom, "Development of 1 Enoch 6–19," 321; Kiel, "*Whole Truth*," 106–109.

121. For an alternate view see Corrie Molenberg, argues that the two stories "do not represent two separate traditions but reflect changing notions of sin within some parts of the Jewish community." See Molenberg, "Study of the Roles," 136–146.

122. Collins, "Apocalyptic Technique," 95, Nickelsburg, "Apocalyptic and Myth," 383; Hanson, "Rebellion in Heaven," 220ff; Dimant, "1 Enoch 6–11," 324; Newsom, "Development of 1 Enoch 6–19," 313–314; Namgung, "Sin and Human," 110.

and producing giant offspring who devastate the earth and victimize human beings (e.g., 7:1–6). As such, human beings are primarily victims of the Watchers' and giants' misdeeds. Alternatively, in the Asael tradition, the Watcher Asael is accused of transmitting forbidden knowledge[123] to human beings, which they in turn use to spread corruption and desolation on the earth. Hence human beings are not victims but rather willing collaborators and perpetrators of sin.

Whether these traditions can be identified precisely and dissected into their original form is another matter. However, in BW 8 the Asael tradition comes to the fore.[124] Asael's teaching of forbidden knowledge and the complicity of human beings in learning them and bringing destruction on earth find mention in BW 8:1–2:

> Asael taught men to make swords of iron and weapons and shields and breastplates and every instrument of war. He showed them metals of the earth and how they should work gold to fashion it suitably, and concerning silver, to fashion it for bracelets and ornaments for women. And he showed them concerning antimony and eye paint and all manner of precious stone and dyes. And the sons of men made them for themselves and for their daughters, and they transgressed and led the holy ones astray. And there was much godlessness on the earth, and they made their ways desolate.

Further, Shemihazah and other angels are attributed with imparting knowledge of the occult art and astronomy (8:3), although this is often considered a later interpolation.[125] Asael's teaching of forbidden knowledge relates primarily to mining and metallurgy and consequently human beings learn to fabricate weaponry and jewellery, as well as the art of cosmetics making from minerals, and dyeing.[126] The products made using the forbidden knowledge fall into two categories: i) weapons of warfare, and ii) materials

---

123. Asael's teaching are called "eternal secrets of heaven" (9:6), and later "worthless mystery" (16:3).
124. For a discussion on the literary history of ch. 8 regarding the Asael tradition, see Nickelsburg, *1 Enoch 1*, 190–191.
125. See Nickelsburg, *1 Enoch 1*, 191.
126. Nickelsburg, 194; Stuckenbruck, *Myth of Rebellious Angels*, 13.

for beautification, probably mainly for women. Having learned the art of weapon making and beautification, human beings "transgressed and led the holy ones astray" (8:1c).

The text in BW 8:1c–2 however is problematic because of textual differences found in the Synkellos/Syncellus, the Panopolitanus or Akhmim, and the Ge'ez mss; they are as follows:

Synkellos (Gk^s)

> 1c καὶ ἐποίησαν ἑαυτοῖς οἱ υἱοὶ τῶν ἀνθρώπων καὶ ταῖς θυγατράσιν αὐτῶν καὶ παρέβησαν καὶ ἐπλάνησαν τοὺς ἁγίους. 2 καὶ ἐγένετο ἀσέβεια πολλὴ ἐπὶ τῆς γῆς καὶ ἠφάνισαν τὰς ὁδοὺς αὐτῶν[127]

> 1c *And the sons of men made them for themselves and for their daughters, and they transgressed and led the holy ones astray.* 2 And there was much godlessness upon the earth and **they made** their ways desolate

Akhmim (Gk^a)

> 2 καὶ ἐγένετο ἀσέβεια πολλή, καὶ ἐπόρνευσαν καὶ ἀπεπλανήθησαν καὶ ἠφανίσθησαν ἐν πάσαις ταῖς ὁσοῖς αὐτῶν

> 2 And there was much godlessness, *and they committed fornication and were led astray* and **they were made** desolate in all their ways

Ge'Ez (E, for Ethiopic)

> 2 And there was much godlessness, *and they committed fornication and were led astray* and **they made** desolate all their ways

As the above variants highlighted in italics show, verse 1c is a variant reading found in the writing of Synkellos. This sentence points to human culpability in the corruption of the world. However, this text is missing in both the Greek of Akhmim and the Ge'ez. Instead, both add the phrase "and they committed fornication and were led astray" in verse 2. In the Akhmim

---

127. Synkellos and Akhmim versions from Bautch, "Decoration," 85.

and the Ge'ez human beings are portrayed as victims and the blame is placed on the angels for leading them astray.[128]

Further, in verse 2 highlighted in bold face, the verb in Akhmim has the passive form, καὶ ἠφανίσθησαν ἐν πάσαις ταῖς ὁσοῖς αὐτῶν ("and they were made desolate in all their ways"), which displaces human responsibility. But in Synkellos the verb is in active form, καὶ ἠφάνισαν τὰς ὁδοὺς αὐτῶν ("and they made their ways desolate"), placing the blame on human beings. The Ge'ez version, although it places the blame on the Watchers for leading human beings astray, similar to the Synkellos' version it preserves the active verb form in the last phrase: *wamāsanu kwellu fenāwihomu* ("and they made desolate all their ways").[129] The active reading places the blame on human beings, and so the Ge'ez version seems to indicate a shared blame understanding. The active form is also similar to the Hebrew verb form in Genesis 6:12 כִּי־הִשְׁחִית כָּל־בָּשָׂר אֶת־דַּרְכּוֹ ("for all flesh had corrupted their way"),[130] and implies human responsibility. As discussed earlier, Bautch's analysis of the Synkellos' reading leads her to conclude that the longer Greek version is a possible authentic variant of a Semitic version and not an addition by an interested later redactor (see above under the heading "Text is Ambivalent"). Nicklesburg likewise states the reading preserved in Synkellos is "ancient," and concludes that the reading preserved in Synkellos "reflects very early tradition" and "not an accidental corruption."[131]

The text in 8:1c–2 of Synkellos clearly places the blame on human beings. This short passage puts forth an idea very different from what is presented in the BW to this point. It states that human beings learned the art of warfare and beautification from Asael, and then they, presumably the women, led the angels astray. This reverses the order of things radically. The implication is that the original sin was not the cohabitation of the Watchers with human women, but the imparting of forbidden knowledge, consequent to which the women seduced the Watchers.[132] Thus it gives primacy to the imparting

---

128. For more details, see Bautch, "Decoration," 79–95 and Nicklesburg, *1 Enoch 1*, 189, 195.
129. Greek and Ge'ez texts taken from Nicklesburg, *1 Enoch 1*, 189.
130. See Bautch, "Decoration," 79–95.
131. Nicklesburg, *1 Enoch 1*, 195–196.
132. Nicklesburg notes these important implications resulting from the Gk[s] text. Nicklesburg, *1 Enoch 1*, 195–196; also see Nicklesburg and VanderKam, *1 Enoch*, 25, n. c.

of knowledge and treats the sin of the cohabiting with human women as its outcome.[133] Synkellos' version that exposes human culpability is also supported by the fact that when God commands Asael's imprisonment Asael is blamed for all of the sins: "And all the earth was made desolate by the deeds of the teachings of Asael, and over him write all the sins" (BW 10:8), whereas in Shemihazah's sentence he and his followers are blamed for mating with human women and having defiled themselves (BW 10:11–15). Nickelsburg and Bautch cite other ancient sources that preserve the similar idea that the angels originally came to earth on some other mission, for instance, to teach righteous living to human beings (Jub 4:15), or to convict human beings of their ingratitude to God (Pseudo Clementine Homilies 8.12)[134], and only after descending do they marry beautiful human women.[135] In Jubilees 4:15; 5:1–3, Targum Jonathan (Gen 6:2), Testament of Reuben 5, and Pseudo Clementine Homilies 8:11–15 women are portrayed as responsible for leading the angels astray, and the idea that women seduced the angels using cosmetics and other adornments is specifically present in Targum Jonathan Genesis 6:2[136] and in Testament of Reuben 5.[137] As such, this strand from Asael tradition in 1 Enoch 8:1c–2 is not easily dismissed, and perhaps the Asael story was woven along with the Shemihazah story to indicate the author's or redactors' conception that the Watchers and the humans share the blame for sin.[138] Hence, the BW

Other scholars who see human culpability being espoused in the Asael tradition are Davidson, *Angels at Qumran*, 47; Wright, *Origin*, 117, Reed, *Fallen Angels*, 31–32; VanderKam, "1 Enoch, Enochic Motifs," 124–125; Namgung, "Sin and Human," 109.

133. It may be noted however that the women are not presented as solely responsible for seducing the Watchers. 1 Enoch 7:1 and 8:3 make women or wives the recipients of the mysteries from the Watchers. However, in these instances the cohabitation of the Watchers with the women precedes the imparting of the knowledge. Moreover, 1 Enoch 8:1 states that men learned the secret arts from Asael and made the adornments for their daughters before the seduction began. Thus, both men and women are implicated. See also Bautch, "Decoration," 91.

134. "The Clementine Homilies," http://www.ccel.org/ccel/schaff/anf08/Page_272.html.

135. Bautch points out that there are witnesses to the contrary in texts such as Irenaeus' *In Demonstration of the Apostolic Preaching 18*, and Cyprian's *On the Dress of Virgins 14* which indicate the Watchers' descent preceding the teaching of forbidden arts. Bautch, "Decoration," 91. This however does not invalidate the testimony of the other texts; it only shows both traditions were well known.

136. Maher, *Targum Pseudo-Jonathan*, 38.

137. See Bautch, "What Becomes," 777; Nickelsburg, *1 Enoch 1*, 195–196.

138. Some of the scholars who come to a similar conclusion are Wright, *Origin*, 8; Reed, *Fallen Angels*, 31–32; Namgung, "Sin and Human," 108–110.

does not unilaterally place the blame for sin on the Watchers but also indicts human beings for the sin and corruption of the world.

Further the Greek Akhmim text in BW 19:2 states, καὶ αἱ γυναῖκες αὐτῶν τῶν παραβάντων ἀγγέλων εἰς σειρῆνας γενήσονται ("And the wives of the transgressing angels will become sirens"). Sirens in antiquity were seductresses, *femmes fatales*, who lured men to their death. In later works sirens came to be associated with death, as singers of dirges,[139] which accords with 1 Enoch 96:2, the only other reference to sirens in 1 Enoch. Both understandings of the term, as seductresses or singers of dirges, present the fate of the human wives of the Watchers in a negative light. The Geʻez rendering preserves a different tradition stating that the wives become "as peaceful": "And their wives, those whom the angels led astray, will become as peaceful." As Bautch points out, the Greek reading is usually preferred[140] because it is understandable how the Greek *vorlage* might have been misread and consequently mistranslated in the Ethiopic – the Ethiopic translator probably misread εἰς σειρῆνας ("(in) siren") as ὡς εἰρηναῖαι ("as peaceful") and thus translated it as *kama salāmāweyāt* ("as/like peaceful").[141] If the Akhmim ms. offers a plausible reading, it could imply that the wives were considered co-conspirators with their Watcher husbands. This is also implied in 8:3 which states that the Watchers revealed the mysteries to their wives and children.[142]

---

139. Bautch, "What Becomes," 771.

140. See Charles, *Book of Enoch*, 43; Nickelsburg, *1 Enoch 1*, verse in 276, textual note in 277.

141. Bautch, "What Becomes," 771–772. However, Bautch challenges both the Greek and the Ethiopic renderings and instead proposes that the Aramaic word שלם in the *pi'el* form, meaning "to complete" or "to bring to an end," lies behind the word translated as "siren" and "peaceful." Accordingly, she offers a possible Aramaic reconstruction – "and the wives of the transgressing angels will be brought to an utter end." This, she suggests, implies the unimportance of the wives since the focus is on the watchers and their punishment. See Bautch, "What Becomes," 778–780. This reading has its merits, except for three points: i) the Aramaic for this passage being not extant there is no evidence that the Aramaic word behind the Greek "siren" or the Ethiopic "peaceful" was indeed שלם, and ii) the wives coming to an "utter end" does seem negative enough to imply a punishment rather than implying unimportance as Bautch suggests, and iii) the Aramaic word שלם in *pi'el* is also translatable as "to restore" (see שלם, in Koehler and Baumgartner, *HALOT*, vol. 2, 1534–1535). As such it could also imply a restoration of the wives, which has a positive connotation. This has a similar effect as the Ethiopic positive reading, "as peaceful," thus probably undoing her effort.

142. The Aramaic does not have that phrase "and to their children" in 8:3 but the Gkˢ (Synkellos) has it, while the text of 8:3 in Gkᵃ (Akhmim) and Geʻez mss. are much shorter and have other variations. See Knibb, *Essays on the Book*, 38.

Hence, it is possible to argue that in the BW human beings were culpable for i) the sins of violence that brought desolation on earth (BW 8:2; 10: 7, 8), ii) the practice and transmission of the knowledge of magical arts and astrology (BW 8:3), and possibly iii) seducing and mating with an ontologically different species. Additionally, through the unlawful union between the mortal women and the immortal Watchers giant offspring were born who further wreaked havoc on the world. While alive, the giants have an insatiable appetite and devour everything, including human beings, and even resort to cannibalism and drinking of blood (BW 7:2–5), which is specifically prohibited in the Torah (Lev 17:10–11). When they are put to death by God's judgment they become evil spirits, because they were a mix of mortal and immortal, and further torment human beings until the end of time (BW 15:8–16:1). Human beings thus bring desolation through wars using weapons created by using forbidden knowledge, mate with immortal beings, and by their unlawful union produces the giants who devastate the earth and all its inhabitants.[143] God therefore responds with retribution not only upon the Watchers (BW21), but also on human beings who willfully participated in and perpetuated the evil practices learned from the Watchers (BW 22). Nickelsburg observes that the supernatural origin of sin is deemphasized in the final form of the book, highlighting instead human responsibility.[144] The righteous, including Enoch, provide a foil to the sinners and the fallen angels. The presence of the righteous in the BW also demonstrates that righteousness was possible, and Enoch, although human, is elevated almost to the status of the angels, having access to the throne of God and to heavenly wisdom and sights. Hence it can be said that divine retribution in BW 22 is based on the deeds of human beings and exhibits characteristics of the anthropocentric aspect.

The anthropocentricity of the divine retribution in BW 22 is further borne out by the fact that retribution is conceived as corresponding not only to the overall deeds of an individual, that is, rewards for the righteous and punishment for the sinner, but is also proportional. It takes into account whether or not the person faced the consequence of those deeds in his or her lifetime and accordingly the souls are segregated to receive punishment in the measure and proportion as deserved by each individual soul (BW 22:9–13). This is

---

143. Nickelsburg, *1 Enoch 1*, 196.
144. Nickelsburg, 47.

evinced by the holding of the souls of the dead sinners not in one but three separate compartments.

There is no indication that among the righteous there would be different categories of reward. They are all presented as a single group, held in the same hollow place that is illuminated and supplied with a fountain of water (BW 22:2, 8). Apart from the brightness of the place and the presence of water, whose significance has been explained above, BW 22 does not supply any other detail about what constitutes the reward of the righteous. However, the chapters following give us a peek into the restored creation. One of the rewards that the righteous will enjoy after the final judgment is access to the tree of life (BW 25:4–6). It is a reversal of the effects of the Fall that included the loss of access to the tree of life (Gen 3:24). The righteous do not have access to the tree of life during the intermediate period in the hollow place, however, after the final judgment (BW 25:4) the tree of life is planted by the house of God (25:4–5) and made accessible to the righteous.[145] Its benefits are spoken of in extravagant terms – it is the most fragrant among all the trees, and its flowers and even its leaves are beautiful (BW 24:4). But most importantly, it provides longevity and healing. It is not clear if eternal life for human beings is envisioned; rather it seems to envision a restoration to the antediluvian period when people enjoyed a long lifespan (BW 25:6).[146]

The souls of the dead sinners, however, are divided into three categories occupying the second to fourth compartments. The sinners who escaped unpunished in their lifetime are held in the second compartment and face the most severe punishment. The specific nature of their sin is not explained;[147] the focus remains on the punishment rather than on the particular deeds. Nonetheless, since they did not suffer the consequences of their sins during their lifetime, they now suffer torments even as they anticipate full and final divine judgment (BW 22:10–11). There seems to be a hint of the idea

---

145. The restored creation also features a tree of wisdom, which Enoch sees from afar as he passes by the paradise of righteousness (32:3–6). It is not clear if the righteous will be given access to it. Macaskill opines that access to the tree of wisdom is not restored to the righteous, which might be inferred because unlike the reference to the tree of life there is no mention of it being given to the righteous. It is accessible only to the "'holy ones' (angels)." Macaskill, *Revealed Wisdom*, 34–35.

146. Nickelsburg states that it suggests a lifespan longer than the pre-flood forefathers. See Nickelsburg, *1 Enoch 1*, 315.

147. Nickelsburg, 308.

of resurrection here in v. 11. The angel Raphael informs Enoch that ὧδε ("here") in the compartment the souls of the sinners are tormented, and in contrast at the final judgment, these souls will be bound ἐλεῖ ("there"),[148] probably a reference to the "accursed valley" (BW 27:1–3). This contrast seems to suggest that the souls will be transferred somewhere else for the final and more severe judgment, and some scholars read this, in conjunction with μετεγερθῶσιν ("raised") in v. 13, which is discussed below, as a possible reference to resurrection.[149]

The third compartment is occupied by souls of individuals who met unjust violent deaths.[150] That the violence against them took place "in the days of the sinners" (22:12) seem to indicate their deaths were unjust. They, like Abel (22:7), make suit before God against their murderers for justice to be served. It seems like v.12 ("the spirits of them that make suit, who make disclosure about the destruction, when they were murdered in the days of the sinners") is drawing on v.7 ("and this is the spirit that went forth from Abel, whom Cain his brother murdered. And Abel makes accusation against him . . ."), and on the narrative of Genesis 4, albeit an exegetically embellished one,[151] and establishing Abel as a prototype for the victims of similar violence in v. 12, particularly in the way these souls and Abel are described – both "make suit" (both verses use forms of the same root ἐντυγχάνω "to appeal, intercede") regarding their murderers.

However, although the souls in this compartment were killed in an unjust violent manner it does not follow that they were also all righteous.[152] Abel may be presented as a type of those who suffered violent deaths, but the text does not make an explicit connection with righteousness. Nickelsburg is perhaps right in suggesting that the connection being drawn between Abel and these souls highlights the "violence of their murderers" and the certainty of the

---

148. Some scholars opine that "there" is a reference to Gehenna, or hell. See Russell, *Method and Message*, 370; Nickelsburg, *Resurrection*, 169.

149. This interpretation is also bolstered by similar references elsewhere in 1 Enoch. See Russell, *Method and Message*, 370–371; Nickelsburg, *Resurrection, Immortality*, 169.

150. See Nickelsburg, *1 Enoch 1*, 308. Wacker, *Weltordnung*, 197–199 cited by Nickelsburg, *1 Enoch 1*, 308.

151. See Byron, "Abel's Blood," 748–749.

152. Nickelsburg, *1 Enoch 1*, 308.

coming judgment.¹⁵³ The two images are also united by the accusation they now continue to make against their murderers. Further, the description of each of the compartments begins with καί οὕτως ("And this" 22:9b,10,12,13), indicating that the compartment of the righteous and the compartment of the souls making suit are distinct. Moreover, v. 2 indicates that only one compartment is illuminated and watered and that is occupied by the righteous (22:9b). As such it indicates that the souls in v. 12 are in one of the dark compartments, which is not really the reward expected for righteous martyrs who were expected to themselves shine like stars (e.g., Dan 11:33–35, 12:3). Hence it would be odd, as Nickelsburg notes, if the souls of martyrs, comparable to Abel in righteousness, were relegated to make their case in a dark place until the time of the final judgment.¹⁵⁴ Alternatively, it has been suggested that these souls were considered ethically neutral but held together in the same compartment as they all share the fate and now seek revenge on their murderers.¹⁵⁵ This interpretation has its appeal, however it also does not explain the condition of their compartment. It is true that Abel, in the history of interpretation, does become the paradigmatic figure for all future righteous victims.¹⁵⁶ However, in BW 22 the immediate context of the darkened compartment of the souls of the murdered ones makes this deduction problematic, if not impossible, especially in light of the larger context that presents retribution that is not only corresponding but also proportionate. The emphasis seems to fall on the fact of the murder and the sustained accusation by the victims of such violence until retribution is meted out. Abel in this case becomes a paradigmatic figure crying out against the wicked murderers. Thus, it is likely that the souls in the third compartment were not considered righteous,¹⁵⁷ but because they themselves are also victims of gross injustice they do not suffer while they await the final judgment when justice would be done, especially regarding their murder.

---

153. See Nickelsburg, 306. However, Nickelsburg elsewhere considers these souls of murdered individuals righteous; see Nickelsburg, *Resurrection, Immortality*, 170–171.

154. Nickelsburg, *1 Enoch 1*, 308.

155. Wacker, *Weltordnung*, 197–199 cited by Nickelsburg, *1 Enoch 1*, 308.

156. Abel is presented as a paradigmatic righteous individual in texts like Josephus (A.J. 1.2.1 §53), 4 Maccabees (18:11–13), and Matthew (23:34–35).

157. Contra Byron who argues that these were souls of innocent victims. Cf. Byron, "Abel's Blood," 748–752.

The fourth compartment also hosted sinners, described as "companions of the lawless" (22:13). This description does not make them any less culpable than the others.[158] However, unlike the sinners in the second compartment, they suffer no torments in their holding place because they have received their punishments during their lifetime. Additionally, they will also not be judged anymore when God comes to execute final judgment upon the souls in the other compartments. Instead, they will not be raised; they will remain in the hollow place forever, and this will be their everlasting punishment.[159] The Greek term translated "raised" is μετεγερθῶσιν (from μετεγείρω, v. 13) and is the only reference to a probable resurrection in BW 22. The verb is used negatively to say the souls in the last compartment will not rise or resurrect at judgment; rather they are to be imprisoned in their compartment forever. The word μετεγείρω itself is not found elsewhere in the NT or the LXX. It seems to be a compound word from μετα + ἐγείρω where ἐγείρω means "to arise, to stand from a sleeping position" with extended meanings such as "to heal, rise to life, restore from dead or damaged state." It appears 144 times in the NT. And although resurrection is not its most common meaning there are several instances when ἐγείρω is used to mean resurrection.[160] For instance, in Matthew 20:19 it is used to describe Jesus' resurrection (ἐγερθήσεται). Similarly, in Matthew 26:32 Jesus refers to his own resurrection using a form of this verb (ἐγερθῆναί).[161] As such, taken together with the reference to a likely transfer of the souls for the final judgment from "here" to "there" in v. 11, it may be referring to some kind of resurrection for the final judgment, or more precisely, non-resurrection in the case of the souls in the last compartment and resurrection for the rest of the souls in the other three compartments. Charles, Nickelsburg, and Outi Lehtipuu all read this as the author's expression in the belief of resurrection. Lehtipuu argues that since resurrection of the wicked alone is not attested anywhere, it is reasonable to deduce the text

---

158. Nickelsburg calls the description a "cliché," Nickelsburg, *1 Enoch 1*, 308.

159. Charles, ed. and trans., *Book of Enoch*.

160. The LXX and the NT also make use of another word that can denote resurrection – ἀνίστημι. The LXX uses ἀνίστημι in Daniel 12:2 and Isaiah 26:19, and it occurs in the NT in Acts 24:15, Luke 14:14, etc. For the usage of ἐγείρω and ἀνίστημι as the most common terms used to describe resurrection see also Lehtipuu, *Debates Over the Resurrection*, 27–35.

161. Also in John 2:22; Acts 3: 15; 4:10; 13:30; Rom 4:24; 6:4, 9; 10:9; 1 Cor 15:12; 2 Cor 4:14; Gal 1:1; Eph 1:20; Col 2:12; 1 Thess 1:10; 2 Tim 2:8; 1 Pet 1:21.

implies resurrection of the righteous.¹⁶² Moreover, Russell states that survival as a disembodied soul or spirit is generally considered only as a transitional phase towards a resurrection of the body as its final state, and the idea that the wicked will burn in hell in their bodies is found in BW 67:8–9.¹⁶³ This coheres well with the picture presented in 1 Enoch 22 since the souls are only intermediately confined in the hollow places while awaiting final judgment.

However, if the idea of resurrection at the final judgment underlies BW 22:11 and 13, the text does not elaborate further. It does not say if the resurrection envisioned involves the reconstitution of the body at resurrection. It could imply that resurrection was a familiar idea to the audience and needed no detailed exposition. However, it cannot be said with certainty. Thus, if μετεγερθῶσιν ("raised" v. 13) is used in the sense of resurrection from the dead, it would imply that the rest of the souls in the other three compartments would also resurrect to face the final judgment and their ultimate fates.

Hence, divine retribution in BW 22 is in response to human deeds. The picture of humanity's role becomes blurry if the focus is only on the Shemihazah story. However, when the Asael story is also brought to bear upon the reading of the account the picture that emerges is more of a shared responsibility between the Watchers and human beings, similar to that of the serpent and Adam and Eve in Genesis 3. Instead of being helpless victims, human beings are portrayed as collaborators with the Watchers who use the knowledge gained from them to bring devastation on earth through violence, use of magical arts, and seduction of the Watchers. It is for these sins that God responds with punishment for the sinners and even after death there is no escaping the divine judgment since retribution is transposed to the post-mortem. Further, there is also a theocentric aspect of retribution in that God provides the laws necessary for man to follow his ways. Thus, while the anthropocentric aspect is at the fore, it is undergirded by the theocratic aspect of divine retribution since God's commandments as the basis of judgment is assumed rather than explained throughout the book.

---

162. Charles, *Book of Enoch*, and Nickelsburg, *1 Enoch 1*, 306; Lehtipuu, *Debates*, 34.
163. For detail see Russell, *Method and Message*, 375.

5.6. Nature of Post-mortem Divine Retribution: Individual or Corporate

The question here is whether the post-mortem divine retribution in the BW is presented as operating on the individual or corporate level. In Deuteronomy, the nature of divine retribution was predominantly corporate so that the consequences of one's deeds could impact others in the family, clan, or even the whole nation. This was understood to be the case because of the largely corporate outlook prevalent in ancient Israelite society and because of the corporate perspective of Yahweh's covenant with Israel. From the foregoing discussion, it may seem that post-mortem divine retribution in BW 22 is individuated since retribution appears to be deeds-based, seen especially in the case of sinners. However, it is not quite as clear. In the BW, several motifs intertwine to giving rise to a complex image of the nature of retribution.

The final judgment is based on adherence to τάς ἐντολὰς αὐτοῦ ("his commandments" or "his laws," BW 5:4), but what exactly constitutes the law is ambiguous. Some scholars consider law as embedded in revealed wisdom, with 1 Enoch being the embodiment of this wisdom. Further, this revealed wisdom has a soteriological function (BW 5:7–8),[164] and is given only to the chosen ones who are the righteous. The issue is further complicated by the contention of some scholars that the chosen righteous refers to the Enochians.[165] In effect, salvation is the exclusive prerogative of the Enochians. This presents an intricate web that needs to be untangled before a reasonable comment on post-mortem divine retribution can be made.

One way to approach this issue is to categorize the scholarly views into two broad groups based on their understanding of ἐντολή (law, commandment) in 1 Enoch – i) law as an entity external to the Torah, and ii) law that assumes the Torah or more broadly assumes the Torah or the Jewish way of life. The first occurrence of the word "law" is in 5:4 in the phrase οὐδὲ ἐποιήσατε κατὰ τὰς ἐντολὰς αὐτοῦ ("nor acted according to his commandments" 5:4). Here the "law" or "commandments" relate to human behavior, and although law is central to the theme of judgment it is not defined. This ambiguity makes it easier to refer to the understanding of law in the first view in terms of

---

164. See Nickelsburg, *1 Enoch 1*, 42, 50–51, 129; Macaskill, *Revealed Wisdom*, 36.

165. Nickelsburg, *1 Enoch 1*, 54; Collins, "Theology and Identity," 57–62, cited by Heger, *Challenges*, 178.

what it is not, that is, law is non-Mosaic. Thus, those espousing the first view understand law as something other than the Torah, variously designated as "law of nature" or "revealed wisdom."[166] This has been discussed earlier under the section on "Torah and 1 Enoch." As concluded earlier, it seemed probable that 1 Enoch does not expound its version of the law because it assumed the familiarity and acceptance of the authority of the already existing law, that is the Mosaic law; that perhaps in speaking of the violation of the commandments it viewed itself as complementary to the Torah, as did the prophets, rather than proposing a new distinct law. Thus, the second view seems preferable.[167]

Moreover, those who prefer the non-Mosaic understanding of the law generally see the righteous chosen as referring to the Enochians. This goes beyond the text into historical reconstruction. For scholars like Boccaccini, Nickelsburg, and Collins, the concept of the chosen ones who are given wisdom and the concept of the righteous in 1 Enoch converge in the Enochians community, that is, those who follow the Enochic law are the chosen righteous.[168] Thus soteriology becomes the exclusive prerogative of the Enochians who possess wisdom. This neat categorization has at least three problems.

First, it divides humanity on ideological grounds, that is, as Enochians and non-Enochians – following the true or false mediator of revelations becomes the criterion. But in 1 Enoch the main dualism is between the righteous and the sinners and hence the basis is ethical or moral, not ideological. For instance, sinners are those who have done wicked deeds (1:9), spoken harsh and proud words (5:4; 27:2). Second, it implies that the rest of the Israelites

---

166. Boccaccini does not explain what law in 1 Enoch is but states that Enochians are the only ones who qualify for salvation. Boccaccini, *Beyond the Essene*, Nickelsburg, *1 Enoch 1*, 50; Collins, "How Distinctive," 30.

167. As cited earlier in the "Torah and 1 Enoch" section, this view is held by scholars like Tigchelaar, "Balaam and Enoch," 94 and Hoffmann, *Das Gesetz*, both cited in Namgang, "Sin and Human," 100–101; Heger, "1 Enoch," 54; Bachmann, *Book of the Watchers*, 18.

168. Boccaccini, *Beyond the Essene*, 171; Nickelsburg, *1 Enoch 1*, 54; Collins, "Theology and Identity," 57–62, cited by Heger, "1 Enoch," 42. Some scholars, like Nickelsburg, see the tension in 1 Enoch between this very particularized view of who constitutes the chosen and the universalistic perspective of wisdom being made available to all; however, he does not elaborate on it. Nickelsburg, *1 Enoch 1*, 54. Whereas for Boccaccini each major ideology is associated with a specific view of individual and corporate retribution, hence he argues that while the Zadokite view human sins as responsible for catastrophes, whether individual and corporate, in the Enochic model, he posits for historical determinism where human behavior is essentially inconsequential. See Boccaccini, *Beyond the Essene*, 171–172; Boccaccini, *Roots of Rabbinic*, 207.

are sinners. For instance, Collins suggests that the Enochians are the chosen righteous while the rest of the Israelites are sinners.[169] This seems unreasonable. Even if there was an Enochic community, which has not been proven yet, it is quite a stretch to argue that all non-Enochians were considered doomed. As Heger points out, the sinners are characterized as worshipping idols and graven images (99:7), and it is improbable that all of Israel, save the Enochians, have turned to idolatry. Third, that 1 Enoch was written in Aramaic, the language of the common people, indicates that the intended audience was most likely not particularly interested in theological issues. As such, it is much more probable to understand the righteous and sinner as being designated as such based on a known law like the Torah and faithfulness to its decrees.[170]

If it is the Torah law that is referred to in the BW, what is the scope of salvation – only Israel or other nations too? Even if the law assumed in the BW, or 1 Enoch for that matter, is the Torah, there are two things that may seem to point to the whole of humanity as its scope: i) the façade of pre-Mosaic Enoch could imply that all humanity was within its purview, and ii) the promise of wisdom to all humanity in the later days, for instance, 1 Enoch 91:14–15 states, "righteous law will be revealed to all the sons of the whole earth ... and all humankind will look to the path of everlasting righteousness" (also see BW 10:21–22) as also the judgment is on all σάρκα (σάρξ "flesh" BW 1:9).[171] This universal scope is also concurrent with what Nickelsburg calls the "three-stage pattern": Noah is saved from the judgment by flood because of the revelation given to him (10:2), from him a plant is planted whose "seed will endure for all generations of eternity" (10:3), the plant being a common metaphor for Israel or the remnant.[172] In the eschaton, "all sons of men will become righteous and all the peoples will worship" (10:21). This three-stage pattern is also seen in the section of 1 Enoch called the Apocalypse of Weeks (93:1–10, 91:11–17).[173] So perhaps in speaking of the giving of wisdom to all

---

169. Collins, "Theology and Identity," 57–62, cited by Heger, "1 Enoch," 42.
170. Heger, *Challenges*, 179.
171. Nickelsburg calls the judgment announced in 1:3c–9 a universal one. Nickelsburg, *1 Enoch 1*, 143.
172. See Nickelsburg, 220.
173. See Nickelsburg, 52–53.

humanity in the final days it was blurring the Israel-other nations distinction and making faithfulness to God's commandments the primary criteria.

Moreover, regardless of how narrow or wide the scope, the more pertinent question is, if righteousness and sinfulness are moral categories, is the nature of retribution individual or corporate? The BW's repeated references to the righteous and sinners seem to be a reference to groups. However, it is possible that these groups were more fluid than appears. Earlier it was mentioned that the book was probably calling for people to return to the right path, to the Jewish way of life. In line with that thought, the BW seems to envision the possibility of sinners becoming righteous upon reception of wisdom. Two aspects indicate this.

First, the righteous are spoken of as recipients of mercy and forgiveness:

> With the righteous he will make peace, over the chosen there will be protection, and upon them will be mercy . . . (BW 1:8; ἔλεος "mercy, pity, compassion")

> . . . But all the chosen will rejoice; and for them there will be forgiveness of sins and all mercy and peace and clemency. (BW 5:6)

These verses indicate that among the righteous there are at least some who needed forgiveness and mercy.

Second, the righteous needed mercy and forgiveness for the sins of godlessness and pride, which is similar to the sins for which the sinners are indicted in BW 1:9 and 5:4. Thus BW 5:8 posits that some of those who constitute the chosen righteous were previously sinners who later "sin no more," and "transgress no more":

> The wisdom will be given to all the chosen; . . . will sin no more through godlessness or pride. . . . And they will transgress no more, nor will they sin all the days of their life, nor will they die in the heat of God's wrath. (BW 5:8)

Understood in this manner, the righteous and the sinners are not fixed groups but in flux. Nickelsburg also considers this possibility. He points out, "There are similarities in the terminology used to describe the sins that are condemned in 1:9 and 5:4, and the sins of the righteous that will be forgiven and no longer committed by them according to 5:8."[174] This unique opportunity to receive forgiveness and mercy is given only to human beings; the Watchers send their petition for forgiveness through Enoch but are denied (BW 13:4–8; 14:4; 16:2–4). Considering this interpretation a possibility, from the final judgment point of view, the nature of post-mortem divine retribution appears to be more individual than corporate – the members who constitute the righteous can be individuals who were previously sinners but stopped sinning.

5.7. Conclusion

BW 22 is a text like no other affording us a glimpse into a strand of Jewish thought concerning post-mortem divine retribution. It portrays the condition of human beings on the other side of death in a vivid manner. This chapter argued that the arguments regarding 1 Enoch as proposing an Enochic Judaism is not convincing enough due to insufficient evidence to corroborate such a radical claim, and the two main components of Enochic Judaism, that of absence of reference to Mosaic elements and the superhuman origin of sin, can be explained in a way that does not necessitate resorting to a non- or anti-Mosaic stance. It was also concluded that although the story of the Watchers predominantly focuses on the sin of the Watchers and hence holds them culpable, human retribution is justified in view of the human responsibility brought to the fore through the Asael tradition.

It was seen that the aspect of divine retribution most prominent in BW 22 is the anthropocentric aspect that emphasizes human actions as the basis for divine retribution. There is ample evidence in favour of this stance, not the least of which is the Asael tradition, especially as preserved in Synkellos' Greek version. Human beings suffer the consequences of their deeds in their post-mortem state even as they await final judgment. This is highlighted especially through the compartmentalization of the dead into distinct categories based on whether they have received the appropriate consequence for their deeds while alive and the reception of different treatment even as

---

174. Nickelsburg, *1 Enoch 1*, 133. Nickelsburg notes that this interpretation is further substantiated by 1 Enoch 101, which is "a warning that verges on a call to repentance" through its call to "observe" and "contemplate."

they await the final judgment. Thus, human actions were determinative for the post-mortem fate of the dead in BW 22.

However, it was also noted that the theocentric aspect underlies the anthropocentric aspect in that the law, based on which judgment is executed on human beings, is given by God, whether one prefers to understand the law as Mosaic or non-Mosaic. Further, judgment is universal and ultimately based on deeds of the individual, and it is these individuals that constitute the righteous or sinners. As such, though the designations "the sinners" and "the righteous" are used throughout, retribution operates individually rather than corporately. Thus, post-mortem divine retribution in BW 22 is largely anthropocentric and individual in nature.

CHAPTER 6

Post-mortem Divine Retribution in 2 Maccabees 7

6.1. Introduction

The previous chapter examined post-mortem divine retribution in the Book of Watchers, particularly as presented in its chapter 22, in relation to the superhuman explanation for the origin of evil and Enoch's cosmic journeys. It is singular in its vivid portrayal of post-mortem divine retribution as not only just, through its moral differentiation of the righteous and wicked, but also proportionate, by segregating the dead according to whether they received their just desserts while alive. As such, post-mortem divine retribution in BW 22 emphasized the anthropocentric aspect, and theocentric aspect. Also, the possibility of sinners receiving forgiveness and mercy and becoming part of the righteous posits that the nature of divine retribution in BW 22 is more individuated rather than the righteous and sinners being a fixed group. Dwelling on a similar theme of post-mortem divine retribution but quite dissimilar in terms of genre is the book of 2 Maccabees.[1] The focus in this chapter is 2 Maccabees 7, which narrates the story of a mother and her seven sons who choose to die rather than violate God's law. Before being put

---

1. The main extant Greek sources for 2 Maccabees are two Greek uncial mss., Codex Alexandrinus, A of the fifth century and Codex Venetus, V of the eighth century CE, and some "Old Latin" and Syriac versions. Zeitlin, *Second Book*, 95; Bartlett, *First and Second Books*, 215.

to death they assert their belief in a post-mortem divine resurrection in what are some of the clearest statements on resurrection in STP Jewish literature.

This chapter examines 2 Maccabees 7 to understand its presentation of the nature of post-mortem divine retribution. The investigation begins with a brief overview of the contents and provenance of 2 Maccabees. It also evaluates the historiographic value of 2 Maccabees to assess its value for the present study. Next, it locates the story of 2 Maccabees 7 in its milieu through a short discussion of the cultural and historical backdrop in which the story unfolds. It then examines the idea of post-mortem divine retribution presented in 2 Maccabees 7 through the concept of resurrection in the speeches of the mother and her seven sons. Since 2 Maccabees 7 is distinct in its emphasis on physical resurrection, the chapter also pays attention to its conception of a physical resurrection in relation to post-mortem divine retribution. This is followed by an examination of the basis and aspect of post-mortem divine retribution in 2 Maccabees 7 in light of the four aspects of divine retribution in Deuteronomy, and a look at whether post-mortem divine retribution operates corporately or individually, which helps analyse the continuities and discontinuities between the concept of divine retribution in Deuteronomy and 2 Maccabees. The chapter ends with an excursus that looks at divine retribution as it applies to Antiochus who is presented in 2 Maccabees as God's agent for punishing the Jews.

6.2. The Book of 2 Maccabees: Contents and Provenance

Second Maccabees is largely a historical narrative, albeit a theological one. It describes the rise of the Hasmonean dynasty in Judea. The book covers a period of 15 years and centres on the city of Jerusalem from the time of the high priesthood of Jason in 175 BCE to the defeat of Nicanor, the Seleucid general and later governor of Judea in 161 BCE.[2] It begins with two letters presumably sent by the Jews of Judea and Jerusalem to fellow Jews in Egypt inviting them to join in the celebration of Hanukkah or the Feast of the Tabernacles (2 Macc 1:1–2:18), as well as a prologue (2 Macc 2:19–32).

---

2. Daniel R. Schwartz, *2 Maccabees*, 3; deSilva, *Introducing the Apocrypha*, 266; Himmelfarb, "Judaism and Hellenism," 21.

This is followed by a narrative recounting of a series of attacks launched by Antiochus IV Epiphanes, the Hellenistic king of the Seleucid Empire (175–164 BCE), on the Jerusalem Temple and its cult, the persecution of the Jews, and the rise and revolt of the Judean military under Judas Maccabeus. It culminates with the defeat and death of Nicanor, the rededication of the Temple (2 Macc 3:1–15:36), and an epilogue (2 Macc 15:37–39). It is in this context of persecution that the concept of post-mortem divine retribution is expressed in this narrative.

The book of 2 Maccabees claims to be an epitome of Jason the Cyrene's five-volume history of Judas Maccabee and his brother, and the Maccabean Revolt (2:23; 19–31).[3] Both 2 Maccabees and Jason the Cyrene's work are considered to have been composed originally in Greek.[4] 2 Maccabees is generally considered to have been written in the BCE, albeit variously dated. For instance, Daniel Schwartz dates it to before 143,[5] Robert Doran dates it to the early years of John Hyrcanus I who reigned between 135/134 and 104 BCE,[6] Hugo Bévenot dates it between 124 BCE and 70 CE,[7] and Jan Willem van Henten between 124 and 63 BCE.[8] John Bartlett considers it impossible to date the book with precision and places it anywhere in the last 150 years BCE.[9] Others have dated the book later than the second century BCE: Nickelsburg dates it to 100 BCE,[10] Jonathan Goldstein's *terminus ad quem* for 2 Maccabees between 78 or 77 and 63 BCE.[11] Otto Eissfeldt dates the composition of Jason's work towards the end of the second century BCE, and 2 Maccabees in its final form, with the addition of the letters and rearrangement by the epitomist, somewhere around 60 BC,[12] and G. Rawlinson

---

3. Jason of Cyrene is otherwise unknown and has been variously evaluated. W. Richnow had argued that the epitomist of 2 Maccabees invented Jason and his work as his source, which Robert Doran argues against; see Doran, *Temple Propaganda*, 81–83; while Jonathan Goldstein attempts to explain Jason's historical methods; see Goldstein, *II Maccabees*, 55–70.

4. deSilva, *Introducing*, 266, 268–270; Zeitlin, *Second Book*, 30.

5. For details see, Schwartz, *2 Maccabees*, 11–15.

6. Doran, *Temple Propaganda*, 111–112.

7. Bévenot, *Die eiden Makkabäerbucher*, 15.

8. See van Henten, *Maccabean Martyrs*, 51–53; deSilva, *Introducing*, 270.

9. Bartlett, *First and Second Books*, 215.

10. Nickelsburg, *Jewish Literature*, 121, 226.

11. Goldstein, *II Maccabees*, 71–83.

12. See Eissfeldt, *Old Testament*, 581.gn 2 Maccabees ional understanding of the afterlife as portrayed in the Hebrew BIble heir

dates it to 80 BCE.[13] Shmuel Shepkaru dates it to the first century BCE,[14] and Werner Dommerhausen to the late first century BCE,[15] while Solomon Zeitlin suggests an even later date, the period of Agrippa (41–44 CE), as the date for the final redaction of 2 Maccabees.[16] As such, with the exception of a few like Zeitlin, the general tendency has been to date 2 Maccabees sometime in the last two centuries BCE.

2 Maccabees consist largely of what can be termed historical narrative. However, the use of the term "history" in describing 2 Maccabees stands in need of qualification, and is discussed briefly below.

6.3. Historiographic Value of 2 Maccabees

The epitomist (abridger) refers to his work as ἱστορία (2 Macc 2:32),[17] which can be translated as "inquiry" or "history"; however, the narrative in 2 Maccabees is not historiography in the modern sense of the word.[18] It is not a disinterested, objective record of past events, as is expected of a modern historiography, rather one that is told from a particular standpoint. There exists a broad consensus among scholars that 2 Maccabees is tendentious, and the author's theological orientation guides his compositional enterprise. For instance, Robert Doran qualifies the description of 2 Maccabees as "history" with the phrase "a highly rhetorical narrative,"[19] Naomi Janowitz calls 2 Maccabees 7 a "triumphalist history,"[20] and G. Rawlinson lists the historical

---

13. Rawlinson, "II Maccabees," 544.
14. Shepkaru, "From after Death," 2.
15. Dommerhausen, *1 Makkabäer 2 Makkabäer*, 9, cited in Doran, *2 Maccabees*, 15.
16. See Zeitlin, *Second Book*, 27–30. Pompey's capture of Jerusalem is dated to 63 BCE, while 2 Maccabees 15:37 states that Jerusalem has been in the hands of the Jews from the death of Nicanor to the time of writing. This, along with the positive view of Rome in the book, seem to suggest, as Goldstein states, that 2 Maccabees was written before Pompey captured Jerusalem. See Goldstein, *II Maccabees*, 71–72.
17. Although termed as the epitomist, Gary Morrison notes that he has been increasingly recognized as also an author to whom the final form can be attributed rather than merely a copyist. See Morrison, "Composition of II Maccabees," 565.
18. The genre of 2 Maccabees was generally considered to be a tragic history, in line with the Hellenistic historiography. However, Doran contends that this classification of 2 Maccabees is forced and suggests that instead of trying to fit it into an existing genre, it should be approached via its topos. See Doran, "2 Maccabees," 107–114.
19. Doran, *Temple Propaganda*, 84ff.
20. Janowitz, *Family Romance*, 16–26.

inaccuracies found in the book.[21] Second Maccabees can be seen as an interpretation of history within the framework of Deuteronomic theological orientation, more of which is discussed below.[22] That the epitomist's theological orientation guides his historiographical enterprise is evident also in the way he rearranges his narrative to suit his purpose. Doran argues that the epitomist heightens the sense of theomachy[23] in 2 Maccabees, especially in the presentations of Antiochus and Nicanor, by reorganizing the events in a slightly different order than how it would have actually happened. Doran's reconstruction of history proposes that Antiochus IV was alive when the request to allow Jews to live by their ancestral law was initially granted. But to heighten the effect of the theomachy pattern, the epitomist reorganized the events in its retelling in 2 Maccabees so that the events are placed after the death of Antiochus IV and Antiochus IV is thus portrayed as having died fighting against God (2 Macc 10:14–11:15).[24] The historiographical motivation is the demonstration of divine justice and establishment of God's people. Therefore, it can be said that the epitomist's interest in presenting the narrative was not purely antiquarian, but to skilfully present the history of his people under Antiochus IV's rule in such a way as to shed light on God's corrective, providential, and protective dealing with his people despite appearances.

This raises the question on the value of the book for the present investigation. This can be resolved by considering two aspects of the book as it relates to this study:

First, the book may not be an objective record of events, however it is history by the measures of ancient historiographies since historiographical standards were different in ancient times.[25] Doran states that 2 Maccabees, with

---

21. For a brief summary of the historical value of the book, see Rawlinson, "II Maccabees," 540–542.

22. Doran, *Temple Propaganda*, 110.

23. From Greek *theos* for "god" and *makhia* for "fight," theomacy denotes a battle among gods in Greek mythology. Here Doran uses it to refer to the topos of a deity defending his/her temple or city against the attacks of earthly rulers, Antiochus IV in this case. He is presented as the arch-villain who opposes or fights against the God of the Jews and his temple.

24. For details see, Doran, *2 Maccabees*, 6–8, 207- 215–216.

25. History writing as a literary genre in the modern understanding is the exact recounting of the events as they *actually happened* in the past. Its credibility is measured against the degree of objectivity and accuracy in portraying past events. Though there is admission of the inescapability from bias on the part of any historian and the impossibility of knowing for certain what happened in the past, McKenzie says the goal and the essential definition of history writing

its interest in divine intervention in history, is characteristic of Hellenistic historiography of the second century BCE.[26] Further, it is not completely devoid of historical value. Scholars agree there is material of genuine historical value and it deserves a hearing and is not to be dismissed.[27] Rawlinson states that 2 Maccabees 3–4:6 is the only record available of the four or five years before the accession of Antiochus IV, which makes it a valuable source.[28] Further, Gary Morrison notes the name Heliodorus mentioned in 2 Maccabees 3 as a minister has been found in a letter from King Seleucus IV, demonstrating that information in 2 Maccabees could be correct.[29] Rawlinson notes that while 2 Maccabees 4:7–7 parallels 1 Maccabees 1:10–64, 2 Maccabees has additional details, and as for 2 Maccabees 8–15 there are "trustworthy details" not found in 1 Maccabees.[30] Hence while the task of discerning the historically accurate parts of 2 Maccabees would still be a challenging task, it is not devoid of historical significance.

Second, the primary interest of this investigation is in the concept of post-mortem divine retribution reflected in the book, rather than in the events

---

nevertheless remains "telling exactly what happened in the past." In contrast to the modern understanding of history as an objective reporting of the past, ancient historiography was "closer to storytelling." Ancient historians had their ideological points to drive home to their audience. This involved interpreting the meaning of the past for the present, "showing how the 'causes' of the past brought about the 'effects' of the present." In Greece historiographies, where close analogues of 2 Maccabees can be found (see Doran for comparisons of 2 Maccabees to the works of Greek historiographers, Doran, *Temple Propaganda*, 84–89), McKenzie says historians used speeches and narrative formula as structuring devices and as such, "speeches typically were invented by historians, in both wording and substance" as was deemed appropriate for the occasion. This was also a prominent feature widely evidenced in the work of fifth century BCE Greek historian Herodotus, who is called the father of history. These ideological intent and fictional elements did not relegate the record of its historical significance, which is inevitably the conclusion drawn when reading the accounts from a modern perspective is attempted; instead, argues McKenzie, a proper understanding of the ancient historiography allows literary freedom for the incorporation of non-historical and fictional elements in their narratives. See McKenzie, "Historiography, Old Testament," 418–420. See also Robert Eric Frykenberg and Philips Long who state that complete objectivity is impossible. Frykenberg, *Belief and History*, 256 and Long, *Art of Biblical History*, 20.

26. See Doran, *Temple Propaganda*, 103–104.
27. Bartlett, *First and Second Books*, 217; Rawlinson, "II Maccabees," 542; Schwartz, *II Maccabees*, 38–44.
28. Rawlinson, "II Maccabees," 542.
29. Morrison, "Composition of II Maccabees," 564.
30. Rawlinson, "II Maccabees," 542.

themselves for their historical insight. As such, regardless of the historicity of the recorded events themselves, the text itself can be regarded as a carrier of ideas and evidence of the presence of the idea of post-mortem divine retribution in Jewish literature during the STP and that suffices for this study. That is to say, instead of looking within the text for history, the text itself becomes part of the witness to the history and thoughts of the period. Hence without making claims to the historicity of its content, the text can still be examined for the concept of post-mortem retribution it portrays as a reflection of the thoughts of that period.

Therefore, even if the historical character of 2 Maccabees were to be considered dubious, its interest in the concept of post-mortem divine retribution is taken for what it is, that is, interest among some circles of that period in the concept of post-mortem divine retribution. With that, we turn to examine the concept as presented in the narrative of 2 Maccabees 7.

6.4. 2 Maccabees 7: Story and Background

The backdrop of story in 2 Maccabees 7 is the cultural-religious clash between Judaism and Hellenism driven to its peak by Antiochus IV's efforts to fully integrate the Jews and the city of Jerusalem into Hellenistic society.[31] The clash resulted from alterations in cultural and religious practices Antiochus imposed on the Jews that were against the Jewish way of life. This in turn led to resistance from the Jews and persecution from Antiochus finally culminating in the Maccabean revolt.

However, it is not to be assumed that there was a rigid distinction between Hellenism and Judaism. The Jews had lived peaceably under the Ptolemies and the Seleucids before Antiochus IV.[32] In fact, Martin Hengel argues to the contrary that all Judaism, including Palestinian Judaism, from around

---

31. Another version of the story is found in 4 Maccabees 8:1–17:6, however, it is not included in this study, except for some cross references when relevant for our investigation on post-mortem divine judgment, as it focuses primarily on the supremacy of pious reason over passion in martyrdom and the immortality of the soul, and is silent about resurrection. See, Crossan, "Resurrection of Jesus," 41; Zeitlin, *Second Book*, 162. Further, it has been noted that the cult practices Antiochus imposed on the Jews were not part of his own religion and scholars have grappled with this puzzle trying to find an answer. For a summary of solutions proposed by various scholars, see Goldstein, *II Maccabees*, 98–112.

32. Gruen, *Construct of Identity*, 333.

the mid-third century BCE on should be termed as "*Hellenistic Judaism*."[33] Collins is right in observing that Hellenism had made inroads into Judea, and certain Hellenistic trappings, for instance the gymnasium which was the centre of Greek education, were even generally accepted by many if not all Jews. It was ultimately the religious persecution under Antiochus that led to the open warfare that was the Maccabean revolt.[34]

Concerning the more immediate events that led to the persecution narrative recorded in 2 Maccabees 7, towards the end of 170 BCE a war broke out between Antiochus IV and the Ptolemaic kingdom in Egypt. Antiochus IV invaded Egypt twice taking Pelusium and Memphis, but later as he laid siege to Alexandria, the Romans force him to withdraw.[35] Meanwhile Antiochus IV hears, correctly or incorrectly, of a revolt in Judea and comes to Jerusalem determined to crush the Jews and their rebellion for good. As William H. C. Frend notes, the religion of the Jews lay at the heart of their resistance and Antiochus IV knew it.[36] Beginning in 167 BCE, he attempted to achieve this by imposing practices that would effectively dissolve the characteristics of Judaism (2 Macc 5:11–6:9), which in the narrative of 2 Maccabees 7 is by forcing the Jews to eat pork against Jewish dietary laws. The narratives of chapters 4–7 deals with the profanation of the Temple through corruption and violence in a bid to gain the office of the high priesthood, the introduction of reforms that were contrary to the Jewish way of life, and climaxing of these events in the persecution of the people. However, the Jews win a decisive victory thwarting Antiochus IV's plan when, first, the mother and brothers choose death over the violation of their law, and again when Antiochus IV's general, Nicanor, is defeated and killed at the end of the book.

The place of martyrdom has been controverted among scholars as there is no clear indication in the text of the setting of the martyrdom of the mother and the seven brothers. Some have suggested that it took place in Jerusalem,[37]

---

33. For interaction between Judaism and Hellenism and Hellenic influence in Palestine, see Hengel, *Judaism and Hellenism*. The above cited matter is from vol.1, 104 and 205.

34. See Collins, *Jewish*, 26–40.

35. Antiochus's father signed a treaty with the Romans following his defeat and hence Antiochus was obliged to withdraw from further attacking Egypt as it was a Roman ally. Frend, *Martyrdom and Persecution*, 40–41; Doran, *2 Maccabees*, 18.

36. Frend, *Martyrdom*, 42.

37. For instance, Doran opines that the text points to Jerusalem as the place of martyrdom and that the epitomist either did not mention Antiochus' return to Jerusalem or

others have preferred Antioch.[38] The preference for Antioch is based primarily on 2 Maccabees 5:21 which reports Antiochus IV's return to Antioch and on 2 Maccabees 6:1 where Antiochus is said to have sent Geron to Jerusalem to compel Jews to leave their ancestral law, implying that he himself was not at Jerusalem. However, even if it is argued that it took place in Jerusalem, the reason for portraying Antiochus at Jerusalem during the persecution is probably not merely a historical inaccuracy but an ideologically strategic placement.[39] It could be an attempt to present the affairs of Jerusalem as of equal importance to Persian ones.

The expansive territory of the Seleucid coupled with the centralization of imperial power in the person of the king necessitated the king's presence in the sight of his people to strengthen their bond and loyalty to him. So important was the king's bodily presence that his coming was considered comparable to an epiphany. Hence, the absence of Antiochus during the persecution in Jerusalem bespeaks of Judea's relative unimportance, and writing him into the persecution scenes elevates the crisis at Judea "to the status of the Persian ones."[40] Moreover, the ambiguity of the place of martyrdom could also add to the adaptability of the story to different locales. Doran notes in a similar vein that the location was not a primary concern as the several rabbinic retellings of the persecution story in different situations shows.[41]

The story in 2 Maccabees 7 portrays such an instance of persecution. It pits Antiochus IV and his soldiers against eight anonymous martyrs, a mother and her seven sons, whom they torture to death for refusing to eat pork in violation of their ancestral law.[42] It was however not just a matter of

---

probably placed the king at the scene to present him as the main opponent it the story. Doran, *Maccabean Martyrs*, 102–103.

38. For Antioch as the place of martyrdom, see, Schatkin, "Maccabean Martyrs," 98–99; also Zeitlin, *Second Book*, 19, 29–30, 49–51, 68.

39. For instance, Rawlinson notes that the presence of Antiochus at Jerusalem during the time of the great persecution is historically incorrect. Rawlinson, "II Maccabees," 541.

40. See Kosmin, *Land of the Elephant*, 175–180; and Kosmin, "Indigenous," 42–43.

41. Doran, *2 Maccabees*, 165. For a study on the various version of the story see Doran, "Martyr: A Synoptic," 189–221.

42. Later rabbinic traditions name the mother as Hannah, in the Midrash she is called Miriam bat Tanchum, she is Solomone or Salomone and its variants in the Greek Christian tradition and Mart Simouni in the Syriac. See Cohen, "Hannah and Her Seven," 36–60; and Zeitlin, *Second Book*, 49; Berger, "Cult of the Maccabees," 114; Young, " 'Woman with the Soul,'" 67. Also, the ages of the sons are unknown, although the description of the youngest brother

a simple dietary change, but a bid to replace the temple sacrifice prescribed by the law with a foreign one.[43] As such, in dying to uphold their law they become martyrs of faith.[44] In the face of death, they assert their conviction in divine retribution and their vindication through resurrection. The story presents the anticipated resurrection in retributive terms as a reward for obedience to God's law even to the point of death. As the above discussion on the historical value of 2 Maccabees indicates, the martyrdoms in chapter 7 are probably not historical; however, as Lester Grabbe mentions, there were indeed occurrences of religious executions and many were unjustly slain during the crisis.[45]

The mother and her sons could be viewed as representative portrayals of all who suffered during this time or as models to be emulated, and the anonymity of the characters is perhaps to be read as a literary device towards that end, that is, pushing the characters from individuals to that of types.[46] In any case, 2 Maccabees 7 presents a situation wherein the absence of any signs of retribution in present life for those who died righteous death during the persecution, divine retribution is deferred or transposed to the afterlife in attempts to wrestle with the question of divine justice, and it is this post-mortem divine retribution in 2 Maccabees 7 that is examined below.

---

as νεανίας ("a young man") and μειράκιον ("a boy") seem to suggest that at least the youngest one was still not an adult. In 4 Maccabees 17:9 they are all referred to as παῖδες ("children").

43. Janowitz, *Family Romance*, 33. Goldstein notes that although the passage does not mention sacrificial meat, it is possible that it is assumed to be so in light of the meat being referred to as σπλαγχνισμός, a pagan sacrificial meal, in 2 Macc 7:42 and 2 Macc 6:7, 18–21. Goldstein, *II Maccabees*, 276, 317.

44. The word martyr comes from the Greek *martys* meaning "witness." Assmann, "Martyrdom, Violence," 52. This study does not include a study on the concept of martyrdom but nonetheless uses the term to designate the mother and the seven brothers.

45. Grabbe, *Judaism from Cyrus*, 224. Jonathan Goldstein also attests to the possibility of such tortures during Antiochus' rule. Cf. Goldstein, *II Maccabees*, 292.

46. So also Nomi Janowitz who argues the namelessness of the mother is deliberate making her a living trope. See Janowitz, *Family Romance*, 11–12; and Doran who calls them "representatives of the underdogs before the oppressor," Doran, *2 Maccabees*, 166; Aharon Ronald E. Agus states it functions as a "typological story"; Agus, *Binding of Isaac and Messiah*, 11.

6.5. Post-mortem Divine Retribution in 2 Maccabees 7

Unlike in the two passages examined from the HB where the presence of the concept of post-mortem divine retribution is debated, 2 Maccabees 7 is quite unequivocal in its elucidation of the concept of post-mortem divine retribution and scholars have recognized the epitomist's interest in that motif.[47] As such, the question is not so much if there is post-mortem divine retribution in 2 Maccabees 7 but rather how this concept is presented. 2 Maccabees 7 uses resurrection as the vehicle through which post-mortem divine retribution is achieved. In Goldstein's view "retribution and resurrection" are the main themes of the narrative in chapter 7 to which even the "theme of the courage of the martyrs" is subordinate.[48] Elledge states the epitomist deals with the problem of theodicy by resting heavily on the hope of resurrection and presents the most graphical picture of physical resurrection available in ancient literature.[49] Kellermann considers resurrection the main theme of chapter 7,[50] Cavallin states that resurrection and post-mortem judgment underly the endurance of the martyrs,[51] while Shmuel Shepkaru also states that resurrection is a "recurrent motif."[52] Hence divine retribution in 2 Maccabees 7 is to be realized through resurrection.

6.5.1. Resurrection in the Speeches of the Mother and Her Seven Sons

The speeches of the mother and her seven sons just before they are put to death reveal that underlying their endurance of torture and acceptance of death is their hope of resurrection. They use various expressions to assert their belief that God will resurrect them (2 Macc 7:9, 11, 14, 23, 29, 36). The second and fourth brothers use similar language of rising up (2 Macc 7:9, 14, 36). Verses 9 and 14 use the verb ἀνίστημι "to raise up" indicating a

---

47. Van Henten, *Maccabean Martyrs*, 163; Ego, "God's Justice," 141–154. Note also Goldstein's comment on Nicanor's fate (15:23–33), that highlights the epitomist's interest in the motif of divine retribution, Goldstein, *II Maccabees*, 502; Assmann, "Martyrdom, Violence," 54.

48. Goldstein, *II Maccabees*, 303.

49. Elledge, *Life After Death*, 16, 18.

50. Kellermann, *Auferstanden in den Himmel*, 39, cited in van Henten, *Maccabean Martyrs*, 123.

51. Cavallin, *Life After Death*, 112.

52. Shepkaru, "From after Death," 3.

resurrection after their death at the hands of Antiochus IV and his soldiers. In verse 9, the phrase εἰς αἰώνιον ἀναβίωσιν ζωῆς ἡμᾶς ἀναστήσει ("raise us up to an eternal reviving of life") is awkward and redundant,[53] and scholars have surmised that it was possibly an attempt to mimic the construction in LXX Daniel 12:2, "... will be raised, some to eternal life."[54] In any case the reference to resurrection is clear and functions retributively as a reward for those who lose their life to keep the divine law.

The third son and the mother express their conviction in divine retribution in terms of getting back (κομίσασθαι/κομίσωμαί vv. 11 and 29 respectively, from κομίζω meaning "receive" or "obtain") their bodies or life. The third brother states that he is offering his body in the hope of receiving it back from the one who gave it to him. Similarly, the mother encourages all her sons to give up their lives in the hope of getting them back, which implies that she too will be resurrected.[55] Further, her words of encouragement to her sons highlight resurrection as a reward for losing their lives in their unwavering fidelity to God's law without regard for their own present suffering (2 Macc 7:22–23, 27–29).[56] Moreover, the speeches of the third brother and mother create a nexus between physical resurrection and creation by placing their hope of resurrection in the one who created the world and their bodies in the first place (discussed below). Hence, they reason that they will have their just reward in resurrection when they will get back what is taken away from them.

The seventh brother speaks of eternal life. However, a part of verse 36 has been variously understood and translated: βραχὺν ὑπενέγκαντες πόνον ἀενάου ζωῆς ὑπὸ διαθήκην θεοῦ πεπτώκασιν (2 Macc 7:36). It has been contested as to whether the genitive ἀενάου ζωῆς ("eternal life") belongs with the preceding noun, πόνον ("pain"), in which case the reading has the sense of the brothers having suffered pain for eternal life. For instance, Goldstein translates:

---

53. "Raise up" and "revive" have the same meaning here and the word "eternal" should qualify "life" rather than "reviving." For the redundancy and grammatical construction of this phrase in Greek, see Goldstein, *II Maccabees*, 305, and Doran, *2 Maccabees*, 157.

54. Goldstein, *II Maccabees*, 305; Schwartz, *2 Maccabees*, 304; Doran, *2 Maccabees*, 157; Baslez, "Origin of the Martyrdom," 128; Sigvartsen, *Afterlife and Resurrection Beliefs*, 45–46.

55. Schwartz, *2 Maccabees*, 313.

56. Van Henten, *Maccabean Martyrs*, 114.

> "My brothers, having borne pain for a short while, now have inherited eternal life under the terms of God's covenant,"[57]

This makes suffering a prerequisite for eternal life – the brothers having suffered enter eternal life.[58] Van Henten states that this reading is preferable because of the proximity of ἀενάου ζωῆς ("eternal life") to πόνον ("pain"), and also because in his opinion this sense is consonant with the idea of resurrection in 2 Maccabees.[59]

The other reading has been to link ἀενάου ζωῆς ("eternal life") with διαθήκην θεοῦ ("covenant of God") that follows it, and thus read as the brothers having suffered and died under God's covenant of eternal life. Schwartz prefers this reading and translates:

> "For our brothers, on the one hand, after undergoing brief suffering have come into God's covenant of eternal life."[60]

This makes eternal life a part of God's covenant.[61] Thus, while one places emphasis on the human act of enduring pain and death, the other emphasizes eternal life as part of God's covenant. In any case both these reading do not contest the basic premise of the presence of the theme of divine retribution in the afterlife.[62] It simply presents two varying emphases: the emphasis on eternal life as a reward for human suffering exhibits the anthropocentric aspect of divine retribution, and the emphasis on eternal life as a blessing included in the covenant reflects the theocentric aspect of divine retribution. These readings cited above generally take the verb πίπτω (lit. "to fall") as having the sense of "coming or falling into one's possession."

However, Doran takes a slightly different approach. He takes the literal meaning of πίπτω ("to fall"). He also laments that not enough consideration has been given to the use of the preposition ὑπό (acc. "under") in this verse. He argues that the locative sense of entering into a place, which the preposition

---

57. Goldstein, *II Maccabees*, 291, 317.
58. This reading is adopted by Bücker, "Das 'ewige Leben,'" 406–412, and Stemberger, *Der Leib der Aufertehung*, 21–22, both cited in Schwartz, *2 Maccabees*, 316–317.
59. Van Henten, *Maccabean Martyrs*, 175, n. 220.
60. Schwartz, *2 Maccabees*, 298, 316.
61. This reading is adopted by Schwartz, *2 Maccabees*, 316–317.
62. Schwartz, 298, 317. Schwartz observes that while scholars have debated the two readings he finds they do not essentially contradict one another.

ὑπὸ can have, cannot be applied to the idea of the covenant. Instead, ὑπὸ in the context of a covenant it would connote "coming under the influence of." He therefore suggests that the translation should be:

> "For our brothers have fallen, having endured under the divine covenant brief pain for eternal life."[63]

The details of this verse may be controverted, nonetheless they are not hugely significant for the overall purpose of our investigation of the presentation of the concept of post-mortem retribution in this narrative. It suffices to emphasize that couched in the words of the youngest brother is a strong conviction in post-mortem compensation through resurrection and adds to the overarching motif of divine retribution in the narrative expressed through the speeches of the other characters. Thus, the concept of post-mortem divine retribution is a major motif in this narrative and is expressed primarily through the concept of resurrection.

6.5.2. Post-mortem Divine Retribution Via Physical Resurrection

Further, not only are there explicit references to resurrection as a post-mortem reward for the martyrs, but the physical aspect of resurrection is quite unapologetically stated as well.[64] The narrative in 2 Maccabees 7 showcases the mother and seven brothers' unswerving fidelity to the law, an idea in complete consonance with traditional Jewish thought. By referring to Moses and repeatedly to the law they embed themselves and their beliefs in the past. However, by speaking so unambiguously of resurrection, and especially of physical resurrection, the text makes a gigantic leap from the traditional understanding of existence beyond death as portrayed in the HB. This text is an important witness to the belief in physical resurrection which became an important tenet in some streams of Judaism.[65] This is interesting since

---

63. Doran, *2 Maccabees*, 148, 162–163.

64. Elsewhere too in 2 Maccabees the belief in bodily resurrection is unambiguously asserted (2 Maccabees 14:41–46). Rhazis, to avoid being captured and humiliated, falls on his sword but does not die before he expresses his conviction that God will give him back his physical body. See, Crossan, "The Resurrection of Jesus," 41.

65. For instance, it is well known that the Sadducees did not believe in it while the Pharisees did. See Setzer, "Resurrection of the Dead," 65-101; Charlesworth, "Our Perennial Yearning," xx.

until now all the texts examined have spoken of resurrection to some degree and in some manner but none has been unequivocal about the physicality of resurrection.

The epitomist makes this concept of physical resurrection clear especially in the speeches of the third brother ("I got these from Heaven, and because of his laws, I disdain them, and from him I hope to get them back again." 2 Macc 7:11, NETS),[66] and echoes of it can be heard in the mother's reference to birth and creation ("Therefore the Creator of the world, . . . will in his mercy give life and breath back to you again, since you now forget yourselves for the sake of his laws." 2 Macc 7:22–23, ". . . accept death so that in his mercy I may get you back again along with your brothers." 2 Macc 27–29, NETS) while speaking of resurrection. The speeches of the other sons do not specify the physical component of the resurrection; nevertheless it may be reasonably assumed that they were all in solidarity in their understanding of the kind of resurrection they anticipated. The third brother offers his tongue and stretches out his hands to be cut off, asserting that he will get them back just as he received them from God in the first place (2 Macc 7:11).

What exactly that body will be is not easily answered. In verse 11, the same demonstrative pronoun (ταῦτα "these") used to indicate the body he offers to be executed is also used to denote the body he expects to get back from God. This emphasizes the belief that the resurrection will be physical,[67] and seem to imply a reconstitution of the same physical body. However, as Goldstein points out, logically speaking it is difficult to conceive how a burnt body would be reconstituted.[68] Perhaps ταῦτα ("these") may be read as a reference to the physical body generally rather than a particular body. Nevertheless, this being a statement of faith rather than a philosophical exposition, within the framework of faith and God's ability to create, such questions of rationality do not really apply. Therefore, the speech is to be taken as indicative of the certainty of their hope of future post-mortem retribution, and like his brother before him he too links his hope of physical resurrection to dying for God's law. That this conviction is rooted in the concept of creation is indicated by the reference to having received the body in the first place from the

---

66. Bartlett, *First and Second Books*, 272; Doran, *2 Maccabees*, 157.
67. Doran, *2 Maccabees*, 157.
68. Goldstein, *II Maccabees*, 308.

heavenly one, that is, God himself (2 Macc 7:11). This resurrection-creation nexus appears even more explicitly in the mother's speech (2 Macc 7:22–23, 27–29). Through the mother's speech, the epitomist expresses the belief in the reconstitution of the physical body on the basis of God's role and power as the creator.

The phrase οὐκ ἐξ ὄντων ἐποίησεν αὐτά ὁ θεός ("God made them out of things that were not" 2 Macc 7:28) has had a long exegetical tradition of being interpreted as a reference to creation *ex nihilo*, Origen being the first one known to interpret it so.[69] Debates concerning the author's intention, or lack thereof, to state the doctrine of creation *ex nihilo* notwithstanding,[70] references to the concept of creation and the development of the embryo in the womb are used effectively to illustrate the certainty of corporal resurrection whether it is the same body they had in life or a new one.[71] Just as God called the world into existence and forms a foetus without anybody's help, not even the mother's since she is unaware (2 Macc 7:22–23),[72] God can and will recreate the mother and her sons and resurrect them in physical form despite the seeming impossibility.[73] The mother's speech is not a philosophical exposition of the doctrine of creation,[74] but a faith statement affirming that even though the process of resurrection is a mystery to human beings God will accomplish it, dismembered and burnt bodies regardless. Within the narrative, as Cavallin states, resurrection functions as "vindication of justice" for those martyred, and hence it is the function of resurrection that

---

69. Schwartz, *2 Maccabees*, 58, 312.

70. Goldstein argues that the text does not warrant a reading of the doctrine of creation *ex nihilo* here. However, he also states that the interpretation of this text as a statement for the doctrine of creation *ex nihilo* by the church fathers "has some foundation" and warrants consideration. He views the doctrine of creation *ex nihilo* as necessitated by a belief in corporal resurrection which required that God could give back the body to the faithful even if the body was totally destroyed in the persecution. For details of the arguments supporting his view see, Goldstein, *II Maccabees*, 307–315. Schwartz argues, contra Goldstein, that there is not enough to dismiss the longstanding history of interpretation of this text as a support for the doctrine of creation ex nihilo, see Schwartz, *2 Maccabees*, 312–313.

71. So also Goldstein, *II Maccabees*, 311.

72. This is more a statement on the mystery of conception rather than ignorance of the reproductive process. Cf. Gen 30:1–2, Eccl 11:5. Doran, *2 Maccabees*, 159. Goldstein sees in verse 23 an allusion to Eccl 8:17. See, Goldstein, *II Maccabees*, 313.

73. Schwartz, *2 Maccabees*, 312–313. See also Goldstein, *II Maccabees*, 309.

74. So also Schwartz, *2 Maccabees*, 312.

takes precedence rather than its nature.⁷⁵ Doran suggests that the absence of a father in the story, and the references to ancestral law in the narrative, further highlight the role of God as the creator and true father of the brothers, who by their obedience to God's law likewise demonstrate that they are his children.⁷⁶

This argument of recreation by referring to creation is in the tradition, albeit a reformulation, of the prophets who argued for God's ability to save the nation by appealing to God's act of creation (for instance, Isa 44).⁷⁷ Hence by juxtaposing the ideas of resurrection, creation of the world, and the growth of an embryo, the narrative puts forth its argument that God is able to bring about a physical resurrection of the martyrs. Further, the retribution envisioned as a physical one is in line with *lex talionis*, albeit, the term *lex talionis* is usually applied in a negative sense to denote the punishment mirroring the crime in kind and degree, here the reward is envisioned as mirroring the sacrifice made – their bodies have been either dismembered or burnt and therefore their resurrection is also a bodily one.

6.5.3. Section Conclusion

The narrative evinces great interest in post-mortem retribution, and expresses it through the concept of resurrection in the speeches of the mother and the brothers. Further this resurrection is envisioned as a physical one; the martyrs who consider their body and lives as worth nothing in comparison to the law will be recompensed by being brought back to life in a corporeal form. Additionally, just as there is reward for the martyrs, the narrative also states that punishment is stored for their persecutors.

6.5.4. Divine Retribution for Antiochus IV

The text is clear that there is divine retribution awaiting Antiochus IV (2 Macc 7:14, 17, 19, 35–36). However, the predictions of Antiochus' fate are relatively vague. In their speeches before they are put to death, the brothers variously warn Antiochus of his coming fate. The sixth and seventh brothers state that Antiochus will not escape divine justice (2 Macc 7:19, 35, 36), expressing their

---

75. Cavallin, *Life After Death*, 113.
76. Doran, *2 Maccabees*, 166.
77. Van Henten, *Maccabean Martyrs*, 177–178.

belief in divine retribution. However, it is uncertain whether divine justice is to be executed in this life or in the afterlife.

Regarding retribution in this life, the epitomist shows that the words of the brothers concerning Antiochus are fulfilled in 2 Maccabees 9. It gives an account of Antiochus's final afflictions and death while he was attempting to rob the temple of Nanaya (Nanea) in Persepolis (9:1–28). The epitomist explains Antiochus's death under these circumstances as God's punishment of Antiochus for his earlier plunder of the Jerusalem Temple led by Menelaus. Correlating two distinct incidents to explain a monarch's death as divine punishment has precedence in the HB's presentation of Sennacherib's murder in the Assyrian temple of Nisroch as Yahweh's punishment for Sennacherib's earlier attack on Jerusalem (2 Kgs 19:36–37; Isa 37:7; 38:1–33).[78]

Historically it is thought that Antiochus died of a disease rather prematurely and his tomb was not found, thus warranting the epitomist's interpretation of the event in retributive terms as having been struck by God.[79] Doran detects the epitomist's delight in 2 Maccabees 9 in presenting Antiochus's afflictions and equating his suffering and death as divine judgment for his previous deeds against the Jews.[80] Beate Ego observes that Antiochus's fate was a mirror of the suffering he had inflicted on others (9:28; 9:6).[81] Hence, predictions that Antiochus will not escape divine justice are shown as fulfilled in the narrative.

Further, the fifth brother warns that Antiochus and his descendants will face divine punishment (2 Macc 7:17). The warning of punishment on Antiochus's descendants does not necessarily preclude a reference to postmortem punishment. However, in light of the words of the fourth brother who claims that Antiochus will not resurrect (examined in the following paragraphs), it is likely that Antiochus is warned that the consequences of

---

78. Kosmin, "Indigenous Revolts," 38.

79. Nickelsburg, *Resurrection, Immortality*, 217. Doron Mendels surmises the possibility of the version of Antiochus' death preserved in 2 Maccabees 9 being a reworking of the Nabonidus' tradition; see Mendels, "Note on the Tradition," 53–56. Further, the details of Antiochus' attempted plunder and death are variously recorded. See Doran, *2 Maccabees*, 186–187. Schwartz also notes the historicity of the account of Antiochus' death recorded in 2 Maccabees 9 is suspect; however, other sources too seem to make a connection between his eastern campaign and a temple attack. See Schwartz, *2 Maccabees*, 352.

80. Doran, *2 Maccabees*, 186.

81. Ego, "God's Justice," 146, 148–150.

his evil deeds will indeed reverberate to impact even his descendants in this earthly life, a reference to the collective outworking of the consequences of one's actions exhibiting the collective nature of Deuteronomic retribution. This can be seen in 2 Maccabees 14:2 and 1 Maccabees 7:2–4 both of which mention that Demetrius ordered Antiochus's son to be put to death along with his guardian Lysias ("And it happened that as he [Demetrius] was going into the royal palace of his fathers, his forces apprehended Antiochus and Lysias.... And the forces killed them, and Demetrius sat on the throne of his kingdom." 1 Macc 7:2–4). While this is only an instance of the death of one of Antiochus's descendants, an early or premature death could be seen as a divine judgment, as implied by Zeitlin.[82] Thus there is a ripple-like effect of Antiochus's deeds against the Jews; it affects him but grows to engulf his descendants as well. However, it does not end here.

Not only will there be judgment in this life for Antiochus, but some kind of post-mortem judgment as well. Nickelsburg's assessment that it could be "either through actual post-mortem punishment or by not being raised from the dead"[83] is right since the statements of the other brothers do not preclude a post-mortem retribution for Antiochus. However, the fourth brother predicts that there will be no resurrection for Antiochus (2 Macc 7:14). According to this claim, Antiochus's punishment consists in not being raised to life again as opposed to the brothers and their mother who will resurrect (2 Macc 7:13, 36). Van Henten is perhaps correct when he states that only the martyrs, who have endured temporary suffering and death for the sake of God and his laws, will resurrect while the king will not be resurrected.[84] Through the words of the fourth brother, the epitomist draws a contrast between the mother and her sons, who will be rewarded with resurrection and reconstitution of their bodies which they now give up, and Antiochus who will not be resurrected, ἀνάστασις (2 Macc 7:14).

Further, in verse 36, the use of μὲν ... δὲ, which denotes a strong contrast and can be translated as "on the one hand ... on the other hand," emphasizes this distinction between the two kinds of fates anticipated for the martyrs and Antiochus: on the one hand the brothers have received eternal life, on the

---

82. See Zeitlin's note on 2 Maccabees 7:17, Zeitlin, *Second Book*, 163.
83. Nickelsburg, "Judgment, Life-After-Death," 149; 2 Maccabees 7:14, 17, 19, 35–37.
84. Van Henten, *Maccabean Martyrs*, 175.

other Antiochus IV will receive his appropriate penalties.[85] Also, verse 14 being the only reference to post-mortem retribution for Antiochus it is probable that the post-mortem retribution envisioned for Antiochus in 2 Maccabees 7 is similar to that in Isaiah 26:14, 19 where non-resurrection itself constitutes and suffices as the post-mortem retribution for the wicked, as opposed to the double resurrection in Daniel 12:1–3. This is also in keeping with the idea of post-mortem retribution posited in 1 Enoch 22 that those who receive their just compensation in life are not raised for post-mortem punishments.[86] Thus having received his just desserts in this life death will be final. There will be no resurrection for Antiochus.

6.5.5. Section Conclusion

In sum, in 2 Maccabees 7 post-mortem divine retribution is expressed through the hope of resurrection which in turn reaffirms the belief in divine justice. It becomes the basis of faith in action in the most extremes of crises. It is singular in its presentation of a physical resurrection for the martyrs and is in consonance with Isaiah 26:14, 19 and BW 22 in envisioning a single resurrection, a resurrection for the faithful alone, and thus functions as the post-mortem reward for the martyrs. Their persecutor does not go scot-free either; Antiochus experiences divine judgment in this life, and possibly cross-generationally, and his existence comes to an end with his earthly life with no prospects of resurrection.

Having discussed the view of post-mortem divine retribution presented in the text, the discussion now turns to examine the basis on which rewards and punishments are disbursed, and if there is any continuity with the Deuteronomic aspects of divine retribution. In this narrative divine response is expected based on the fact of their forfeiting their lives to uphold the divine law, hence the hope of post-mortem divine retribution is closely linked to dying for the sake of the law.

---

85. Doran, *2 Maccabees*, 162.
86. So also Nickelsburg, *Resurrection*, 217.

6.6. Basis and Aspects of Post-mortem Divine Retribution

To understand the basis and aspect of the post-mortem divine retribution in this account, one must begin by seeking the underlying reasons that motivate the mother and the brothers to choose death. The speeches of the mother and the brothers reveal two reasons why the martyrs readily give up their lives: i) for the sake of the law, and ii) for their sins. These become the motivating factors of their action and consequently the basis upon which a favourable divine response is expected.

6.6.1. Dying for the Law: Anthropocentric Aspect of Divine Retribution

The first reason, that of accepting death for the sake of the law, seems to indicate that the basis of divine retribution is their act of dying for the law, which would mean that the anthropocentric aspect of divine retribution at work. To recall, the anthropocentric aspect of divine retribution is characterized by God responding to human action. This aspect of divine retribution highlights human beings as the initiator, that is, human beings initiate an action to which God responds with either reward or punishment as appropriate. What follows is an examination to see if this initial finding is substantiated by the narrative.

In this narrative, the mother and each of the seven brothers when faced with a choice decide to die rather than transgress against God and his law. It is in the context of this act of ultimate loyalty to God that they confidently affirm that God will respond by bringing them back to life. That the law is the central motivation[87] for giving themselves up to death is made explicit in the speeches of the mother and four of the seven brothers – the first, second, third, and seventh brothers (2 Macc 7:2, 9, 11, 23, 30, 37). They portray the belief that adherence to the law is more important than life itself, and speak of their hope of being bestowed with eternal life after death precisely because they lose their earthly life for the sake of the law (2 Macc 7:9, 11, 23, 29).

The word νομος ("law") is used in a variety of ways in the narrative. It appears six times in 2 Maccabees 7, in the singular form (2 Macc 7:23, 30) as well as the in the plural (2 Macc 7:2, 9, 11, 37), and in some instances with the word πάτριος ("ancestral, hereditary, of or belonging to one's father," in

---

87. So also van Henten, *Maccabean Martyrs*, 132, 200.

2 Macc 7:2, 30, 37). In the singular νομος is generally considered a reference to the Torah.[88] Van Henten considers the possibility that the plural could refer to the laws of the city of Jerusalem or the ethos of the Jews; however, he states that such a definitive difference in usage is difficult to determine with certainty.[89] Schwartz notes that πάτριοι νόμοι ("ancestral laws") as used in 7:2 was typically a Greek term and probably used intentionally because it was commonly known that a violation of such laws was considered inexcusable. Using this term would therefore more effectively convey to the audience, including non-Jews, the implications of these martyrs violating the law.[90]

The term πάτριοι νόμοι ("ancestral laws") appears in 2 Maccabees 6:1 as well where it is used interchangeably with θεοῦ νόμοις ("laws of God") with reference to being governed by it (πολιτεύεσθαι "live or conduct oneself"). Van Henten concludes that whether in singular or plural the word in 2 Maccabees "always refers to divine law."[91] Schwartz too views the term πάτριοι νόμοι as used for explanatory reasons to better convey the gravity of the situation and does not see a difference between ancestral law and God's Law.[92] Since in Jewish polity the religious and the political were fused together, to be governed by the ancestral laws was the same as being governed by the Torah.[93] As such, in this narrative, the word "law" in both its plural and singular forms refers to the divine law, and it is to uphold this law that the mother and the seven brothers give up their lives.

Coming back to anthropocentric aspect of divine retribution in this account, the words of the mother and four brothers show that resurrection as post-mortem retribution for the martyrs is based on their having forfeited their earthly lives for the sake of God's law. The eldest brother speaks first and his words set the tone for the unfolding of the rest of the episode.[94] He declares a readiness to give up their lives for the sake of the ancestral laws.

---

88. For a helpful discussion on the use of νομος in Hellenistic Judaism see Segal, "Torah and Nomos," 19–27.

89. For further details, see van Henten, *Maccabean Martyrs*, 134–135.

90. Schwartz, *2 Maccabees*, 275.

91. For further details, see van Henten, *Maccabean Martyrs*, 134–135.

92. Schwartz, *2 Maccabees*, 275.

93. Doran makes a similar observation, Doran, *2 Maccabees*, 133; van Henten, *Maccabean Martyrs*, 134, 200; John Collins also states "religion and national identity went hand in hand," Collin, *Between Athens and Jerusalem*, 1.

94. So also, Agus, *Binding Isaac*, 13.

He does not speak of resurrection as their divine recompense; however, his assertion is subsequently authenticated in deed by all the brothers and the mother, several of whom link dying for the law to their expectation of resurrection. Therefore, even though the first brother barely has a chance to speak a couple of sentences before he is tortured and executed, he is rightly called the προήγορος ("spokesperson" 2 Macc 7:2, 4) of all the others who connect dying for the law to their hope of resurrection.

The second brother, addressing his last words to the king, connects the hope of eternal life to their dying ὑπὲρ ("for, on behalf of") the laws of the king of the universe (2 Macc 7:9). Identifying God as τοῦ κόσμου βασιλεὺς ("the king of the universe or world") conveys at least three points: i) it draws a contrast with Antiochus whose kingly status is limited to a small territory on earth,[95] ii) their refusal to obey the laws of an earthly king is contrasted with their obedience to the heavenly law, and iii) the law thus described as of the king of the universe carries with it political as well as religious connotations. In effect, it subordinates Antiochus' law under the supremacy of God's law and sets Antiochus up against God himself for demanding that the Jews obey him by violating of God's laws.[96] Further, the hope of resurrection is linked to their voluntary death for the sake of the law – while the earthly king releases (ἀπολύω "release, free from") them from their earthly life for not obeying his commands, the king of the universe will raise them up to an eternal life for dying for his laws. The life that the earthly king takes away unjustly the king of the universe will restore in his divine justice. Their hope of resurrection to an eternal life is thus a divine recompense for losing their earthly life for the sake of God's law, exhibiting the anthropocentric aspect of divine retribution.

Explicit connection between the readiness to die for God's law and the expected resurrection is made in the speech of the third brother as well.[97] His speech is the clearest articulation of the physicality of the expected

---

95. Goldstein, *II Maccabees*, 305; Doran, *2 Maccabees*, 157.

96. Similarly, van Henten, *Maccabean Martyrs*, 114.

97. This speech is omitted in some mss., and some have considered it a gloss and preferred to excise it. However, van Henten rightly warns of the dangers of presuming the ability to distinguish the gloss from the original on the basis of logic for such a story as this. See van Henten, *Maccabean Martyrs*, 113. Although not commenting specifically on this verse Cavallin also speaks of the impossibility to differentiate between the work of the original author from that of the epitomist's; Cavallin, *Life After Death*, 111.

resurrection. His ὑπεροράω ("disregard" 2 Macc 7:11, also in v. 23) for his suffering is in contrast to God regarding or watching over them and having compassion on them (2 Macc 7:6).[98] He takes no notice of his suffering while God notices it. He reasons that he received his body from οὐρανός ("heaven"), here used as an epithet for God, and he now gladly offers it for the sake of God's laws, therefore he is confident that his body will be given back to him. As such, his speech exhibits the confidence that since he gives up his body for God, God will respond by giving it back to him, evincing the anthropocentric aspect of divine retribution.

The last few references to the law are made by the mother and the youngest brother (2 Macc 7:23, 30, 37). The youngest brother remains resolute in his willingness to die rather than transgress the law. But Antiochus, being down to the seventh and the last of the brothers, and seeing how fear of torture and death were not bringing about the desired result, makes one desperate attempt by luring the young man with prosperity (2 Macc 7:24). Antiochus' offer of wealth, career, and status to the seventh son in exchange for violating the law were not mere words. There were instances of Jews abandoning their ancestral faith to partake completely in what Hellenistic civilization had to offer. Such an instance is Tiberius Julius Alexander, Philo's nephew, who forsook Judaism for a successful career in government.[99] Thus what Antiochus was offering was a real possibility.

However, Antiochus' posing of material wealth as an alternative to God's law does not even receive an acknowledgment, implying that there is nothing comparable to the law in the eyes of the youngest brother. His address to the king is the longest among the brothers and he, like his brothers, explains that his obedience is to the law given by Moses (2 Macc 7:30). The young man's rejection of the king's offer is an added testament to his faith and commitment to God and his law as he chooses to instead offer his σῶμα καὶ ψυχὴν ("body and soul") for the sake of the law (2 Macc 7:37). He does not speak of his own resurrection but claims that the brothers' suffering for the law were brief; but that in exchange they now have eternal life (2 Macc 7:36; see above for a discussion on this verse). Doran notes that the perfect form of the verb πίπτω (variously translated as "to fall" or "coming into one's possession," see

---

98. Doran, *2 Maccabees*, 157.
99. Cohen, *From the Maccabees*, 33.

above) seems to indicate that the brothers are already enjoying eternal life.[100] Hence in the speech of the youngest brother as well, because the brothers died for the sake of the law they can expect to enjoy eternal life, making it a divine reward for their devoted act.

Finally, the mother is said to have been encouraging all her sons to embrace death rather than transgress (2 Macc 7:21). She likewise urges her youngest to embrace death ἵνα ("so that" denoting purpose or goal, 2 Macc 7:29) she may receive him back with the rest of her sons, emphasizing resurrection as a reward for their martyrdom (2 Macc 7:22–23, 25–29). She advises her son, just as Antiochus tells her to, but she encourages her son to urgently do exactly the opposite of what Antiochus asks of her, that is, to save himself (2 Macc 7:25, 27–29).[101] She encourages him to give up his life just as his brothers have so that he too will be resurrected with them. In the Jewish tradition, her willingness to give up her sons has been compared to Abraham's willingness to sacrifice Isaac.[102] She derives her strength from her conviction that the same God who created the universe and brought life into it is able to raise her sons up and form them if they die without violating the law. The mother, having encouraged all her sons to lay down their lives, also likewise dies.[103] Her speech and her deeds, that of giving up her seven sons as well as her own self, makes resurrection dependent on their act of dying for the law thus exhibiting the characteristics of anthropocentric divine retribution, albeit post-mortem in this narrative.

The foregoing discussion shows that the hope of resurrection is based on the mother and the seven brothers giving up their lives for the sake of the law. Their resurrection is presented as "a reward for long torture and sufferings"

---

100. Doran, *2 Maccabees*, 148.

101. Van Henten, *Maccabean Martyrs*, 115.

102. See Agus, *Binding of Isaac*, 11–32, Assmann, "Martyrdom, Violence," 53; Young, "'Woman with the Soul,'" 79–80. However, Young's reference to the mother is from 4 Maccabees. It is interesting to note that later the writer of the book of Hebrews too would see in Abraham's willingness to sacrifice his son a reasoning that appeals to the resurrection power of God, much like the mother in this narrative (Heb 11:17–19). The reading of the *Akedah* in Hebrews 11:17–19 as a prefiguration of resurrection is seen in Christian tradition. For instance, see Cockerill, "Better Resurrection," 215–234. For a comparison on how Isaac's "martyrdom" tradition developed differently in Rabbinic and Christian exegetical traditions, see Segal, "'He Who Did Not,'" 169–84.

103. In 4 Maccabees 17:1 the mother is described as having thrown herself into the fire.

they endured.[104] Nickelsburg also states the reason for resurrection is the persecution they suffered.[105] As such, resurrection is not for all Jews, not even for all faithful Jews. Rather resurrection is presented as a reward reserved for martyrdom – those who lost their bodies and lives for the sake of God's law will receive their lives and bodies back. Resurrection is thus presented as a reward attendant not upon the righteous in general but uniquely upon the martyrs.

6.6.2. Section Conclusion

In sum, it can be said the expectation of resurrection is based on the martyrs having forfeited their lives to uphold the divine law. This link between their act and the expected divine retribution is explicit in the speeches made by the mother and the brothers before being put to death. Their obedience to the law is seen as a demonstration of faithfulness to God for which God rewards them; it is their act that elicits the divine response. This is characteristic of the anthropocentric aspect of divine retribution wherein the facet of retribution in focus is the deeds of humankind to which God responds. However, death being imminent their just recompense remains unrealized in this life on earth. The martyrs overcome this through their conviction that God who is "all-seeing" (9:5) will reward them in the afterlife by giving them back their bodies which they sacrificed for his law. Divine retribution thus remains viable and God's justice is upheld by moving the reward of the martyrs to the afterlife.

Further, there is an undeniable covenant underpinning in the way retribution is presented in this narrative. It was mentioned above that the speeches of the mother and the brothers reveal two reasons why the martyrs readily give up their lives: i) for the sake of the law, and ii) for their sins. Having examined the first reason, the focus now turns to the second reason, that of dying for their sins. The second reason for the mother and the brothers choosing to die defying Antiochus IV's orders was for their sins and this brings out two points. First, that there is a covenant underpinning to their act of martyrdom. The covenant underpinning highlights the theocentric aspect of divine retribution, which emphasizes God's initiative in his dealing with

---

104. Baslez, "Origin of the Martyrdom," 128.
105. Nickelsburg, *Resurrection, Immortality*, 217.

people. Here God is no longer seen as responding to human action, rather he is the initiator; his actions are directed to achieving his own purposes and are no longer dependent on the deeds of human beings. Second, the interplay between the deeds of individuals and the fate of the Jewish nation brings out the corporate nature of divine retribution, although not post-mortem *per se*. the corporate nature of retribution refers to instances when the consequences of the deeds of an individual affect others who are in relations to him – family, clan, or even the whole nation. Each of these two points are examined in separate sections under the theocentric aspect of divine retribution and the nature of divine retribution.

6.6.3. Dying for Their Sins: The Theocentric Aspect of Divine Retribution

The theocentric aspect of divine retribution that operates within the framework of the covenant, which is God's initiating act towards human beings independent of human actions. The contention here is that there is a covenant underpinning in the narrative of 2 Maccabees 7 that gives it its theocentric bend. However, to demonstrate this it first needs to be seen if the sins for which the martyrs die has a collective or individual sense.

It has been examined that the first motivating factor for their choice to die was for the sake of the law. Now, the second motivating factor for the choice made by the martyrs to die is explained as the bearing of responsibility for "their sins." Their suffering at the hands of Antiochus is understood to be the consequence of their sins against God. This awareness of sin is seen in the speeches of the two youngest brothers (2 Macc 7:18, 32; also implied in v. 38). It is not immediately evident whose sin is in view – the sins of the individual martyrs or the collective sins of the Jewish nation. Beate Ego states that it remains unclear if the faithful were suffering for their own sins or because of their participation in the sins of those who were unfaithful.[106] A closer look at the narrative suggests that the reference here is probably to the sins of the Jewish people as a whole, and the martyrs were taking ownership of the collective sin of the people. This is indicated by the following points:

i) There is no mention of the sins of the individual martyrs, but the book tells of the sins of some of the Jewish leaders who bring corruption into the

---

106. Ego, "God's Justice," 153.

temple (2 Macc 1:8; 4:10–17; 8:33), and more generally to the sins of the people (2 Macc 5:17).[107] Van Henten is also of the view that "sins" here refer more to the sins of the people, who have been led to this state because of the deeds of some of their leaders like Simon, Jason, Menelaus, and others, rather than to that of the individual martyrs.[108] This is similar to the Deuteronomic understanding of collective responsibility wherein the sins of the leader or a king can affect the whole clan or nation.

ii) The martyrs are presented as ideal Jewish figures whose self-sacrifice brings peace to the nation. The narrative structure, which places the success of Judas Maccabaeus (2 Macc 8) right at the heels of the death of the martyrs, implies that their death has begun to positively impact the fate of the nation.[109] They represent model Jews from every section of society, young and old, men and women.[110] This is not to say they were sinless, but their sin is presented as deriving from having so identified with the people. Thus, while they are not sinless they are ideal in that the narrative presents them as standing firm in their allegiance to God and taking the sins of the whole nation upon themselves.

iii) That the martyrs are taking collective responsibility is also reflected in the youngest brother speaking of the wrath of God ἐπὶ τὸ σύμπαν ἡμῶν γένος ("upon our whole race" 2 Macc 7:38). It is this divine anger that has befallen the whole nation and that they hope to reverse through their deaths. Considering that the whole of the Jewish people was groaning under the new policies of Antiochus, it is likely that they would have read their situation in

---

107. 2 Maccabees also mentions the sins of the leaders like Simon whose words eventuate in Heliodorus' attacked on the Temple treasury (2 Macc 3), Menelaus, who plans the murder of Onias, the high priest, and mistreats his fellow Jews (2 Macc 4:34; 5:23), Jason, who along with his men, kills several Jews (2 Macc 5:6), Lysimachus who robs the temple on several occasions (2 Macc 4:39), and Alcimus who incites king Demetrius against Judas Maccabeus and his people (2 Macc 14).

108. Van Henten, *Maccabean Martyrs*, 137.

109. Van Henten, 142.

110. Also among the martyrs is Eleazar who is not discussed here. Van Henten argues that the martyrs are presented as exemplary figures who in refusing to obey Antiochus' command choose a specific way of life. He compares non-religious depictions of self-sacrifice and martyrdom in the Graeco-Roman period non-Jewish literature, and Josephus' praise for the faithfulness of the Jews to the law, to show that the martyrs here were also being presented as national heroes. See van Henten, *Maccabean Martyrs*, 201, 212–225, 268. Doran also briefly notes the idea of a noble death. He states that exhibiting the virtues especially of courage and righteousness, and the willingness to die, make the martyrs' deaths similar to the worthy death found in the Graeco-Roman literature of that time in Doran, *2 Maccabees*, 164.

light of the Scriptures that warn of national oppression under foreign rulers for apostasy (Deut 32).

iv) Finally, if the martyrs were dying for their individual sins, the youngest brother's claims that their suffering is a temporary divine discipline, and God will reconcile with them (2 Macc 7:32–33) is left with little meaning since the mother and the brothers all die.[111] Hence it makes better sense to understand that they were speaking of the sins of the whole nation, which will be paid for by their death and consequently bring about God's mercy and reconciliation on them, the nation (2 Macc 7:38).[112]

As such, the concept of sin here is used in a collective sense rather than referring to the sins of the individual martyrs. The sins of some of the leaders of the Jews affects the whole Jewish community and reflects a covenantal understanding of the whole community having entered into the covenant with God as one. Hence, the sins here refer to the sins of the Jews, and the martyrs are presented as bearing the punishment of the whole people.

The expected outcome for dying for the sins of the nation is that God's wrath will come to an end and he will have mercy on the people, resulting in peace for the Jewish nation (2 Macc 7:32–33). This understanding of God's dealing with them through the intertwining of individual actions and the fate of the nation has a strong covenant underpinning and is alluded to twice in the narrative at crucial junctures.[113] First, when the eldest brother is tortured and killed the mother and other brothers console themselves and bolster their faith and decision to go through death by referring to the Song of Moses (2 Macc 7:6).[114] The reference in verse 6 to the song which confronts as a witness reflects Deuteronomy 31:21 and is the title of the Song of Moses in Deuteronomy 32. Covenant underpinning appears the second time in the words of the youngest brother who asserts that their suffering is a training and

---

111. Van Henten, *Maccabean Martyrs*, 138–139.

112. The idea of dying for the sins of others recalls the suffering of the Servant in Isaiah 53:1–12 which was examined briefly in chapter 1. Some scholars have read the voluntary death of the mother and brothers on behalf of the nations as a vicarious sacrifice. For instance, see, McClellan, "Reevaluation of the Structure," 81–95. However, there are others who do not see the death of the Maccabean figures as vicarious; for instance Seeley, *Noble Death*, 87–89.

113. Whether the nation is held as having sinned because of the sins of its leaders or the deeds of the mother and the brothers affecting the peace of the nation, the deeds of individuals are seen as altering the fate of the nation.

114. See Goldstein, *II Maccabees*, 304; Doran, *2 Maccabees*, 156.

God will soon reconcile with them, which echoes the ideas of Deuteronomy 32:36 (2 Macc 7:33).[115] By hemming in their martyrdom with Deuteronomy 32 at the death of the first and the last brothers, the covenant becomes the framework within which their deaths are understood. Thus, the theocentric aspect envelops the acts of martyrdom.

Further, the narrative as a whole evinces a view that history progresses under God's purview, and the expectation of peace for the people stems from it. This view of history has strong reverberations of Deuteronomy 32 that ties the fate of the nation to their faithfulness to God,[116] and has been noted by scholars.[117] There are ample allusions to Deuteronomy in this short account that makes it reasonable to assume that the concept of covenant undergirds

---

115. Van Henten states the verb καταλλάσσω ("to reconcile"; passive in 2 Macc 7:33, καταλλαγήσεται) here refers to divine-human reconciliation as opposed to an inter-human reconciliation. He argues that in view of the defunct temple cult, and the use of the passive form of the verb, καταλλαγήσεται, the narrative presents the martyrs as having affected reconciliation by their deeds. Van Henten, *Maccabean Martyrs*, 141–142. In any case, even if the martyrs' deeds initiate the reconciliation, it is only possible because God first promised to turn to them when they have suffered enough (Deut 32:36, 42). Therefore, they expected reconciliation with God after a time of suffering as already enshrined in God's promise to his people.

116. Deuteronomy 32 describes God's marvelous works for his people who in turn responds with apostasy because of which God turns away from them and consequently punishes them. However, it also tells of God's compassion and vindication for his people and the subsequent punishment of those who oppressed them. It is perhaps also worth noting that the passage that praises Yahweh's power to kill and to bring to life, which was discussed briefly in the introductory chapter as a text that though not speaking of a literal afterlife expressed Yahweh's potentiality, occurs in Deuteronomy 32:39, and Deuteronomy 32 is now alluded to here in 2 Maccabees 7, a text that speaks explicitly of resurrection.

117. Goldstein states the brothers had Deuteronomy 32 in mind even as they declared their convictions before Antiochus prior to being put to death (see Goldstein, *II Maccabees*, 303). David deSilva states the book tries "to demonstrate the ongoing legitimacy of Deuteronomy's philosophy of history" – a theological interpretation of history that affirms adherence to ancestral law for "national security and prosperity" (deSilva, *Introducing*, 266, 271, 273–274). Schwartz notes that this "understanding of history" that is based upon Deuteronomy 32 is basic to the book and prominent especially in 2 Maccabees 7 (Schwartz, *2 Maccabees*, 21–22, 298). Van Henten observes the correspondence between the portrayal of the development of history in in the narrative of the martyrs and that of the Deuteronomist. He also states that Deuteronomy 31–32 links the fate of the nation to their faithfulness to God's law, which in the context of chapter 7 implies that the distinction is made not only between Antiochus and the Jews but between those who remain faithful to God's laws and those who do not (see van Henten, *Maccabean Martyrs*, 140, 110–111, 136–137, 163). Nickelsburg proposes that the whole book is structured on a Deuteronomistic pattern (Nickelsburg, *Jewish Literature*, 118). Whether or not one agrees with Nickelsburg's suggested structure, the epitomist's Deuteronomic orientation to history is evident in that he portrays the erosion of the covenant way of life as the greatest threat to the peace and security of the nation (Doran, *Temple Propaganda*, 110). Also cf. Goldstein's discussion on the use of Deuteronomy 32 in 1 Maccabees and Testament of Moses in crisis settings; Goldstein, *II Maccabees*, 294–295; Schwartz, *2 Maccabees*, 21–22, 298; Also see Doran,

this story of martyrdom and the expectation of peace for the Jews is based on covenant promise: the partial quotation of Deuteronomy 32:36 in 2 Maccabees 7:6 as mentioned, the references to the collective sins of the people and the expectation of mercy and reconciliation after a time of suffering alludes to Deuteronomy 32 (2 Macc 7:18, 32–33), and the references to the all-seeing God who "watches over us" as a trope appearing several times in the book (2 Macc 1:27; 7:6, 35; 8:2; 9:5; 12:22; 15:2).[118] The understanding is that God is always watching over his people, but Antiochus is able to oppress them because the sins of the people have caused the Lord to look away momentarily (Deut 32:20). It is because of this deuteronomic understanding of history and God's dealing with them as covenanted nation that the brothers can claim that their suffering is not evidence of God's abandonment but rather a temporary discipline, and God will soon be reconciled with his servants (2 Macc 7:33).[119]

6.6.4. Section Conclusion

Dying for the collective sins of the nation reveals a covenant underpinning which highlights the theocentric aspect of divine retribution. Therefore, it can be said the conviction of the martyrs that God will have compassion on the nation is based on the promise God had already made to the people in the covenant. In other words, human actions can elicit divine response because God had already made that provision in his promise. This shows that the theocentric aspect, which emphasizes God's benevolent actions towards human beings independent of their deeds, undergirds the anthropocentric aspect of divine retribution, which emphasizes human action. As such, although there is a strong anthropocentric aspect at play in that resurrection is a post-mortem reward for the deeds of the martyrs, the anthropocentric aspect is presented within the overarching framework of the theocentric

---

2 Maccabees, 156; Downing, "Jesus and Martyrdom," 281–283; Young, "'Woman with the Soul,'" 70–71; Sigvartsen, *Afterlife and Resurrection Beliefs*, 29, 41, 45.

118. Schwartz, *2 Maccabees*, 205, 302.

119. There is also another aspect of divine retribution evident here – the dissolution aspect wherein God's dealings with his people are seen not primarily as rewards or punishments, but as serving other purposes such as teaching or chastisement of the nation. Hence, though they have sinned and the suffering is punitive, it is also to be understood as a divine discipline (v. 33). However, since this aspect of divine retribution is experienced only in this life and is not related to post-mortem retribution it is not studied here.

aspect of divine retribution through the covenant which God had initiated with the people.

Thus, the death of the martyrs for the sins of the people brings about peace from oppression for the Jewish nation according to the provisions in the covenant and exhibits the theocentric aspect of divine retribution. National peace is not post-mortem retribution for the martyrs *per se* in that they do not experience the peace themselves; rather it is experienced by those who survive the persecution. It is post-mortem for the martyrs only in the sense that it is retribution for their deaths and comes into force only through and after their death. This covenant underpinning suggests that the martyrs' self-sacrifice and their expectation of resurrection and peace all happens within this covenantal understanding and as such there is a theocratic aspect of retribution underlying the expectation of divine retribution.

6.7. Nature of Post-mortem Divine Retribution: Corporate and Individual

Divine retribution in 2 Maccabees 7 evinces both the corporate and the individualistic nature by intertwining the fates of the nation and individuals. The corporate nature of divine retribution refers to instances when the consequences of the deeds of an individual affect others in the community who are related to him – family, clan, or even the whole nation, and this is examined first.

6.7.1. Corporate Nature of Divine Retribution

The study of Deuteronomistic divine retribution in chapter 2 found that the nature of divine retribution in Deuteronomy is predominantly, though not exclusively, corporate. This corporate nature is seen in 2 Maccabees 7 as well. That the community would suffer the consequences of the deeds of individuals, especially in cases where that individual has a place of prominence in the community, is found in the Deuteronomistic and chronistic historiographical presentation of the regnal accounts, as Ven Henten rightly observes, where the actions of the kings determine the fate of the nation as well.[120] For instance,

---

120. Van Henten, *Maccabean Martyrs*, 137–138.

the Deuteronomistic historian eventually places the blame for Judah's exile to Babylon on King Manasseh (2 Kgs 23:26–27; 24:1–4).

In 2 Maccabees 7, divine retribution displays a collective nature in two ways. Negatively, the sins of the apostatizing individuals in leading positions bring punishment on the nation, as mentioned above. The nation is said to be suffering for their sins (2 Macc 7:18, 32) and the persecution under Antiochus is portrayed as divine ἐπιπλήξεως καὶ παιδείας (from ἐπίπληξις "rebuke," and παιδεία "training" 2 Macc 7:33). This collective understanding is emphasized by the use of the word ἑαυτοῦ (reflexive pronoun) in the plural form (2x in v. 18, and 1x in v. 32).[121] This reflects the covenantal understanding of the people's relationship with God, as stated above.[122] Hence the disaster on the Jews is understood as "punitive, but corrective, discipline rather than destructive judgment" (2 Macc 7:16b, 33–35).[123] Further, the epitomist sees the reforms brought in during the period of Jason's and Menelaus' high priesthood as a setting aside of the Torah prescribed way of life and thus constituting apostasy. As such, the narrative presents the view that the nation is ripe for divine chastisement and the sins of these Jewish leaders result in God's wrath falling on the whole nation. This effect of collective retribution in 2 Maccabees 7 is not post-mortem since the suffering is experienced while alive; however, it is eventually what leads to the death of the martyrs.

Divine retribution in its corporate nature also works the other way around so that the consequences of actions of individuals can positively affect others. In the narrative, the collective nature of divine retribution is also at work in the belief that the deaths of the martyrs would bring peace for the Jews (2 Macc 7:38) as seen above. The martyrs,[124] although presumably model Jews

---

121. Verse 18: "on account of *ourselves* we suffer, having sinned against *our* God"; verse 32: "we suffer on account of *our* sins"; translation and italics mine.

122. Doran, *2 Maccabees*, 158, 161.

123. deSilva, *Introducing*, 275. So also Ego, "God's Justice," 153–154. She notes that two kinds of justice are at play in 2 Maccabees – God's justice on the oppressors of the Jewish people is more measure for measure so that the judgments on them is definitive, whereas judgments upon the Jews themselves is more pedagogical, aimed at teaching and correcting.

124. While the present study is limited to the study of the martyrs in chapter 7, van Henten is correct in also including the deaths of Eleazar and Razis within the purview of his discussion of the martyrs as the saviours of the Jewish people. See van Henten, *Maccabean Martyrs*. Goldstein is even more pointed in stating that the mother and the brothers' suffering are part of the suffering of the whole of Israel and do not constitute a separate special sacrifice that brings an end to the persecution. According to him the reference to Deuteronomy 32 implies

themselves, suffer and die for the sins of the nation,[125] and in doing so bring an end to the oppression, which is implied by the victory of Judas Maccabeus in 2 Maccabees 8.

Thus, divine retribution in 2 Maccabees 7 exhibits a corporate nature with the consequences of the deeds of individuals affecting the whole community both positively and negatively. This can be attributed to the covenant underpinning of the narrative discussed above which gives it its corporate outlook. The corporate outworking of divine retribution is not post-mortem since the effects of divine retribution play out within history, both in terms of suffering for the sins of the apostates, and experiencing peace as a result of the martyrdoms. However, this corporate nature of retribution leads to the death of the faithful Jews which propels divine retribution into the afterlife in a more individualist manner, as shall be seen next.

6.7.2. Individual Nature of Post-mortem Divine Retribution

In the post-mortem, divine retribution becomes individualized through resurrection which is presented as the reward particularly for the martyrs for standing firm in their faith and allegiance to the law during persecution.[126] The narrative seems to indicate that only those individuals who died at the hands of Antiochus have the hope of resurrection. Assmann expresses a similar view when he states that "dying for God comprises the idea of personal salvation."[127] Doran also notes that 2 Maccabees is a "radical change" in the conception of what happens after death by proposing individual resurrection, especially in the third brother's assertion that he will receive back his body (2 Macc 7:11; also 14:46).[128] Similarly, Sigvartsen views the resurrection belief in the book as deriving from an "individualist interpretation" of the Deuteronomic retribution principle,[129] while van Henten states that there is an "obvious connection" between the deeds of an individual and their retribution in 2 Maccabees.[130]

---

that it is the suffering of the people as a whole, to which is added the suffering of the mother and the brothers, which brings about the end of persecution. See Goldstein, *II Maccabees*, 316.

125. deSilva, *Introducing*, 275. Van Henten, *Maccabean Martyrs*, 210–213.
126. Nickelsburg, *Resurrection, Immortality*, 217.
127. Assmann, "Martyrdom, Violence," 54.
128. Doran, *Temple Propaganda*, 110.
129. Sigvarten, *Afterlife and Resurrection*, 48.
130. Van Henten, *Maccabean Martyrs*, 163.

In the story, the brothers consistently link their hope of resurrection to their dying for the law. This is especially evident in the speeches of the second and third brothers and the mother (2 Macc 7:7, 11, 23), implying that resurrection is specifically connected to martyrdom. The third brother unequivocally states that he considers losing his body for the sake of the law as nothing because he hoped (ἐλπίζω "to hope"; ἐλπίζω v. 11; ἐλπίδας v. 14) to get his body back from God, while the mother speaks of the creative power of God as she urges her sons to disregard themselves for the sake of the law because of the hope (ἐλπίδας v. 20) she has that God would give them back to her (2 Macc 7:23). The narrative makes it quite apparent that the physical resurrection envisaged is for those whose body and life were forfeited in the persecution. All these point to resurrection being connected to martyrdom; it is a personal reward for the martyrs. Thus, in the narrative of 2 Maccabees 7, post-mortem retribution via the concept of resurrection is a reward specifically for the martyrs.

As van Henten states, the vindication of the martyrs in this narrative is comparable to the portrayal of the exemplary faithfulness and piety and the suffering righteous in the biblical tradition (for instance, Abraham in Gen 22; also 15:6; Daniel and his friends in Daniel 3, 6) and early post-biblical tradition (for instance, Susanna in Susanna 3), except that the "rescue" of the suffering righteous in this case happens post-mortem via resurrection.[131] This transposition of the reward to the afterlife is a decisive break from the deuteronomic traditional conception that retribution works out in history, even inter-generationally. Seen from this perspective personal divine retribution in the afterlife is a "completely new" idea as Assmann puts it,[132] albeit there are precursors in Isaiah 26 and Daniel 12 in the HB.

This is perhaps to be explained from the perspective of divine justice. In the context of the narrative, post-mortem divine retribution is necessitated by the absence of justice in the present life.[133] The martyrs reaffirmed their

---

131. Van Henten, *Maccabean Martyrs*, 129, 131, 298. While Doran agrees that both Daniel and the martyrs in 2 Maccabees 7 are heroes, he finds the difference between being rescued and being put to death, or the killing of oneself, a radical one that needs to be studied as separate forms rather than grouping them all together indiscriminately. Doran, "Martyrs," 189–190.

132. Assmann, "Martyrdom, Violence," 54.

133. Eugene Coetzer and Pierre Jordaan argue that the story of the martyrs is an attempt to makes sense of the divine absence in the face of torture and death of his people. They state

belief that God was watching over them even as they were tortured to death (2 Macc 7:6); hence justice, if it does not prevail in their lifetime, will do so after death. Thus the great injustice suffered by the martyrs in losing their lives for their allegiance to God and his law is resolved through the concept of physical resurrection which allows divine justice to be maintained by transposing the just reward of the martyrs to the afterlife.[134] C. K. Barrett states that the belief in resurrection came from the conviction that God would uphold his justice, and since accepting death meant dissolution of the hope of earthly retribution and of the possibility of participation in the national peace, hope of post-mortem individual reward arose.[135] Similarly, van Henten states the idea of post-mortem retribution has its roots in the belief that God is omniscient and himself executes divine retribution in its "appropriate time."[136] Assmann observes that the death of the martyrs represents the ultimate kind of loyalty to God and his laws, as such a historically distant retribution is deemed as insufficient in this case. He states, "the deficiency of meaning within this life is experienced as so unsustainable that it sends forth a command for immediate fulfillment." God's justice required that the martyrs receive their recompense after death.[137] This implies that resurrection as divine retribution is individuated so that the ones who lose their life and bodies are the ones who are rewarded with life and body, thus reflecting the individual nature of retribution.

6.7.3. Section Conclusion

In 2 Maccabees 7 divine retribution while alive is experienced collectively; whether it is suffering together for the sins of the apostates or receiving divine

---

that immortality and existence beyond death is an answer to the questions raised by God's absence in crisis. See Coetzer and Jordaan, "Selling Religious Progress," 189.

134. So also deSilva, *Introducing*, 277; Crossan argues that since the martyrs were publicly humiliated and their bodies mutilated, justice requires that they be vindicated in a like manner through "a public, visible, *and* bodily" resurrection. See Crossan, "Resurrection of Jesus," 42–43. Agus states that resurrection is necessitated by the fact that the martyrs were "deeply wronged" and suffered profoundly. Agus, *Binding of Isaac*, 14–16.

135. Barrett, "Immortality and Resurrection," 9. Norman Snaith, although not specifically discussing 2 Maccabees 7, similarly agues the belief in Sheol was replaced by ideas of afterlife because of the need for individual justice. Snaith, "Justice and Immortality," 313–314, 317.

136. As opposed to Koch's act-consequence nexus or consequence producing sphere of deeds; see van Henten, *Maccabean Martyrs*, 163.

137. Assmann, "Martyrdom, Violence," 54–55.

mercy because of the martyrdom of a few, the nation goes through it together. In contrast, in the afterlife divine retribution is experienced individually – only those who died for the law will resurrect as a recompense for the persecution they suffered. There is no indication that all the Jews or even all the righteous will take part in this resurrection. However, since the death of the martyrs also affects the collective fate of the nation, their death is like a double-edged sword: i) it affects the post-mortem fate of the individual martyrs through resurrection as a reward for their martyrdom, and ii) it affects the collective fate of the nation by restoring peace. Thus in 2 Maccabees 7 the divide between life and death becomes more fluid. Instead of a definite break between life and death, both life and death lie on a continuum, with the act of dying affecting both sides of death, that is, life and afterlife. Therefore, while the corporate as well as the individual nature of divine retribution is operative in the narrative, divine retribution when pushed to the afterlife exhibits the characteristic of the individual nature of divine retribution.

Finally, it was discussed earlier that there is divine retribution for Antiochus for his oppression of the Jews; however, it was also later seen that the brothers claimed the oppression was divinely imposed as a punishment for their sins and Antiochus was a mere agent. This raises the question: why should a mere agent be punished? On that question, a brief explanation follows.

6.8. Excursus: Divine Retribution for the Agent of Divine Punishment

There is an apparent contradiction in saying the suffering of the Jews is a just punishment from God, as well as claiming that the perpetrators of the persecution will face judgment. If ultimately the reason for the suffering of the Jews is beyond Antiochus's control,[138] in that he is merely an unwitting agent in God's hands, a punishment for being an agent seems unjustified.

This seeming inconsistency is resolved if it is understood that his punishment is not for acting as God's unwitting agent but for overstepping his divine mandate. Antiochus IV is an agent of God's punitive measure on the Jews, and hence the suffering of the Jews was ultimately God-ordained. But he becomes guilty of overreaching himself. Initially Antiochus IV is described

---

138. Doran, *2 Maccabees*, 161.

in the role of an agent in God's hand, almost in a positive light, when he acts against the murder of the pious priest Onias (2 Macc 4:37–38). Thus, in this capacity Antiochus IV was God's instrument used to punish his people, as were the Assyrians and the Babylonians. However, Antiochus IV later mirrors the Assyrians described in Isaiah 10:5–19, in his overstepping the limits of executing God's punishment to the Jews.[139] In persecuting the Jews for their loyalty to their God and his law, he was setting himself up against God, for which he brings on himself divine wrath.[140] Moreover, Antiochus is described as being filled with pride, φρυαττόμενος ἀδήλοις ἐλπίσιν ("puffed up with uncertain hope," 2 Macc 7:34; also cf. 5:17, 21; 9:4). He is described as presuming to have the ability to command the seas, weighing the mountains, of touching the stars, and considering himself to be godlike (2 Macc 9:8, 10, 12). These descriptions are elsewhere used of God himself (Job 38:8–11; Isa 40:12; 51:15),[141] and for his overweening ambition he is held accountable. Scholars have also found this description of Antiochus's arrogance and downfall as reminiscent of Isaiah 14:12–14.[142]

Hence, this seemingly contradictory view that the Jews were suffering under Antiochus for their sins can be held in juxtaposition with the understanding that Antiochus will not go unpunished for his violence against them. Antiochus who was the unwitting agent of God's judgment on the Jews for their infidelity to the LORD goes overboard and thus becomes the object of God's judgment. His punishment however, unlike the reward for the martyrs, is completed on earth and there is no resurrection to eternal damnation for Antiochus.

6.9. Conclusion

This chapter shows that the narrative manifests a great interest in the concept of divine retribution, which is both anthropocentric and theocentric, individualistic as well as corporate, and works out in terms of reward and

---

139. Goldstein, *II Maccabees*, 293.

140. Zeitlin, *Second Book*, 48; Bartlett, *First and Second Books*, 273; van Henten also views Antiochus as having set himself up against God; see van Henten, *Maccabean Martyrs*, 175.

141. Ego, "God's Justice," 150.

142. Goldstein, *II Maccabees*, 293; van Henten, *Maccabean Martyrs*, 167; Ego, "God's Justice," 150; Doran, *2 Maccabees*, 158, 188–189.

punishment in the afterlife as well as in this life. As a reward, divine retribution is post-mortem and is expressed through the concept of resurrection. It is unique in its assertion of a physical resurrection as a reward for martyrdom. It serves to affirm the belief in divine justice to the effect that even when divine retribution, particularly reward, is not realized in this life it remains viable in the afterlife. Further, divine retribution also includes punishment for the perpetrator, Antiochus IV, but the outworking of the punishment is achieved on earth so that there is no post-mortem hope for the persecutor, who ultimately was fighting against God himself. Punishment may not come instantaneously but the narrative posits that it will eventually work itself out in this life, possibly engulfing his descendants too.

The account of the martyrs in 2 Maccabees 7 shows both continuity and discontinuity from the deuteronomic understanding of divine retribution. First, divine retribution in 2 Maccabees 7 exhibits the characteristics of the anthropocentric as well as theocentric aspects of divine retribution, similar to deuteronomic divine retribution. The martyrs demonstrate an unswerving allegiance to God in their deeds by dying for his law, and are consequently rewarded with resurrection. This explicit linking between human action and divine response exhibits the anthropocentric aspect of post-mortem divine retribution. However, this anthropocentrism – the fact that human actions can elicit divine response – is firmly situated in the covenant that Yahweh initiated with Israel and thus highlights the theocentric aspect of this human divine interaction. It presents a perspective of history that is framed by the covenant so that their understanding of the unfolding of the events under Antiochus, the suffering, their future expectation for their actions, and the fates of the Jewish nation as well as that of Antiochus are all informed by this understanding of their covenantal relationship with God.

Second, divine retribution in 2 Maccabees 7 is both corporate and individual. Concurrent with the deuteronomic understanding, divine retribution in history is corporate. The nation both suffers persecution and experiences peace from oppression collectively for the deeds of the few individuals; that is, persecution is ultimately traced back to the sins of the leaders, and martyrs who die for the collective sin serve to bring peace to the nation. However, when the realization of divine retribution is transposed to the afterlife in the case of the martyrs who do not enjoy this peace, divine retribution becomes individualized so that the recipients of the rewards are the martyrs themselves and does not include anyone else. In asserting such a confidence in individual post-mortem retribution, this narrative pushes the traditional boundary of the concept of God's justice. The consequence of their deaths leads to their resurrection and also brings peace to the Jewish nation which is experienced by others who are still alive. As such, in 2 Maccabees 7, the consequences of their deaths by so reverberating in both life and the afterlife soften the divide between life and death and turn the diametrically opposite states of life and death into a continuum of life and afterlife.

CHAPTER 7

Conclusion

7.1. Introduction

This study attempted a thoroughgoing examination of the nature of the post-mortem divine retribution in the HB and selected STP Jewish literature, specifically by reading the post-mortem texts of Isaiah 26:19, Daniel 12:1–3, Book of the Watchers 22, and 2 Maccabees 7 alongside the aspects of divine retribution in the book of Deuteronomy. Post-mortem divine retribution is a point of confluence of two major themes in biblical studies, that is, the theme of divine retribution and the afterlife. However, post-mortem divine retribution in biblical studies is a relatively unresearched subject, emerging mainly in existing works by way of incidental references in studies relating to the afterlife. There is no other work known yet in the field of biblical studies that specifically investigates this subject. The specific contribution of this study is that it connects the themes of divine retribution and the afterlife and proposes that some elements of earthly divine retribution continue to function similarly even when divine retribution is transposed to the afterlife while the others elements become defunct with the cessation of life. In doing so this study calls attention to texts that push the boundary of divine retribution from life to afterlife and highlights the continuities and discontinuities between earthly and post-mortem divine retribution.

To conclude the investigation, it is relevant to highlight the contours of the presentation of post-mortem divine retribution in the four post-mortem texts as they relate to the aspects of divine retribution in Deuteronomy.

7.2. Summary of the Chapters

Chapter 1 set out the orienting elements of the thesis by defining the basic concept of retribution, outlining its method, and selecting the texts with post-mortem references to be examined. It was decided that the term retribution would be used as referring to both reward and punishment, which is often how it is used in biblical studies, and was defined as one of the ways in which God's justice and the divine-human interaction is experienced in a tangible way by human beings. The chapter also looked at the ways in which intertextuality has been appropriated as a method in biblical studies from the world of literary theory where it had its beginnings in Kristeva. The use of intertextuality as a method in biblical studies diverges broadly into two categories: production-centred, which is diachronic in its approach to texts, and reception-centred, which is synchronic. It was concluded that the thesis will primarily use the reception-centred perspective to read the texts, but will take into account the production-centred features of texts when it is explicit in the texts.

Chapter 2 discussed the concept of divine retribution in the HB, focusing especially on the book of Deuteronomy. It argued as untenable the monochromatic presentation of the concept of divine retribution in the HB that characterizes retribution as divine interventions to reward or punish human deeds. It also examined Koch's proposition that retribution in the HB is not a judicial process but rather a mechanical one, that is, deeds have built-in consequences and inevitably result in disastrous consequences without any need for divine intervention. It was concluded that this dynamistic or impersonal expression of retribution is a part of divine retribution but diverged from Koch's view in asserting that it was not the only kind of retribution evinced in the HB. Instead the chapter argued that divine retribution is more nuanced, allowing for different emphases or aspects to emerge in its expression in various instances. This move towards a nuanced understanding of divine retribution was observed in the works of several scholars. With respect to the book of Deuteronomy, it was seen that there are at least four aspects of divine retribution and each of the four aspects were illustrated with a textual example from Deuteronomy.

The first is the impersonal aspect of divine retribution in which the expression of divine retribution emphasizes the natural consequence of deeds rather than God's direct intervention. This aspect was illustrated through an examination of Deuteronomy 21:1–9 that describes the case of an unsolved homicide within the Israelite boundary that was said to incur bloodguilt on the residents. The second is the anthropocentric aspect which emphasizes the human act as the initiating factor and God appears mainly as a reactor to human action. Deuteronomy 11:13–21 was used to illustrate this aspect of divine retribution, which is an exhortation to love Yahweh once they enter the land, and lays down the blessings and punishments that would be attendant upon their obedience or disobedience. The third is the theocentric aspect, which balances the anthropocentric aspect by emphasising God's action towards human beings that is independent of human deeds, and directed instead by God's own purposes. This aspect was exemplified through the examination of Deuteronomy 7:6–11 which explains Israel's elected status as something that was God's gracious initiative and not one contingent on Israel's merits. The last aspect was the dissolution of retribution wherein the sufferings and blessings that people experience were explained as not directly related to their actions but expressed as functioning pedagogically, and in such cases reward and punishment ceases to be viable expressions for conveying the reasons behind these experiences. The study used Deuteronomy 8:1–20 to illustrate instances when sufferings and prosperity were instruments of testing and teaching rather than purely retributive.

It was further noted that these aspects may operate either at an individual level, where only the person responsible for the deeds faced the consequences, or at a corporate level in which case the consequences of the deed affected people other than the one who committed it. As such, it was demonstrated that divine retribution in Deuteronomy is best understood as a multi-faceted concept with each aspect revealing a different emphasis.

Having highlighted from the text that the nature of divine retribution in Deuteronomy is nuanced and consists of various aspects, the study examined the concept of post-mortem divine retribution by reading the selected texts that contain post-mortem reference *vis-à-vis* these aspects of divine retribution. This was done in the next four chapters, each dealing with one text that presented an avenue for a discussion of the post-mortem divine retribution.

Chapter 3 dealt with Isaiah 26:19. Although the post-mortem reference in Isaiah 26:19 is not as clear as in the other three texts examined in this study, there was enough to make a case for such an investigation. It began by examining the issue of dating the Isaiah 24–27 complex. It was observed that assigning a date to this complex remains largely indeterminate and since the interpretation was not completely dependent on the assigned date, the text was examined from the perspective of its temporal orientation, that is, whether it was speaking of the past or the future. The study proceeded by adopting a future perspective to read the text. It also examined the grammatical difficulties and the issue of the identity of the speaker in Isaiah 26:19 which influences the interpretation. It was argued that the speaker in v. 19 was the prophet who was speaking on behalf of Yahweh bringing the salvation oracle to the people.

Next, the arguments for and against literal resurrection interpretation were examined. It was argued that the resurrection language is used literally to refer to an actual resurrection of the dead rather than metaphorically to a national restoration. This conclusion was arrived at by considering several interpretational difficulties posed by the metaphorical reading that are better understood when read literally. The metaphorical interpretation generally roots the text in the sixth- or fifth-century BCE exilic context, reads the lament as a cry for national restoration, and the response as Yahweh's promise to restore the nation. However, it was argued that the people's lament cannot be used as an interpretative scope for Yahweh's response and that basing the interpretation on a debatable date of the Isaiah 24–27 complex was shaky at best. Further, it was observed that the cluster of death-life terms in v.19 made a metaphorical reading difficult. Hence, it was argued that literal interpretation made better sense in this text.

In looking at the literal interpretation, it was noted that post-mortem divine retribution is presented in terms of resurrection and non-remembrance. Thus, in Isaiah 26:19 resurrection functions as the reward for the righteous whereas the wicked will not rise and will be forgotten. It was argued that those who will resurrect were part of the righteous lamenting community of God's people. The identity of those who will not rise was arrived at by studying Isaiah 26:13–14 together with v. 19, and it was concluded that it referred to the dead foreign rulers, the *rephaim*, who were often thought to have some power to bestow favours. Further, the description of the recipients of resurrection as "righteous" seemed to imply that the basis for the differentiation between those who would resurrect and those who would not is a moral one. However, the corporate manner of identifying the righteous made it difficult to ascertain if and to what extent nationalistic or ethnic considerations come into play.

In other words, is divine retribution based on morality or ethnicity? It was proposed that the basis of retribution is possibly a composite of moral as well as national identity, that is, Israel as a community is considered righteous. If there was any division or conflict within this community, it did not emerge in the text itself. Additionally, it was found that the identity of those who will not resurrect is not diametrically opposite of Israel as a religious political entity, that is, they are not the other nations. Rather those who will not rise are the *rephaim*, the dead and divinized foreign rulers who vied for Israel's allegiance. The fate of the *rephaim*, however, is not only non-resurrection but also non-remembrance, and thus indicating a double death. They were to be relegated to forgetfulness with no one to call their names. The cessation of their memories thus consigned to death after death.

Thus the study highlighted that in Isaiah 26:19, the emphasis of post-mortem divine retribution seemed to be on the anthropocentric aspect as it highlighted the deeds of the people in moral terms. The people were identified as righteous and characterised as trusting and teachable, and faithful in the face of competing claimants to their allegiance. As such resurrection is the reward for their faithfulness to Yahweh. The punishment of the *rephaim* was also Yahweh's response for their attempt to set themselves up as competitors for Israel's allegiance. However, this portrayal of divine retribution also seemed to indicate a theocentric underpinning in speaking corporately of divine retribution toward a covenanted community. The corporate identity and outlook of Israel was one that was forged through the covenant, an act of grace that Yahweh initiated independent of Israel's merits. Hence, underlying the anthropocentric emphasis of post-mortem divine retribution in Isaiah 26:19 was the theocentric aspect. Further, as noted, the post-mortem divine retribution operated corporately, with Israel functioning as a single entity.

Therefore, in Isaiah 26:19, the concept of divine retribution transitions from being operational in this world to being viable even after death. However, in this text, the ideas of post-mortem reward and punishment are not eternal life and eternal suffering. Instead, resurrection itself functions as the reward for God's people, while the punishment consists of the intensification of the concept of death for God's enemies. Further, divine retribution in the afterlife, similar to divine retribution in Deuteronomy, continues to consider human deeds as a criterion for retribution, thus evincing the anthropocentric aspect. The theocentric aspect also continues to influence retribution in that those who do receive the post-mortem rewards belong to a specific community. However, the impersonal and dissolution aspects of divine retribution in Deuteronomy appear to be defunct when divine retribution is transposed to the afterlife, since the final judgment leaves scope neither for a mechanical outworking of the consequences of human deeds nor for pedagogical training. Although Isaiah 26:19 offers but a small glimpse into post-mortem divine retribution, it nonetheless pushes the boundary of the earth-bound divine retribution that typifies Deuteronomy by taking a step, albeit a small one, into the afterlife making post-mortem divine retribution possible.

With Daniel 12:1–3 the concept of post-mortem divine retribution is on firmer ground. This text was examined in Chapter 4. The vision and assurance of post-mortem divine retribution in Daniel 12:1–3 is given in the context of crisis, although it is difficult to identify which specific historical event lies behind it. Since the interpretation of the book of Daniel depends quite significantly on the date and context one places it in, the study began with a discussion of the issue of the date of the book. While the differences in opinion concerning the date and consequently the interpretation of the text are divergent, it was found that both the early and late date views largely agree that Daniel 11:1–35 corresponds to the Seleucid period under Antiochus IV and the issue boils down, broadly speaking, to whether after v. 35 the text is to be interpreted eschatologically or historically. The chapter proceeded to present the text from both perspectives, that is, Daniel 12:1–3 as read as an eschatological prophecy and as a prophecy regarding Antiochus IV's expected end.

Despite posing some interpretational problems, Daniel 12:1–3 is comparatively much clearer than Isaiah 26:19 regarding its concern for post-mortem divine retribution. It discussed both the literal and metaphorical interpretation and found that the waking up of those asleep in the dust is better explained as a reference to an actual resurrection of the dead as opposed to a metaphorical reference to the reconstruction of Israel. Further it was concluded that the text posited a resurrection of both the faithful and the wicked, in contrast to the idea presented in Isaiah 26:19, so that they can be assigned to their final destinies, the righteous rising to eternal life and the wicked to eternal condemnation. From the eschatological prophecy point of view, resurrection in Daniel is a reference to the second coming of Jesus, while the historical prophecy view reads it as an answer to the theological and historical problem of persecution under Antiochus IV. It was also noted that among the faithful who rise to life is a sub-group simply called "the wise," which seemed to be a designation for the teachers and leaders of the community who lead others in the way of righteousness. They are to be singled out for special distinction and bestowed with additional glory, although the specifics were unclear. The resurrection of the wicked leads to punishment which is not elaborated but it was surmised that it was probably eternal in terms of both duration and quality. Thus, in Daniel resurrection is no longer an end in itself, but facilitates the outworking of the post-mortem rewards and punishments.

Regarding the aspect of divine retribution, it was argued that in Daniel 12:1–3 the emphasis in divine retribution falls on the anthropocentric aspect in that retribution focuses on faithfulness rather than on ethnicity or national identity. This emphasis emerges noticeably in the sub-category within the faithful, that is the wise ones, who are distinguished from the rest of the faithful based mainly on their deeds in life of bringing others to righteousness. The wise who do or risk more during their lifetime are thus rewarded proportionately with additional glory. The anthropocentricity is further emphasised by the fact that belonging to Israel does not guarantee eternal life. The "many" who rise could imply a total or partial resurrection. But regardless of whether the resurrection is envisaged as for all or limited only to some, allegiance to God is seen as determinative. Thus, it is the faithfulness to the covenant that becomes the defining criterion betraying its anthropocentric emphasis. However, this anthropocentricity is again embedded in the theocentric aspect in that the retribution is measured by their faithfulness to the covenant, which is God's initiative; that is, retribution operates within the covenant that is corporate in its outlook. Thus overall, post-mortem divine retribution in Daniel 12:1–3 exhibits the anthropocentric as well as the theocentric aspects of divine retribution.

Further, post-mortem divine retribution in Daniel 12:1–3 is predominantly individuated unlike divine retribution in Deuteronomy which exhibited a predominantly corporate nature. The distinction of the people as faithful and wicked rather than on lines of national or ethnic identity as the criterion for retribution demonstrates this retributive justice is individuated. However, post-mortem divine retribution in Daniel does not completely lose sight of the corporate interest. The covenantal underpinning also points to its underlying corporate perspective. While the division is on the basis of faithfulness to the covenant, the overall concern in the book of Daniel is for the fate of the nation of Israel. Moreover, eventually the resurrection of the faithful ones is seen as the triumph of the nation, albeit reconstituted of only the faithful ones since the wicked by transgressing the bounds of the covenant and aligning themselves with the interest of the foreign elements relegate their Jewish identity. Hence, while the post-mortem divine retribution is individuated, it culminates in victory for God's people as a whole.

Chapter 5 commenced the examination of the STP texts with BW 22 which gives an insight into a peculiar formulation of the post-mortem retribution. The BW, as it now stands, is a part of the collection called 1 Enoch. The reception history of 1 Enoch involves a claim that it is a literature of a different strand of Judaism called Enochic Judaism which proposes Enoch (the person) and 1 Enoch (the collection) as the revealer of wisdom as opposed to Moses and the Torah. One of the main reasons for proposing an Enochic Judaism is the absence of the Mosaic figure and institutions in the Enochic collection. The place of BW in this line of interpretation is that it also contains an explanation of the origin of evil, which places the responsibility of sin on angels who cohabited with women, rather than on human beings as in the Torah. The thesis first argued that absence of explicit mentions of Moses and Torah does not equal to opposition. Since Enoch predates Moses in the biblical narratives, the books attributed to Enoch could not explicitly mention Moses without dropping the authorial façade and claims to Enochic authority. Further the absence of the mention of Moses or the Torah in other books of the HB are not considered as distinct from the Mosaic tradition. It also highlighted that there are several instances in the Enochic collection which allude to the Mosaic Torah, and despite the claims that Torah is displaced by revealed wisdom it does not present an alternative body of law according to which the judgments are to be carried out. Hence, it was concluded that similar to the prophetic literature, it is likely that the general terms law and commandments are used in 1 Enoch to refer to the Mosaic law rather than to espouse a new revelation.

Concerning the second point, it was argued that the BW does not completely absolve human beings of the responsibility for sin, but rather the BW's origin of sin is a conflation of two traditions, the Asael and Shemihazah. While the Shemihazah tradition holds angels responsible for the origin of sin, the Asael tradition presents human beings as culpable. Further it was argued that divine retribution on human beings at the end assumes culpability and the reason for retribution was not based on ideological differences, following Enoch as opposed to Moses, but on moral grounds, as righteous and wicked.

Having addressed the question of 1 Enoch's relation to Moses and the Torah, the thesis proceeded to examine the presentation of post-mortem divine retribution in BW 22. BW 22 presents post-mortem divine retribution in the context of Enoch's cosmic journey where he arrives at places of punishments prepared for the rebel Watchers and transgressing stars, and later at a cave-like place prepared for holding dead human beings. The thesis studied the interest of BW 22 in the post-mortem divine retribution by highlighting four aspects: i) its interest in the spirit of the souls of the dead, who, it was concluded, were conscious individual beings awaiting final judgment; ii) its presentation of differentiated dead who were held in a compartmentalized repository, separated into four compartments not only as righteous and sinners, but further segregated based on whether or not the dead ones had experienced consequences appropriate to their deeds during their lifetime; iii) and the souls of the dead were not only divided as they awaited their final post-mortem fate, but they also already experience a foretaste of their final retribution. The compartment containing the souls of the righteous is well lit and provided with water, both elements being significant, with light probably referring to God's presence and water to its life-giving qualities. The wicked remain in compartments that are dark, and the souls of the dead who did not experience any punishment for their evil deeds while alive are tormented even as they wait for final judgment; and iv) there is a final and full judgment waiting for the souls of the dead even though they already experience some degree of retribution in their holding compartments.

The thesis argued that BW 22 exhibited the anthropocentric and theocentric aspects of divine retribution. The theocentric aspect was seen in the presumption of the Torah undergirding of the book. The divine judgment which is a major theme of the BW is based on the law and commandments. It was argued that the law in BW was a reference to the Torah God gave so that human beings might know and act according to his commandments, and as such underlined the anthropocentric aspect. In BW 22 while the souls of the dead receive and will receive retribution according to their deeds, it was not clear what exactly those deeds are. This was examined by exploring other parts of the BW. It was argued that the Asael tradition in BW 8:1–2 preserved in the Greek version of the chronographer George Synkellos pointed to human culpability in the corruption of the world. Human beings learned various arts and skills that Asael taught, and used the knowledge to spread evil. The women are especially implicated as having seduced the Watchers by adorning themselves with makeup and jewellery. While this version is preserved in only one Greek ms. in the Enochic collection, this descent of the angels to originally teach human beings and later leading to cohabitation with women is preserved in other ancient documents as well. It was thus concluded that this variant reading is likely authentic rather than a corruption or later addition, and hence the BW indicts human beings for the origin of sin rather than solely placing the blame on the Watchers. As such post-mortem divine retribution on human beings can be traced back to their sins of violence, use of magical arts and astrology, and for mating with the ontologically different creatures, the Watchers, which in turn produced the giants who wreaked havoc on the earth. Further the righteous, of whom Enoch is a prime example, provide a foil to the sinners demonstrating that participation in the spread and perpetuation of evil was wilful and that righteousness was possible. Hence, it was concluded that the narrative also highlighted human choice and responsibility exhibiting the anthropocentric aspect.

It was further seen that the division of the souls of the dead into different compartments was based not only on their deeds but also on whether they experienced the appropriate consequences while alive. While the righteous seemed to be kept only in one compartment, the sinners were segregated into three different compartments: i) those who did evil and did not face any negative consequences in life, who now are tormented in their intermediate state even as they await final punishment; ii) those who died violent deaths, although it is not immediately clear if they were sinners or righteous. However, since their compartment is dark like that of the other sinners it was concluded that they were probably also sinners, but because they also suffered gross injustice in the nature of their death, they did not experience other punishments while in their compartment; and iii) those who sinned and received due punishment on earth and hence neither suffer punishment in their compartment nor will be resurrected at the final judgment. Such segregation based on the deeds and appropriateness of the punishment exhibits great interest on the human side of the divine retributive action and hence emphasizes the anthropocentric aspect of divine retribution.

It was further observed that post-mortem divine retribution in BW 22 was individual in nature. The study argued against the view that salvation was the prerogative of Enochians alone, but instead that the BW seemed to have the whole of humanity in its purview. Pertaining more specifically to the question of the nature of retribution, it was argued that the righteous and the sinners were not fixed groups in the BW but fluid. The text indicated a possibility that the sinners can becomes righteous by receiving wisdom, and more so by the fact that the righteous are said to have been recipients of forgiveness and mercy. As such the emphasis is on individuals with members of the righteous being constituted in part at least by those who were previously sinners but received forgiveness and mercy, and hence an emphasis on the individuated nature of divine retribution.

Chapter 6 looked at 2 Maccabees 7 that contains one of the clearest assertions of physical resurrection couched in the story of the martyrdom of a mother and her seven sons. Antiochus IV and his soldiers try to force the mother and the sons to eat pork in violation of the Jewish dietary regulation, which becomes the centre of contention. Post-mortem divine retribution is presented through the concept of resurrection. Resurrection is conceived as a reward for martyrdom, and the hope of resurrection is presented as the reason for the perseverance of the faithful protagonists in the face of death. Further, resurrection is also conceived of explicitly in physical terms. The mother and sons profess their unswerving fidelity to God's law in conjunction with the hope of being resurrected physically. While such fidelity and expectation of a just reward is consonant with the teachings of the Torah, the narrative makes a remarkable jump in speaking of the afterlife in terms of such clear physical post-mortem existence. The physicality of the expected resurrection is clearly referred to in the speech of the youngest brother; however, the exact nature of the body is not as clear. In the speech of the mother the text further conflates the resurrection, creation, and growth of an embryo in the womb so that the resulting concept of resurrection is one of re-creation.

The text also speaks of retribution against Antiochus for his treatment of the Jewish people, although the conception of punishment pales in comparison to the clarity with which the reward of the martyrs is presented. Divine justice for Antiochus is certain. His premature death is interpreted as a divine retribution, especially in the text where his death is placed in the context of an attempt to loot a temple. This is seen as poetic justice for his crimes of plundering the Jerusalem temple. His son is also killed by Demetrius, though the incident is recorded in 1 Maccabees rather than in 2 Maccabees. Premature death is generally perceived as divine punishment and hence the consequence of Antiochus' sins not only affects him but also seemingly engulfs his descendant. Further, the punishment for Antiochus involves non-resurrection as well, which the text sharply contrasts with the physical resurrection of the martyrs, which is considered as a reward.

The post-mortem divine retribution in the narrative of 2 Maccabees 7 exhibits an emphasis on the anthropocentric aspect with an underlying theocentric aspect. The text repeatedly presents the hope of resurrection and eternal life as a reward based specifically on the deaths of the mother and her sons for the sake of the law, which in 2 Maccabees 7 refers to the divine law. As such, in this narrative, resurrection as reward is not democratised for all the righteous but is the special reward for martyrdom so that those who lose their life and bodies for the sake of God will receive them back again from God. Hence divine retribution in 2 Maccabees 7 is dependent on the deeds of human beings and resurrection is the specific reward for martyrdom.

The theocentric aspect was detected in the covenant framework that undergirds the whole narrative. It was argued that the sins for which the mother and her sons die is that of the people and their leaders against God. The text does not dwell on the individual sins of the martyrs, rather it speaks of the sins of the Jewish nation against God for which the martyrs bear the responsibility and pay the price. Hence, even when the focus is not on the sins of the individual martyrs, the corporate outlook of the covenant means that the martyrs are seen as bearing responsibility for the sins of the whole people, and their deaths will cause God to have mercy on the nation and reconcile with them. Further this conviction and expectation of God's mercy and reconciliation evinces a view of history expressed in Deuteronomy 32, which espouses that oppression by the foreign nations is divinely allowed because of the sins of the people and God will reconcile with his people soon. This interweaving of the national fate and individual deeds has echoes of the covenant, and the reference to Deuteronomy at the deaths of the first and the last brothers strengthen this covenantal feature in the narrative. Thus, although there is a strong anthropocentric emphasis in the narrative, it also exhibits the theocentric aspect of divine retribution through its covenantal underpinnings.

The intertwining of the fates of the nation and the individuals means that the nature of retribution is both corporate and individual. The corporate nature of divine retribution comes to the fore in the fact that the consequences of the deeds of the individual, both negative and positive, impacts the whole community and this is seen predominantly in the earthly life. The persecution of the Jewish people is presented as a result of the sins of the apostatizing individuals in leading positions within the community, and conversely the martyrdom of a few ideal citizens restores the peace of the community. While this corporate outworking is not post-mortem *per se* the restoration of peace to the community is a post-mortem effect of the death of the martyrs.

The individual nature of retribution is highlighted through the conception of resurrection as a reward specifically for those who forfeited life and body for God and his law. It was argued that resurrection is a vindication of the martyrs comparable to the suffering and rescue of the righteous characters in the biblical tradition, except the rescue is transposed to the afterlife. This was explained from the point of view of divine justice. The mother and the sons would have expected divine justice in keeping with the biblical tradition, but acceptance of death to maintain fidelity to the law meant the dissolution of that very hope. Hence, while the martyrs bring national peace, they themselves cannot participate in the corporate expression of divine retribution; as such the hope of individual divine retribution emerges, making divine justice possible even after death.

Thus, post-mortem divine retribution in 2 Maccabees 7 is predominantly anthropocentric with an emphasis on human deeds of martyrdom as the basis for divine retribution, although there are undertones of the theocentric aspect as well. Further, divine retribution in this narrative exhibits the corporate nature in its earthly expressions but is individuated when transposed to the afterlife, the effect of which also reverberates in the national life and is experienced as restoration of peace by those alive.

7.3. Overall Observations

In tracing the contours of the aspects of the post-mortem divine retribution in the four texts of the HB and the STP Jewish literature in light of the aspects of divine retribution in Deuteronomy, certain patterns emerge which are summed up below.

7.3.1. Post-mortem Divine Retribution Is Predominantly Anthropocentric

Four texts were examined for their presentation of the post-mortem divine retribution, namely, Isaiah 26:19, Daniel 12:1–3, BW 22, and 2 Maccabees 7. In all these texts, the aspect of divine retribution most prominent was the anthropocentric aspect according to which God responds to human deeds; human beings initiate the action and God reacts or responds accordingly. Hence, the emphasis in such cases of retribution is on human action. Each of the texts described the people in moral terms, albeit in varying degrees.

For instance, in studying Isaiah 26:19 morality as well as national identity seemed to play a role, for though the people are described in moral terms and their deeds are also described, the community is taken as a single entity. Whether the whole community was righteous or not the text presents the whole of Israel as delivered without any hint at division within that community. On the other end of anthropocentricity is 2 Maccabees 7, wherein divine retribution in the form of resurrection is not even said to be for all the righteous, rather it is for a handful of people who fall into the category of martyrs, a very specific act on the part of human beings. Further, in contrast to Isaiah 26:19, Daniel 12:1–3's anthropocentric aspect makes a distinction between the faithful and the apostates within the community so that, while the purview of deliverance is still within the community, the deeds of the individuals are determinative for divine retribution, with those who risked their lives to bring others to righteousness receiving special reward. In BW 22 the anthropocentric aspect is highlighted rather distinctly through the segregation of the dead into four different categories so that the post-mortem divine retribution would be commensurate with the deeds of the individuals and their lot in life. If 2 Maccabees 7 reserves divine retribution only for the ideal Jews and for the most wicked enemies like Antiochus so that there is no reference to resurrection for the faithful Jews or divine punishment for the soldiers, BW 22 goes to the other extreme wherein the scope of possible salvation seems to be universal.

7.3.2. Theocentric Aspect of Divine Retribution Underlies the Anthropocentric Aspect

In each case of post-mortem divine retribution, the anthropocentricity was offset by a theocentric undergirding. The theocentric aspect of divine retribution emphasizes God's initiative in dealing with people independent of human actions; it is directed at achieving his own purposes. For instance, God initiating the covenant, or God extending mercy to an undeserving people. The specific divine initiative that demonstrates the theocentric aspect in all the above examined instances of post-mortem divine retribution is the covenantal framework that underlies post-mortem divine retribution.

In Isaiah 26:19 and Daniel 12:1–3 the covenant underpinning is evident in their focus on the community. While the Isaianic text emphasizes the deliverance of the community, the Danielic text indicates division within the community between the faithful and the apostates. The theocentric aspect in BW 22 and 2 Maccabees 7 is brought out through their focus on the divine law. On one hand the pre-Mosaic façade of the BW precludes one from definitively identifying the focus community as Jewish; rather it gives it a more universal scope and hence divine retribution has a sense of being applicable to all humanity. However, even in this broadened scope of retribution it is the divine law which serves as the basis on which judgment is pronounced. In 2 Maccabees 7 on the other hand the law, and the martyrs' adherence to its regulations, lead to their death and resurrection. Post-mortem retribution is not universal, it does not even have the whole of the Jewish people in view, only the martyrs will receive the reward of resurrection. Also, the intertwining of the deeds of the individuals and the fate of the nation evinces a covenantal understanding of identity and responsibility.

Hence, the theocentric aspect of divine retribution is expressed through the covenantal nature of the Jewish community, and this comes out with different emphases in the selected texts, balancing the anthropocentricity of the post-mortem divine retribution.

7.3.3. The Impersonal and the Dissolution Aspects Become Defunct

The other two aspects of divine retribution found in Deuteronomy, the impersonal aspect and the dissolution of retribution, do not figure when divine retribution is pushed to the afterlife. The impersonal aspect focuses on instances of retribution that are expressed as natural consequences of the deed, and the dissolution of retribution are instances when God's interaction with human beings in their experience of blessing or suffering cannot be explained through the retributive lens but are for teaching. These two aspects are understandably non-functional in the post-mortem since the final judgment leaves scope neither for a mechanical outworking of the consequences of human deeds nor for pedagogical training. In post-mortem divine retribution, the judgments are all presented as executed through divine intention. In Isaiah 26:19 the prophet speaks the salvation oracle on behalf of Yahweh, in Daniel 12:1–3 the word of the coming resurrection and judgment is brought by the angel Michael, in BW 22 the places of judgment and repository are already prepared, and in 2 Maccabees 7 the martyrs are sure that God will reward them. There is nothing in these texts to indicate a mechanical outworking of the consequences of deeds. Further, there is also no room for the dissolution aspect of retribution since the enjoyment of reward or the sufferings of punishments in these texts are clearly retributive. The rewards and the punishments do not function pedagogically since the final judgment leaves no scope for any further learning.

7.3.4. Post-mortem Divine Retribution Is Both Corporate and Individual in Nature

Divine retribution in Deuteronomy is predominantly corporate in nature, but the divine retribution on the individual remains in tandem with the corporate expressions. Similarly, when divine retribution is moved to the afterlife, it exhibits both the corporate and individual nature, but with an emphasis on the individual nature.

The corporate nature of post-mortem divine retribution is clearest in the Isaianic text. The community as a whole is chastised, seeks Yahweh, and is promised deliverance. In the other three texts, the individual nature is more evident. The Danielic text divides the community between the faithful and the apostates at resurrection so that the basis for post-mortem divine retribution is individual faithfulness and not communal or national identity. In the BW, the individual nature of post-mortem divine retribution is made evident in the segregation of the dead into compartments, and the coming final judgment is presented as depending on the deeds of the individual as well as whether each has experienced the consequences in life commensurate to their deeds. The presentation of post-mortem divine retribution in 2 Maccabees 7 is so individuated that it proposes resurrection as applicable not even to the righteous or faithful, but only to those who lose their life for the sake of the law. However, unlike the BW, the three texts from Isaiah, Daniel, and 2 Maccabees see positive retributive rewards as operating only within the covenanted community, while the retributive punishments have the other nations or communities in view. This view in the Isaianic text is evident. In Daniel and 2 Maccabees too only those within the Jewish community can expect the reward for their faithfulness to Yahweh. It is only in the BW that the scope seems more inclusive and the distinction between the righteous and the wicked is not made on communal or national identity lines and is presented as relatively fluid, with sinners becoming righteous on reception of wisdom and mercy and forgiveness from God.

This study of the nature of post-mortem divine retribution can be fruitfully explored in the NT as well, and below is a brief look at the direction it could take.

7.4. Potential for Further Research: The Nature of Post-mortem Divine Retribution in the New Testament

Post-mortem divine retribution is a prominent feature in the NT and can be examined in line with the foregoing discussion. The study so far posed three broad questions to each of the HB and STP text examined: i) is there a discernible post-mortem reference in the text? ii) what is the basis of post-mortem divine retribution? and iii) is the nature of post-mortem divine retribution corporate or individual? The discussion that followed demonstrated that there was a burgeoning, if variegated, view of afterlife that emerged in the HB and flourished during the STP. This can be said to have been propelled at least in part by the need for a viable post-mortem divine retribution and developed in many different directions during the STP. Once the concept of post-mortem divine retribution became an accepted part of some of the streams of Judaism it carried on into the NT, and the scope for the study of the nature of post-mortem divine retribution in the NT is extensive.

The three questions referred to earlier could direct the examination of post-mortem divine retribution in NT studies as well. What follows is a suggestion of a potential research topic. It does not presume to answer questions but rather it only raises them in relation to the NT's presentation of post-mortem divine retribution. It takes a cursory look at various texts in the NT that speak of some kind of post-mortem judgment and asks the three questions to present some tentative directions which the research could take. The theme of post-mortem judgment often appears in tandem with other concepts such as resurrection, Parousia, eternal life, Gehenna, and so on, and hence are examined briefly first. These concepts have been studied in their own right, but they can also be approached from the perspective of the light they shed on the concept of post-mortem divine retribution.

7.4.1. Discerning Post-mortem Divine Retribution in the NT

Post-mortem divine retribution in the NT can be seen in the separation of the people into two distinct groups of some kind destined for two radically distinct fates, one group for reward and the other for punishment. This concept of two groups of people receiving two different fates figures prominently in its conception of the concepts mentioned above such as resurrection, eternal life, Gehenna, Parousia.

7.4.1.1. Resurrection

The resurrection of Jesus is foundational to the NT faith and its conception of the future expectation of resurrection for all. It is the first stage and the basis of the general resurrection to come. However, in terms of post-mortem divine retribution, it is the resurrection of the people that is of interest. In the texts of the HB and the STP that were examined, it was observed that while some texts envisaged the resurrection only of the righteous (as in Isa 26:19) others spoke of the resurrection of both the righteous and the wicked (as in Dan 12:1–3). Similarly, in the NT both these views of resurrection are present.

The understanding that only the righteous will rise at resurrection is a view found in the gospels as well as the Pauline literature. The Gospel of Luke speaks of resurrection as only of the righteous (Luke 14:14); only those who are worthy attain resurrection (Luke 20:34–35).[1] This seems to also appear

---

1. Chaim Milikowsky examines the differences in the portrayal of Gehenna in the gospels of Matthew and Luke. Milikowsky, "Which Gehenna," 243.

in the Gospel of John where Jesus speaks of resurrection to eternal life but mentions only those who believe in him (John 6:39–40, 54), although in other passages the Gospel of John seems to picture a resurrection of both believers and unbelievers (see next paragraph). Regarding the Pauline literature, Murray Harris argues that the view most characteristic of the Pauline corpus is that resurrection is only for οἱ τοῦ Χριστοῦ ("those who belong to Christ" 1 Cor 15:23).[2] 1 Thessalonians 4:13–18 also refers to the resurrection of οἱ νεκροὶ ἐν Χριστῷ ("the dead in Christ" 1 Thes 4:16), and although this passage does not deny the resurrection of unbelievers, it also does not mention it.[3]

In contrast to the view that only the just or the righteous will be resurrected, the NT also features the resurrection of the both the righteous and the wicked. The Gospel of John, along with passages that seemingly speak of the resurrection only of the just mentioned above, also clearly conceives of the resurrection of both the righteous and the wicked to two separate fates. It states that all who are in the grave will rise; the righteous will rise to life while the wicked will rise to condemnation (John 5:28–29). This passage is set in the context of Jesus as the judge in the present (John 5:19–24) as well as in the eschaton (John 5:25–30).[4] The book of Revelation also presents this segregation of the people into two groups. At the scene of the final judgment of the dead, those whose names are not found in the book of life are thrown into the lake of fire to experience a second death (Rev 20:11–15).

7.4.1.2. *Eternal Life, Gehenna, Parousia*

At other instances the post-mortem rewards and punishments occur in relation to concepts such as eternal life, Gehenna or hell, and Parousia among others. The concept of Gehenna or hell which in the HB was a geographical

---

2. Harris further notes the resurrection of the dead is closely connected to the resurrection of Christ, which is not only the first fruit or a foretaste of the coming more general resurrection, but also the resurrected are described as being raised "with Christ" or "with him" (Col 3:1; 2:12; Eph 2:6). Harris, "Resurrection and Immortality," 150–151, 156.

3. Pesler discusses the apparent inconsistency in Paul's eschatology regarding imminent Parousia and the resurrection of the dead. Pesler proposes the possibility that Paul initially expected a very imminent Parousia and the teaching of resurrection of the dead became more important over time in the face of the death of believers. Pesler, "Resurrection and Eschatology," 37–46. If one accepts the proposition that Paul's eschatology developed over time, this line of argument could shed light on why in the Pauline corpus the focus is on the resurrection of believers alone.

4. Osborne, "Resurrection," 934.

location associated with apostasy (see Chapter 4, section 4.4.1) and began to gain some eschatological significance in Isaiah (see Chapter 1 which discusses Isaiah 66:24), becomes an important feature in the NT's conception of post-mortem divine retribution. For instance, the gospels begin with John the Baptist preaching fire for those who will not repent (Matt 3:10–12). The idea of segregation of the people into two groups for two distinct fates similarly appears in the parable of the weeds (Matt 13:24–30, 36–43), which likens the "sons of the evil one" to the weeds. At the end of the age they are thrown into the fiery furnace while the fate of the righteous is glory with their Father (so also in the parable of the net in Matt 13:47–50). The other well-known passage that is usually related to the eschatological judgment is Matthew 25:31–46, the parable of the sheep and the goats, which portrays the nations being separated into two groups and receiving two distinct eternal fates. Portraying this division at a more individual level is the parable of the rich man and Lazarus (Luke 16:19–31). In the afterlife, the rich man ends up tormented in hell, while the poor man is carried to Abraham's side. So also, Jesus' warning in Matthew 18:8–9 and Mark 9:43–47 uses the singular "you" as the subject of the address, and uses the hand, foot, and eye as metaphors to teach the disciples to resist temptation so as to enter life rather than hell, which is described in the words of Isaiah 66:24.[5] The book of Revelation assigns the worshippers of the beast to hell, vividly describing it as a place of perpetual torment with burning sulphur (Rev 14:10–11). Thus, in the NT the concept of post-mortem punishment centres on the idea of hell, which is now clearly designated as a place of active punishment featuring fire, worms, and weeping and gnashing of teeth.[6]

The division of people into two groups also appears in relation to the theme of Parousia or the Second Coming of Jesus. Since the timing of Parousia is unknown the exhortation is to remain vigilant. Matthew's Olivet Discourse uses three short parables (men in the field, two women grinding, two persons in a bed) to illustrate that the hour is unknown (Matt 24:40–44, also Lk 17:34–37). However, what is of interest here is that it also portrays two contrasting fates by stating that "one will be taken, the other left" indicating that there will be those who receive salvation and those who are doomed for

---

5. Osborne, "Resurrection," 934.
6. O'Callaghan, *Christ our Hope*, 193.

judgment. This theme of post-mortem divine retribution is further seen in the parable of the good and wicked managers (Matt 24:45–51 and Lk 12:41–46). At the master's return the faithful servant is given greater authority while the fate of the wicked servant is described quite graphically as being dismembered and placed with the unbelievers.[7]

There are indications of a diverse understanding of post-mortem existence in the NT; however what emerges is that post-mortem divine retribution was a well-known and accepted concept in the theological thoughts of the NT writers. They envisioned some kind of reward and punishment in the eschaton notwithstanding the differences in the specifics. As such, the presence of the concept of post-mortem divine retribution is clearly presented in the NT.

Since there is ample evidence of post-mortem retribution in the NT, the next step would be to explore what the NT presents as the basis for this retribution.

7.4.2. The Basis of Post-mortem Divine Retribution in the NT

The question of the standard of judgment in the NT presents a more complex picture than has been encountered until now and is often seemingly contradictory. It presents a consistent teaching that one is saved by grace through faith in Christ aside from works but also affirms that judgment will be according to, or at least take into account, one's deeds in life. These two apparently diametrical teachings are held in tension with no proposal for resolution gaining significant favour among the scholars. It will make for an intriguing study to see what light these passages can shed on the NT's conception of the basis of post-mortem divine retribution. Below is a brief look at of some of the key passages that focus on the basis of retribution, whether it is spoken of from a work or ethical standpoint or purely from a relational perspective.

7.4.2.1. Work-Based Retribution

The ethical perspective on the fate attendant upon one in the afterlife is stated in several passages in the NT. If the emphasis is on human deeds as a decisive criterion for divine judgment, it would highlight the anthropocentric aspect of divine retribution wherein God's response is dependent on human action.

---

7. Osborne, "Resurrection," 934.

Such expressions with emphasis on human deeds come to the fore in passages like Matthew 5:29–30 and 18:8–9 and Mark 9:43–47, which speak of cutting off parts of the body to refrain from sinning as preferable to ending up in hell because of the sins one commits. These seem to suggest deeds committed in life can merit one a post-mortem fate in Gehenna.[8] The eschatological judgment in the parable of the sheep and the goats (Matt 25:31–46) portrays the nations being separated into two groups and receiving two distinct eternal fates. The distinguishing characteristics between these two groups is their charity (or lack of) towards the dispossessed and the marginalized. Those who served the poor and the needy are said to have served Christ himself and this becomes the criterion for their being welcome into eternal life. In the parable of the rich man and Lazarus (Luke 16:19–31), although there is no reference to their deeds in life, in the afterlife as the rich man suffers in hell he asks for Lazarus to go and warn his brothers so they would not also end up in hell. The answer he receives is that the brothers have Moses and the Prophets, which is probably a reference to the Torah, to teach them. It seems to imply that obedience to the law is necessary and perhaps sufficient to avoid hell. Further, Luke 14:14 was cited earlier as presenting a view of the resurrection of the righteous alone. This verse occurs in the context of conduct at banquet (Luke 14:7–14) which concludes with Jesus saying that God will reward at the resurrection those who invite to their banquet the marginalized people in the community who cannot repay them for the invitation. All these make for an interesting exploration of what could be the basis of post-mortem retribution.

Moreover, although Paul is the advocate of justification by faith, there are statements in the Pauline corpus that seem to indicate that deeds were not out of his purview as well. Paul's statement in Romans 2:6–8, 13 uses retributive terminology. He states that to those who by persistence in doing good seek glory, honour and immortality God will give eternal life. Thus, he links ἔργου ἀγαθοῦ ("good work") to ζωὴν αἰώνιον ("eternal life") in a way that seems to highlight the anthropocentric aspect of divine retribution. How are such statements to be interpreted – literally, hypothetically, as a foil to the point he is actually making, as just another word for faith, or is it a matter

---

8. Milikowsky examines the differences in the portrayal of Gehenna in the gospels on Matthew and Luke in Milikowsky, "Which Gehenna?"

of inconsistency on the side of Paul? Further complicating the issue is the question of audience; who is Paul addressing here? These matters are key for the interpretation of this passage and are debated.[9] However, it provides ample room for discussion as to what is presented as the basis of post-mortem divine retribution in the Pauline corpus.

This deed-based retribution appears in James and Revelation as well. The epistle of James makes deeds a major component of faith and constitutes his primary message. However, scholars like Serge Ruzer argue that James's epistle does not have an eschatological point of view, a claim which will have implications on the topic under study.[10] In Revelation, in the scene of the final judgment of the dead (Rev 20:11–15), judgment as to whether one is to be thrown into the lake of fire is made by consulting the books – one that recorded the deeds of the people during their lifetime and the other listed the names of people in the book of life.[11] That the dead are judged by what they had done during their lifetime is repeated twice (vv. 12–13). This emphasis on a person's deeds or conduct as the basis of divine retribution is also seen in Revelation 22:12.

Hence, there seems to be a place for the discussion of the anthropocentric aspect of divine retribution in the NT. Not all the passages cited above may stand the test, and there are others not mentioned here. Nevertheless, it does demonstrate that there is room for discussion of the anthropocentric emphasis in the NT's conception of post-mortem divine retribution that cannot be easily dismissed.

7.4.2.2. Relation-Based Retribution

Balancing the NT's focus on deeds as a possible factor in post-mortem divine retribution is its emphasis on grace and faith as the basis for justification and salvation. This is often seen as a distinctive marker of the Kingdom of God that Jesus proclaimed, and seems to exhibit characteristics of the theocentric aspect of divine retribution wherein God's dealings with human beings are

---

9. For instance, Kent L. Yinger mentions the variety of ways in which scholars have attempted to interpret this passage. See Yinger, *Paul, Judaism, and Judgment*, 146–147. Also, Sanders, *Paul and Palestine Judaism*; Donfried "Justification and Last Judgment," 90–110; Snodgrass, "Justification by Grace, 72–93; Scholtus, "Jewish Legalism," 81–100.

10. See Ruzer, "James on Faith," 79–104.

11. Mealy, *After the Thousand Years*, 169–170.

no longer dependent on human deeds; rather, God initiates acts of grace or mercy in order to achieve his own purposes.

The NT is generally perceived as being replete with such expressions. In the Gospel of John, one of the earliest teachings of Jesus is that eternal life is given to those who believe in the Son (John 3:16, so also in 5:24). Here ζωὴν αἰώνιον ("eternal life") is now linked with πιστεύων ("believing"), and as such eternal life is clearly stated as attendant on those who hear and believe in him. As mentioned earlier, Pauline letters do speak of judgment according to works, but Paul's theology is generally understood as being centred on justification by faith and is largely characterized by an emphasis on God's saving grace. This juxtaposition of faith and works in Pauline letters has generated much scholarship.[12] Paul argues that the sole condition for salvation is faith in "the saving power of Jesus' death and resurrection and confession of Jesus' lordship" (Rom 3:21ff, esp. vv. 24, 28; 10:9–10).[13] In his letter to the Galatians Paul argues that it is by faith in Christ and not law that one is justified, going on to even say that Christ's death would be meaningless if righteousness could have gained by keeping the law (Gal 2:16, 21). Michael Bird states that, while the role of works is not denied in Paul, for Paul the eschatological judgment "has already been executed in the sacrificial death of Jesus" (Rom 5:1; 8:1), and as such vindication at the eschaton is based purely on Christ's death and resurrection.[14]

The NT presents two seemingly contradictory views on what constitutes the basis of salvation and hence of post-mortem divine retribution. This antinomy is a rich and complex field for research and could be studied for its implications on the theme of post-mortem divine retribution in the NT.

7.4.3. Nature of Divine Retribution: Corporate or Individual

The nature of divine retribution in terms of whether it operates corporately – so that the consequences of one's deeds impacts others, or individually – in which case the retribution only affects the individual, is another area to consider. In the examination of texts in the HB and the STP Jewish literature it

---

12. Stendahl, "Justification," 1–7; Travis, *Christ and the Judgment*; Davies, *Faith and Obedience*.

13. Bird, "Judgment and Justification," 313.

14. Michael Bird, *Saving Righteousness of God*, 173–174

was seen that in Isaiah 26:19 divine retribution has a corporate outlook with the community of God's people being addressed as one. However, in the other three texts, Daniel 12:1–3, BW 22, and 2 Maccabees 7, post-mortem divine retribution was more individuated.

Preliminary research indicates a more individuated post-mortem divine retribution in the NT. For instance, in the parable of the rich man and Lazarus (Luke 16:19–31), the rich man's request to have his brothers warned to avoid a fate in hell portrays an individuated post-mortem divine retribution; each one is responsible for their own fate. Further, Paul also states that ἕκαστος ("each one") will give an account of himself to God (Rom 14:12).[15] The word ἕκαστος ("each one") appears again in the context of the eschatological judgment in Revelation which says that each one will be judged according to what they had done (Rev 20:13). Whichever basis of retribution is in view, whether inclusive of work or exclusive of it, there seems to be no evidence that the consequences of an individual's act or faith impacts the post-mortem fate of another person or group of persons. The people may be conceived of corporately during their lifetime as a church or a community of believers, and in the afterlife the people may again constitute a corporate body of believers or saints and are referred to collectively with terms such as "the righteous" (Matt 13:43; 25:37), or alternatively "the sinners" (Matt 13:49), however there is no indication that in the final judgment itself the consequences of one's deeds or faith are transferrable to others. Thus post-mortem divine retribution in the NT seems to be conceived of in a predominantly individuated manner.

7.4.4. Section Conclusion

A brief discussion based on a cursory look at the NT indicates that there is a potential for such an investigation and the subject of post-mortem divine retribution would benefit from a careful examination to specifically highlight what the NT texts have to say regarding the nature of post-mortem divine retribution in the NT. The proposition laid out here is tentative and preliminary and a proper study would show if it holds, what nuances and differences

---

15. This verse is in the context of Paul addressing the matter of eating, and judgment amongst believers regarding it. However, the implication to divine retribution stands – that God will judge each one.

emerge, and how the Christ-event impacts the understanding of post-mortem divine retribution in biblical studies.

7.5. Conclusion

Divine retribution in Deuteronomy was nuanced and exhibited at least four aspects. Further, divine retribution in Deuteronomy was seen as operating corporately with the consequences of a deed affecting others in the community as well as individually where only the person responsible faced the consequences. The perspective and outworking of divine retribution in Deuteronomy, however, is limited to the earthly life. As such it can be said that divine retribution is more nuanced in the earthly life signalling, perhaps among other things, divine patience in interacting with his people.

However, when divine retribution is transposed to the afterlife, it is two-dimensional, exhibiting only the anthropocentric and the theocentric aspects; the impersonal and the dissolution aspects of divine retribution seem to become defunct. Consequently, one's deeds in life become determinative for one's post-mortem fate. Thus, while divine retribution in earthly life is experienced in more varied ways, post-mortem divine retribution is rather straightforward depending primarily on the individual deeds within the boundary of the covenant. There is scope neither for an extension of mercy, nor for a natural outworking of the consequences of the deeds. Also, suffering and blessing are not a pedagogical exercise as it sometimes is when God deals with human beings in this life; these aspects of divine retribution end with the cessation of earthly life. Therefore, post-mortem divine retribution as seen in the selected texts of the HB and the STP Jewish literature is anthropocentric with a theocentric undergirding, and is predominantly individual in nature.

APPENDIX

Annotated Bibliography for the Themes of Divine Retribution and Afterlife in the Hebrew Bible and Second Temple Period Jewish Literature

Introduction

The concept of post-mortem divine retribution sits at the intersection of two broad themes, divine retribution and the afterlife in the HB and STP Jewish literature, and there is a rich body of works available on both these themes. What follows is an annotated bibliography of some of the works in these two areas: i) divine retribution and ii) afterlife and related themes.

Divine Retribution

The topic of divine retribution in the HB is well researched. Chapter 2 of this dissertation provides an overview of the trajectory which the study on the concept of retribution in the HB has followed, and hence the annotated bibliography does not repeat those. Divine retribution in the HB is typified by its focus on the earthly life, and concerns related to divine justice with an interest in the collective level or the individual. These studies on divine retribution concentrate on specific books, such as Deuteronomy, Chronicles, Proverbs, Job, Ezekiel, and Tobit. Others like Eichrodt and Jose Krasovec treat it thematically in the whole of the HB, and still others focus on a particular genre, such as the prophetic or wisdom tradition in HB and the STP Jewish literature.

Darr, Katheryn Pfisterer. "Proverb Performance and Transgenerational Retribution in Ezekiel 18." In *Ezekiel's Hierarchical World: Wrestling with a Tiered Reality* SBLSS 13, edited by Stephen L. Cook and Corrine L. Patton, 199–223. Atlanta: Society of Biblical Literature, 2004.

Katheryn Pfisterer Darr examines the concept of divine transgenerational retribution encapsulated in the "sour grapes" proverbs using the rhetorical and reader-response criticism. She uses the understanding of the nature and power of proverbs to determine behaviour, and interprets the function of the "sour grapes" proverbs in the context of Ezekiel 18 as an exhortation towards repentance to the despairing exiles.

Kidner, Derek. "Retribution and Punishment in the Old Testament, in the Light of the New Testament." The Second Finlayson Lecture.

Derek Kidner looks at the ways in which the term retribution is used in the OT and in the NT. He differentiates the term retribution from vengeance, examines the vocabulary used in relation to the concept of retribution, and the execution of retribution mainly in the Deuteronomic legal section. In the NT, the article focuses on the teachings of Jesus, and examines the human administration of justice as a mirroring or foreshadowing of divine judgment.

Kaminsky, Joel S. *Corporate Responsibility in the Hebrew Bible.* JSOTSup 196. Sheffield: Sheffield Academic Press, 1995.

Kaminsky challenges the view that corporate responsibility is an older, more primitive and peripheral theology later replaced by the idea of individual responsibility. He seeks to reexamine this evolutionary view of the individual-corporate dynamic with regards to divine retribution in ancient Israel. He studies the relationship between the covenant and corporate perspective in Deuteronomy and Deuteronomistic History to demonstrate that the corporate perspective was central, especially in the conception of divine retribution, and also the connection between covenant and other concepts such as divine wrath, holiness, bloodguilt, etc. Turning to examine the individualizing tendency, he argues that the emergence of an emphasis on individualism is not a radical one, but that in both Deuteronomy and DtrH (Deuteronomist

History), as also in Jeremiah 31 and Ezekiel 18, emphasis on the individual occurs within the context of a corporate view of divine retribution. As such the growing emphasis on individual responsibility was not a rejection of corporate responsibility but an attempt to qualify the demands on the individual while still maintaining a corporate outlook.

Kaminsky, Joel S. "Would You Impugn My Justice? A Nuanced Approach to the Hebrew Bible's Theology of Divine Recompense." *Interpretation: A Journal of Bible and Theology* 69, no. 3 (2015): 299–310.

Joel Kaminsky argues against a mechanistic view of divine retribution. He demonstrates how a nuanced understanding of the concept of retribution in the HB can illuminate the arguments made in the Book of Job.

Kapfer, Hilary Claire. "Collective Accountability Among the Sages of Ancient Israel." PhD Diss., Harvard University, 2013.

Hilary Claire Kapfer states that the concept of collective retribution is generally considered as belonging to the domain of the narrative, legal, and prophetic traditions in Israel, but she argues that collective retribution is operative within Israel's wisdom tradition as well.

Kelly, Brian E. "'Retribution' Revisited: Covenant, Grace and Restoration." In *The Chronicler as a Theologian: Essays in Honor of Ralph E. Klein*, edited by Matt Patrick Graham, Steven L. McKenzie, and Gary N. Knoppers, 206–227. JSOTSup 371. London: T and T Clark, 2003.

Brian Kelly argues against the often-held notion that the Chronicler unilaterally advocates mechanical and immediate divine retribution by highlighting the Chronicler's presentation of God's mercy to the repentant. He views this provision for the repentant within the framework of the Davidic covenant.

Kiel, Micah D. *The "Whole Truth": Rethinking Retribution in the Book of Tobit*. LSTS 82. London: T and T Clark, 2012.

Micah Kiel studies the view of retribution presented in the Book of Tobit, mainly attempting to demonstrate that the rigid or mechanical view often presented as the only view of retribution in Tobit and especially touted as Deuteronomic as an oversimplification which is a disservice to the complex picture that emerges with a careful reading of the book and to Deuteronomy's view on retribution. Kiel's also highlights the different aspects of divine retribution in Deuteronomy to make his case for a more nuanced presentation. Being a study of Tobit, the retribution examined here is earthly.

Krašovec, Jože. *Reward, Punishment, and Forgiveness: The Thinking and Beliefs of Ancient Israel in the Light of Greek and Modern Views.* VTSup 78. Leiden: Brill, 1999.

Jose Krasovec's literary comparative analysis of the concepts of reward, punishment, and forgiveness spans the whole of the HB, with the exception of a few books. It situates the examination of these concepts within the cultural contexts of ancient Israel and Greece and modern philosophical and theological interpretation. It deals briefly with Isaiah 26:19, one of the passages this dissertation investigates, interpreting it as a post-mortem judgment passage (see pp. 517–519).

Patrick Miller, *Sin and Judgment in the Prophets: A Stylistic and Theological Analysis.* SBLMS 27. Chico: Scholars Press, 1982.

Patrick Miller shows that the prophetic writings use various theological motifs and stylistic elements to express the appropriateness of the punishment and the correspondence between sin and their punishment.

Wong, Ka Leung. *The Idea of Retribution in the Book of Ezekiel.* VTSup, vol. 87. Leiden: Brill, 2001.

Ka Leung Wong demonstrates that the concept of retribution as operative in the Book of Ezekiel is governed by what he calls three principles of retribution: i. covenant (that is, retribution is in accordance with the terms of the covenant), ii. the disposal of impurity (that is, retribution gets rid of the impurity generated by the wrongful act), and iii. poetic justice (that is, retribution has the element of mirroring some aspects of the crime or wrongful act). *This work is detailed and makes a valuable contribution to the study of retribution in Ezekiel that is not often examined, but it is focused on retribution in this life.*

Yona, Shamir. "The Influence of Legal Style on the Style of Aphorism: The Origin of the Retribution Formula and the Clause lō' yinnāqeh 'He Will Not Go Unpunished' in the Book of Proverbs." *Birkat Shalom* (2008): 413–423.

Shamir Yona examines the origin of the retribution formula *lo yinaqqeh* (לֹא יִנָּקֶה) where the verb *niqqa* (נִקָּה) in legal context means to acquit someone in a court of law. Retribution is a central theme in the wisdom literature. However, he argues that the retribution formula does not originate from the Wisdom tradition, wherein the teaching regarding retribution is mainly to refrain from taking revenge. This is similar to other ANE wisdom literature which likewise forbid retaliation. Instead he states that the retribution formula originates from the legal codes, and the wisdom style is influenced by the legal style. Where the formula does occur in the Wisdom literature it either refers to offenses that were to be taken up by the court of law, or in situations where the retribution is left in God's hands.

Afterlife and Related Themes

The other main area of investigation in this cross-section that is related to post-mortem divine retribution is the study of the concept of afterlife which often occurs in tandem with other themes in biblical interpretation such as resurrection, death, shades, body, soul, Sheol and hell.

Bauckham, Richard. "Jewish Visions of Hell." *JTS* 41 (1990): 355–356.

In this article, Richard Bauckham engages with Martha Himmelfarb's *Tours of Hell* and attempts to establish a closer relationship between the tours of hell tradition and the larger context of tour apocalypses. He posits that this can be done by examining visions of hell which are not tours of punishments in hell, and by examining other references to visions of hell. He examines cosmic tour texts which contain visions of hell, and argues that in these texts, initially the interest in the fate of the wicked was portrayed through the belief that the wicked will be punished in the future on the day of last judgment. This was expressed through the portrayal of visits to holding places for the wicked as they await judgment, a visit to hell, or a vision of last judgment when the wicked were thrown into hell. However, this portrayal of future punishment at the last judgment is gradually replaced by the belief that the wicked already experience punishment in their intermediate state even as they await final judgment. This change he argues is concomitant with the emergence of tours of hell.

Bernstein, Alan E. *The Formation of Hell: Death and Retribution in The Ancient and Early Christian Worlds*. Gower Street, London: UCL Press, 1993.

Alan Bernstein, a medieval historian, examines the history of the formation of the concept of hell in three societies: ancient Greco-Roman, ancient

Judaism and early Christianity. He asserts that though the concept of hell in Greco-Roman and the ancient Judaism developed simultaneously they were mostly independent. He sees both the Greco-Roman and ancient Judaism as holding in tension the fundamentally opposing concepts of *neutral death* – the dead live on without any distinction between the good and the bad, and *moral death* – the dead face post-mortem retribution. Hell brings about a measure of justice for those who seem to escape into death, suffering no consequence for their evil life. It implies an order in the universe which corrects the apparent excess of evil. The author states that one of the problems of studying ancient literature as a background for the concept of hell is that the authors of these early sources did not directly address this issue. If and when hell was mentioned, it was in the process of discussing other matters and they happened to lightly touch upon this issue. So, if these authors at all "anticipated" hell, it was logically, not purposely.

Bronner, Leila Leah. *Journey to Heaven: Exploring Jewish Views of the Afterlife*. Jerusalem: Urim Publication, 2015.

Using a historical approach, Bronner traces the development of the idea of afterlife in the Jewish textual history, including the HB, STP writings, rabbinic texts, rationalist philosophers in the medieval period, Jewish mysticism Kabbalah and theological thinking among modern Jews. With an eye on the social and cultural contexts from which these texts grew, she examines concepts such as Sheol, resurrection, immortality, judgment, messianism, and *olam haba* or the World to Come. By associating each literature or period with a concept of afterlife, whether it is expressed only in a veiled manner or as speculation, surfaces through debates, or is asserted clearly, she shows that the afterlife has been an important part of the Jewish thought and conversation throughout the ages.

Finney, Mark T. *Resurrection, Hell and the Afterlife: Body and Soul in Antiquity, Judaism and Early Christianity*. New York: Routledge, 2016.

Mark Finney's thesis is that resurrection of the body is a Greco-Roman construct rather than a Jewish one, and that conception of the afterlife in STP Judaism was focused on the soul alone. He investigates the ideas of resurrection, hell and the afterlife in antiquity, HB, STP Qumran and Rabbinic sources and the NT, with a thrust into the body-soul debate. His main contention is that the generally accepted understanding that the Jewish view of afterlife is a physical post-mortem existence and the Greco-Roman view as non-physical needs to be re-evaluated. He argues that post-mortem existence in physical form is a Greco-Roman conception, mainly drawing from Homer, and that Judaism primarily conceived of afterlife in terms of soul. His perspective on STP Judaism afterlife is shaped by his analysis of four texts from the HB from which he concludes that where there is indication of afterlife it is only of the soul and that where bodily resurrection appears it is used as a metaphor for national restoration. Hence STP Judaism afterlife, with the exception of the writings of Josephus, is focuses on the soul. Finney uses this analysis to argue that Pauline resurrection in 1 Corinthians 15 focuses on the resurrection of Jesus's soul, and that the idea of bodily resurrection appears in the gospels in Matthew and especially in Luke who attempted to present Jesus's resurrection in a Greco-Roman perspective for his audience, and the resurrection of the body gained prominence and became part of the orthodoxy.

Friedman, Richard Elliot and Shawna Dolansky Overton. "Death and Afterlife: The Biblical Silence." In *Judaism in Late Antiquity: Part 4, Death, Life-After-Death, Resurrection and the World-to-Come in the Judaism of Antiquity*, edited by Alan J. Avery-Peck and Jacob Neusner, 35–60. Leiden: Brill, 2000.

Friedman and Overton rightly note that the Hebrew Bible has confusingly very little to say about something as common as death. The authors assert that unlike the popular assumption, there was belief in the afterlife in Israel and the presence of this belief is corroborated by textual and archeological data – apertures in the ceiling of the tombs through which to give offerings to the dead or the jars placed over the head of the corpses were seen as indication of the existence of the cult of the dead. The authors compare the existence of such practices in Egypt and Ugarit, and state that Biblical references to maintenance of ancestor graves, cults of the departed spirit or divination with the help of departed spirits and high places in general all add up to a much greater significance for popular Israelite beliefs in the afterlife and the cult of death then assumed to be present so far.

Hays, Christopher B. *A Covenant with Death: Death in the Iron Age II and Its Rhetorical Uses in Proto-Isaiah*. Grand Rapids, MI: Eerdmans, 2015.

Christopher B. Hays combines literary and archaeological perspectives to examine the rhetoric of death as presented in Isaiah 1–39 in light of the imagery and perceptions of death in the ANE during Second Iron Age, which he considers to be the period of composition of most of proto-Isaiah. Hays shows that although the imagery of death in proto-Isaiah is rooted in the surrounding religious and cultural contexts, it neither simply absorbs nor blindly opposes them. He observes that proto-Isaiah exhibits several transformations of the beliefs of its neighbours regarding death and afterlife and the need to consider these for a fuller understanding and appreciation of the imagery of death in proto-Isaiah. His analysis of Isaiah 24–27 is particularly relevant to the present study although we diverge at several points.

Himmelfarb, Martha. *Tours of Hell: An Apocalyptic Form in Jewish and Christian Literature,* Philadelphia: University of Pennsylvania Press, 1983.

This book examines texts that contain tours of hell, seventeen texts in all, in an attempt to reconstruct the history of the tours of hell tradition in the Jewish and Christian writings from the first century BCE to the Middle Ages. She examines the origin of the tours of hell tradition, locating it in the Book of Watchers or 1 Enoch 17–36, and concludes that while there are elements of Greek influence, it is rooted in the Jewish and Christian tradition. She traces two shared features among these texts – the narrative structure and the sin-and-punishment motif, which she further sub-divides into measure-for-measure and environmental punishments (fire, worms, beasts, angels).

Johnston, Philip S. *Shades of Sheol: Death and Afterlife in the Old Testament*. Downers Grove: InterVarsity Press, 2002.

Philip Johnston examines the conception of death, the underworld, the shades who inhabit the underworld, and the afterlife in the HB. He deals with all the relevant texts, looking at them in light of the mourning customs of ancient Israel. He argues against the view that the Israelite conceptions of death might been influenced by the beliefs and conceptions of the neighbouring nations. He concludes that Sheol was predominantly a place for the wicked, while the fate of the godly is unclear. He contends that death and the afterlife were not central concerns for the Israelites; rather they were more focused on Yahweh and communion with him which eventuated in the emergence of the hope of an afterlife. Some of his conclusions are overdrawn but his treatment of the issue in terms of textual examination is comprehensive if not very detailed.

Saggs, H. W. F. "Some Ancient Semitic Conceptions of the Afterlife." *Faith and Thought* 90 (1958): 157–182.

Saggs describes three stages in the Roman afterlife belief, the first two stages discernible in the Semitic conception of afterlife. He deals with archaeological data, retribution on the basis of rituals rather than morality, a comparison of *rephaim* with Ugarit *rpum*, and the Mesopotamian myths to shed light on the possibility of understanding the OT understanding of afterlife. He states that in the OT, barring Isaiah 66:24 and Daniel 12:2–3, the picture is that all went to Sheol (169–170).

Bibliography

"Actus Primus," *Catholic Online, Catholic Encyclopedia*, Encyclopedia Volume, http://www.catholic.org/encyclopedia/view.php?id=166.

Adams, Samuel L. *Wisdom in Transition: Act and Consequence in Second Temple Instructions*. JSJSup 125. Leiden: Brill 2008.

Agus, Aharon Ronald E. *The Binding of Isaac and Messiah: Law, Martyrdom, and Deliverance in Early Rabbinic Religiosity*. Albany: State University of New York Press, 1988.

Albright, W. F. and C. S. Mann, *Matthew: A New Translation and Introduction*. AB. Vol. 26. Garden City: Doubleday, 1971.

Alexander, T. Desmond. "נְבֵלָה." In *NIDOTTE*, edited by Willem A. VanGemeren, 15–18. Vol. 3. Carlisle: Paternoster Press, 1997.

Ali, Jephet Ibn. *A Commentary on the Book of Daniel*. Translated by D. S. Margoliouth. Oxford: Clarendon Press, 1889.

Allen, Graham. *Intertextuality: The New Critical Idiom*. London: Routledge, 2000.

Allen, Leslie C. *Ezekiel 20–48*. WBC. Vol. 29. Dallas: Word Books, 1990.

———. "שכח." In *NIDOTTE*, edited by Willem A. VanGameren, 104. Vol. 4. Carlisle: Paternoster Press, 1996.

Allison Jr., Dale C. *Studies in Matthew: Interpretation Past and Present*. Grand Rapids: Baker Academic, 2005.

Armerding, Carl. "Asleep in the Dust." *Bibliotheca Sacra* (1964): 153–158.

Arnold, Bill T. "The Love-Fear Antinomy in Deuteronomy 5–11." *VT* 61, no. 4 (2011): 552.

Assmann, Jan. "Martyrdom, Violence, and Immortality: The Origins of a Religious Complex." In *Dying for the Faith, Killing for the Faith: Old-Testament Faith Warriors (1 and 2 Maccabees) in Historical Perspective*, edited by Gabriela Signori, 39–59. BSIH. vol. 206. Leiden: Brill, 2012.

Aune, D. E., T. J. Geddert and C. A. Evans, "Apocalypticism." In *DNTB*, edited by Craig A. Evans and Stanley E. Porter. 45– 58. Downers Grove: IVP Academic, 2000.

Bachmann, Veronika. "The Book of the Watchers (1 Enoch 1–36): An Anti-Mosaic, Non-Mosaic, or Even Pro-Mosaic Writing?" *JHS* 11, no. 4 (2011): 2–23.

Bailey, Daniel P. "The Intertextual Relationship of Daniel 12:2 and Isaiah 26:19: Evidence from Qumran and the Greek Versions." *Tyndale Bulletin* 51, no. 2 (2000): 305–308.

Bailey, Lloyd R. "Gehenna: The Topography of Hell." *The Biblical Archaeologist* 49, no. 3 (1986): 187–191.

Baker-Brian, Nicholas J. *Manichaeism: An Ancient Faith Rediscovered*. London: T and T Clark International, 2011.

Bakhtin, Mikhail Mikhailovich and P. N. Medvedev. *The Formal Method in Literary Scholarship*, translated by Albert J. Wehrle. Baltimore: Johns Hopkins University Press, 1978.

Baldwin, Joyce G. *Daniel: An Introduction and Commentary*. TOTC. Vol. 23. Leicester: Intervarsity Press, 1978.

———. *1 and 2 Samuel: An Introduction and Commentary*. Vol. 8. TOTC. Leicester: Intervarsity Press, 1988.

Barnes, William H. *1–2 Kings*. Tyndale Cornerstone Biblical Commentary. Vol. 4b. Carol Stream: Tyndale House Publishers, 2012.

Barré, Michael L. "Bullutsa-rabi's Hymn to Gula and Hosea 6:1–2." *Orientalia*, Nova Series 50, 3 (1981): 241–245.

———. "New Light on the Interpretation of Hosea VI 2." *VT* 28, no. 2 (1978): 129–141.

———. "Textual and Rhetorical-critical Observations on the Last Servant Song (Isaiah 52:13–53:12)." *CBQ* 62, no. 1 (2000): 1–27.

Barrett, C. K. "Immortality and Resurrection," *London Quarterly and Holborn Review* 190 (1965): 91–102.

Barrett, Robert Carl. "Disloyalty and Destruction: Religion and Politics in Deuteronomy and the Modern World." PhD thes. Durham University, 2007. Available at Durham E-Theses, http://etheses.dur.ac.uk/2141/

Barthes, Roland. *Image, Music, Text*. Translated by Stephen Heath. New York: Hill and Wang, 1977.

Bartlett, John R. *The First and Second Books of Maccabees*. The Cambridge Bible Commentary on the New English Bible. Cambridge: Cambridge University Press, 1973.

Barton, John. "Déjà Lu: Intertextuality, Method or Theory?" In *Reading Job Intertextually*, edited by Katharine Dell and Will Kynes, 1–16. LHBOTS 574. New York: Bloomsbury T and T Clark, 2013.

———. *Ethics in Ancient Israel*. Oxford: Oxford University Press, 2014.

———. "Historical Criticism and Literary Interpretation: Is There any Common Ground?" In *Crossing the Boundaries: Essays in Biblical Interpretation in*

Honour of Michael D. Goulder, edited by S. E. Porter, P. Joyce, and D. E. Orton, 3–15. Leiden: Brill, 1995.

Baslez, Marie-Francoise "The Origin of the Martyrdom Images: From the Book of Maccabees to the First Christian." In The Book of the Maccabees: History, Theology, Ideology: Papers of the Second International Conference on the Deuterocanonical Books, Papa, Hungary, 9–11 June 2005, edited by Geza G. Xeravits and Jozef Zsengeller, 113–130. JSJSup. Vol. 118. Leiden: Brill, 2007.

Bauckham, Richard J. "Apocalypses." In *Justification and Variegated Nomism: Vol. 1 – The Complexities of Second Temple Judaism*, edited by D. A. Carson, Peter T. O'Brien, and Mark A. Seifrid, 135–188. WUNT 2.14. Tübingen: Mohr Siebeck, 2001.

———. "Life, Death, and the Afterlife in Second Temple Judaism." In *Life in the Face of Death: The Resurrection Message of the New Testament*, edited by Richard N. Longenecker, 80–95. Grand Rapids, MI: Eerdmans, 1998.

Bautch, Kelley Coblentz. "Decoration, Destruction and Debauchery – Reflection on 1 Enoch 8 in Light of 4QEn^b." *Dead Sea Discoveries* 15 (2008): 79–95.

———. "What Becomes of the Angels' 'Wives'? A Text-Critical Study of '1 Enoch' 19:2." *JBL* 125, no. 4 (2006): 766–780.

Beal, Timothy K. "Glossary." In *Reading Between Texts: Intertextuality and the Hebrew Bible*, edited by Danna Nolan Fewell, 21–24. LCIB. Louisville: Westminster, 1992.

———. "Ideology and Intertextuality: Surplus of Meaning and Controlling the Means of Production." In *Reading Between Texts: Intertextuality and the Hebrew Bible*, edited by Danna Nolan Fewell, 29–39. LCIB. Louisville: Westminster, 1992.

Beckwith, Roger T. "The Earliest Enoch Literature and its Calendar: Marks of Their Origin, Date and Motivation." *Revue De Qumrân* 10, no. 3, 39 (1981): 365–403. www.jstor.org/stable/24607867.

Bedenbender, Andreas. "The Place of the Torah in the Early Enoch Literature." In *The Early Enochic Literature*, edited by Gabriele Boccaccini and John J. Collins, 65–79. JSOJSup. Vol. 121. Leiden: Brill, 2007.

Berger, Albrecht. "The Cult of the Maccabees in the Eastern Orthodox Church." In *Dying for the Faith, Killing for the Faith: Old-Testament Faith Warriors (I and 2 Maccabees) in Historical Perspective*, edited by Gabriela Signori, 105–123. BSIH. Vol. 206. Leiden: Brill, 2012.

Bernstein, Alan E. The Formation of Hell: Death and Retribution in the Ancient and Early Christian Worlds. Grower Street, London: University College London Press, 1993.

Beuken, Willem A. M. "Mount Zion: A Comparison of Poetic Visions in Isaiah 24–27, 52, and 66." In *The Desert Will Bloom: Poetic Visions in Isaiah*, edited by A. Joseph Everson and Hyun Chul Paul Kim, 91–107. Atlanta: Society of Biblical Literature, 2009.

Bevan, Anthony Ashley. *A Short Commentary on the Book of Daniel*. Cambridge: Cambridge University Press, 1892.

Bird, Michael. "Judgment and Justification in Paul: A Review Article." *Bulletin for Biblical Research* 18.2 (2008): 299–313.

———. Saving Righteousness of God: Studies on Paul, Justification, and the New Perspective. Paternoster Biblical Monographs. Eugene: Wipf and Stock Publishers, 2007.

Black, Matthew. *The Book of Enoch or 1 Enoch 1: A New English Edition with Commentary and Textual Notes*. Leiden: Brill, 1985.

Blenkinsopp, Joseph. Isaiah 1–39: A New Translation with Introduction and Commentary. AB. Vol. 19. New York: Doubleday, 2000.

Bloch-Smith, Elizabeth M. "The Cult of the Dead in Judah: Interpreting the Material Remains." *JBL* 111/2 (1992): 213–224.

Block, Daniel I. "Beyond the Grave: Ezekiel's Vision of Death and Afterlife." *Bulletin for Biblical Research*. Vol. 2 (1992): 113–141.

Boase, Elizabeth. *The Fulfilment of Doom? The Dialogic Interaction between the Book of Lamentations and the Pre-Exilic/Early Exilic Prophetic Literature*. New York: T and T Clark, 2006.

Boccaccini, Gabriele. *Beyond the Essene Hypothesis: The Parting of Ways Between the Qumran and Enochic Judaism*. Grand Rapids: Eerdmans, 1998.

———. *Roots of Rabbinic Judaism: An Intellectual History, from Ezekiel to Daniel*. Grand Rapids: Eerdmans, 2002.

Boston, James R. "The Wisdom Influence upon the Song of Moses." *JBL* 87 (1968): 198–2021.

Box, G. H. *The Book of Isaiah: Translated from a Text Revised in Accordance with the Results of Recent Criticism*. New York: Macmillan, 1909.

Branson, R. D. "יסר *yāsar*." In *TDOT*, edited by G. Johannes Botterweck and Helmer Ringgren, 129. Vol. 6, translated by David E. Green. Grand Rapids: Eerdmans, 1990.

Brensinger, Terry L. "נסה." In *NIDOTTE*, edited by Willem A. VanGemeren. Vol. 3. Grand Rapids: Zondervan, 1997.

Breytenbach, Cilliers. "The Septuagint Version of Isaiah 53 and the Early Christian Formula 'He Was Delivered for Our Trespasses.'" *Novum Testamentum* 51, no. 4 (2009): 339–351.

Bruce, Andrew. Davidson, *The Theology of the Old Testament*. New York: 1907.

Brueggemann, Walter. "A Shape for Old Testament Theology: 1, Structure Legitimation; 2, Embrace of Pain." *CBQ* 47, no. 1 (1985): 28–46.

———. *Deuteronomy*. AOTC. Nashville: Abingdon Press, 2001.

———. *First and Second Samuel*. Interpretation: A Bible Commentary for Teaching and Preaching. Louisville: JKP, 1990.

———. *Isaiah 1–39*. Westminster Bible Companion. Louisville: WJKP, 1998.

———. "Unity and Dynamic in the Isaiah Tradition." *JOST* 29 (1984): 89–107.

Butler, Trent. *Hosea, Joel, Amos, Obadiah, Jonah, Micah*. Holman Old Testament Commentary. Nashville: Holman References, 2005.

Byron, John. "Abel's Blood and the Ongoing Cry for Vengeance." *CBQ* 73 (2011): 743–756.

Cartledge, Tony W. *1 and 2 Samuel*. SHBC. Macon: Smyth and Helwys, 2001.

Carpenter, Eugene. "Daniel." In *Ezekiel, Daniel*. Tyndale Cornerstone Biblical Commentary, 285–469. Vol. 9. Carol Stream: Tyndale House Publishers, 2010.

Carson, Alexander. "The Word 'Aphar as a Determinative for the Study of Job XIX: 25–27," *Review and Expositor* 28, no. 4 (1931): 387–97.

Cavallin, Hans Clemens Caesarius. *Life After Death: Paul's Arguments for the Resurrection of the Dead in 1 Cor 15, Part 1: An Enquiry into the Jewish Background*. ConBNT 7. Lund: CWK Gleerup, 1974.

Chalmers, Aaron Jonathan. "A Critical Analysis of the Formula 'Yahweh Strikes and Heals.'" *VT*, 61, no. 1 (2011): 16–33.

Chapman, Stephen. "Reading the Bible as Witness: Divine Retribution in the Old Testament." *Perspectives in Religious Studies* 31, no. 2 (2004): 171–190.

Charles, R. H. *The Book of Enoch, or 1 Enoch: Translated from the Editor's Ethiopic Text, and Edited with the Introduction Notes and Indexes of the First Edition Wholly Recast Enlarged and Rewritten; Together with a Reprint from the Editor's Text of the Greek Fragments*. Oxford: Clarendon Press, 1912.

Chase, Mitchell L. "'From Dust You Shall Arise:' Resurrection Hope in the Old Testament." *SBJT* 18, no. 4. (2014): 9–29.

Chester, Andrew. "Resurrection and Transformation." In *Auferstehung – Resurrection*, edited by Friedrich Avemarie, Hermann Lichtenberger, 47–77. WUNT 135. Tübingen: Mohr Siebeck, 2001.

Childs, Brevard S. *Introduction to the Old Testament as Scripture*. Philadelphia: Fortress Press, 1979.

———. *Isaiah*. OTL. Louisville, Kentucky: Westminster John Knox Press, 2001.

Christensen, Duane L. *Deuteronomy 1:1–21:9*. 2nd ed. WBC. Vol. 6a. Nashville: Thomas Nelson Publishers, 2001.

Claassens, L. Juliana M. "Biblical Theology as Dialogue: Continuing the Conversation on Mikhail Bakhtin and Biblical Theology." *JBL*. Vol. 122, no. 1 (2003): 127–144.

"The Clementine Homilies," Christian Classical Ethereal Library, http://www.ccel.org/ccel/schaff/anf08/Page_272.html.

Clements, Ronald E. *Isaiah 1–39*. NCB. Grand Rapids: Eerdmans, 1980.

Coetzer, Eugene, and Pierre Jordaan. "Selling Religious Progress to a Nostalgic Nation: Jewish Doctrinal Revolution in 2 Maccabees 7." *Ekklesiastikos Pharos*, 91 (2009): 170–190.

Cogan, Mordechai and Hayim Tadmor. *2 Kings*. AB. Vol. 11. New York: Doubleday, 1988.

Cohen, Gerson David. "Hannah and Her Seven Sons in Hebrew Literature." In *Studies in the Variety of Rabbinic Cultures*, edited by Gerson David Cohen, 39–60. Philadelphia: JPS, 1991.

Cohen, Sahye J. D. *From the Maccabees to the Mishnah*. 2nd ed. Louisville, KY: WJKP, 2006.

Collins, John J. "Introduction: Towards the Morphology of a Genre." *Semeia* 14 (1979): 1–20.

Collins, John J. *Apocalyptic Imagination: An Introduction to Jewish Apocalyptic Literature*. 2nd ed. Grand Rapids: Eerdmans, 1998.

———. "Apocalyptic Technique: Setting and Function in the Book of Watchers." *CBQ* 44, no.1 (1982): 91–111.

———. *Between Athens and Jerusalem: Jewish Identity in the Hellenistic Diaspora*. Grand Rapids: Eerdmans, 2000.

———. *Daniel*, Hermeneia: A Critical and Historical Commentary on the Bible. Minneapolis: Fortress, 1993.

———. *Daniel, 1-2 Maccabees*. Old Testament Message: A Biblical-Theological Commentary. Wilmington, Delaware: Michael Glazier Inc., 1981.

———. Daniel: With an Introduction to Apocalyptic Literature. FOTL 20. Grand Rapids: Eerdmans, 1984.

———. "An Enochic Testament? Comments on George Nickelsburg's Hermeneia Commentary." In *George W. E. Nickelsburg in Perspective: An Ongoing Dialogue of Learning*, edited by Jacob Neusner and Alan J. Avery-Peck, 373–378. Vol. 2. JSJSup 80. Leiden: Brill, 2003.

———. "The Eschatology of Zechariah." In *Knowing the End from the Beginning: The Prophetic, the Apocalyptic and Their Relationships*, edited by L. L. Grabbe and R. D. Haak, 74–84. JSOP 46. Clark International, London, 2003.

———. *Jewish Cult and Hellenistic Culture: Essays on the Jewish Encounter with Hellenism and Roman Rule*. JSJSup. Vol. 100. Leiden: Brill, 2005.

———. "How Distinctive was Enochic Judaism." *Meghillot: Studies in the Dead Sea Scrolls* 5–6 (2008): 17–34.

Collins, John J. and George W. E. Nickelsburg. *Ideal Figures in Ancient Judaism: Profiles and Paradigms*. SBLSCS 12. Chico: Scholars Press, 1980.

Cook, Stephen L. *The Apocalyptic Literature*. IBT. Nashville: Abingdon Press, 2003.

———. "Deliverance as Fertility and Resurrection: Echoes of Second Isaiah in Isaiah 26." In *Formation and Intertextuality in Isaiah 24–27*, edited by J. Todd

Hibbard and Hyun Chul Paul Kim, 165–182. SBL Ancient Israel and Its Literature 17. Atlanta: Society of Biblical Literature, 2013.

Cooper, Derek and Martin J. Lohrmann, eds. *1-2 Samuel, 1-2 Kings, 1-2 Chronicles*. Reformation Commentary on Scripture. Old Testament. Vol. 5. Downers Grove: IVP Academic.

Craigie, Peter C. *The Book of Deuteronomy*. NICOT. Grand Rapids: Eerdmans, 1976.

———. *Psalms 1-50*. WBC. Vol. 19. Nashville: Thomas Nelson Publishers, 1983.

Crenshaw, James L. "Love Is Stronger Than Death: Intimations of Life beyond the Grave." In *Resurrection: The Origin and Future of a Biblical Doctrine*, edited by James H. Charlesworth and others, 53–78. Faith and Scholarship Colloquies Series. New York: T and T Clark, 2006.

Cross, Frank Moore. *Canaanite Myth and Hebrew Epic*. Cambridge: Harvard University Press, 1973.

———. New Direction in the Study of the Apocalyptic. *JTC* 6 (1969): 157–165.

Crüsemann, Frank. "The Unchangeable World: The 'Crisis of Wisdom' in Koheleth." In *God of the Lowly: Socio-Historical Interpretations of the Bible*, edited by W. Schottroff and W. Stegemann, translated by M.J. O'Connell, 57–77. Marynoll: Orbis Books, 1984.

Culler, Jonathan. "Presupposition and Intertextuality." *MLN*. Vol. 91, no. 6, Comparative Literature (1976): 1380–1396.

Dahood, Mitchell. "Isaiah 53,8–12 and Massoretic Misconstructions." *Biblica* 63, no. 4 (1982): 566–570.

———. *Psalm I, 1-50*. AB. Vol. 16. Garden City: Doubleday, 1966.

———. *Psalm II, 51-100*. AB. Vol. 17. Garden City: Doubleday, 1968.

Darby, John Nelson. *Studies on the Book of Daniel: A Course of Lectures*, 3rd ed. London: John B. Bateman, 1864.

Davidson, Andrew Bruce. *The Theology of the Old Testament*. New York: 1907.

Davidson, M. J. *Angels at Qumran: A Comparative Study of 1 Enoch 1–36, 72–108 and Sectarian Writings from Qumran*. JSPSup 11. Sheffield: JSOT Press, 1992.

Davies, Glen. *Faith and Obedience in Romans: A Study in Romans 1–4*. JSNTSup 39. Sheffield: JSOT Press, 1990.

Day, John. "אורת טל in Isaiah 26:19." *Zeitschrift für die alttestamentliche Wissenschaft* 90, no. 2 (1978): 265–269.

———. "Da'at 'Humiliation' in Isaiah LIII 11 in the Light of Isaiah LIII 3 and Daniel XII 4, and the Oldest Known Interpretation of the Suffering Servant." *VT* 30, no. 1 (1980): 97–103.

———. *Yahweh and the Gods and Goddesses of Canaan*. JSOTSup 265. Sheffield: Sheffield Academic Press, 2000.

De Ru, G. "The Conception of Reward in the Teaching of Jesus." *Novum Testamentum*, vol. 8, no. 2/4 (1966): 202–222.

De Vaux, Roland. *Ancient Israel: Its Life and Institutions*, translated by John McHugh. Grand Rapids: Eerdmans, 1997.

Declaisse-Walford, Nancy, Rolf A. Jacobson and Beth Laneel Tanner. *The Books of Psalms*. NICOT. Grand Rapids: Eerdmans, 2014.

Dell, Katharine, and Will Kynes, "Introduction." In *Reading Job Intertextually*, edited by Kathrine Dell and Will Kynes, xv- xxiii. LHBOTS 574. New York: Bloomsbury T and T Clark, 2013.

deSilva, David A. *Introducing the Apocrypha: Message, Context, and Significance*. Grand Rapids, Mich.: Baker Academic, 2002.

Dimant, Devorah. "1 Enoch 6–11: A Methodological Perspective." *SBL Seminar Papers 1978.*, edited by Paul J. Achtemeier, 323–339. SBLSP 18. Missoula, MT: Scholars Press, 1978.

Dix, G. H. "The Enochic Pentateuch." *JTS* 27 (1926): 29–42.

Doak, Brian R. *The Last of the Rephaim: Conquest and Cataclysm in the Heroic Ages of Ancient Israel*. Boston: Ilex Foundation, 2012.

Dominic, Crossan John. "The Resurrection of Jesus in Its Jewish Context." *Neotestamentica* 37, no. 1. 2003: 29–57.

Donfried, K. P. "Justification and Last Judgment." *ZNW* 67 (1976): 90–110.

Doran, Robert M. and Robert C. Corken, eds. *Collected Works of Bernard Lonergan: Early Works on Theological Method 1*. Toronto: University of Toronto Press, 2010.

Doran, Robert M. *Temple Propaganda: The Purpose and Character of 2 Maccabees*. CBQ Monograph Series, 12. Washington, D.C.: The Catholic Biblical Association, 1981.

———. *2 Maccabees: A Critical Commentary*. Hermeneia: A Critical and Historical Commentary on the Bible. Minneapolis: Fortress Press, 2012.

———. "2 Maccabees and 'Tragic History.'" *Hebrew Union College Annual*. Vol. 50 (1979): 107–114.

———. "The Martyr: A Synoptic View of the Mother and Her Seven Sons." In *Ideal Figures in Ancient Judaism: Profiles and Paradigms*, edited by John J. Collins and George W. E. Nickelsburg, 189–221. SBLSCS 12. Chico, CA: Scholars Press, 1980.

———. "The Second Book of Maccabees." *NIB*. Vol. IV. Nashville: Abingdon Press, 1996.

Downing, John. "Jesus and Martyrdom." *JTS*. New Series 14, no. 2 (1963): 279–293.

Doyle, Brian. *The Apocalypse of Isaiah Metaphorically Speaking: Isaiah 24-27*. Leuven: Leuven University Press, 2000.

Driver, R. S. *Deuteronomy*. ICC. Edinburgh: T and T Clark, 1901.

———. *Isaiah, His Life and Times, and the Writings Which Bear His Name*. New York, 1888.

Ego, Beate. "God's Justice: The 'Measure for Measure' Principle in 2 Maccabees." In The Book of the Maccabees: History, Theology, and Ideology: Papers of the Second International Conference on the Deuterocanonical Books, Papa, Hungary, 9–11 June, 2005, edited by Geza G. Xeravits and Jozsef Zsengeller, 141–154. JSJSup. Vol. 118. Leiden: Brill, 2007.

Eichrodt, Walter. *Ezekiel*. OTL. Philadelphia: Westminster, 1970.

———. *Theology of the Old Testament*. Translated by John A. Baker. OTL. Vol. 2. Philadelphia: Westminster, 1967.

Eising, Münster H. "זָכַר zākhar." Translated by David E. Green. In *TDOT*, edited by G. Johannes Botterweck and Helmer Ringgren, 67. Vol 4. Grand Rapids: Eerdmans, 1980.

Eissfeldt, Otto. *The Old Testament: An Introduction, Including the Apocrypha and Pseudepigrapha, and Also the Works of Similar Type from Qumran: The History of the Formation of the Old Testament*. Translated by P. R. Ackroyd. Oxford: Basil Blackwell, 1965.

Elledge, Casey Deryl. *Life After Death in Early Judaism: The Evidence of Josephus*. Tubingen: Mohr Siebeck, 2006.

———. "Resurrection of the Dead: Exploring out Earliest Evidence Today." In *Resurrection: The Origin and Future of a Biblical Doctrine*, edited by James H. Charlesworth and others, 35–52. New York: T and T Clark, 2006.

Ernest G. Clark, translator. *Targum Pseudo-Jonathan, Deuteronomy*. Vol. 5B. The Aramiac Bible. Edinburgh: T and T Clark, 1997.

Eslinger Lyle. "Inner-Biblical Exegesis and Inner-Biblical Allusion: The Question of Category." *VT* 42, no. 1 (1992): 47–58.

———. "Watering Egypt (Deuteronomy XI 10–11)," *VT* 37, no. 1 (1987): 85–90.

Evans Craig A. and Peter W. Flint. "Introduction." In *Eschatology, Messianism, and The Dead Sea Scrolls*, edited by Craig A. Evans and Peter W. Flint, 1–3. Grand Rapids: Eerdmans, 1997.

Feder, Yitzhaq. "The Mechanics of Retribution in Hittite, Mesopotamian and Ancient Israelite Sources." *JANER* 10, no. 2 (2010): 119–157.

Fewell, Donna Nolan. "Introduction: Reading, Writing, and Relating." In *Reading Between Texts: Intertextuality and the Hebrew Bible*, edited by Donna Nolan Fewell, 11–20. LCIB. Louisville: Westminster, 1992.

Finney, Mark. *Resurrection, Hell and the Afterlife: Body and Soul in Antiquity, Judaism and Early Christianity*. New York: Routledge, 2016.

Firth, David. *1 and 2 Samuel*. AOTC. Vol. 8. Nottingham: Apollos, 2009.

Fischer, Stefan. "How God Pays Back: Retributive Concepts in the Book of Job." *Acta Theologica* 20/2 (2000): 26–41.

Fishbane, Michael. "Inner Biblical Exegesis: Types and Strategies of Interpretation in Ancient Israel." In *Midrash and Literature*, edited by G. H. Hartman and S. Budick, 19–37. New Haven: Yale University Press, 1986.

Fonrobert, Charlotte. "Review: Roots of Rabbinic Judaism: An Intellectual History, From Ezekiel to Daniel." *Shofar* 22, 4 (2004): 156–59.

Fox, Michael V. "The Rhetoric of Ezekiel's Vision of the Valley of the Bones." *Hebrew Union College Annual* 51 (1980): 1–15.

Freidman Richard Elliott, and Shawna Dolansky Overton. "Death and Afterlife: The Biblical Silence." In *Judaism in Late Antiquity: Death, Life-After-Death, Resurrection and The World to Come in the Judaisms of Antiquity*, edited by Alan Avery-Peck and Jacob Neusner, 35–59. Vol. 4. JLA. Leiden: Brill, 2000.

Frend, William Hugh Clifford. *Martyrdom and Persecution in the Early Church: A Study of Conflict from the Maccabees to Donatus*. Oxford: Basil Blackwell, 1965.

Fritz, Volkmar. *1 and 2 Kings*. A Continental Commentary. Translated by Anselm Hagedorn. Minneapolis: Fortress, 2003.

Frykenberg, Robert Eric. *Belief and History: The Foundations of Historical Understanding*. Grand Rapids: Eerdmans, 1996.

Fudge, Edward. "The Final End of the Wicked." *JETS*, 27/3 (1984): 325–334.

Gammie, John G. "Theology of Retribution in the Book of Deuteronomy." *CBQ* 32, no. 1 (1970): 1–12.

Gardner, Anne. "Daniel 12:1e–2 or How to Reverse the Death Curse of Genesis 3." *Australian Biblical Review* 40 (1992): 1–19.

Garrett, Duane A. *Hosea, Joel*. NAC. Vol. 19A. Nashville: Broadman and Holman, 1997.

George G. Nicol, "Watering Egypt (Deuteronomy XI 10–11) Again," *Vetus Testamentum* 38, no. 3 (1988): 347–348.

Gese, Hartmut. "The Crisis of Wisdom in Koheleth." In *Theodicy in the Old Testament*, edited by James L. Crenshaw, translated by L. L. Grabbe, 141–153. London: SPCK, 1983.

Giessen Gerstenberger, "עָנָה II *'ānâ*." Translated by David E. Green. In *TODT*, edited by G. Johannes Botterweck, Helmer Ringgren, and Heinz-Josef Fabry, 237. Vol. XI. Grand Rapids: Eerdmans, 2001.

Ginsberg, H. L. "The Oldest Interpretation of the Suffering Servant," *VT* 3 (1953): 400–404.

Goff, Matthew. "1 Enoch." In *The Oxford Encyclopedia of the Books of the Bible*, edited by Michael David Coogan, 224–237. Vol. 1 Acts – LXX. Oxford: OUP, 2011.

Goldingay, John. *Daniel*, WBC. Vol. 30. Nashville: Thomas Nelson, 1996.

———. "Death and Afterlife in the Psalms." In *Judaism in Late Antiquity 4: Death Life-After-Death, and the World to Come in the Judaisms of Antiquity*, edited by Alan J. Avery-Peck and Jacob Neusner, 61–85. Leiden: Brill, 2000.

Goldstein, Jonathan A. *II Maccabees: A New Translation with Introduction and Commentary*. AB. Vol. 41A. New York: Doubleday, 1983.

Gordon, Robert P. "The Gods Must Die: A Theme in Isaiah and Beyond." In *Isaiah in Context Studies in Honour of Arie van der Kooij on the Occasion of His Sixty-Fifth Birthday*, edited by Michaël van der Meer, Percy van Keulen, Wido Th. Van Peursen, and Bas Ter Haar Romeny, 45–61. VTSup 138. Leiden: Brill 2010.

———. *I and II Samuel: A Commentary*. LBI. Grand Rapids: Regency Reference Library, 1986.

Grabbe, Lester L. *Judaism from Cyrus to Hadrian Vol. 1: The Persian and the Greek Period*. Minneapolis: Fortress Press 1992.

Gray, George Buchanan. *A Critical and Exegetical Commentary on the Book of Isaiah 1–27*. ICC. Edinburgh: T and T Clark, 1980.

Gray, John. *1 and 2 Kings: A Commentary*. 2nd ed. OTL. Philadelphia: Westminster, 1970.

Greenfield, Jonas C. and Michael E. Stone, "Enochic Pentateuch and the Date of the Similitudes," *HTR* 70 no. 1–2 (1977): 51–65.

Greenspoon, Leonard J. "The Afterlife in the Septuagint." In *Heaven, Hell, and the Afterlife: Eternity in Judaism, Christianity, and Islam*, edited by J. Harold Ellens, 43–59. End Time and Afterlife in Judaism. Vol. 1. Santa Barbara, CA: Praeger, 2013.

———. "The Origin of the Idea of Resurrection." In *Traditions in Transformation: Turning Points in Biblical Faith*, edited by Baruch Halpern and Jon D. Levenson, 247–321. Winona Lake, Indiana: Eisenbrauns, 1981.

Grehard F. Hasel, "Resurrection in the Theology of Old Testament Apocalyptic," Zeitschrift für die Alttestamentliche Wissenschaft, vol. 92, 2 (1980): 267–283.

Grohamann, Marianne, and Hyun Chul Paul Kim. "Introduction." In *Second Wave of Intertextuality and the Hebrew Bible*, edited by Marianne Grohamann and Hyun Chul Paul Kim, 1–20. Atlanta: SBL Press, 2019.

Grossfeld, Bernard. translator. *Targum Onqelos: Deuteronomy*. The Aramaic Bible. Vol. 9. Wilmington: Michael Glazier, 1988.

Gruen, Erich S. *The Construct of Identity in Hellenistic Judaism Book Subtitle: Essays on Early Jewish Literature and History*. DCLS. Vol. 29. Berlin: De Grutyer, 2016.

"H5038 גבלה," Strong's Hebrew Lexicon Number, https://studybible.info/strongs/H5038.

Hanger, Donald A. *Matthew 14–28*. WBC. Vol. 33b. Dallas: Word Books, 1995.

Hanson, Paul D. *The Dawn of Apocalyptic: The Historical and Sociological Roots of Jewish Apocalyptic Eschatology*. Philadelphia: Fortress, 1975.

———. "Rebellion of Heaven, Azazel and Euhemeristic Heroes in 1 Enoch 6–11." *JBL* 96 (1977): 197–233.

Harris, Murray J. "Resurrection and Immortality in the Paulin Corpus." In *Life in the Face of Death: The Resurrection Message of the New Testament*, edited by Richard N. Longenecker, 147–170. Grand Rapids: Eerdmans, 1998.

Hartman, Lars. *Asking for a Meaning: A Study of 1 Enoch 1–5*. ConBNT 12. Lund: Gleerup, 1979.

Hartman, Louis F. and Alexander A. Di Lella, *The Book of Daniel*. AB. Vol. 23. New York: Doubleday, 1978.

Hayes, Richard B. "Forward to the English Edition." In *Reading the Bible Intertextually*, edited by Richard B. Hayes, Stefan Alkier, Leroy A. Huizenga, xiii. Waco, Texas: Baylor University Press, 2009.

Hays, Christopher B. *A Covenant with Death: Death in the Iron Age II and Its Rhetorical Uses in Proto-Isaiah*. Grand Rapids: Eerdmans, 2015.

———. "The Date of Isaiah 24–27 in Light of Hebrew Diachrony." In *Formation and Intertextuality in Isaiah 24–27*, edited by J. Todd Hibbard and Hyun Chul Paul Kim, 7–24. SBL Ancient Israel and its Literature 17. Atlanta: SBL, 2013.

Heger, Paul. *Challenges to Conventional Opinions on Qumran and Enoch Issues*. Leiden: Brill, 2012.

———. "1 Enoch – Complementary or Alternative to Mosaic Torah?" *JSOJ* 41 (2010): 29–62.

Heider, George C. *The Cult of the Molek: A Reassessment*. JSOTSup 43. Sheffield: JSOT Press, 1985.

Helfmeyer, "נָסָה *nissaâ*; מַסּוֹת *massôt*; מַסָּה *massâ*." In *TDOT*, edited by G. Johannes Botterweck and Helmer Ringgren, Vol. IX. Grand Rapids: Eerdmans, 1998.

Helyer, Larry R. *Exploring Jewish Literature of the Second Temple Period: A Guide for New Testament Students*. Downers Grove: IVP, 2002.

Hengel, Martin. *Judaism and Hellenism: Studies in their Encounter in Palestine During the Early Hellenistic Period*. Vols. 2. Translated by John Bowden. London: SMC Press, 1974.

Hertzberg, Hans Wilhelm. *I and II Samuel*. OTL. Louisville: WJK Press, 1964.

Hibbard, J. Todd. *Intertextuality in Isaiah 24–27: The Reuse and Evocation of Earlier Texts and Traditions*. FAT 2/16. Tübingen: Mohr Siebeck, 2006.

Hiers, Richard H. "Eschatology." In *The HarperCollins Bible Dictionary*, edited by Paul Achtemeier, 302–305. New York: HarperCollins, 1996.

Himmelfarb, Martha. *A Kingdom of Priests: Ancestry and Merit in Ancient Judaism*, Jewish Culture and Contexts. Philadelphia: University of Pennsylvania Press, 2006.

———. "Judaism and Hellenism in 2 Maccabees." In *Poetics Today*. Hellenism and Hebraism Reconsidered: The Poetics of Cultural Influence and Exchange I. Vol. 19, no. 1 (1998): 19–40.

———. "Temple and Priests in the Book of the Watchers, the Animal Apocalypse, and the Apocalypse of Weeks." In *The Early Enoch Literature*, edited by Gabriele Boccaccini and John J. Collins, 219–235. JSJSup. Vol. 121. Leiden, Brill: 2007.

Hinds, Stephen. *Allusion and Intertext: Dynamics of Appropriation in Roman Poetry*. Cambridge: Cambridge University Press, 1998.

Hogeterp, Albert L.A. "Resurrection and Biblical Tradition: Pseudo-Ezekiel Reconsidered." *Biblica* 89, no. 1 (2008): 59–69.

Hooke, S. H. "The Theory and Practice of Substitution." *VT* 2, no. 1 (1952): 2–17.

Hubbard, David Allan. *Hosea: An Introduction and Commentary*. TOTC. Leicester, UK: IVP, 1989a.

Irwin, William. "Against Intertextuality." *Philosophy and Literature* 28, no. 2 (2004): 227–242.

Ironside, H. A. *Lectures on Daniel the Prophet*. Reprint ed. New York: Loizeaux, 1950.

James Baxter. *The Book of Deuteronomy and Post-modern Christianity*. Eugene: Wipf and Stock Publishers, 2013.

Janowitz, Naomi. *The Family Romance of Martyrdom in Second Maccabees*. London: Routledge, 2017.

Jobes, Karen H. and Moises Silva. *Invitation to the Septuagint*. 2nd ed. Grand Rapids: Baker Academics, 2000.

Johnson, Dan G. *From Chaos to Restoration: An Integrative Reading of Isaiah 24–27*. JSOTSup 61. Sheffield: JSOT Press, 1988.

Johnston, Philip S. *Shades of Sheol: Death and Afterlife in the Old Testament*. Downers Grove: IVP, 2002.

Joyce, Paul. *Divine Initiative and Human Response in Ezekiel*. JOSTSup 51. Sheffield: JSOT Press, 1989.

Kaiser, Otto. *Isaiah 13–39: A Commentary*. OTL. Philadelphia: The Westminster Press, 1974.

Kaminsky, Joel S. *Corporate Responsibility in the Hebrew Bible*. Sheffield: Sheffield Academic Press, 1995.

———. "Review: Roots of Rabbinic Judaism: An Intellectual History, From Ezekiel to Daniel." *Hebrew Studies*. Vol. 43 (2002): 289–292.

———. "Would You Impugn My Justice? A Nuanced Approach to the Hebrew Bible's Theology of Divine Recompense." *Interpretation: A Journal of Bible and Theology* 69, no. 3 (2015): 299–310.

Keller, Edmund B. "Hebrew Thoughts on Immortality and Resurrection." *IJPR*. Vol. 5, 1 (1974): 16–44.

Kelly, Brian E. *Retribution and Eschatology in Chronicles*. JSOTSup 211. Sheffield: Sheffield Academic Press, 1996.
Key, Andrew F. "The Concept of Death in Early Israelite Religion." *JBR*, vol. 32, 3 (1964): 239–247.
Kiel, Micah D. "Interpreting Tobit Two Ways: Inner Biblical Exegesis and Intertextuality." In *Intertextual Explorations in Deuterocanonical and Cognate Literature*, edited by Jeremy Corley and Geoffrey David Miller, 293–318. Berlin: De Gruyter, 2019.
———. *The "Whole Truth": Rethinking Retribution in the Book of Tobit*. Library of Second Temple Studies, 82. London: T and T Clark, 2012.
Kissane, Edward. *The Book of Psalms: Translated from a Critically Revised Hebrew Text with a Commentary*. Vol. 1 (Psalms 1–72). Dublin: Browne and Nolan, 1953.
Klein, Ralph W. *1 Samuel*. WBC. Vol. 10. Waco: Word Books, 1983.
Knibb, Michael A. "The Book of Enoch or the Books of Enoch? The Textual Evidence for 1 Enoch." In *The Early Enochic Literature*, edited by Gabriele Boccaccini and John J. Collins, 21–40. Leiden: Brill, 2007.
———. "Christian Adoption and Transmission of Jewish Pseudepigrapha: The Case of '1 Enoch.'" *Journal for the Study of Judaism in the Persian, Hellenistic, and Roman Period* 32, no. 4 (2001): 396–415. www.jstor.org/stable/24668772.
———. *Essays on the Book of Enoch and Other Early Jewish Texts and Traditions*. Studia in Veteris Testamenti Pseudepigrapha. Vol. 22. Leiden: Brill, 2009.
Koch, Klaus. "Is there a Doctrine of Retribution in the Old Testament?" In *Theodicy in the Old Testament*, edited by James L. Crenshaw, 57–87. London: SPCK, 1983.
Koehler, Ludwig and Walter Baumgartner. *The Hebrew and Aramaic Lexicon of the Old Testament*. Vol. 2, ת – פ (Leiden: Brill, 2001).
Koopmans, William T. "בעל." In *NICOTTE*, edited by Willem A. VanGemerem. Vol. 1. Carlisle, Cumbria: Paternoster Press, 1996.
Kosmin, Paul J. "Indigenous Revolts in 2 Maccabees: The Persian Version." *Classical Philology* 111 (2016): 32–53.
———. *The Land of the Elephant Kings: Space, Territory, and Ideology in the Seleucid Empire*. Cambridge: HUP, 2014.
Krašovec, Jože. *Reward, Punishment, and Forgiveness: The Thinking and Beliefs of Ancient Israel in the Light of Greek and Modern Views*. Leiden: Brill, 1999.
———. "Is there A Doctrine of 'Collective Retribution' in The Hebrew Bible?" *Hebrew Union College Annual* 65 (1994): 35–89.
Kraus, Hans-Joachim. *Psalms 1–59: A Commentary*. Translated by Hilton C. Oswald. Minneapolis: Augsburg Publishing House, 1988.
Kristeva, Julia. *Revolution in Poetic Language*. Translated by Margaret Waller. New York: Columbia University Press, 1984.

———. "Word, Dialogue and Novel." In *Desire in Language: A Semiotic Approach to Language and Art*, edited by Leon S. Roudiez, translated by Thomas Gora, Alice Jardine, and Leon S. Roudiez, 64–91. New York: Columbia University Press, 1980.

Kvanvig, Helge S. "Enoch – From Sage to Visionary Apocalyptist." *Henoch* 30 (2008): 48–51.

———. "Enochic Judaism: A Judaism Without the Torah and the Temple?" In *Enoch and the Mosaic Torah: The Evidence of Jubilees*, edited by Gabriele Boccaccini and Giovanni Ibba, 163–177. Grand Rapids: Eerdmans, 2009.

Kynes, Will. "Job and Isaiah 40–55: Intertextualities in Dialogue." In *Reading Job Intertextually*, edited by Katharine Dell and Will Kynes, 94–105. LHBOTS 574. New York: Bloomsbury T and T Clark, 2013.

Laato, Antti. "Theodicy in the Deuteronomistic History." In *Theodicy in the World of the Bible*, edited by Antti Laato and Johannes C. De Moore, 183–235. Leiden: Brill, 2003.

LaCocque, André, and Paul Ricoeur. Translated by David Pellauer. *Thinking Biblically: Exegetical and Hermeneutical Studies*. Chicago: University of Chicago Press, 1998.

Lehtipuu, Outi. *Debates Over the Resurrection of the Dead: Constructing Early Christian Identity*. Oxford Early Christian Studies. Oxford: Oxford University Press, 2015.

Leonard, Jeffery M. "Identifying Inner-Biblical Allusions: Psalm 78 as a Test Case." *JBL* 127, no. 2 (2008): 241–265.

Lester, G. Brooke. *Daniel Evokes Isaiah: Allusive Characterization of Foreign Rule in the Hebrew-Aramaic Book of Daniel*. London: Bloomsbury T and T Clark, 2015.

Leupold, H. C. *Exposition of the Psalm*. UK: Evangelical Press, 1977.

Levenson, Jon Douglas. *Resurrection and the Restoration of Israel: The Ultimate Victory of the God of Life*. New Haven: Yale University Press, 2006.

Levine, Baruch A., and Jean-Michel De Tarragon. "Dead Kings and Rephaim: The Patrons of the Ugaritic Dynasty." *JAOS* 104, no. 4 (1984): 649–659.

Lewis, Theodore J. *Cults of the Dead in Ancient Israel and Ugarit*, Harvard Semitic Monograph, 39. Atlanta: Scholars Press, 1989.

Lim, Bo H. and Daniel Castelo, *Hosea*. The Two Horizons Old Testament Commentary. Grand Rapids: Eerdmans, 2015.

Lindenberger, James M. "Daniel 12:1–4." *Interpretation* 39, no. 2 (1985): 181–186.

Long, Philips V. *The Art of Biblical History*. Grand Rapids: Zondervan, 1994.

Longman III, Tremper. *The Book of Ecclesiastes*. NICOT. Grand Rapids: Eerdmans, 1997.

———. *Psalms*. TOTC. Vols. 15–16. Downers Grove: IVP Academics, 2104.

Lucas, Ernest. *Daniel*. Apollos Old Testament Commentary. Downers Grove: IVP Academic, 2002.

Lundbom, Jack R. *Deuteronomy: A Commentary*. Grand Rapids: Eerdmans, 2013.

Macaskill, Grant. "Priestly Purity, Mosaic Torah, and the Emergence of Enochic Judaism." *Henoch* 29 (2007): 67–89.

———. *Revealed Wisdom and Inaugurated Eschatology in Ancient Judaism and Early Christianity*. JSOTSup Text and Studies. Vol. 115. Leiden: Brill, 2007.

Maher, Michael, translator. *Targum Pseudo-Jonathan: Genesis*. The Aramaic Bible. Vol. 1B. Edinburgh: T&T Clark, 1992.

"Manichaeism: Ancient Religious Movement," *Encyclopaedia Britannica*, https://www.britannica.com/topic/Manichaeism.

Martin Irvine, "Mikhail Bakhtin: Main Theories: *Dialogism, Polyphony, Heteroglossia, Open Interpretation*: A Student's Guide." http://faculty.georgetown.edu/irvinem/theory/Bakhtin-MainTheory.html.

Martin-Achard, Robert. *From Death to Life: A Study of the Development of the Doctrine of Resurrection in the Old Testament*. Translated by John Penny Smith. Edinburgh: Oliver and Boyd, 1960.

Martone, Corrado. "The Enochic Tradition and the Diversity of Second Temple Judaism." *Henoch* 30 (2008): 51–55.

May, H. G. "The Fertility Cult in Hosea." *The American Journal of Semitic Languages and Literatures* 48, no. 2 (1932): 73–98.

Mays, James Luther. *Psalms*. Interpretation: A Bible Commentary for Teaching and Preaching. Louisville: JKP, 1994.

McAffee, Matthew. "Rephaim, Whisperers, and the Dead in Isaiah 26:13–19: A Ugaritic Parallel." *JBL* 135. 1 (2016): 77–94.

McCann Jr, J. Clinton. "The Book of the Psalms." *NIB*. Vol. 4. Nashville: Abingdon Press, 1996.

McClellan, Daniel O. "A Reevaluation of the Structure and Function of 2 Maccabees 7 and its Text-Critical Implications." *Studia Antiqua* 7, no. 1 (2009): 81–95.

McConville, J. Gordon. "Retribution in Deuteronomy: Theology and Ethics." *Interpretation: A Journal of Bible and Theology* 69, no. 3 (2015): 288–298.

McNamara, Martin, translator. *Targum Neofiti 1: Deuteronomy*. The Aramaic Bible. Vol. 5A. Edinburgh: T and T Clark, 1997.

Mealy, J. Webb. "After the Thousand Years: Resurrection and Judgment in Revelation 20." *JSNTSup* 70. Sheffield: JSOT Press, 1992.

Meek, Russell L. "Intertextuality, Inner-Biblical Exegesis, and Inner-Biblical Allusion: The Ethics of a Methodology." *Biblica* 95, 2 (2014): 280–291.

Mendels, Doron. "A Note on the Tradition of Antiochus IV's Death." *Israel Exploration Journal*, vol. 31, no. 1/2 (1981): 53–56.

Merrill, Eugene H. *Deuteronomy*. NAC. Vol. 4. Nashville: Broadman and Holman, 1994.
Michael. *Biblical Interpretation in Ancient Israel*. Oxford: Clarendon Press, 1985.
Milik, J. T. ed., with Matthew Black. *Books of Enoch Aramaic Fragments of Qumran Cave 4*. Oxford: Clarendon Press, 1976.
Milikowsky, Chaim. "Which Gehenna? Retribution and Eschatology in the Synoptic Gospels and in Early Jewish Texts." *New Testament Studies*. Vol. 34, no. 2 (1988): 238–249.
Millar, W. R. *Isaiah 24–27 and the Origin of Apocalyptic*. HSM 11. Missoula: Scholars Press, 1976.
Miller Jr., Patrick D. *Deuteronomy, Interpretation Series*. Louisville: Westminster John Knox Press, 1990, 2012.
———. *Sin and Judgment in the Prophets: A Stylistic and Theological Analysis*. SBLMS 27. Chico: Scholars Press, 1982.
Miller, Stephen R. *Daniel*, NAC Vol. 18. Nashville: Broadman and Holman, 1994.
Miscall, Peter D. "Isaiah: New Heavens, New Earth, New Book." In *Reading Between Texts: Intertextuality and the Hebrew Bible*, edited by Donna Nolan Fewell, 40–56. LCIB. Louisville: Westminster, 1992.
Mitchell, David C. "'God Will Redeem My Soul from Sheol': The Psalm of the Sons of Korah." *JSOT*. Vol. 30. 3 (2006): 365–384.
Molenberg, Corrie. "A Study of the Roles of Shemihaza and Asael in 1 Enoch 6–11." *JJS* 35 (1984): 136–146.
Mombert, Jacob Isidor. "On Job Xix. 25–27." Journal of the Society of Biblical Literature and Exegesis (1882): 27–39.
Montgomery, James A. *A Critical and Exegetical Commentary on the Book of Daniel*. ICC. New York: Charles Scribner's Sons, 1927.
Moor, Johannes C. de. *Intertextuality in Ugarit and Israel: Papers Read at the Tenth Joint Meeting of the Society for the Old Testament Studies and Het Oudtestamentisch Werkgezelschap in Nederland en Belgie held at Oxford, 1997*. Leiden: Brill, 1998.
Moore, Michael S. "Resurrection and Immortality: Two Motifs Navigating Confluent Theological Streams in the Old Testament (Daniel 12, 1–4)." *Theologische Zeitschrift* (1983): 17–34.
Morrison, Gary. "The Composition of II Maccabees: Insights Provided by a Literary Topos." *Biblica* 90, no. 4 (2009): 564–72.
Murphy, Ronald. *Ecclesiastes*. WBC. Vol. 23A. Dallas: Word Books, 1992.
Murray, Francesca Aran. *1 Samuel*. BTCB. Grand Rapids: Brazos, 2010.
Najman, Hindy. "Review of Gabriele Boccaccini, Beyond the Essene Hypothesis: The Parting of Ways Between the Qumran and Enochic Judaism." *AJS Review* 26, no. 2 (2002): 352–354.

Namgung, Young. "Sin and Human Accountability in Second Temple Judaism." PhD diss, University of Pretoria, 2018.

Nelson, Richard. *Deuteronomy*. OTL. Louisville, London: Westminster John Knox Press, 2002.

———. *Double Redaction of the Deuteronomistic History*. JSOTSup 18. Sheffield: JSOT Press, 1981.

Neusner, Jacob. "Comparing Judaisms." *History of Religions* 18, no. 2 (1978): 177–191.

Newman, Carey C. "Divine Retribution." In *Holman Bible Dictionary*. http://www.studylight.org/dictionaries/hbd/d/divine-retribution.html.;

Newsom, Carol A. "Bakhtin, the Bible, and Dialogic Truth." *The Journal of Religion* 76, no. 2 (1996): 290–306..

———. "The Development of 1 Enoch 6–19: Cosmology and Judgment." *CBQ*, 42, no. 3 (1980): 310–329

Nickelsburg, George W. E. "Apocalyptic and Myth in 1 Enoch 6–11." *JBL* 96 (1977): 383–405.

———. "Enochic Wisdom: An Alternative to the Mosaic Torah?" In *Hesed ve-Emet. Studies in Honor of Ernest D. Frerichs*, edited by Jodi Magness and Seymour Gitin, 123–132. Brown Judaic Studies 320. Atlanta: Scholars Press, 1998.

———. Jewish Literature Between the Bible and the Mishnah. Philadelphia: Fortress Press, 1981.

———. "Judgment, Life-After-Death and Resurrection in the Apocrypha and Non-Apocalyptic Pseudepigrapha." In *Judaism in Late Antiquity: Death, Life-After-Death, Resurrection and the World to Come in the Judaisms of Antiquity*, edited by Jacob Neusner, Alan J. Avery-Peck and Bruce Chilton, 141–162. Vol. 3. JLA. Leiden: Brill 2001.

———. *1 Enoch 1: A Commentary on the Book of 1 Enoch Chapters 1–36; 81–108*. Hermeneia: A Critical and Historical Commentary. Minneapolis: Fortress Press, 2001.

———. *Resurrection, Immortality and Eternal Life in Intertestamental Judaism and Early Christianity*. HTS 56, exp. ed. Cambridge: Harvard University Press, 2006.

Nickelsburg, George W. E. and James C. VanderKam. *1 Enoch: The Hermeneia Translation*. Minneapolis: Fortress Press, 2012.

Nicole, Emile. "בחר." In *NIDOTTE*, edited by Willem VanGemeren, 638. Vol. 1. Cumbria: Paternoster Press, 1996.

Noble, T. A. "Eschatology." 296–299. In *The New Dictionary of Theology: Historical and Systematic*, edited by Martin Davie and others. 2nd ed. Downers Grove: IVP Academic, 2016.

O'Callaghan, Paul. *Christ our Hope: An Introduction to Eschatology*. Washington, DC: Catholic University of America Press, 2011.

Ollenburger, Ben C. "If Mortals Die, Will they Live Again? The Old Testament and Resurrection." *Ex Auditu* 9 (1993): 29–44.

Olyan, Saul M. "Fire and Worms: Isaiah 66:24 in the Context of Isaiah 66 and the Book of Isaiah." In *Supplementation and the Study of the Hebrew Bible*, edited by Saul M. Olyan, Jacob L. Wright, 147–157. Providence, Rhode Island: Brown Judaic Studies, 2018.

Oropeza, B. J. "Intertextuality: A Brief History of Interpretation." https://www.academia.edu/35554463/Intertextuality_A_Recent_History_of_Interpretation.

Osborne, Grant R. "Resurrection." In *DNTB*. Edited by Craige A. Evans and Stanley E. Porter. 931–956. Downers Grove: IVP Academic, 2000.

Oswalt, John. *The Book of Isaiah 1–39*. NICOT. Grand Rapids: Eerdmans, 1986.

Papaioannou, Kim. *The Geography of Hell in the Teaching of Jesus: Gehena, Hades, the Abyss, the Outer Darkness Where There is Weeping and Gnashing of Teeth*. Eugene: Pickwick Publications, 2013.

Parry, Jason Thomas. "Desolation of the Temple and Messianic Enthronement in Daniel 11:36–12:3." *JETS* 54, no. 3 (2011): 485–526.

Patai, Raphael. "The 'Egla 'Arufa or the Expiation of the Polluted Land," *The Jewish Quarterly Review*, New Series, 30, no. 1 (1939): 59–69.

Paton, Lewis Bayles. "The Hebrew Idea of the Future Life: V. Yahweh's Relation to the Dead in the Later Hebrew Religion." *The Biblical World*. Vol. 35, no. 5 (1910): 339–352.

Pesler, G. M. M. "Resurrection and Eschatology in Paul's Letters." *Neotestamentica* 20 (1986): 37–46.

Peterson, Robert A. *Hell on Trial: The Case for Eternal Punishment*. Philipsburg: Presbyterian and Reformed Publishing Company, 1995.

Phillips, Anthony. *Deuteronomy*. Cambridge: Cambridge University Press, 1973.

Polaski, Donald. *Authorizing an End: The Isaiah Apocalypse and Intertextuality*. Leiden: Brill, 2001.

———. "The Politics of Prayer: A New Historicist Reading of Isaiah 26." *Perspectives in Religious Studies* 25, no. 4 (1998): 357–371.

Porteous, Norman W. *Daniel*. OTL. Philadelphia: Westminster Press, 1965.

Preuss, H. D. עוֹלָם, 'ôlām; עָלַם 'ālam. Translated by David E. Green and Douglas W. Stott. In *TDOT*, edited by Johannes Botterweck, Helmer Ringgern and Heinz-Jossf Fabry. Vol. 10. Grand Rapid: Eerdmans, 1999.

———. "שָׁכַח šākah." Translated by Douglas W. Stott. In *TDOT*, edited by G. Johannes Botterweck, Helmer Ringgren, and Heinz-Josef Farby, 674. Vol. 14. Grand Rapids: Eerdmans, 2004.

Prusak, Bernard P. "Heaven and Hell: Eschatological Symbols of Existential Protest." *Cross Currents* (1975): 475–491.
Rankin, O. S. *Israel's Wisdom Literature: Its Bearing on Theology and the History of Religion*. New York: Schocken, 1969.
Rawlinson, G. "II Maccabees: Introduction and Commentary." In The Holy Bible According to the Authorized version (A.D. 1611) with Explanatory and Critical Commentary and A Revision of the Translation, by Clergy of the Anglican Church: Apocrypha, edited by Henry Wace. Vol. 2. Ecclesiasticus to Maccabees. London: John Murray, 1888.
Redditt, Paul. "Isaiah 26." *Review and Expositor* 88 (1991): 195–199.
Reed, Annette Yoshiko. *Fallen Angels and the History of Judaism and Christianity: The Reception of Enochic Literature*. Cambridge: Cambridge University Press, 2005.
———. "The Textual Identity, Literary History, and Social Setting of 1 Enoch: Reflections on George Nickelsburg's Commentary on 1 Enoch 1–36; 81–108." *ARG* 5 (2003): 279–396.
Roberts, Jimmy Jack McBee. *First Isaiah: A Commentary*. Hermeneia: A Critical and Historical Commentary on the Bible. Minneapolis: Fortress Press, 2015.
Rogerson, J. W. and J. W. McKay. *Psalm 1–50*. CBC on the New English Bible. Cambridge: Cambridge University Press, 1977.
Rottenberg, Ephraim. "Reward and Punishment." In *20th Century Jewish Religious Thought: Original Essays on Critical Concepts, Movements and Beliefs*, edited by Arthur Allen Cohen and Paul Mendes-Flohr, 827–832. Philadelphia: JPS, 2009.
Roubin, Rachel. "On Canaanite Motifs in the Book of Hosea (Hosea 5:14–6:4)." *Hebrew Abstracts* 14 (1973): 109–110.
Routledge, Robin L. "Death and Afterlife in the Old Testament." *JEBS* 9, no. 1 (2008): 22–39.
Russell, D. S. *The Method and Message of Jewish Apocalypse: 200 BC – AD 100*. Philadelphia: Westminster Press, 1964.
Ruzer, Serge. "James on Faith and Righteousness in the Context of a Broader Jewish Exegetical Discourse." In *New Approaches to the Study of Biblical Interpretation in Judaism of the Second Temple Period and in Early Christianity*. Edited by Gary A. Anderson, Ruth A. Clements, and David Satran. STDJ. Vol. 106. 79–104. Leiden: Brill, 2013.
Sacchi, Paolo. "The Book of the Watchers as an Apocalyptic and Apocryphal Text." *Henoch* 30 (2008): 9–26.
———. *Jewish Apocalyptic and Its History*. JSPSup 20. Sheffield: Sheffield Academic Press, 1997.
Sanders, E. P. *Paul and Palestine Judaism: A Comparison of Patterns of Religion*. Philadelphia: Fortress, 1977.

Sarna, Nahum M. *On the Book of Psalms: Exploring the Prayers of Ancient Israel.* New York: Schocken Books, 1993.

Sarna, Nahum Mattathias. "Psalm 89: A Study in Inner Biblical Exegesis." In *Biblical and Other Studies*, edited by Alexander Altmann, 29–46. Cambridge: Harvard University Press, 1963.

Satlow, Michael L. *Creating Judaism: History, Tradition, Practice.* New York: Colombia University Press, 2006.

Sawyer, John F. A. *Isaiah.* DSBS. Vol. 1. Philadelphia: Westminster Press, 1984.

Schaper, Joachim. *Eschatology in the Greek Psalter.* WUNT I, 2.76. Tübingen: J.C.B. Mohr, 1995.

Schatkin, Margaret. "The Maccabean Martyrs." *Vigiliae Christianae.* Vol. 28, No. 2 (1974): 97–113.

Schearing, Linda S. and Steven L. McKenzie, eds. *Those Elusive Deuteronomists: The Phenomenon of Pandeuteronomism.* JSOTSup 268. Sheffield: Sheffield Academic Press, 1999.

Schmid, Konrad. "Review of Christopher B. Hays, Death in the Iron Age II and in First Isaiah (FAT, 79; Tübingen: Mohr Siebeck, 2011)." *JHS.* Vol. 12 (2012). http://www.jhsonline.org/reviews/reviews_new/review614.htm.

Schmidt, Brian B. "Afterlife Beliefs: Memory as Immortality." *Near Eastern Archaeology* 63, no. 4 (2000): 236–39.

———. *Israel's Beneficent Dead: Ancestral Cult and Necromancy in Ancient Israelite Religion and Tradition.* Winona Lake: Eisenbrauns, 1996.

———. "Memory as Immortality: Countering the Dreaded 'Death after Death' in Ancient Israelite Society." In *Death, Life-after-Death, Resurrection and the World-to-Come in the Judaisms of Antiquity*, edited by Alan J. Avery-Peck and Jacob Neusner, 87–100. Vol. 4. JLA. Boston: Brill Academic Publishers, 2001.

Schmitz, Philip C. "The Grammar of Resurrection in Isaiah 26:19a-c." *JBL* 122, no. 1 (2003): 145–149.

Schnabel, Eckhard J. "Review of Gabriele Boccaccini, Beyond the Essene Hypothesis: The Parting of the Ways Between Qumran and Enochic Judaism." *JBL* 120, 2 (2001): 372–373.

Scholtus, Silvia C. "Jewish Legalism and the 'New Perspectives on Paul.'" *Parousia* 7 (2018): 81–100.

Schwartz, Daniel R. *2 Maccabees.* CEJL. Berlin: Walter de Gruyter, 2008.

Seeley, David. *Noble Death: Graeco-Roman Martyrology and Paul's Concept of Salvation.* JSOTSup 28. Sheffield: JSOT, 1990.

Segal, Alan. *Life After Death: A History of the Afterlife in the Religions of the West.* New York: Doubleday, 2004.

———. "Torah and Nomos in Recent Scholarly Discussion." *SR* 13/1 (1984): 19–27.

Seitz, Christopher. *Isaiah 1–39*. Interpretation: A Bible Commentary for Teaching and Preaching. Louisville: Westminster John Knox Press, 1993.

Seow, Choon-Leong. *Ecclesiastes*. AB. Vol. 18c. New York: Doubleday, 1997.

Setzer, Claudia. *Resurrection of the Body in Early Judaism and Early Christianity: Doctrine, Community and Self-Definition*. Boston: Brill, 2004.

———. "Resurrection of the Dead as Symbol and Strategy." *JAAR*. Vol. 69, 1 (2001):65- 101.

Shepkaru, Shmuel. "From after Death to Afterlife: Martyrdom and Its Recompense." *AJS Review* 24, no. 1 (1999):1–44.

Shipp, R. Mark. *Of Dead Kings and Dirges: Myth and Meaning in Isaiah 14:4b–21*. SBL Academia Biblica 11. Leiden: Brill, 2002.

Sigvartsen, Jan Age. *Afterlife and Resurrection Beliefs in the Apocrypha and Apocalyptic Literature*. JCTCRS 29. London: T&T Clark, 2019.

———. Afterlife and Resurrection Beliefs in the Pseudepigrapha. JCTCRS 30. London: Bloomsbury T and T Clark, 2019.

Smith, Gary. *Isaiah 1–39*. NAC. Vol. 15a. Nashville: Broadman and Holman, 2007.

Smith, Janet. *Dust or Dew: Immortality in the Ancient Near East and in Psalm 49*. Cambridge: James Clarke and Co., 2011.

Snaith, Norman Henry. "Justice and Immortality," *SJT* 17 (1964): 309–324.

Snodgrass, Klyne R. "Justification by Grace – To the Doers: An Analysis of the Place of Romans in the Theology of Paul." *NTS* 32 (1986): 72–93.

Sommer, Benjamin D. "Exegesis, Allusion and Intertextuality in the Hebrew Bible: A Response to Lyle Eslinger." *VT* 46/4 (1996): 479–489.

Sonne, Isaiah. "Isaiah 53:10–12." *JBL* 78, no. 4 (1959): 335–342.

Spronk, Klaas. *Beatific Afterlife in Ancient Israel and in the Ancient Near East*. Kevelaer: Butzon and Bercker, 1986.

———. "Good Death and Bad Death in Ancient Israel According to Biblical Lore." *Social Science and Medicine* 58 (2004): 987–995/10–13.

Stahlberg, Lesleigh Cushing. *Sustaining Fiction: Intertextuality, Midrash, Translation and Literary Afterlife of the Bible*. LHB 486. New York: T and T Clark, 2008.

Stele, Artur S. "Resurrection in Daniel 12 and its Contribution to the Theology of the Book of Daniel." PhD Diss., Andrews University, 1996.

Stendahl, Krister. "Justification and the Last Judgment." *Lutheran World* 8 (1961): 1–7.

Stevenson, Kenneth and Michael Glerup, eds. *Ezekiel, Daniel*. Ancient Christian Commentary on Scripture. Old Testament. Vol. XII. Downers Grove: IVP, 2008.

Stone, Michael Edward. "Book of Enoch and Judaism in the Third Century B.C.E." *CBQ*. Vol. 40, no. 4 (1978): 479–492.

Strong, John T. "Egypt's Shameful Death and the House of Israel's Exodus from Sheol (Ezekiel 32.17–32 and 37.1–14)." *JSOT*. Vol. 34, no. 4 (2010): 475–504.

Stuart, Douglas. *Hosea and Jonah*. WBC. Vol. 31. Waco: Word Books, 1987.

Stuckenbruck, Loren T. "The Book of Enoch: Its Reception in Second Temple Jewish and in Christian Tradition." *Early Christianity* 4 (2013): 7–40.

———. *The Myth of Rebellious Angels: Studies in Second Temple Judaism and New Testament Texts*. WUNT 335. Tübingen: Mohr Siebeck, 2017.

Suter, David W. "Fallen Angel, Fallen Priest: The Problem of Family Purity in 1 Enoch 6–16." *HUCA* 50 (1979): 115–135.

———. "Temples and the Temple in the Early Enoch Tradition: Memory, Vision, and Expectation." In *The Early Enoch Literature*, edited by Gabriele Boccaccini and John J. Collins, 195–218. JSJSupp. Vol. 121. Leiden, Brill: 2007.

Sweeny, Marvin A. *Isaiah 1–39 With an Introduction to Prophetic Literature*. FOTL. Vol. XVI. Grand Rapids: Eerdmans, 1996.

———. *Reading the Prophetic Books: Form, Intertextuality and Reception in Prophetic and Post-Biblical Literature*. FAT 89. Tubingen: Mohr Siebeck, 2014.

———. "Textual Citations in Isaiah 24–27: Toward an Understanding of the Redactional Function of Chapters 24–27 in the Book of Isaiah." *JBL* 107 (1988): 39–52.

Talley, David. "חשק" in *NIDOTTE*, edited by Willem A. VanGemeren, 318. Vol. 2. Carlisle: Paternoster Press, 1996.

Tate, Marvin. *Psalms 51–100*. WBC. Vol. 20. Grand Rapids: Zondervan, 1991.

Thiessen, Matthew. "A Buried Pentateuchal Allusion to the Resurrection in Mark 12:25." *CBQ* 76 (2014): 273–290.

Thompson, Deanna A. *Deuteronomy: A Theological Commentary on the Bible*. Louisville: Westminster John Knox Press, 2014.

Tigay, Jeffery H. *Deuteronomy*. The JPS Torah Commentary. Philadelphia: The Jewish Publication Society, 1996.

Tigchelaar, Eibert. "Balaam and Enoch." In *The Prestige of the Pagan Prophet Balaam in Judaism, Early Christianity and Islam, edited by* G. H. van Kooten, and J. van Ruiten, 87–99. Leiden: Brill, 2008.

———. "Wisdom and Counter-Wisdom in 4QInstruction, Mysteries, and 1 Enoch." Gabriele Boccaccini and John J. Collins (eds.), *The Early Enochic Literature*, JSJSupp. Vol. 121. Leiden, Brill: 2007, 177–193.

Tiller, Patrick. "George Nickelsburg's '1 Enoch: A Commentary on the Book of 1 Enoch: Chapters 1–36; 81–108'." In *George W. E. Nickelsburg in Perspective: An Ongoing Dialogue of Learning*, edited by Jacob Neusner and Alan J. Avery-Peck, 365–372. Vol. 2. Leiden: Brill, 2003.

Tomasino, Anthony. "עוֹלָם." In *NIDOTTE*, edited by Willem A. VanGemeren. Vol. 3. Grand Rapid: Zondervan, 1997.

Tooman, William A. *Gog of Magog: Reuse of Scripture and Compositional Technique in Ezekiel 38-39*. FAT 2. 52. Tübingen: Mohr Siebeck, 2011.

Towner, Sibley W. *Daniel*. Interpretation. Atlanta, GA: John Knox Press, 1984.

———. "Retributional Theology in the Apocalyptic Setting." *Union Seminary Quarterly Review*. Vol. XXVI, no. 30 (1971): 203-214.

Travis, Stephen T. *Christ and the Judgment of God: Divine Retribution in the New Testament*. Basingstoke, UK: Pickering, 1986.

Turner, Alice K. *The History of Hell*. San Diego: Harcourt Brace and Company, 1993.

van der Kooij, Arie. "Isaiah 24-27: Text-Critical Notes." In *Studies in Isaiah 24-27: The Isaiah Workshop – De Jesaja Werkplaats*, edited by Hendrik Jan Bosman and Harm van Grol, 13-15. OTS 43 Leiden: Brill, 2000.

van der Woude, Annemarieke. "Resurrection or Transformation: Concepts of Death in Isaiah 24-27." In *Formation and Intertextuality in Isaiah 24-27*, edited by J. Todd Hibbard and Hyun Chul Paul Kim, 143-164. SBL Ancient Israel and its Literature 17. Atlanta: SBL, 2013.

van Henten, Jan Willem. *The Maccabean Martyrs as Saviours of the Jewish People: A Study of 2 and 4 Maccabees*. JSJSupp. Vol. 57. Leiden: Brill, 1997.

VanderKam, James C. *Enoch: A Man for All Generations*. Columbia, SC: University of South Carolina Press, 1995.

———. "Enoch Traditions in Jubilees and Other Second-century Sources." In *SBL Seminar Papers 1978*, edited by Paul J. Achtemeier, 228-251. Vol.1. Missoula, Scholars Press, 1978.

———. *From Revelation to Canon: Studies in the Hebrew Bible and Second Temple Literature*. Boston: Brill, 2002.

———. "1 Enoch, Enochic Motifs, and Enoch in Early Christian Literature." In *The Jewish Apocalyptic Heritage in Early Christianity*, edited by James C. VanderKam, and W. A. Adler, 124-125. Minneapolis: Fortress 1996.

Venter, Pieter M. "Allotted Place and Cursed Space in 1 Enoch 12-36." *OTE* 27, no. 2 (2014): 666-683.

von Rad, Gerhard. *Deuteronomy*. OTL. Philadelphia: Westminster, 1966.

———. *Deuteronomy: A Commentary*. OTL. Bloomsbury, London: SMC Press, 1966.

———. *Old Testament Theology*. Vol. 1. London: SCM Press, 1975.

Wächter, L. "שְׁאוֹל šᵉʾôl." Translated by Douglas W. Stott. In *TDOT*, edited by G. Johannes Botterweck, Helmer Ringgren, and Heinz-Josef Fabry, 243-246. Vol. 14. Grand Rapids: Eerdmans, 2004.

Wallis, "חָשַׁק hasaq" In *TDOT*, edited by G. Johannes Botterweck, Helmer Ringgren, and Heinz-Josef Fabry, 262. Vol. 5. Grand Rapids: Eerdmans, 1968.

Walton, John H. "Retribution." In *Dictionary of the Old Testament: Wisdom, Poetry & Writings*, edited by Tremper Longman III and Peter Enns, 647. Downers Grove: IVP, 2008.

Walvoord, John F. "The Resurrection of Israel." *Bibliotheca Sacra* 124, no. 493. (1967): 3–15.

Warmuth, Kiel. "נָקִי." In *TDOT*, edited by G. Johannes Botterweck, Helmer Ringgren, and Heinz-Josef Fabry, 558. Vol. IX. Grand Rapids: Eerdmans, 1998.

Waschke, G. "קוה." Translated by Douglas W. Stott. In *TDOT*, edited by G. Johannes Botterweck, Helmer Ringgren, and Heinz-Josef Fabry, 569. Vol. 12. Grand Rapids, MI: Eerdmans, 2003.

Wegner, Paul. "ענה." In *NIDOTTE*, edited by Willem A. VanGemeren, 450. Vol. 3. Grand Rapids: Zondervan, 1997.

Weinfeld, Moshe. *Deuteronomy 1–11*. AB. Vol. 5. New York: Doubleday, 1991.

Weiser, Artur. *The Psalms: A Commentary*. Translated by Herbert Hartwell. OTL. Philadelphia: Westminster, 1962.

Weitzman, Steven. "Lessons from the Dying: The Role of Deuteronomy 32 in Its Narrative Setting." *HTR* 87, no. 4 (1994): 377–393.

Westermann, Claus. *Isaiah 40–66: A Commentary*. Translated by David M. G. Stalker. OTL. Philadelphia: Westminster Press, 1969.

Wielenga, Bob. "Eschatology in Malachi: The Emergence of a Doctrine." *In die Skriflig* 50, no. 1, a2091 (2016): 1–10.

Wieringen, Archibald L. H. M. van. "'I' and 'We' Before 'Your' Face: A Communication Analysis in Isaiah 26:7–21." In *Studies in Isaiah 24–27: The Isaiah Workshop – De Jesaja Werkplaats*, edited by Hendrik Jan Bosman, Harm van Grol, and Johannes C. de Moor, 239–251. OTS 43. Leiden: Brill, 2000.

Wijngaards, J. "Death and Resurrection in Covenantal Context (Hos. VI 2)." *VT* 17, no. 2 (1967): 226–239.

Wildberger, Hans. "בחר bhr to choose." In *Theological Lexicon of the Old Testament*, edited by Ernest Jenni and Claus Westermann. Translated by Mark E. Biddle, 216. Vol. 1. Peabody: Hendrickson, 1997.

———. *Isaiah 13–27*. Translated by Thomas H. Trapp. A Continental Commentary. Minneapolis: Fortress Press, 1997.

Willis, Amy Merrill. *Dissonance and the Drama of Divine Sovereignty in the Book of Daniel*. LHB 520. New York: T and T Clark, 2010.

Willis, Timothy M. *Elders of the City: A Study of the Elders-Laws in Deuteronomy*, SBLMS 55. Atlanta: Society of Biblical Literature, 2001.

Wolde, Ellen van. "Texts in Dialogue with Texts: Intertextuality Between Ruth and Tamar Narratives." *Bib Int* 5, no. 1 (1997): 1–28.

———. "Trendy Intertextuality?" In *Intertextuality in Biblical Writing: Essays in Honour of Bas van Iersel*, edited by Sipke Draisma, 43–49. Kampen: Uitgeversmaatschappij J. H. Kok, 1989.
Wong, Ka Leung. *The Idea of Retribution in the Book of Ezekiel*. VTSup 8. Leiden: Brill, 2001.
Woods, Edward J. *Deuteronomy*. TOTC. Vol. 5. Downers Grove: IVP, 2011.
Wright, Archie T. *Origin of Evil Spirits: The Reception of Genesis 6:1–4 in Early Jewish Literature*. WUNT, 2 Reihe, 198. Tübingen: Mohr Siebeck, 2005.
Wright, Christopher J. H. *Deuteronomy*. NIBC. Peabody: Hendrickson Publishers, 1996.
Wright, David P. "Deuteronomy 21:1–6 as Rite of Elimination." *CBQ* 49, no. 3 (1987): 387–403.
Wright, George Ernest. "The Law-Suit of God: A Form-Critical Study of Deuteronomy 32." In *Israel's Prophetic Heritage: Essays in Honor of James Muilenburg*, edited by Bernard W. Anderson and Walter Harrelson, 26–67. New York: Harper and Brothers, 1962.
Wyatt, N. "The Concept and Purpose of Hell: Its Nature and Development in West Semitic Thought." *Numen* 56, no. 2/3 (2009): 161–184.
Yinger, Kent L. *Paul, Judaism, and Judgment According to Deeds*. SNTS Monograph Series 105. Cambridge: Cambridge University Press, 1999.
Young, Edward J. *The Book of Isaiah: The English Text, with Introduction, Exposition, and Notes*. Vol. 2. Chapters 19–39. Grand Rapids: Eerdmans, 1969.
———. *Daniel*. The Geneva Series of Commentaries. Carlisle, Pennsylvania: The Banner of Truth Trust, 1949.
Young, Ian. "Collectives: Biblical Hebrew." In *Encyclopaedia of the Hebrew Language and Linguistics*, edited by Geoffrey Khan, 477–479. Vol. 1: A-F. Leiden: Brill, 2013.
Young, Robin Darling. "The 'Woman with the Soul of Abraham': Traditions about the Mother of the Maccabean Martyrs." In *"Women Like This": New Perspectives on Jewish Women in the Greco-Roman World*, edited by Amy-Jill Levine, 67–81. SBL Early Judaism and its Literature. Atlanta: Scholars Press, 1991.
Zeitlin, Solomon. *The Second Book of the Maccabees*. Translated by Sidney Tedesche. New York: Harper and Brothers, 1954.
Zevit, Ziony. "The 'Eglâ Ritual of Deuteronomy 21:1–9." *JBL* 59, no.3 (1976): 377–390.

Subject Index

A
afterlife 12, 17, 176, 224, 233, 235, 237, 239, 260
Akhmim 168, 182, 185
angels 145, 159, 167, 184
Antiochus IV 124, 203, 206, 215, 235
apocalypse 89, 124

C
collective retribution 51
  collective 225, 231
corporate retribution 53
  corporate 106–107, 117, 151, 192, 225, 230, 237, 241–243, 251, 254, 263
covenant 3, 63, 67, 72, 79, 149, 163, 211, 224, 227, 237, 245, 250, 253

D
dead 17, 19, 95, 104, 107, 110–111, 175, 247, 252
death 7, 10, 13, 15–16, 56, 99, 115, 128, 226, 235, 262
death after death 109, 111, 115
Deuteronomic 3, 45, 55, 226, 229, 233, 237
divine retribution 2, 47, 51, 53, 132, 151, 179, 186, 191, 215, 231, 239
  aspects of 45, 54

anthropocentric aspect 61–62, 106, 117, 149, 180, 191, 211, 219, 224, 237, 241, 243, 245, 247, 250, 252, 259
dissolution aspects 244
dissolution of retribution 72, 75, 241, 253
impersonal aspect 54, 240, 253
post-mortem 2, 84, 119, 131, 140, 175, 176, 209, 218, 233, 242, 244, 249, 255
theocentric aspect 67, 72, 75, 140, 180, 191, 211, 225, 237, 239, 241, 243, 247, 250, 253

E
Enochic Judaism 160, 166, 172, 246
eschatological 10, 14, 27, 92, 124, 244
eschatology 125
eternal life 129, 210, 221, 260, 262

F
fire 27, 135, 257

G
Ge'ez 168, 182, 185
Gehenna 26, 136, 257
giants 159, 186

H
hell 26, 136, 191, 260

301

Hellenism 205
Hellenistic 121

I
individual 151, 192, 195, 232, 237, 241, 249, 251, 254, 262
individual retribution 53, 71
intertextuality 32–33, 40, 43
  production-centred 40
  reception-centred 41

J
judgment 159, 170–171, 178, 261
justice 2–3, 188, 224, 233

L
law 162, 164, 192, 206, 212, 219–222, 233, 246

M
martyrdom 224, 228, 233, 250
martyrs 207, 220, 225, 231–232, 237

O
origin of evil 166, 170

P
parousia 258
punishments 2, 26, 50, 52, 70, 75, 115, 135, 174, 177, 187, 235, 240, 257

R
rephaim 104, 107, 109, 112, 114, 176, 243
resurrection 5, 13, 23, 30, 98, 103, 107, 127, 133, 139, 141, 188, 190, 209, 212, 221, 232, 242, 244, 249, 256
rise 9, 22, 96, 104, 112, 114, 190, 242
rising 209
retribution 49
reward(s) 2, 30, 52, 71, 78, 103, 115, 143, 177, 187, 212, 232, 240, 257
righteous 8, 95, 103, 105, 176, 187, 195, 242

S
Seleucid period 124
shades 101, 176
Sheol 19, 116
sleep 128
sleeping 101, 190
soul(s) 175, 187, 247
spirit 175
Synkellos 168, 182, 248

T
Torah 160, 162, 164, 167, 192, 220, 246

U
Ugarit 109
Ugaritic 145
underworld 116, 136, 176

W
Watchers 167, 171, 180, 183, 248
wicked 134, 137, 177
wisdom 3, 16, 29, 106, 165, 192

Scripture Index

OLD TESTAMENT

Genesis
4:10–12 57
18:17–32 2

Deuteronomy
7:6–11 67
8:1–20 73
11:13–21 62
21:1–9 56
32 227
32:39 5

1 Samuel
2:6 6

Job
19:25–27 16
42:5 17

Psalm
1:5 8
16:10–11 10
17:15 11
49:15 12
73:24 14

Ecclesiastes
3:21 16

Isaiah
16:14 104
24–27 .... 85, 91

26:14 114
26:19 .... 84, 94, 104, 112, 252
53:10–12 24
66:24 .... 26, 135

Ezekiel
32:18; 21–23 18
37:1–14 20

Daniel
11 123
12:1–3 .... 119, 126, 252

Hosea
6:1–2 21

NEW TESTAMENT

Matthew
3:10–12 258
13:24–30 258
13:36–43 258
24:40–44 258
24:45–51 259
25:31–46 .... 258, 260

Luke
14:14 256
16:19–31 258
20:34–35 256

John
3:16 262
5:24 262
5:28–29 257
6:39–40, 54 257

1 Corinthians
15:23 257

Romans
2:6–8, 13 260
10:9–10 262
14:12 263

Galatians
2:16, 21 262

1 Thessalonians
4:16 257

Revelation
14:10–11 258
20:11–15 261
20:13 263

SECOND TEMPLE PERIOD LITERATURE

1 Enoch 156, 160, 162, 164, 169, 192, 246

2 Maccabees
7 .... 199, 212, 230, 249, 252, 255
7:28 214
7:32–33 227
7:36 210

Book of Watchers
BW 22 .... 158, 182, 249, 255

Langham Literature, with its publishing work, is a ministry of Langham Partnership.

Langham Partnership is a global fellowship working in pursuit of the vision God entrusted to its founder John Stott –

> *to facilitate the growth of the church in maturity and Christ-likeness through raising the standards of biblical preaching and teaching.*

Our vision is to see churches in the Majority World equipped for mission and growing to maturity in Christ through the ministry of pastors and leaders who believe, teach and live by the word of God.

Our mission is to strengthen the ministry of the word of God through:
- nurturing national movements for biblical preaching
- fostering the creation and distribution of evangelical literature
- enhancing evangelical theological education

especially in countries where churches are under-resourced.

Our ministry

Langham Preaching partners with national leaders to nurture indigenous biblical preaching movements for pastors and lay preachers all around the world. With the support of a team of trainers from many countries, a multi-level programme of seminars provides practical training, and is followed by a programme for training local facilitators. Local preachers' groups and national and regional networks ensure continuity and ongoing development, seeking to build vigorous movements committed to Bible exposition.

Langham Literature provides Majority World preachers, scholars and seminary libraries with evangelical books and electronic resources through publishing and distribution, grants and discounts. The programme also fosters the creation of indigenous evangelical books in many languages, through writer's grants, strengthening local evangelical publishing houses, and investment in major regional literature projects, such as one volume Bible commentaries like the *Africa Bible Commentary* and the *South Asia Bible Commentary*.

Langham Scholars provides financial support for evangelical doctoral students from the Majority World so that, when they return home, they may train pastors and other Christian leaders with sound, biblical and theological teaching. This programme equips those who equip others. Langham Scholars also works in partnership with Majority World seminaries in strengthening evangelical theological education. A growing number of Langham Scholars study in high quality doctoral programmes in the Majority World itself. As well as teaching the next generation of pastors, graduated Langham Scholars exercise significant influence through their writing and leadership.

To learn more about Langham Partnership and the work we do visit **langham.org**

www.ingramcontent.com/pod-product-compliance
Lightning Source LLC
Chambersburg PA
CBHW070429260426
43673CB00068B/1783